MW00603684

They Came to Rockingham

To Janet & Don, dear friends!
Love,
Liz
"Elisabeth Wilson Hodges"

Elisabeth Wilson Hodges

They Came to Rockingham

Elisabeth Wilson Hodges

ISBN 1890306770

Library of Congress Control Number: 2004116502

WARWICK HOUSE PUBLISHERS
720 Court Street
Lynchburg, VA 24504

Blanche Odessa Miller Wilson and James Moore Wilson

Dedication

Had I my life to begin again, I would not choose for myself a different childhood. As early as the third grade I began to see that I was a lucky little girl indeed when one of my textbooks revealed that, at the time of its publication, a great many people in the United States did not have electricity, central heating, telephone service, and indoor plumbing. My family had all of them! This was only the first of such realizations. It took me many years, including some rebellious ones, to sense that all of these things, and many which were more important than these, were results of the efforts of the great parents with which I had been blessed. It is to the memory of these parents that I dedicate this book.

At the time of their deaths Blanche Odessa Miller Wilson and James Moore Wilson, her husband, had four grown children, thirteen grandchildren, and at least one great-grandchild. Each of these individuals, except perhaps the youngest, had an impression of my parents with which they will live their lives. I find it an awesome task to try to redefine them in the face of so many varying impressions. I have asked my siblings for guidance, and receiving some suggestions, I shall now interpret our parents through my eyes and experience, without apology.

Blanche and Moore were introduced by his cousin, Bill Moore, who had met this attractive teacher from Rockingham County; and Moore, who had an on-going flirtation with what sounded to me like the whole nursing staff of King's Daughters' Hospital in Staunton, paused to take a second look. The two were married in Spring Creek at the home of her mother in June of 1928, and honeymooned, as was the custom in those days, at Niagara Falls.

Because Blanche was a teacher at the Virginia School for the Deaf and the Blind, they looked at property on which to settle in Staunton, but because Moore was a farmer with obligations to his widowed mother and his family they ultimately bought acreage in Raphine, in Rockbridge County. While they built their home they lived, rather uncomfortably for all, I fear, with Moore's mother, Emma Amelia Wade Wilson, and two of her adult children. They were still living there at the time their firstborn, James Moore Wilson, Jr., arrived but soon moved into their new Dutch Colonial home a mile or so down the winding road.

The rest of us, three daughters, were born in that new house. Mother had been reared very closely and privately and had no desire to return to the public hospital experience she had had with the birth of her son. So, on two occasions a nurse was employed and the doctor, a personal friend, was lined up to come on short notice to the house to deliver twins (to the great surprise of all), and four years later, me.

Mother and Daddy were very careful parents. Our health and safety were their first consideration, with our "upbringing" a close second. Daddy abandoned the garage which had been built under the house so there would be no question of one of us ever "getting under the wheels" of the car. Mother sheltered us from the snakes that naturally inhabited the wooded area around our home by calling Daddy from anywhere he happened to be in the community to come home and kill the offender, even if she had spotted the hapless creature across the road on the neighbor's property. Mother also sheltered us from thunderstorms by lining us up like small sparrows on the living room sofa until all signs of the event had passed.

As we grew to be teenagers Mother sheltered us from every conceivable danger, real or imagined. She wrung her hands over requests that we be allowed to go to friends' homes or driving in their cars. We might never have gone, but Daddy would say, in the style of Mark Twain,

"If I was born to be drowned, I'll never be hanged," and his gentle, patient word usually won the day.

Daddy *was* gentle and somewhat reserved. He had been raised to understand that the impressions of others made a difference, and he was very careful that we understood that. We were not allowed to say darn or any of the relatively tame words we brought home from school in those days, and I remember the pain in his expression when I wore bright red fingernail polish to the dinner table one day. His curfews were conservative, even when his daughters were triple-dating, which we often did, and the boys moved out fairly quickly when his voice was heard from the bedroom above.

The male of the species held a special place in the Scotch-Irish family of the time, as it had for generations. It was even more important that our brother fit the family mold than it was for the girls, and Daddy not only served as a good role model, but saw to it that Jim had a few extra advantages. First he was provided with a scooter and the freedom to use it, and later, a convertible! We girls might have been jealous, but we didn't think of it in time. That was just the way it was, and anyhow, our brother would take us out in that convertible sometimes.

Mother was a bit of a challenge for Daddy. She didn't really like being parked in rural Rockbridge County so far away from her big Rockingham family, and so far away from the city which she had come to enjoy in her teaching days. And she was "Victorian," and helplessly feminine about many things. She not only never learned to drive; mechanical things, in general, frightened her. She didn't like to push an elevator button or open a casement window. Daddy usually bought the furniture, and with her list, chose the groceries. She never voted. She needed Daddy for many decisions and even more tasks. And she was often dissatisfied.

The dissatisfaction weighed heavily on Daddy, but he loved her with a tremendous patience, and drove for miles even to kill the neighbor's black snakes. After her death, he made our home a memorial to our mother. He displayed the old pictures of the two of them, and quietly moved things back where Mother had left them after his daughters had changed things around to make them more convenient for him.

Both Mother and Daddy were strong in their faith and one had to be pretty sick to be kept at home from any church activity. If the church door was unlocked, there was a pretty good chance one or all of us was there. Daddy was a Deacon and an Elder, in turn, and supported the work of the church even if he did think some of the changes made in the building and furnishings were pretty frivolous. Mother attended circle meetings and taught Sunday School, and we were all at the church from the beginning to the end of a Sunday morning. We children needed little encouragement to attend Vacation Bible School and Young Peoples' activities for the church provided much of our society in rural Rockbridge County.

Historically, education was very important to the Scotch-Irish, as well as to the other cultures which influenced our upbringing, and our parents gave high priority to that facet of our lives. I early found out that reading a book was a pretty good way to avoid the chores which were always pressing on the farm. Martha suggested, correctly, that we grew up knowing we were going to college, even before we knew what it was.

It was Daddy who contributed the most to my beliefs and to any moral strengths I may possess. I'm not sure how he did it; he certainly did not preach to his family and I can't recall many religious discussions being held. I suppose his message was delivered through example, because he lived his faith as well as anyone I have ever known.

We probably never lived up to Mother's and Daddy's expectations. Both of them had come from proud old families, and they had worked hard to see that their little brood lacked for naught. I suspect they thought we could carry their combined genes to new heights - the dream of every parent. I think of Mother and the endless hours she spent over her White treadle sewing machine, before Daddy surprised her with the tonnage of the "portable" electric Singer. She made us beautiful dresses, functional and attractive play clothes, reversible quilted bath robes, a barn dance skirt for me with a flounce *this wide*- everything! She spent hours making long rope curls in hair that cared not for such discipline. Or she plaited three sets of braids, put us in the starched white blouses and checked pinafores that she had made, and carried us anywhere, with pride. She never tired of having us with her; I have heard her say that she didn't want us to grow up.

We went to community programs, community barbeques, community Christmas carolings where Santa appeared, horse shows, cake walks, and a few events at the school, athletic and otherwise. I recall one school-sponsored farce in which the adults played the roles of school-aged children, and my Daddy played a naughty little boy! When we went to the city for educational purposes we had many more opportunities, these on a somewhat more sophisticated level. We went to plays and symphony concerts; we haunted movie houses; and I, for one, joined the YMCA and learned what I had not learned on the farm - to swim. If their children were involved in any activity Mother and Daddy were there to see and support.

I mentioned that education was very important to both Mother and Daddy, though Mother had had the greater opportunity there. Daddy had been taken out of school as a youngster when his father, Samuel McCown Wilson, had become ill. His older brothers were in the military, serving in World War I, and he was the only one at home to take on the job of two family farms his father had been managing. Only briefly did Daddy ever get away from the frustratingly difficult job of farming. Once he went to Florida where he got a job with the engineers who were busy, even then, clearing the Florida wetlands. He loved that and said he would have liked engineering, but he was needed back on the farm, and this time he never got away. He told me, a year or so before his death, that he had never wanted to farm. I felt winded. Imagine pouring so much of oneself into a difficult, often thankless, job that one never would have chosen to do! Yet he had never complained, and he had worked hard, and he was pretty successful. He sent four kids to college!

He had help. Mother taught before she was married and sixteen years later she taught again, this time with her growing family around her. Being dissatisfied with the quality of the education available to her children in the county schools, she went back to the school for the deaf, got a teaching position, rented an apartment, and spent the week marshalling children- all by herself- and teaching. She was disappointed when our brother decided that he wanted to finish high school in the county; I'm pretty sure the rest of us weren't given a choice. Daddy concurred and drove us into town early Monday mornings and retrieved us on Friday evenings. It was a hard life for both Mother and Daddy, but each of them was convinced that this was the thing to do for our educations. I feel sure the additional opportunities provided made a major difference in my life.

They worked together to give us opportunity, and they were proud of everything we accomplished, to the time of their deaths. Mother would write a letter telling with pride what one of the other family members had done. Daddy showed pride and support too, but his praise was typically less effusive than Mother's. I recall an evening during my freshman year in college when Mother and Daddy had met my bus in Staunton and we three went to see *The Robe* before going home to Raphine. I had made the Dean's List in my first semester and I knew they would be pleased, as I was. Mother had gone on and on about my achievement as we walked toward the theater, and Daddy had said nothing. I had to hear his approval, so I asked what he thought of my grades. His response was characteristic. There was pride, but he wanted to maintain perspective. He answered, "If that's the best you can do. . ." I've never forgotten it.

They were of another generation. Daddy thought it unsuitable for one of his daughters to go to nursing school. He said that teaching and becoming a housewife were the only two suitable occupations for young ladies. And that in the 1950's! Many things in our lives were fashioned by tradition.

They were nice, both of them. They enjoyed people and met them well. They liked to do good things for others. The code of the community said that one helped his neighbor if the neighbor was unable to help himself, and my father farmed other men's fields at all hours when he was needed.

Mother loved her relatives and reflecting on her early years. She greatly enjoyed her teaching, though it became harder for her as she grew older. She loved parties and good times, in moderation. She loved cooking good food and serving it to those who were dear to her. She loved her flower garden and winning blue ribbons at the Garden Club. She reveled in beautiful things and all that was sweet and good.

Daddy loved his family in his reserved way. He loved his God and the wonders of the world around him. He was fascinated by the advancements in industry and technology. He thought man's flight was the most marvelous development he had witnessed, and he was by his television set when man set foot on the moon! It would have been interesting to hear his thoughts at that moment. He loved flowers, as Mother did, and enjoyed working with her in her Garden Club endeavors.

And, happily for us, they loved their children and were good parents to us. We owe them a great deal.

It is to these, my parents, that this book is dedicated.

Contents

Introduction

Why would one subject oneself to hundreds of hours of research and organization in order to write a book? Writing a spinetingler or a juicy novel might be fun, but a research document? But here it is. I didn't do it by myself, however. This book is the compilation of years of research on the part of a number of people, most particularly my mother, Blanche Odessa Miller Wilson, and my sister, Emma Wilson Jordan. But Martha Wilson Black, our sister, has helped too, and certainly my husband, William Long Hodges, deserves kudos for research as well as for patience and encouragement. Many others, enumerated in the acknowledgements following, have also helped or encouraged.

The product could be considered regional history, since the names in its index are names that were found in the documents of Augusta and Rockingham Counties in Virginia as early as the 1700's. These same names are found repeated in 2004 in the columns of their telephone books. Those in this book who bore those names were involved in all facets of the life of their communities, and their lives are representative of those communities.

In a limited way it is European history, for care has been given to tell something of the areas from which these ancestors came to America, if the areas are known, and of the conditions of their lives there. A sneak peek into the world at large has also been provided at the opening of many of the chapters so that the reader may relate things that were happening on the very narrow scale of the few families who found their way into our area of interest to things that were taking place all over the globe during their lifetimes. This backdrop may give more accurate, and presumably, more interesting perspective to the lives presented.

It is also family history, intended to honor the memories of my parents and to share the family data and stories with their children, grandchildren, g-grandchildren, g-g-grandchildren, and generations yet to come. Interesting ancestors will entertain present and future generations, provide for them a more personal view of history through ancestral trials and triumphs, remind them who they are by exposing their proud origins, and as Stonewall Jackson suggested, provide for each of them a model for living. If these things are made possible by this writing, my time will not have been wasted.

Even as I compose this introduction, they are all shaking their heads. "She will never finish it," they are saying. And my family has some reason for concern. This study began over thirty years ago, when Blanche Miller Wilson, my mother, became genealogically recharged because I was asked to join the Daughters of the American Revolution. I went to Mother with the application papers - where else? The four of us, my two sisters, my brother, and I, as children, had been saturated with family stories. We had heard most of them, repeatedly, from a lady who had learned to revere her family at the knees of her grandmother, Caroline Virginia Coakley Kiracofe. Once Mother got into the generational enumeration of her forebears, she branched out into Daddy's line, with equal enthusiasm. He knew something about his family, and was duly proud of every one of those old Scotch-Irish Presbyterian Valley-of-Virginians, but it was Mother who dug out the details of all the lines, with deeply-ingrained determination.

One problem: Mother didn't drive. She had laughed over her failure to learn to drive a horse and buggy in her youth, and she was just too helplessly "feminine" to even attempt a horseless vehicle. So she needed help. When she could divert our father from his busy schedule, she took him along. Otherwise, she ensnared either Emma or me, depending on which of us was at hand and moving slowly enough to be caught. We went to court houses, libraries, and archives. We visited and helped to entertain long lost relations. We dug through many dusty books, letters, and documents. Mother's enthusiasm was still greater than that of the rest of us, but we were becoming more interested, more subject to the addiction.

As her health became progressively worse, Mother became less and less able to keep up with her compelling, and much adored, study. She became easily confused and frustrated, and her attempts at recording things became equally confused and repetitious. Finally it had to stop, and for several years before her death and quite a few after, her many notes shifted from pile to pile and box to box, until we finally closed our childhood home. All of Mother's family records were piled into a box and set carefully aside, perhaps forever.

But no, it was not to be. For some reason, I had become the genealogist-apparent. Perhaps I was self-appointed; perhaps the responsibility was placed on me because I had recharged Mother's only-slightly-depleted batteries in the first place; but I was holding both Mother's box and a file of my own from our earlier treking. One night during a visit, my sister Emma said, "We really have to do something with all that stuff." We started that night, neither one of us really able to recite the names of any of our ancestors beyond our grandparents, and, with the materials we had on hand, we traced two families back to the Atlantic Ocean.

"Way leads on to way," and our simple beginnings and the enthusiasm which has resulted from our successes has taken us from a sure knowledge of four grandparents that first night to the identification and documentation of well over three hundred direct-line "grandparents."

From my point of view, we as a family are a fairly typical result of the "melting pot" that is American culture. The vast majority of our ancestors were simple, hard-working, and, happily, reasonably successful individuals. There were few who held notable wealth or power. There were no national leaders; but there were many who were local leaders, and almost all appear to have been good neighbors within their communities. There were probably no saints, but there were some who made immense sacrifices for the good of their families, their beliefs, the cause of freedom, and ultimately, for us, their descendants.

This book exposes one documented horse thief, and, as suggested above, there were some other individuals who did things about which we could not brag as we reflect on them from the enlightenment of the twenty-first century. There were some medieval Welshmen, for example, ancestors of the Gaineses of Virginia, who held tremendous power, which they wielded against others when those others were not wielding tremendous power against them. Some of them look pretty bad from this vantage point. If they had not been tyrants, would their exploits have been recorded? No. Only because they had power and wealth do we have any idea who they were. Their stories are interesting.

Then there were the Englishmen of the Coakley line who were all too glad to overpower the Irish, occupy their lands, and subjugate them in the name of their queen. The Scotsmen did some of that also. And there were others.

I don't know how you feel about those acts and others you will encounter, but you, in this book, have the opportunity to come to terms with a few individuals, most of them admirable, some perhaps flawed, whose genetic material you may share. If they appear flawed, know that history never brought charges against them, for during their time, and under the conditions in which they found themselves, most of their acts were not only condoned, but supported and encouraged as rightful acts. *Do* read about them. They, too, are interesting.

The people you will meet in generations six, seven, and eight (Chapters 1-3), along with a very few who arrived on American shores at an earlier time, came to Rockingham County by many routes from Switzerland and Germany, and from England, Scotland and Ireland. In spite of the different cultures they represented, and the particular body of experiences that led each to choose a perilous journey and an uncertain future over the less tolerable situation in which he found himself, these men and women shared a desire for personal freedom in a land of more opportunity than any of them had known before. Each of them was heroic.

Some facts I have come to face in the collecting of material and in the writing of this book, and the next one, which will deal with our father's family, are these:

- We **will never finish this book**. There is a tremendous amount of information available and, although we may have accumulated the most easily found, we will not live long enough to plumb the depths. Some of you may wish to continue our work, which has really been play.
- We have a kinship with many, many people in Rockingham County, in Virginia, in the country, and, more illusively, in Europe. I have found

direct connections with a number of people whom I had known before and with whom I would never have guessed I shared kinship. Being a Virginian has a great deal to do with that; many families left roots here as they moved westward through this state.

- There are a great number of people who are interested in genealogical research, and they are some of the most helpful people anywhere. There may be a few people who have been kind enough to help me who have been unintentionally omitted in the listing of credits below. If you are one of these, please forgive me and then tell me of my error. I want to have the opportunity to apologize and to thank you personally for your assistance.

Acknowledgements

Historical research, by nature, is never accomplished alone. I have received the instruction and support of every author whose work I have read and every individual I have consulted. Kathryn and Floyd Mason have been most generous in their support, as has John Colclough of Dublin; and Esther Lancaster of Nova Scotia and her late father, Charles Coakley. In addition I am considerably indebted to Calvin Sutherd, Lula Mae Miller, Dr. John Wayland, Dr. Paul Glick and C. E. May for their definitive works. The bibliography enumerates many other authors and contributors after whom I read and whose work I admire. In addition there were Marion Coakley, Mary Hollen, Williette Firebaugh, Leila Maxwell Miller, Irene Bixler, Galen Miller, Charles Miller, Joan Owen, Michael Buggy, Sally Roseveare, Mrs. Roy Simmons, Jim Wooddell, Anne Serrett, and my friends at Jones Memorial Library and the Bedford Public Library.

I am further indebted to members of my family who provided information, and especially to my sisters and my husband who traveled and searched with me. Jim Black set me up on the computer, and bailed me out at all hours when I had problems.

An old friend, Bob Womack, was a superior proofreader, while his son, Tom Womack, worked with my old, old pictures. Many of my new e-mail friends who were helpful are known by only one name or an address. They are appreciated, nonetheless.

Abbreviations and Such

b. born
bpt. baptized
chr. christened
m. married
d. died
c1900 "about" 1900
bef1900 before 1900
aft1900 after 1900
bet1800/1900 between1800 and 1900
MP Member of Parliament
MS Municipal Surveyor (best guess)
John Doe (5/3/1900-5/3/1966) John's birth and death dates (mo/da/yr)
Jane Doe (1/1/1900-1/1/1967) 12/25/1925 Jane's birth and death dates followed by the date of her marriage to John
Jane Doe (-1/1/1967) Jane's birthdate unknown; death date given
John Doe (5/3/1900-) John's death date unknown; birth date given
G-g-grandfather Great-great-grandfather (5th generation)
Elizabeth__ last name unknown
__Brim first name unknown
Bold Name direct line ancestor
LDS Latter Day Saints

Chapter 1
Generation 8

Where does one begin when writing the complex history of one's *being*? I have discovered no perfect way to begin the story of this composite family whose known record spans, in one line, more than twenty generations.

We, in the United States of America, tend to focus on our experience on these shores. We have studied the history of our country and most of us enjoy reading stories or seeing films about the rugged early days of the nation. We can relate to life as it was then, at least in some small measure. So there we will begin, examining the circumstances that brought Blanche Odessa Miller's many families together in what we now call Rockingham County, Virginia. During our investigation of the conditions that caused the early forebears to risk everything in order to take their chances in a new nation, we will meet the individuals who took the risks, as well as their descendants, even unto the present generation.

We have no knowledge of what caused some of our ancestors to leave their native lands. We cannot look for the records in the villages and towns from which they departed, because, although we can identify the country from which each family came, we cannot be sure of the specific area in some cases. We are certain about others, however, including the Millers.

For these *Muellers*, Johann Michael and his family, the unrest that motivated emigration was germinated when Protestantism gained a strong hold in the areas we now know as Switzerland and Germany. Until that time the Catholic Church had retained control of the state and its people, spiritually and politically. The new principle introduced by Protestantism dictated that religion be presented in such a way as to appeal to individual human reason, and liberated minds spawned all sorts of new religious organizations, and immense problems.

"Each faction became intolerant of all the others and persecution, plunder, and war followed in swift succession to compel all dissenters to the acceptance of now this, and now another form of worship."[1] This was the Thirty-Years' War of 1618-1648. Pious Germans in the valley of the Rhine suffered the horrors of persecution and worse until the Treaty of Westphalia of 1648 when Catholics, Lutherans and members of the Reformed Churches reached some accord.

War did not end at that time, regrettably. The Rhine Valley went on to experience the carnage of the wars of Frederick the Great which continued

---

[1] Martin Grove Brumbaugh, A.M., PhD, *A History of the German Baptist Brethren in Europe and America* (Elgin, Ill., Brethren Publishing House, 1906), p. 2.

until 1688, and the seemingly unending French wars, fought largely over the location of the border between France and Germany. The war-weary people moved to avoid the impossible situations in which they found themselves, only to find that similar situations existed where they next settled.

Worse yet, the intolerance which had supposedly been resolved by the Treaty of Westphalia rekindled. The state churches, now *three* in number, denied to all others the right to exist in the German Empire.[2]

"Whoever found his religious convictions running counter to these (of the state churches); whose faith was of a different sort; who interpreted his Bible in another sense; who worshiped God in his own way; found life a burden and a cross; Church and State vied in their zeal to persecute dissenters. The harmless Mennonites. . .the Pietists. . .(and others) were alike reviled, persecuted, and regarded as fit subjects for insane asylums or prisons. What happened to these in the closing years of the seventeenth century became also the fate of the Taufers (German Baptists) in the opening third of the eighteenth century."[3]

"Upon these God-fearing, conscientious people fell the full power of church and state. Their sufferings were awful. The flaming torch of persecution nightly lighted the valley of the Rhine for a hundred miles. The agonized prayers of burning saints were heard on every side. Sturdy, devout, God-strengthened men and women these, who heroically suffered and died for the religion they loved. There were no cowards in the procession that marched through howling mobs to the stake."[4]

These martyrs and their kind were known as Anabaptists. The German Anabaptists included several sects, differing from one another in their interpretation of the Bible and in the amount of authority they chose to give to the leadership within their churches.

As the printed Bible became more and more available to the common people, they expressed increasing dissatisfaction with the abuses of the state churches. Consequently, additional disastrous, state-inflicted sanctions limited personal freedom and social and economic livelihood in many areas of Europe, not only in Germany, but in Switzerland and France, and to a lesser extent in England and the Netherlands. In a large portion of Europe there were people expelled from their lands and threatened with execution for their beliefs.

Depressed economic conditions were the result of many years of war and mayhem. Because of a scarcity of laborers, the rulers in some areas found it *practical* to practice religious tolerance in order to attract settlers. Such a

---

[2]Oswald Seidensticker, *The First German Emigration to America,* as reported by Brumbaugh, p. 3.
[3] Brumbaugh, p. 3.
[4] Brumbaugh, p. 5.

place was the Palatinate area of northwestern Germany. In the early 18th century, the village of Schwarzenau, in the Rhine Valley, became a sanctuary for our Anabaptist forebears. They came to build small huts and to organize a new congregation "with the Bible as the rule and guide in all things."[5] There, under the protection of a "mild" count, liberty of conscience was allowed and the people prospered.

As soon as it was known that the area was a "Valley of Peace," it was sought by yet more people. By 1720 the group of dissenters was large enough to be conspicuous, and once more the people knew persecution. The German Baptist group then fled to Westervain in West Friesland, where it flourished for nine years before hearing of the opportunities to be had in Pennsylvania. The leaders promptly chartered the good ship *Allen* with her master, James Craigie, and sailed 7/7/1729 from Rotterdam, touching in at Cowes, England, and finally landing in Philadelphia, Pennsylvania on 9/15/1729. The ship carried 59 families, 126 people. So far as I know, none of our grandparents sailed with this group, but there were many other sailings, many other groups. Ludwig Treiber, Sr., for instance, came in 1749, as a young man of 19, from Rothenstein, Germany aboard the *Fayne*.

There were other congregations of the German Brethren which developed in such places as Marienborn, Krefeld, Eppstein and Solingen. G-g-g-g-g-grandfather John Nicholas Long/Lang came to America from Solingen, a city a few miles southeast of Dusseldorf.

The first hazards in the process of migration lay in the escape from Germany. "The passage down the Rhine to Holland took from four to six weeks. This journey was beset with many delays and inconveniences. Fees and tolls were frequently demanded. . .Ever present too must have been the fear that the authorities would halt them temporarily for some trifling matter, as often occurred, or turn them back definitely, as frequently threatened. . .On the other hand philanthropic assistance was not lacking. Along the river the Palatines were presented with money and food by pious countrymen, many of whom regarded the pilgrims with envious eyes, wishing they too might be seeking their fortune in the new World."[6]

Johann Michael Mueller, father of the immigrant Miller ancestor, was

---

[5]Brumbaugh, p. 25.

[6] Gottlieb Mittelberger, *Journey to Pennsylvania* (Philadelphia, 1898) p. 18, quoted by Walter Allen Knittle, PhD, *Early Eighteenth Century Palatine Emigration: A British Government Redemptioner Project to Manufacture Naval Stores* (Baltimore, Genealogical Publishing Co., 1965), pp. 47-50.

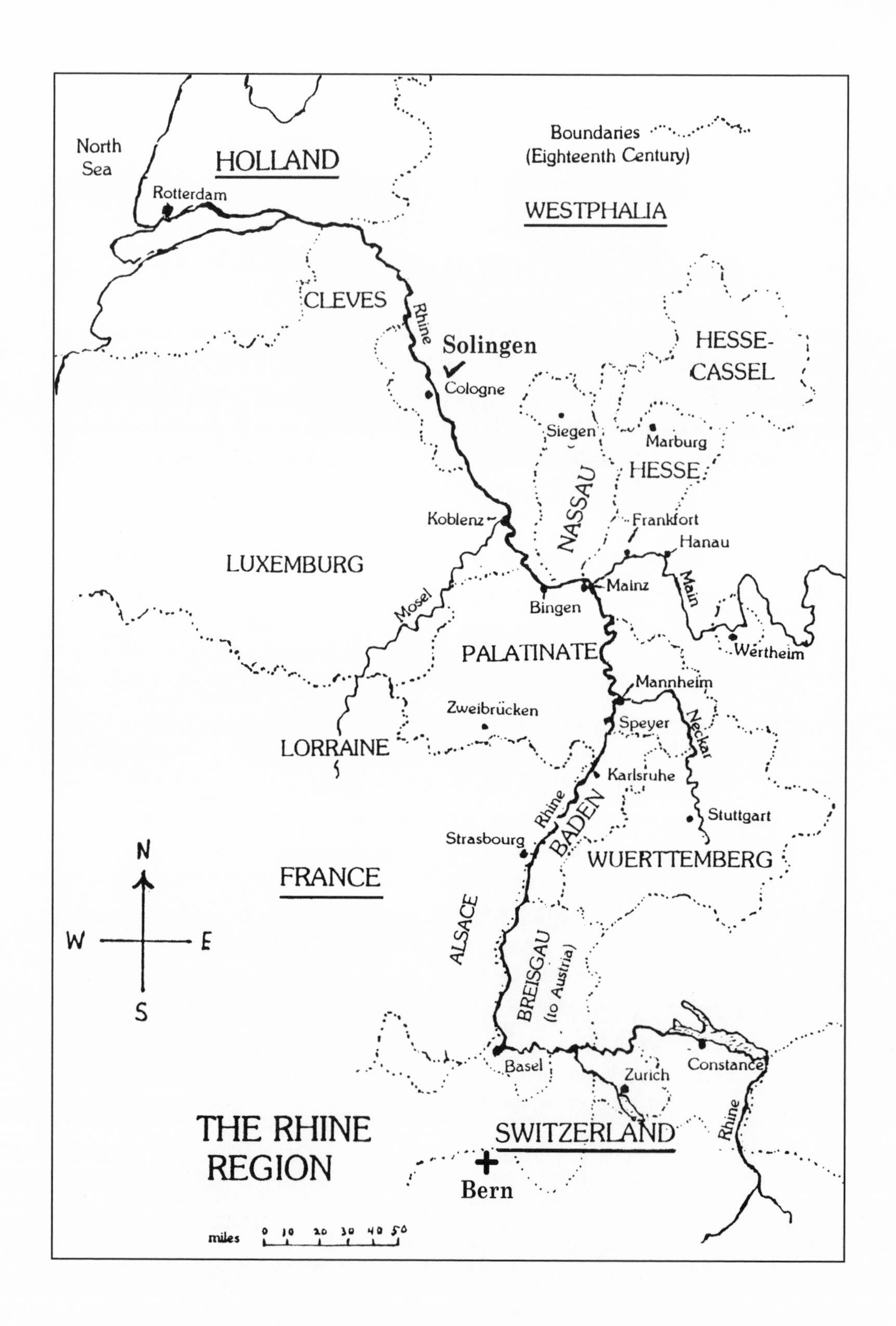

North Sea
HOLLAND
Boundaries (Eighteenth Century)
Rotterdam
WESTPHALIA
CLEVES
Rhine
Solingen
HESSE-CASSEL
Cologne
Siegen
Marburg
HESSE
NASSAU
Koblenz
Frankfort
Hanau
LUXEMBURG
Mosel
Mainz
Main
Bingen
PALATINATE
Wertheim
Mannheim
Zweibrücken
Speyer
Neckar
LORRAINE
Karlsruhe
Rhine
BADEN
Stuttgart
Strasbourg
WUERTTEMBERG
N
FRANCE
W
E
ALSACE
BREISGAU (to Austria)
S
Basel
Zurich
Constance
THE RHINE REGION
SWITZERLAND
Rhine
Bern
miles 0 10 20 30 40 50

born near Bern, Switzerland. Very likely the experiences of his family were similar to those described above. It has even been suggested that the Swiss group had experienced imprisonment for their Anabaptist beliefs and that some were actually deported to America.[7] Whatever the reason for their escape from Switzerland, Michael's father took the family to Steinwenden, Germany. From Steinwenden Michael emigrated, arriving in Philadelphia on 10/3/1727 aboard the *Adventurer.*

Of these early German immigrants it was said, "They are contented with very ordinary food, their bread being brown and their meat of the coarsest sort, which, with a few herbs, they eat with much cheerfulness and thankfulness. On the whole, they appear to be an innocent, laborious, peaceable, healthy and ingenuous people, and may be rather reckoned a blessing than a burden to any nation where they shall be settled."[8]

John Greenleaf Whittier celebrated the courage and the principles of the very early Anabaptist and Quaker adventurers in his verse. From "Pennsylvania Hall," these lines reflect their sorrows, their hopes, and their social consciousness:

"Meek-hearted Woolman and that brother-band,
The sorrowing exiles from their 'Fatherland,'
Leaving their home in Kriesheim's bowers of vine,
And the blue beauty of their glorious Rhine,
To seek amidst our solemn depths of wood
Freedom from man and holy peace with God;
Who first of all their testimonial gave
Against the oppressor, for the outcast slave.
Is it a dream that such as these look down
And with their blessings our rejoicings crown?"

John Greenleaf Whittier
from "Pennsylvania Hall"[9]

Opportunities in Penn's Country

---

[7] Todd and Goebel, p. 226, quoted by Knittle, op. cit. (Baltimore, Genealogical Publishing Co., 1965), p. 103.
[8] *The State of the Palatines*, 27; Eccles. Rec., III, 1831, quoted by Knittle, p. 70.
[9] John Greenleaf Whittier, "Pennsylvania Hall," as quoted by Oscar Kuhns in *The German and Swiss Settlements of Colonial Pennsylvania: A Study of the So-Called Pennsylvania Dutch* (Ann Arbor, Michigan, Gryphon Books, 1971), p. 40.

As we searched for our immigrant ancestors, we found it surprising that so many of them entered America through the port of Philadelphia and settled first in Pennsylvania. The Germans shared this practice with the Scotch-Irish and others. It seemed the thing to do, and there was good reason.

Harvey Lawrence Long in his publication about *The Big Long Family in America* referred to William Penn, founder of the state of Pennsylvania, as "the Father of religious liberty in America." Penn, an English Anabaptist, of a sect known as Quakers, was a man of means and connection. In 1681 he came into possession of 40,000 square miles of territory in the American wilderness. Here he began his "holy experiment."

Aware that more than 3000 Quakers had been imprisoned in England in the reign of Charles II (1660-1685), and that every American colony except Rhode Island had severe laws against those of the religion, resulting in cruel and unjust treatment of them, Penn planned a colony where Christianity could flourish without the structure of a state church. He caused a tract to be published in which he advertised the colony, and this tract was circulated in France, Germany, Holland and England. In it he offered favorable terms and complete religious liberty to all. He welcomed the persecuted of every land, the Quakers, the Mennonites, the German Baptists, and others, regardless of their beliefs. In this colony, all oppressed people were invited to live together in freedom and peace.

Our ancestors, most of them oppressed people, whether due to religious, economic or cultural reasons, or all of the above, flocked to Pennsylvania. Here they were dazzled by the prospect of owning land. They could buy 5000 acres for 100 pounds sterling, and perhaps a one shilling per 100 acre "quit rent" each year, which allowed these men of modest means to own from 200 to 1000 acres. And they no longer had to serve a feudal landlord! The land was their own!

After the rough huts, which were built on the land to provide the barest protection for the new landowner and his family, log cabins were built. By 1700 some of the houses were of stone or brick. A number of the early houses, many of them simple, but sturdy, can still be seen today, as can the large and functional barns. Folks in the Shenandoah Valley, during my youth, would tell that the immigrant farmer built the barn, moved into it his cows, sheep, and family, and, as he earned his living, would proceed with the building of the house. At that time, these families probably had the highest standard of living of any farm laborers in the world.

"Michael" Muller/Mueller/Miller was one of these men, along with several other g-g-g-g-g-grandparents you will encounter in generation eight.

(Hans) Johann "Michael" Miller

b. 10/5/1692 probably in Steinwenden, in the Rhineland-Pfaltz area of southern Germany, where his family had emigrated upon leaving Switzerland.

son of **Johann Michael Mueller** (1655-1/31/1695) and **Irene Charitas**.
Anna Loysa Regina (Johann, Sr.'s second wife) was Michael's step-mother and Jacob Stutsman II's mother. After Johann Michael Miller's (Sr.'s) death she had married Hans Jacob Stutzman (c1660-) 11/29/1696.[10]

brother of Johann Nichel Mueller (6/5/1685-6/6/1685)
Johann Abraham Mueller (6/9/1686-)
Samuel Mueller (4/30/1687-died same day)
Catharine Barbara Mueller (6/7/1688-6/29/1691)
Eva Carharine(?) Mueller (4/29/1691-6/29/1691)
Michael was the only one of the children to survive beyond infancy!
step-brother of Jacob Stutsman II (1706-1773)

m. (1)**Susannah Agnes Bechtol** (Bechtol/Bechtel) (5/3/1688-c1752);
(2)Elizabeth Gerber/Garber, widow of his friend, Nicholas Garber. Elizabeth had no children with Michael.[11]

father of John Peter Miller (1715-1794)
Hans Jeremiah Miller (1717-1781)
David Miller (1719-1785) moved to Ohio
Hans Michael Miller (1720-1784) m. Elizabeth__
George Miller (1722-1798) m. Catherine__
Lodowich Miller (c1724-1792) m. Barbara Long (c1727-)
Philip Jacob Miller (1726-1799) m. Magdalena Rochette
Michael Miller II (1728-1792)[12] m. Elizabeth__
Barbara Miller (1733-1808) m. John H. Garber (1728/1732-1787) c1752

---

[10] Floyd R. Mason and Kathryn G. Mason, *The Michael Miller and Susanna Bechtol Family Record* (Bridgewater, VA, Bridgewater Beacon Printing, Inc., 1993), pp. 10, 20.
[11] Ibid., p. 53.
[12] Two of Michael Miller's boys, Michael and Philip Jacob, are said to have appeared together, along with Simon Stucky and others, on 4/10/1767 in Lancaster County, Maryland, to take the Oath of Affirmation and state that they are residents of Frederick County of that state. (*Pennsylvania Archives,* 2nd Series, vol. 2, p. 467, quoted by Walter Carlock in *The Studebaker Family in America, 1736-1976*, Tipp City, OH, The Studebaker National Family Association, 1976), p. 677.

Jacob Miller (1735-1815) naturalized in 1747 with Lodowich; moved to Franklin County, Virginia c1765
Eva Elizabeth Miller m. Michael Danner (Tanner) (1696-1777) - his second wife
Maria Elisabeth Miller (3/19/1754-)[13]

"The step-brothers, Michael Miller and Jacob Stutsman, having lived in Germany, came to America 10/3/1727 on the ship *Adventurer*."[14] There were actually two dates of arrival for Michael Miller, this being the first, and the second being 9/23/1732, again on the *Adventurer*. Travel was not a leisure activity in those days, so Michael must have had some very good reason for this second trip. This devout German Baptist may have returned to Germany in order to tell those whom he had left behind of the successful migration of those who had found peace in Penn's country. Such "recruitment" was not unheard of during this period.

One of the more titillating finds in the search for Michael Miller was a copy of the ship list of the *Adventurer*, October 2, 1727. (Note the one day difference in the material pertaining to the ship's arrival. You will find that I am faithful to my sources, whatever they be. One day could not have made a great deal of difference, anyway.) The first name on the list is that of Michael Muller, followed by names of 30 other men, from what one can tell from the nearly illegible signatures. There is no doubt about Michael's name, however, clearly first on the list. In my imagination I could see this man, smaller in stature, perchance, than his modern-day counterpart, bouncing down the gangplank in his enthusiasm for the new opportunities in his life. I liked him immediately.

Elsewhere, however, I found another ship's list showing the name of Alexander Mack in the first position. Recognizing the importance of Alexander Mack[15] to the German Baptist movement; knowing that Michael was sent as far as South Carolina, a goodly distance considering the lack of roads and ready transportation, to help in the establishment of new congregations of the German Brethren; and having evidence that he was an associate of Mack, I decided it was possible that Michael was a leader of this group aboard the *Adventurer*. This did not make him any less appealing to my imagination.[16]

---

[13] Mason, *Miller Record*, p. 20.

[14] Floyd R. Mason, compiler, *Michael Miller of 1692 and His Descendants* (Bridgewater, VA, 1986), p. 2.

[15] Alexander Mack was the spiritual leader of the German Baptist movement. His son, Alexander, Jr. led the church after the death of his father.

[16] Ralph Beaver Strassburger, *Pennsylvania German Pioneers: A Publication of the Original Lists of Arrivals in the Port of Philadelphia from 1727 to 1808*, vol. 1, William John Hinke, ed. (Baltimore, Genealogical Publishing Co., 1980), p. 4.

It might be emphasized at this point that Michael had *signed* his name, as had others of the German people with whom he arrived in the American colonies. Several authors have commented that the German immigrants were better schooled than were some of our other forebears whose wills were signed with a mark. The German Baptists stressed the value of individual worship, including the reading of the Bible, so education was important in their lives.

The Masons, authors of the *Michael Miller Family Record*, conducted an extensive search for Michael's land records. They reported no evidence of land ownership before 1744, although Michael paid a tax on land in Chester County, Coventry Township, Pennsylvania for the years 1732-1740. He was also known to have taken a warrant for another 200 acres of land in 1737, but apparently had never obtained a patent for the property.[17]

Land purchases over the years by Michael Miller included:

1744..shared 100 acres with Samuel Bechtol in York County, Pennsylvania northeast of Hanover; sold in 1752 at which time he was living in Frederick County, Maryland. Nicholas Garber was also involved in this transaction.

1745..“Ash Swamp” 150 acres near Hagerstown; resurveyed to sons, John, Philip Jacob, and Lodowich in 1752, probably after the death of Susannah.[18]

1749.. “Millers Fancy” a 36 acre grant located at the mouth of Little Antietam where it joins Antietam Creek between Skipton on Craven and Resurvey of Well Taught; he and Elizabeth lived there until his death in 1771 after which it was deeded to Elizabeth's son-in-law.

1749..“Skipton on Craven” 180 acres. In 1765 he deeded it to Jacob Good and John Rife, Elizabeth's sons-in-law.

1755..“Resurvey of Well Taught” 409 acres. This land was described as limestone land on the Antietam which includes the site of Leitersburg, Maryland. Michael lived on 8 of the 409 acres, on the east side of Antietam Creek, and the 36 acres mentioned above, called "Miller's Fancy." This land also became the property of sons-in-law.

1760..“Blindman's Choice” a grant, surveyed, 50 acres. He gave this to

[17] Mason, *Miller Record,* p. 14.

[18] “We have no death date for Susanna Bechtol…but an administrative record in the Orphan's Court of York County, Pennsylvania states that in 1754 Elizabeth Garber, the widow of Nicholas Garber, is now the wife of Michael Miller and that he is administering the accounts for (Nicholas Garber's) will…12/10/1754.” Mason, *Miller Record,* p. 12.

Michael Miller, Jr.

____...had "Range" surveyed, 50 acres believed to be on Piney Creek; sold in 1765 to Michael and Eve Tanner. There is speculation that Eve (Eva) was one of Michael Miller's and Susanna Bechtol's daughters.[19]

Considering Michael's obvious desire that his and Elizabeth's offspring own land, it is not surprising to read that he gave his son Hans Michael Miller 1000 pounds to purchase what must have been a sizeable parcel of land called Pleasant Gardens, located near Maugansville, Maryland.

Michael was paying taxes on Skipton on Craven, Miller's Fancy and Resurvey of Well Taught as late as 1763. By 1765 he had deeded all of this land to one child or another, although he continued to live on Miller's Fancy and 8 acres of Survey of Well Taught until his death in 1771. The fact that his heirs paid the taxes due on the property from 1769 until the time of his death seems to indicate that he was physically or financially unable to handle this responsibility, or that he had come to some agreement with his heirs before deeding the land to them.

"We found that after the death of Michael Miller (Sr.) in 1771, both Michael Miller Jr. and Hans Michael Miller were paying the tax in succeeding years. (In addition) Philip Jacob Miller was paying taxes on the 290 acres of 'Ash Swamp' and Lodowich Miller was paying taxes on land that he had bought near Taneytown, Maryland."[20]

Our German forebears, as well as those from other cultures, were hungry for independence and willing to work hard for wealth. There was certainly no dishonor associated with working the land. In fact, as previously mentioned, these families found land ownership and the labor that accompanied it a privilege. Members of each family worked hard together to make a living. They were typically frugal and in many cases set aside the funds that would enable at least one member of the family to study in order to be able to render service to the total community.[21] The Miller family produced many preachers.

"When (Michael Miller and his peers) got around to establishing churches a few years after they settled in the American colonies, they did so with vigor, sending men on missionary tours into the backcounty in the 1720's. Some of them, including Michael Miller, traveled as far as South

---

[19] Mason, *Miller Record*, p. 14.

[20] Mason, *Miller Record*, pp. 13-14.

[21] Mason, *Miller Record*, p. III.

Carolina for this purpose. One of the institutions founded, the Ephrata cloister (in Pennsylvania), became, by 1775, one of the outstanding Protestant monasteries in America, a strong influence on the Brethren settlements from Pennsylvania and Maryland to North and South Carolina."[22]

The Miller family, along with the Garbers, are thought to have attended the German Baptist churches in Coventry Township, Chester County; in Manheim Township, York County; and in Frederick (later called Washington) County, Maryland.

"Some think that Michael Miller...and some of his sons were members at Little Conewingo and the Antietam congregations. Elder Nicholas Martin, the elder of the churches in the area where they lived, reported on the health of Michael Miller and Jacob Stutsman in his letters to Alexander Mack, Jr...."[23]

d. 1771

It was reported in a letter from Nicholas Martin written in Conococheague 5/24/1772 that. . ."dear Brother Michael Miller died a year ago."[24]

Michael is believed to be buried on the plantation where he lived or in the family cemetery on John Miller's section of Ash Swamp, but "(s)ome records say (Jacob Stutsman II and Michael Miller) lived and were buried at Conococheaque, Washington County, near Hagerstown, Maryland."[25]

Aside from the responsibilities this energetic man assumed in relation to his family and his church, he also served his community as Constable in the area of Upper Antietam Hundred in 1760.[26]

G-g-g-g-g-grandfather- 8th generation

Susanna Agnes Berchtol/Bechtel

b. 5/3/1688 in Krottelbach, Germany

daughter of **Hans Berchtoll** (-6/15/1711) and **Anna Christina** (-bef 1686)

---

[22] Roger E. Sappington, *The Brethren in Virginia: The History of the Church of the Brethren in Virginia* (Harrisonburg, The Committee for Brethren History, 1973), pp. 1-7.
[23] Mason, *Miller Record*, p. 10.
[24] Donald F. Durnbaugh, ed., *The Brethren in Colonial America* (Elgin, Illinois, The Brethren Press, 1967), p. 255.
[25] Mason, *Miller Record*, p. 20.
[26] Mason, *Miller Record*, p. 54.

sister of Hans Jacob Berchtoll (1686-1739) m. Anna Marie Glosselloss
Hans Peter Berchtoll (5/1/1690-)(twin) m. Maria Elizabeth Zimmer
Hans Heinrich Berchtoll (5/1/1690-)
Barbel (Barbara) Berchtoll (c1693-)
Ursula Berchtoll (1696-)

The Berchtol family was Mennonite, attending the Konken Church.[27]

m. **(Hans) Johann "Michael" Miller** (1692-1771)

mother of John Peter Miller (1715-1794)
Hans Jeremiah Miller (1717-1781)
David Miller (1719-1785)
Hans Michael Miller (1720-1784) m. Elizabeth__
George Miller (1722-1798) m. Catherine__
Lodowich Miller (c1724-1792) m. Barbara Long (c1727-)
Philip Jacob Miller (1726-1799) m. Magdalena Rochette
Michael Miller II (1728-1792)
Barbara Miller (1733-1808) m. John H. Garber (1728/1732-1787) 1752
Jacob Miller (1735-1815)
Eva Elizabeth Miller m. Michael Danner (Tanner) (1696-1777). She was his second wife.
Maria Elisabeth Miller (3/19/1754-)

d. c1752, probably in Pennsylvania[28]

G-g-g-g-g-grandmother- 8th generation.

John Nicholas "Nikol" Lang

b. c1702

Our immigrant in this line, John probably started for the New World from Solingen, Germany, a town north of Cologne just off the Rhine River

---

[27] Mason, *Miller Record*, p. 9.
[28] We believe (Susanna) died in 1752 at the time that Michael had land, 'Ash Swamp', in Maryland resurveyed for the three sons, John, Philip Jacob and Lodowich. This explains why there is no wife's signature on the deeds...and perhaps why the land was divided." Mason, *Miller Record*, p. 12.

near the French border. He arrived on the ship *Harle* 9/1/1736 at age 34. Embarking from Rotterdam, they had stopped briefly at Cowes, England, as had other German emigrants of the period. On this boat, small by our standards, were packed 388 immigrants: 151 men, 65 women, and 172 children.[29] Most of these people were Pietist dissenters from the established Catholic and Lutheran churches in the area along the Rhine known as the Palatinate.[30]

m. **Anna Maria Studebaker** (bpt.10/15/1702-bef1776) probably in Germany

father of **Barbara Long/Lang** (c1727-) m. Lodowich Miller (c1724-1792)
John Long (1728-) m. (1)Anna Catharina Studebaker; (2)Margaret__;
of "Baker's Lookout," old homestead in Maryland.
Frederick Long (c1732-) m. Elizabeth Studebaker (c1737-)
David Long (c1738/40-1763) m. Maria Christina Studebaker
(11/9/1734-)

d. 1776

G-g-g-g-g-grandfather- 8th generation

Anna Maria Studebaker

bpt. 10/15/1702

daughter of **Casper Stutenbecker** (c1646-1710) and **A. Gertrude von Staden** (c1670-1706) from the vicinity of Hagen, Germany.

Anna Maria was listed as Marie Langin, aged 33, when she arrived in Philadelphia 9/1/1736. The name Langin includes a feminine ending, accounting for the difference in spelling from that of her husband's name. This family arrived with the family of Peter Studebaker, Clement and Heinrich Studebaker, and with Johannes Gerber, who is most likely G-g-g-g-g-grandfather John Garber.

sister or half-sister of Peter Studenbecker (c1698-)

---

[29] Harvey Lawrence Long, AB, MA, JD, *The Big Long Family in America, 1736-1976: A Host of Descendants of John Long 1728-1791* (Ogle County, IL, 1981), pp. xv-18.
[30] Walter Carlock, *The Studebaker Family in America, 1736-1976* (Tipp City, OH, The Studebaker National Family Association, 1976), p. 3.

Clement Studenbecker (c1700-)[31]
half-sister of Heinrich Studebaker (bpt. 9/19/1708-)[32]

m. **John Nicholas "Nikol" Lang**

mother of **Barbara Long** (c1727-) m. Lodowich Miller (c1724-1792)
John Long (1728-) of Baker's Lookout m. (1)Anna Catharina Studebaker; (2)Margaret__
Frederick Long (c1732-) m. Elizabeth Studebaker (c1737-)
David Long (c1738/40-1763) m. Maria Christina Studebaker (11/9/1734-)

d. bef1776

G-g-g-g-g-grandmother- 8th generation

Michael Sprenkle (Sprenckel)

b. in Switzerland

m. **Ann Margaretha Mueller**

father of **Anna Barbara Sprenkle** (1737-c1781) m. Ludwig Treiber (Lewis Driver, Sr.)(c1728-bef1772) bef1754

This family settled first in Conestoga (at another mention, Codorus) Township, Lancaster, Pennsylvania. Michael "took up" 500 acres of land along Codorus Creek in York County, situated on the west side of the Susquehanna River. In 1747 he added 200 adjoining acres to that tract.

Michael was a signatory of a letter that a number of German settlers in the Kreutz Creek Valley wrote to the Governor of Maryland.

---

[31] Carlock, p. 3.

[32] Anna's brother, Heinrich, is remembered in the annals of Pennsylvania history because he and his pregnant wife were massacred in an Indian raid. It seems that General Braddock and George Washington, in a failed attempt to drive the troublesome French and Indians from lands west of the Alleghanies in 1755, succeeded only in stirring up serious trouble for the settlers along their route. In the raid on the Studebaker home, in what is now Franklin County, Pennsylvania, all of the children were captured, except the eldest daughter who was visiting away from home. In 1764 two of the children were returned, but they had lost all memory of their lives before the Indians and one, a daughter named Elizabeth, ran away and returned to the Indians.

d. c1748. His wife, Margaret, survived him.[33]

G-g-g-g-g-grandfather- 8th generation

Ann Margaretha Mueller

m. **Michael Sprenkle**, immigrant

mother of **Anna Barbara Sprenkle** (1737-c1781) m. Ludwig Treiber (Lewis Driver, Sr.)(c1728-c1772)

d. aft1748

G-g-g-g-g-grandmother- 8th generation

Hans Gerber/Garber

b. 1700 in Switzerland

Hans possibly immigrated in 1726 from Switzerland, by way of Germany, settling in the Colebrook Valley in Coventry Township, Chester County, Pennsylvania by 1729. On 5/10 of that year he petitioned, along with a group of settlers, for protection from Indian attacks near Falckner's Swamp and Goschenhoppen.[34] The signature of Johannes Garber on the petition is identical to the signature on his will, written in 1748.

brother of Niclaus Gerber (1698-1748) m. Elizabeth __, who became the second wife of Michael Miller (10/5/1692-1771)

At some time prior to 1728 he married, but we know not where or to whom. Those of the children who have been identified as belonging to this family began to appear, however, at about that time. They were:

Johannes H. Garber (1728/1732-1787) m. Barbara Miller (1733-1808) c1752

---

[33] Carolyn Click Driver and Bertha Driver Gassett, *Descendants of Ludwig Treiber (Lewis Driver) and Barbara Sprenkle in The Shenandoah Valley of Virginia The United States of America,* 1990, pp. 3-3B.

[34] Steven R. Garber and Jerry R. Masters, "Gerber, Garber and Garver Progenitors in Pennsylvania," *Pennsylvania Mennonite Heritage*, vol. 22, no. 3, July 1999, pp. 25, 30.

Martin Garber (c1733-c1800) m. Anna (Preston?)
possibly Nicholas Carver (1742-); moved to Virginia in 1783

By 1744 Hans moved with his brother Nicholas to a Mennonite settlement in Heidelberg Township, York County, Pennsylvania. Nicholas had bought a 100 acre farm, and this he shared with his brother, Hans. An inventory dated 4/26/1748 indicates that Nicholas owned the farm, valued at 150 pounds, on which Hans owned improvements valued at 115 pounds.[35]

"Some researchers contend the name (Garber) is derived from the German word which means to tan, polish or curry, while others propose that it is derived from a similar word which means 'to gather into sheaves.' "[36]

d. 1748

G-g-g-g-g-grandfather- 8th generation

James Cokeley

It is reported in our family that the Daniel James Coakley who settled in the Shenandoah Valley by 1810 was named for his grandfather. We have always assumed that the immigrant's name, therefore, was exactly the same as his. And it may have been so. Or, on the other hand, perhaps the "James" only was received from his grandsire. We do know that our immigrant ancestor used the name James, or James, Sr., for this is the way we find him in those records which remain.

James may have been born in Ireland. Charles Coakley of Nova Scotia, a researcher who spent considerable time in Ireland and in England and who met members of the family there, stated that James was the second son of John Coakley of "southern" Ireland. There is information that is missing here, however, in spite of considerable efforts to find it.[37] James might even have been born in the West Indies.

The Irish Coakleys/Cokeleys/Colcloughs are traditionally associated

[35] Garber and Masters, p. 25.

[36] Garber and Masters, p. 30.

[37] John Colclough of Dublin, a most knowledgeable genealogist, feels that we may be descendants of Sir Patrick Colclough through his son, Adam of Boley; or of Thomas of Currach, Patrick's brother, through Caleb Coakley of Currach; or perhaps of Caesar "the Great" Colclough, Patrick's grandson through the line of Dudley of Duffrey. Caesar was known to have had a dalliance or two. Caesar's brothers, John of Ballyteige and Henry of Kildavin are also candidates, though I think they are less likely than others named here.

with Tintern Abbey, a wonderful old Cistercian Abbey in County Wexford, in the southeastern corner of Ireland. Bill and I have visited there twice, once with patient friends who were willing to miss lunch, just once, to humor me in my excitement; again, with my sister, Martha, and her husband. It was a thrill on both occasions, and I am assured by those there who know the family history, that, one way or another, this will prove to be the family seat.

But who were James's parents? What of John Coakley, Adam, or Caleb, for that matter? Was one of those the father of "James"? I have scoured libraries, at home and abroad, and found no answers. Two researchers have been employed, one in County Wexford and one in the Bahamas, and so far, there is no conclusive response.

Family members have visited with me the plantation that belonged to James in King George County, Virginia. There a distant cousin, Joan Owen, descendant of James's son, William, assisted us. We drove through the area that belonged to James. We saw what we assume to be the house site. We looked at the shore to see it as this man must have seen it when he first sailed up the Potomac River. We have found James, but his parentage remains a mystery.

How could a man who was given a grant of 3000 acres of land for a plantation on Andros Island; who was outfitted with two sailing vessels, one for his family, another for slaves who would work the plantation, or who had the personal means to outfit himself in this manner; who has, to this day, a town bearing his name on the island of Andros; whose name, Coakley, is used by island residents who are presumably descendants of the slaves that were left behind there; who subsequently owned 1300 acres of land that is now a part of King George County, Virginia and who left descendants there; *how could there be no records* to tie this man to his Irish family? Where *does* one go to find them?

According to a letter from Marion Coakley of 1/6/1967: "A tradition has been carried down that Daniel James Cokeley came with his wife and family to America from Ireland and settled in the eastern part of Virginia, east of Fredericksburg, the land being located in the counties of Spotsylvania and Caroline. Two figures have been given as to the size of the plantation they owned: one, 1300 acres, another 3000, and it has been said that they owned many slaves." There are obvious flaws in that "tradition," but one cannot afford to cast out ideas until all have been thoroughly investigated.

Many of our problems stem from the fact that records in the parishes of eastern Virginia have been destroyed. After the British were defeated there was among the colonists considerable hard feeling toward them and their rule. Many sought to destroy everything British, and in so doing, destroyed their own court and parish records, to the extent that they were able. There was also destruction of courthouses and many other properties at the time of the Civil War. And, of course, there were the occasional accidental fires and discardings that happen over time.

Charles Coakley says that James was brother of: Henry Coakley, who left Ireland for America in 1745, never to be heard of again;
William Coakley, who went to New Zealand, where his descendents still live;
Richard Coakley, who went to Brazil, where his descendents still live; and
John Coakley, who stayed in Ireland, becoming the ancestor of the Nova Scotia family of Coakleys.

I cannot reproduce the research that is reported here.

m. (1)**Margaret Antonison** 6/30/1745 on Antigua;[38] 2)Violet Buttridge 1/12/1786 [39]

father of **Benjamin(e) Coakley** (c1750-11/21/1782) m. Catherine__
William Coakley m. Mildred Sullivan 2/4/1781
James Coakley, Jr. (bpt.1/12/1746/7-)[40] m. 1)Nancy Wilson (bef4/9/1787-bef1798); 2)Susannah Dishman 1/10/1798[41]
John Coakley (c1760-1820) who appeared in the 1810 Census of Spotsylvania County; m. Mary_, possibly Mary Smallwood 5/30/1772, St. Michael, Barbados
and possibly Elizabeth Cockley, who was found, along with John, witnessing a ten acre land transaction[42]

According to tradition, James started his adventure with his wife and sons, his personal possessions and his farming tools in one ship, and 100 slaves in another. He went to Andros Island, just north of Cuba in the

[38] James and Margaret were reportedly married at St. John's, an Anglican church which was then a simple wooden building, "devoid of beauty or comfort," built in 1683-1684. (Vere Langford Oliver, MRCS, &c., *Caribbeana; Being Miscellaneous Papers Relating to the History, Genealogy, Topography, and Antiquities of the British West Indies,* vol. 3, London, Mitchell Hughes and Clarke, 1910, p. 236.)

[39] John Bailey Calvert Nicklin, *St. Paul Parish Register: Stafford and King George Counties, 1715-1798* (Baltimore, Genealogical Book Co., 1962), p. 10.

[40] Upon writing to a library I discovered on the internet, I received a copy of a scrap of paper, giving no citation. From all evidence, it was copied from a register showing three baptisms which took place between 1/4/1746 or 47 and 1/12/1746 or 47 in Saint John's Parish in Antigua. It reported, "James the son of James Coakley and Margt. His Wife." Only that and the date.

[41] From the notes of Walter Coakley, genealogist.

[42] *King George County Deed Book 6,* 1745-1784, p. 13.

Bahamas, where he took possession of 3000 acres of land he had been given by the English government.[43] It would have been his intention to grow tobacco, sugar cane, cotton, and sweet potatoes for the English market. He built on the island, spawning a community called Coakley Town, but abandoned his plans after five years because three hurricanes, during those five years, had destroyed his crops and one of his ships. He left, taking with him his family, a few trusted servants, and those possessions he could carry on his remaining ship. He sailed to the Virginia colony, promising his slaves that he would return for them. He never did.

Arriving in Virginia he is said to have disposed of his ship and acquired 1300 acres of land along Poplar Road, which was then an old crooked buffalo trail.[44] The plantation buildings stood near the present location of the village of Ninde. One building, a mill built of stone, survived until it was torn down in the 1960's to make way for the new road between Colonial Beach and Fredericksburg. The mill was powered by a stream which is now the county line between King George and Westmoreland counties. The Cokeley plantation extended from the Potomac to the Rappahannock River in that area known as the Northern Neck today.

James Cokeley's name is first found in Virginia on a petition in which he and 121 other colonists asked the "Honourable Convention of Virginia" to establish a new ferry crossing at Gibsons in King George County because "thro' Caprice ill-Nature or perhaps from selfish Views" Mr. Miller, the "obstinate and Preverse" ferryman had moved the landing to an inconvenient, and possibly dangerous place on the Rappahannock River.[45] This undated petition was presented to the convention on 6/1/1776.[46]

During the Revolution citizens often contributed foodstuffs and supplies to the militia and continental armies. In the more difficult times these things might be confiscated. Certificates were provided to the "contributor" so that he might be reimbursed later. James Cokeley apparently held a certificate

---

[43] I was disappointed to find no evidence of so large a grant of land until Bill and I read that many of the grants made in the name of the crown were actually made by local officials in the islands. And as we found in the Bahamas, many of those early records no longer exist.

[44] A slice of life in those days: "Docks on the Rappahannock River were...crossroads for commerce between (growers) and shipping owners. Tobacco was a major crop...Hogsheads drawn by oxen were pulled over 'rolling roads' made with logs...Farmers came to market day with the season's harvest...Quilts (covered) the tobacco to keep it moist..." (Mary Tod Haley, *Caroline County, A Pictorial History,* Norfolk, Donning Co., Publishers, 1985), p. 11.

[45] *Fifth Virginia Convention Proceedings* and notes 4-5.

[46] This petition was granted in 10/1776 in "An Act for Establishing Several New Ferries, and for Discontinuing a Former Ferry," as reported by William Waller Hening, *The Statutes at Large; Being a Collection of the Laws of Virginia from the First Session of the Legislature in the Year 1619* (Richmond, 1821), pp. 233-235.

for 275 pounds of beef that he provided.[47]

The family sold quite a bit of the land but lost more of it by "going security" during the Revolution. In the records of the King George County Court of November 1782[48] there are lists of . . . "persons whose property was seized or taken for public use. . . Among the names is one James Cokly."[49] Most of these seizures took place in 1781 during the Yorktown Campaign. Activity resulting from the Revolution caused considerable hardship for big land owners, and the Civil War, later, was likewise disastrous, because no one was left to work the land and there were problems of high taxation.[50] We do not know how each of these events specifically impacted the Coakley family.

In the *King George County Order Book 4* of 5/4/1786, Benjamin Johnson sued James Cockly, Sr. for debt, this after the Cokeley property had been confiscated.[51]

On 8/3/1787 the Executor of the John Pick estate was awarded a judgment, presumably for debt, against James Cockly, Sr. and his attorney, Thomas Hailes.[52]

In spite of conditions of relative poverty after the Revolution, James seems to have maintained his standing in the community. In 1784 he witnessed a land transaction involving a 557 acre plantation;[53] and in 1786 he remarried!

In 1787 James, along with his sons William and James, Jr., were taxed in King George County; John was taxed in Fredericksburg Town.[54] Benjamin was deceased.

At this time James paid a tax on 2 horses and 3 cows.

d. 1788

"James, Sr." apparently left no will, and after his death the settlement of his affairs became a problem. Thomas Hailes, his attorney, caused James's

---

[47] Janice L. Abercrombie and Richard Slatten, compilers, *Virginia Publick Claims: King George County* (Athens, GA, Iberian Publishing Co., 1991), p. 17.
[48] Lyon G. Tyler, MA, LLD, ed., *Tyler's Quarterly Historical and Genealogical Magazine,* vol. 5 (Richmond, Richmond Press, Inc., 1924), pp.54-56.
[49] Walter Coakley notes.
[50] Information contributed by Marion Coakley, Dayton, VA, 1994.
[51] *King George County Order Book 4A*, p. 279, as cited by Walter Coakley.
[52] *Ibid*., p. 365.
[53] *King George County Deed Book 7*, 1785-1793, p. 56.
[54] Netti Schreiner and Florene S. Love, compilers, "King George County Personal Property Tax 1787, List B" from the *1787 Census of Virginia,* vol. 1 (Springfield, VA, Genealogical Books in Print, c1987), p. 370.

son William to be summoned to appear in order to serve as executor for his father's estate.[55] Since William, the "heir at law," did not respond to the summons, his brother, James, Jr., was likewise summoned, not once but twice.[56] He, also, failed to come forward, and in the end Thomas Hailes, himself, posted bond in the amount of one hundred pounds and administered the estate.

Why James's sons refused to administer his estate remains a puzzle. Ill health might have been a reason, or inconvenience, though it is known that William lived nearby; or it may be that there was some risk to an heir in settling an indebted estate. I have read of such an occurrence.

G-g-g-g-g-grandfather- 8th generation

The Coakleys left their mark on the land which James owned when he arrived in the American colonies. Between the years of 1884 and 1918 there was a Coakley Post Office near Ninde in King George County, Virginia.[57]

Andros Island

The Bahamas were "discovered by a Genoese sailor in 1492, depopulated by the Spanish, resettled by Bermudian adventurers, held hostage by rapscallion bands of buccaneers, cultivated by Loyalist refugees from the American Revolution and African slaves, bloated by profits from Civil War blockade-running, devastated by everything from insects to hurricanes, and, finally, resurrected by tourism. . . ."[58]

One of approximately 700 islands, Andros is the largest of the Bahamas, approximately 104 miles long and 40 miles wide, with pine and mahogany forests, creeks and prolific bird life. Hans Hannau, in his book *Islands of the Bahamas* referred to it as one of the largest unexplored tracts of land in the Western Hemisphere. Andros is, according to native Indian myth, the exclusive home of the *Chickcharnies*, three-fingered, three-toed, red-eyed Bahamian elves that make mischief for people if disturbed.[59]

Coakley Town, and most of the other development on the island, is located on the east coast. It, along with Andros Town and Fresh Creek, is

---

[55] *King George Order Book 4A,* p. 425.
[56] *King George Order Book 4A*, pp. 434, 436.
[57] "Post Offices," *The Virginia Genealogist*, vol. 23, January/March 1979, pp. 55-57.
[58] Peter Benchley, "The Bahamas," *National Geographic,* vol. 162, no. 3, (Sept. 1982), p. 373.
[59] Hans W. Hannau, *Islands of the Bahamas* (New York, Hastings House Publishers, n.d.), pp. 105-106.

compressed into a small area, to the extent that one town is indistinguishable from another. The land lies on a large stream called Fresh Creek, and faces the world's second largest coral barrier reef. Adjacent to the reef, which is, in places, twenty thousand feet thick, is the "Tongue of the Ocean," a thousand fathom deep crevasse in the Atlantic, which has been used since 1963 as the site for the Atlantic Undersea Testing and Evaluation Center to test undersea devices and nuclear submarines.[60] The town sites, the naval testing center, and a dazzling white beach on which we briefly strolled, interrupting the activities of a couple of conch hunters, are all likely to have been on the land once granted by "the king" to James Cokeley.

In 1718 Captain Woodes Rogers convinced the English Crown to buy out other countries which still held title to the lands of the Bahamas, and it was he who became the first honest and effective governor. After his term in office, the problems of the Bahamas alluded to above wore down a succession of governors. By 1741, about the time of James's arrival, there were 2,303 settlers, along with a goodly number of slaves, in the islands. And there were inconveniences: ". . .there was not one mason, . . .there were no wheeled vehicles, . . .war with Spain recurred. . ."[61]

And there were the hurricanes. "The greatest natural killer in the Bahamas has always been hurricanes. . .often caus(ing) more devastation than a war. . .in 1866 on Nassau 601 houses were demolished and 600 damaged. . . Of 200 ships at anchor in Nassau Harbour, 199 were sunk or smashed to splinters. . .Hurricanes in the 1920's damaged farming and the sponge industry on the Bahamas' largest island, Andros, which, with 2,300 square miles, constitutes 43 percent of all the land in the country."[62] Considering his own experience with loss to hurricanes and the general history of the weather of the islands, it is not surprising that James decided this was not the location for a successful plantation.

There was undoubtedly another good reason for his abandonment of the land grant on Andros. James's intent was to make his fortune as a planter. I can imagine his feelings when he saw and scratched at the land he had been given. It is filled with rock, and of a very coarse texture. We saw no place where one might cut a row for planting, the land appearing to be more like concrete than soil. Much of the terrain is swampy, and whether swampy or not, it is heavily covered with mangrove thickets. There are few trees, but bush-like entanglements are everywhere, the narrow road on which we traveled having been cleared through them. We asked if people gardened there and were

---

[60] *1990 Caribbean Islands Handbook* (Prentice Hall, 1989), p. 55.

[61] Hannau, pp. 16-19.

[62] Benchley, p. 390.

assured that there were some family gardens. It seems that the would-be gardener cuts down the vegetation with a machete and burns it on the ground where it is cut. Then he plants anywhere he can get into the soil. With the technology available to James, operating a plantation on Andros would likely have been infeasible. The soil in Virginia must have been a welcome sight after that experience.

A Rediscovery of Andros

On the morning of March 7, 2001, my husband, Bill, and I stood outside the small airport at Andros (Town) on the island of the same name. We had flown over from Nassau, where we were vacationing and researching the history of the Coakley family. Two or three taxis were waiting for fares, and the driver of one of them, Irvin Mackey, was gently insistent that he could find people for us to interview and had the day to dedicate to the task. He was hired, and we discovered that the choice we had made was a good one. We would surely have been proverbial "fish out of water," had we not an experienced guide who knew the roads and the people of the area. He took us first to Small Hope Bay Lodge, a diving and snorkling resort, where the proprieters were interested in our mission. They arranged for us to meet two of their employees, one of whom was named Rudolph Coakley.

After introducing ourselves and telling Mr. Coakley of our mission, he volunteered information that was as corroborative as any that I have found of the oral tradition of the Coakley family of Virginia. He stated that the story his family had passed down was that the "master" had brought his family from England, stopping by Eleuthra on the way, and had settled on Andros. I am not sure that I asked all that I should have after this discovery, for I was thrilled to hear a story that seemed to confirm the oral tradition of our own family. I do not think Rudolph Coakley knew what had happened to the "master," but I failed to ask.

I did tell Mr. Coakley that I had had some concern about how the slaves would have felt about being abandoned in the islands as the slave master sailed off without them. Mr. Coakley seemed to think that this would not have been very upsetting to them. After all, they then became freedmen, and, as we discovered in the land and survey office on Nassau, the next time the king granted the land that James had abandoned as he left for calmer waters, it was awarded to Peter Coakley, Galem Coakley, Catherine Coakley, Jupiter Coakley, and George Coakley, among others, all of them descendants of the freed former slaves of Andros. The grants made at this time by King George

III, presumably c1790, were considerably smaller in size than the 3000 acre one allotted to James, but were probably portions of the same land that had been granted to him almost fifty years before. The records of these grants constitute the first written record of the land holdings on Andros Island to be found there. Much of this land is still owned by members of the Coakley family today.

I asked Mr. Coakley if he had any impressions that had been handed down in his family's oral tradition about what kind of man the master had been or how his former slaves had felt about him. The only evidence as to these feelings that the two of us discovered was found in the fact that to his generation, his family is still making use of the given names which my family used in Virginia. This use of names was reported to me by other branches of the Bahamian Coakley family, as well, in telephone or personal interviews. Those names which are recurrent are Benjamin, John, William, Daniel, and James.

After we had exhausted our list of people to interview and spots to view on Andros, Mr. Mackey drove Bill and me to a beautiful beach where the locals hold their festivals. It was a short distance from the towns and pristine in its isolation and in the beauty of its jade waters and brilliantly white sands. I was later told that this beach would likely have belonged to James. Perhaps his family had enjoyed that spot, as we did.

Margaret Antonison

Nothing is known of Margaret, except that she was married to James on the island of Antigua on 6/30/1745 in St. John's Parish. It is therefore assumed that she had lived there with her parents who, like James and his family, had come to seek their fortunes in the Leeward Islands. Many Europeans were drawn there by land which was readily available. The name Antonison could be either Danish or Scottish. Having searched in vain for it in Danish records,[63] and having found a number of Scottish Antonisons, spelled in a number of ways, I am inclined to think that Margaret's family must have been Scottish.[64]

[63] Among the directors of the Danish company responsible for establishing colonies in the West Indies was Ferdinand Anthon, appointed in 1723, then again in 1732, to serve until 9/12/1732. Family tradition includes a Danish princess somewhere along the way. Could Margaret have been that "princess?" Not likely, but an interesting coincidence nonetheless. I really believe Margaret was a Scottish lassie. (Waldemar W. Westergaard, *The Danish West Indies Under Company Rule, 1671-1754*, New York, Macmillan Co., 1917, pp. 290-291.)

[64] George Suckling, a lawyer who tried to establish a system of law on Tortola, had little good to say about the planters, whom he felt were not interested in law because it might actually work to

probable mother of **Benjamin**(e) **Coakley** (c1750-11/21/1782) m. Catherine__
William Coakley m. Mildred Sullivan 2/4/1781
James Coakley, Jr. (bpt. in Antigua 1/12/1746/7-) m. (1)Nancy Wilson (bef4/9/1787-bef1798); (2)Susannah Dishman 1/10/1798
John Coakley who appeared in the 1810 census of Spotsylvania County; m. Mary_, possibly Mary Smallwood 5/20/1772 in St. Michael, Barbados
probably Elizabeth Cockley, who was found, along with her brother John witnessing a ten acre land transaction

d. bef1786

G-g-g-g-g-grandmother- 8th generation

William Bridges

father of **Ann Bridges** m. William Vigar (-bef3/21/1829)
Matthew Bridges m. Elizabeth Jarvass; co-executor of his father's estate
Thomas Bridges, co-executor of his father's estate
Mary Bridges

lived in Spotsylvania County, Virginia

d. 11/8/1792

His will, which was proved in Spotsylvania County c1794, named Matthew and Thomas, his sons, and William Vigar, his son-in-law, as executors. His heirs were his wife, and the children named above, with the exception of Matthew.[65]

---

their disadvantage because of their careless financial practices. He felt differently about the ladies, however, and reported that their "behavior is polite and their conversation entertaining, sprightly, but very delicate and modest, their dress is very neat, but not gaudy…they have a tender manner of treating their servants and slaves…no people in the West Indies are better obeyed then they." (Florence Lewisohn, *Tales of Tortola and the British Virgin Islands*, Hollywood, FL, International Graphics, 1966, p. 20.)

[65] William Armstrong Crozier, *Spotsylvania County Records 1721-1800* (Baltimore, Southern Book Co., 1955), p. 50.

A William Bridges appears in the annals of Prince George County and twice in the records of Westmoreland County. A William Bridges, the Elder, was also found in Surry County, as was William, the Younger.

Brumfield Long, Jr.

b. c1721 in Richmond County, Virginia.

son of **Brumfield Long, Sr.** (c1695-bef8/1/1763) and **Elizabeth Reynolds** (bef1713)

brother of Reuben S. Long (1716-probably bef1762)
William Long (1718-bef1767) m. Ann Durrett (c1726-)
John Long (1726-aft1762) m. Isabella__
Benjamin Long (1728-aft2/20/1804) b. in King George County; m. Mary Bond 1748
Henry Long (c1730-)
step-brother of Mary Long (c1736-) m. John Payne, Jr.
Sarah Long (c1738-) m. Thomas Vaughan aft1757; moved to Halifax County, Virginia
Martha Long (c1740-) m. __Kay
Elizabeth Long (c1742-) m. __Apperson

m. (1)**Elizabeth Bond** (c1732-bef1773) of Culpeper County, Virginia; (2)Sarah__, c1773, who, after Brumfield's death married Hezekiah Brown in 1786; she was widowed again by 1821.

father, with Elizabeth Bond, of:
Reuben Long (c1748-) served in a campaign against the French and Indians in 1756
John Bond Long (c1749-) m. Mary Haynes, daughter of William Haynes of Bedford County, Virginia.
Benjamin Long (c1750-1773)
Gabriel Long (c1752-)
Brumfield Long (c1754-)
Nancey Ann Long (c1756-) m. Richard Chism/Chisholm[66]
Mildred (Millie) (c1764-) m. Benjamin Head (-1808) 7/19/1785
Elizabeth Long (c1740-aft1831) m. Robert Gaines

[66] *Culpeper County Deed Book K 1779-1781*, pp. 181-183.

(1740-45 to1806-08)

Richard Long (c1768-) m. Elizabeth, a daughter of Benjamin Long and with Sarah__, 2nd wife:

Thomas Long (1775-)- Sarah's "dutiful and affectionate son" m. Bathsheba D. Moxley

This family lived in Orange County on Brook's Run. This area became Culpeper County in 1749.

Brumfield, like his father, was a blacksmith.[67]

Brumfield moved to be with his father, Brumfield, Sr. in Spotsylvania County in 1746. Attracted by his father's word that he (Bromfield, Sr.) would help his son "get an Overseers place," he left his protesting wife, Elizabeth, and his family in Spotsylvania and sought greener pastures. His father had said of him that he ". . .was like to be a good man and that none of his other children were so promising as him, and therefore he intended to advance him."[68]

For a strange and sticky court case which resulted from this move, see Brumfield Long, Sr. in chapter eight.

On 5/19/1767 Brumfield bought 116 acres on Brook's Run from the Alexander Spotswood estate.[69] On 4/14/1776 he purchased "for Robert Latham, Jr." another 100 acres of the Spotswood estate, this time the "Mine Tract" along the Rapidan River in Orange County.[70]

Brumfield Long, known as Sr. after the death of his father, paid taxes in 1777 on 1 slave over 16 years of age, 1 slave under 16 years of age, 2 horses and 3 cows.[71]

Bromfield's (Brumfell, Brumfield, Bromfell, Bloomfield) Last Will and Testament was written on 1/21/1778 and recorded in Culpeper County 7/20/1778. The will, as recorded by Richard Chissam, Nancey Ann Long's husband, mentions for the first time his Beloved Wife, Sarah, whom he undoubtedly had wed after the death of Elizabeth Bond. If he should predecease Sarah and she married she was ". . .to enjoy only one third part. . .

---

[67] Paul C. Buchanan, *Long Families on the Rappahannock River Before 1800* (1987), pp. 11-12.

[68] *Spotsylvania County, Virginia, Order Book 2*, p. 17, as quoted by Paul C. Buchanan and Susie M. Owens, "Henry Long and Some Descendants of Colonial Virginia: Third Generation: Children of Bloomfield Long," *The Virginia Genealogist*, vol. 38, p. 192.

[69] *Culpeper County, Virginia Deed Book E*, p. 377 as quoted by Buchanan and Owens, p. 193.

[70] *Orange County, Virginia Deed Book 16,* p. 414-416, as quoted by Buchanan and Owens, p. 193.

[71] Schreiner, *1787 Census*, p. 710.

and the other two thirds to be lodged in the hands of my two sons John Long and Bromfield Long to maintain and educate my children out of the profits of the same in the best manner they can and at the death of . . .Sarah Long if my son Thomas Long should be of lawfull age I desire that my whole estate. . .be sold at the best price and equally divided amongst my children. . ." His blacksmith tools and his "Gunn" were to be given to his son Bromfield. Before that division, fifty pounds was to be deducted from his son Reuben's portion, and thirty pounds from his daughter, Nancey (Ann) Chissam's part. The estate could not be divided until Thomas, then underaged, became 21.[72] In October of 1821 Sarah gave her one-third of Brumfield's estate to her only son, Thomas Long.

"While sons John and Brumfield were named as executors, 'not being in place to qualify, on the motion of Sarah Long,[73] widow of the dec'd, certificate (was) granted her for obtaining letters of administration. . .till the executors qualify'."[74]

Brumfield's estate was appraised 4/29/1779. The listing included, along with the "gunn" and the smithing tools, 32 hogs, 22 sheep, 15 cattle and three horses. The total estate was valued at 1980 pounds.

d. 1/21/1778 in Culpeper County, Virginia

G-g-g-g-g-grandfather- 8th generation

There was, and perhaps still is, a parish known as Bromfield Parish. It is felt that this name may be associated with a family of the same name, and that the names of Brumfield, I and II, had their origin there.

Elizabeth Bond

b. c1732 in Spotsylvania County, Virginia

daughter of **John Bond** (c1702-c1760) and **Mary Parks** (1706-aft1779)[75]
3/2/1730

John Bond had special affection for "his girls" for on 11/16/1749, while

---

[72] *Culpeper County Will Book K* 1779-1781, pp.182-183.
[73] Sarah, the second wife of Brumfield, is listed as a Patriot by the Daughters of the American Revolution for selling beef to a corporal on 10/14/1781 for two pence per pound!
[74] Buchanan, pp. 10-11.
[75] Computer records from The Church of the Latter Day Saints, Salt Lake City, Utah.

making a gift to them, he mentioned them in this manner: ". . .(F)or love and affection which John Bond hath to Mary his now wife and to his daughter Elizabeth wife of Blumfield Long the Younger and to his daughter Mary the now wife of Benjamin Long. . ."[76]

sister of Mary Bond (c1734-) m. Benjamin Long (c1730-)[77]
Isaac Bond m. (1)Sarah__ (1744-); (2)Lydia__ (10/17/1762-)

m. **Brumfield (Bromfield) Long, Jr.** (c1721-1/21/1778)

mother of Reuben Long (c1748-)
John Bond Long(c1749-) m. Mary Haynes
Benjamin Long (c1750-1773)
Gabriel Long (c1752-)
Brumfield Long (c1754-)
Nancey Ann Long (c1756-) m. Richard Chism
Mildred (Millie) Long (c1764-) m. Benjamin Head (-1808) 7/19/1785
Elizabeth Long (c1740-aft1831) m. Robert Gaines (1740-45 to 1806-08)
Richard Long (c1768-) m. Elizabeth, a daughter of Benjamin Long

d. bef1773 Culpeper, Virginia

G-g-g-g-g-grandmother- 8th generation

Capt. Robert Gaines

Although Sutherd's research, as quoted in several places in this book, was very helpful, Robert's birthdate, given as c1720-1725, is in error. We have proof that he died in 1744. It is unlikely that he would have accomplished all that he did if he had lived only 24 years.

son of **Richard Gaines** (1686-1755/56) of Culpeper County, Virginia
and **Catherine Rawlins**

brother of William Gaines (1705-1796) m. Isabella Pendleton (1712-1775)

[76] *Culpeper County, Virginia Deed Book A*, pp. 108-109, as quoted by Buchanan and Owens, p. 192.
[77] LDS

Thomas Gaines m. Dorothy "Dolly" Broaddus__
Francis Gaines (c1708-1775) m. Dorothy__; became the clerk of the vestry on which Robert served as of 8/3/1743.
James Gaines (1/18/1719-3/10/1786) m. Mary Pendleton
Richard Gaines (1726-2/1/1802) m. Mildred Hollinger
John Gaines
Roger Gaines m. Martha Rallings
Henry Gaines m. Mrs. Mariah Wood Stepp; served in the French and Indian War

We have as yet discovered no reason for the title of Captain, which is regularly appended when Robert's name is written in the parish records of Stratton Major Parish. Titles were sometimes given as a mark of respect for the individual, but Robert was quite young, even when he died. I prefer to think that he earned his rank as a member of the militia.

m. **Ursula**[78] **Bridges** [79](-aft1767)

Since there are records that prove that Robert served on the vestry of the Stratton Major Parish from 10/1732 until shortly before his death in 1744, it is assumed that he was also living in or near King and Queen County.

father of William Gaines (-1813) m. Jane Robinson
Robert Gaines (c1740-c1808) m. Elizabeth Long (c1740-aft1831) c1770
Mary Gaines (given a deed of gift of goods and chattels by her mother, Ursula Gaines, the same as her brother, Robert)
Alice Gaines m. John Robinson (-1811)
Ursula Gaines m. Elijah Carter
Lucy Gaines living and unm in 1776[80]

We have no idea of the order of the births of these children, except Robert, who was certainly one of the last to be born.

There is evidence provided in two instances below that Robert Gaines was a skilled carpenter or builder. And, as it is assumed in the case of all gentlemen of this era, he was likely to have been a "planter" also, growing

---

[78] Raleigh Travers Green, compiler, *Genealogical and Historical Notes on Culpeper County, VA* (Baltimore, Regional Publishing Co., 1983), p. 14.
[79] Notes from Irene Bixler.
[80] Calvin E. Sutherd, *A Compilation of Gaines Family Data with Special Emphasis on the Lineage of William and Isabella (Pendleton) Gaines* (Ft. Lauderdale, August 1972), p. viii.

tobacco, the money crop, and other things needed to thrive in the colonies.[81]

From the records of King and Queen County we learn that Henry Gaines contracted to build Stratton Major Church for a fee of 1300 pounds of tobacco. The building was to be "fifty by eighty feet, with corresponding height and with galleries." Bishop Meade determined that the Gaines family had one of the pews and that both Robert and his brother Francis served on the vestry there.[82]

We gained an interesting chronology of Robert's public activities from these records:

In 1732 Robert undertook to repair and "redecorate" the interior of the Stratton Major Parish Church. He agreed to fix ". . .plaister & whitewash what is broaken down on the inside & the said Gaines Obliges himself ye Same Shall hold Tite the Space of Seven Years for which he is to be paid Seven hundred pounds of Tob.(acco) in the next levy."

On Tuesday, 10/10/1732 Capt. Robert Gaines was appointed to the Vestry of the parish. He, along with Capt. Philip Roots, "came in & took the oaths appointed & Signed to conform to the Church of England as by law Established, & were added to this Vestry."

Monies passed hands in interesting ways in the early church. Most of the vestry members seemed to have some duty that required them to pay out or receive legal tender, whether it was in coin, tobacco, or some other medium of exchange. In October 1734 "Capt Gaynes received 240 pounds (of tobacco, probably), by account; on 10/11/1736 "Capt Robt Gaynes received 1600 pounds; in 1738 he was awarded 4 pounds "for work done at ye Glebe;" on 10/10/1740 the Vestry was "ordered y(superscript t) the Church-Warden to pay to Capt. Gaines 23 pounds 18 shillings; on 4/10/1741 Capt. Gaynes was ordered to pay Thomas Garrett 1 pound 6 shillings as per account, and Mary

---

[81] Another "slice of life" reported by Haley, as quoted from King's *Highlights of History*...: "...A series of catastrophes befell Virginia which the colonists called 'the plagues.' In the spring of 1728 a multitude of caterpillars spread...east of the Blue Ridge and threatened to destroy all plant life. Superstitious settlers believed the Lord had sent these...to punish them for ...wickedness... Destruction of plant life by caterpillars paved the way for the second plague. Shortage of food in the forest caused famished deer to descend on the crops which...planters strove to protect. These animals came in such great numbers that in many places it was impossible for the alarmed freeholders to drive them off. The only solution was to kill (the deer). The carcasses brought on the third plague, the wolves, which concentrated...to enjoy feasts...Unfortunately, the wolves did not clean up the...deer and move on. Instead, they stayed and preyed on the settler's livestock and sometimes attacked the children and even older members of the family...(T)he bounty on wolf scalps (was raised) to 100 pounds of tobacco each...at a time when a laboring man only made 30 pounds of tobacco for working from sun to sun..." (Haley, *Caroline County*, pp. 10-12).

[82] Bishop William Meade, *Old Churches and Families of Virginia* (Philadelphia, J. B. Lippincott, 1857, p. 375.

Walden 1 pound 3 shillings "Toward the Support of her Family," but Capt. Dudley and Major Rootes were both to pay Capt. Gaynes, each a different amount.

Church and state were not at all separate. Tithes were collected through the church for governmental purposes, and administered according to the dictates of the Vestry and the court. One such order reads: "Pursuant to an Order of King & Queen County Court, dated the 12th Day of July 1743, requiring the Several Vestries in each respective Parish in this County to divide their Parishes into precincts for processioning every Person's Land therein as by the Law in that Case is directed-

"Ordered that the inhabitants of the Several Precincts hereafter Mentioned do go in Procession of the Lands as followeth Viz."

Several times Capt. Robert served as a processioner. His orders, on one occasion, read: "It's Order'd that Capt. Gaynes, Mr. Wm. Lyne & John Thack or any two of them do meet on the 3d friday in Xber. Next and go in procession off and see all & every persons land Between the Western Branch of Arracacoe Swamp & Tarsatyans Swamp plainly mark'd Continuing their proceedings in all Suitable weather untill the whole precinct be finish'd, and that all the Inhabitants of the Said precinct do attend the Said processioners according to Law, and the Said processioners are further ordered to Make and return to this Vestry at their Next Sitting after the Last of March Next a true acct. of what Lands processioned, What Not the reasons in Case of Failure and What persons present in their Whole proceedings." It was later noted the "Capt. Robert Gaines, Mr. Wm. Lyne and Jno Thack processioners return'd their report and it was order'd to be register'd."

At that same meeting of the Vestry, on 10/10/1740, "Mr. Richd Anderson and Capt. Robt. Gaines are Appointed Church Wardens and Mr. Anderson is Appointed Collector for this Present Year."

It was recorded in the Vestry minutes in 1739 that "The Levies being Settled this Present Year are found to amount to 31,431 lb of Tob(superscript o). it being Levied upon 835 Titheables at 38 lb per Poll and there remains a fraction in the Collectors hands of 299 lb of Tobo." One would assume that they were unable at this report to collect 299 pounds of the levy.

The church exercised other authority, as well. On 4/16/1734, "being Easter week," the Vestry announced that "Capt. Robt. Gains & his wife (Ursula) Mr. Richd Shackelford & his wife Mr. Wm. Lyne & his & Mr. John Ware are appointed to Sit in the pew next above the pulpit & that Mr. John Smith & his wife Sit with his mother."

Henry Gaines's name appears now and then in vestry business, and Francis Gaines, another brother of Robert and Henry, became "Clark of this

Vestry" 8/3/1743. Another name of interest is Collo.(Colonel) John Robinson (sometimes, Esq.), whose name appears both on and off the Vestry roster. This gentleman is probably the father of John Robinson who married Robert's daughter Alice, and Jane Robinson, who married Alice's brother, William.

In October 1744 it is reported in Vestry Minutes that Richard Corbin, Gentleman and Will Hunt have been appointed to serve on the church vestry in place of Gawin Corbin Esq. and Rob.' Gaines decd. [83]

"Adm. bond 100 lbs. Ursula Gaines admx. of Robert Gaines, deceased, with Joseph Herndon, July 5, 1763."[84]

G-g-g-g-g-grandfather- 8th generation

Ursula (Bridges)

We are uncertain of Ursula's maiden name; an adequate search has not been made to confirm this one. I received the name Bridges from an excellent, if most unlikely source, and feel that, because Irene Bixler's[85] information helped to straighten out a century-old mistake in the records of our family, her information in this matter is also likely to be accurate. There is, as documented herein, one William Bridges and his daughter Ann Bridges. These were also from Spotsylvania County, where Ursula was living at the time of her death.[86]

There is also a strong possibility that Ursula could have been a Broaddus. Her husband's brother, Thomas Gaines, m. Dorothy Broaddus, and more than one marriage between families was common in those days, probably for reasons of demographics. In fact, Ursula could well have been the daughter

---

[83] *The Vestry Book of Stratton Major Parish, King and Queen County, Virginia*, 1729-1783 (Richmond, The Library Board, 1931), pp. 11-63.

[84] Crozier, *Spotsylvania Records*, p. 61.

[85] How Irene Bixler came to play such an important role makes an interesting story. A gentleman, whose name is lost to me, talked with my sister, Emma, and me in the Rockingham Historical Association Library. He suggested that Catherine Bixler, a Gaines descendant, could help us in our confusion about the Gaines family. But he had no good address, only the name of a town in Ohio. I called the historical facility in that town and was told that Mrs. Bixler had died, but that they would put me in contact with her daughter. I wrote to this individual, who apparently passed the letter on to her father's second wife, Irene Bixler. This incredible lady took the time to research her predecessor's files in order to dig out considerable information for me. With this information I was able to correct a mistake made by G-g-grandfather Austin Coakley.

[86] There was a Briggs/Bridges family in Stafford County; one William Bridges appears in the annals of Prince George County and twice in the records of Westmoreland County. A William Bridges, the Elder, is also found in Surry County, as is William the Younger. All of these might be descended from, or at least related to, one Nich(olas) Bridges who had arrived in colonial Virginia by 8/25/1655. (Nell Marion Nugent, *Cavaliers and Pioneers, Abstracts of Land Patents and Grants, 1623-1800*, vol. 3, Richmond, Dietz Printing, 1934, p. 312.)

of __Broaddus, who, in 1766, "sold out" a number of his neighbors who were in his debt. It is suggested by the author of *Colonial Caroline* that "Broaddus' attitude may (have been) accounted for, in part, by the fact that his father, William Broaddus, died heavily in debt to William Shackleford and James Gaines, and he had to pay this debt before coming into his share of the estate."[87]

m. **Robert Gaines** who died in King and Queen County in 1744.

Robert and Ursula were active in the Stratton Major Parish in King and Queen County. Ursula's will is recorded in Spotsylvania County 22 years after her husband's death. Their g-g-granddaughter, Caroline Virginia Coakley, was told, and told my mother in turn, that she was named for the beloved County of Caroline, which lies in a thirty-mile wide band between the other two counties. I believe that the Gaines' place of residence for at least a portion of their lives may have been Caroline County, a county whose records were damaged heavily during the War Between the States. I believe that their son, Robert (husband of Elizabeth Long) may have had fond memories of that county, which influenced the naming of his g-granddaughter.

mother of William Gaines (-1813) probably m. Jane Robinson

- **Robert Gaines** (1740-45 to 1806-08) m. Elizabeth Long (c1740-aft1831) c1770
- Mary Gaines (also given a deed of gift of goods and chattels by her mother, Ursula Gaines, as was her brother Robert)
- Alice Gaines m. John Robinson (-1811)
- Ursula Gaines m. Elijah Carter
- Lucy Gaines, living and unm in 1776

The order of the births of these children is unknown.

The quotation "Adm. bond 100 lbs. Ursula Gaines admx. of Robert Gaines, deceased, with Joseph Herndon, July 5, 1763."[88] indicates that Ursula served as the administrator of her husband's estate.

It was bothersome to me for some time that "Urshula" administered Robert's estate in 1763, since he had died in 1744. It becomes more reasonable when one realizes that her son, Robert, at least, would have come of age at that time. I must conjecture that Ursula waited for her children to mature before

[87] T. E. Campbell, *Colonial Caroline: A History of Caroline County, Virginia* (Richmond, Dietz Press, 1954), p. 408.
[88] Crozier, p. 61.

settling her husband's estate. We have not found Robert's will. He died young, perhaps intestate.

"April 29, 1767 Ursley (X) Gaines of St. George Parish of Spotsylvania County to her son Robert Gaines. Deed of gift goods and chattles. Wit: Wm. Robinson, Thomas Rowe. . . ."[89]

d. aft1767, perhaps in Spotsylvania County, Virginia

G-g-g-g-g-grandmother- 8th generation

Edward Erwin, (Sr.)

b. 1700, in Ulster, Ireland. Irvin B. Crews estimates this date to have been c1689-90.

Edward is said to have left Ireland with his wife and five sons on the same ship as the Currys (McCurrys), intent on settlement in the American colonies. They were said to have arrived in Philadelphia.

m. **Frances**__ c1728 in Ireland

father of John Erwin (-c1761) m. Jane Williams prior to 8/16/1756
Robert (Irving) Erwin (-1789) m. Ann Crockett
Andrew Erwin (-c1765) m. Anna__; land adjoined his father's
Edward Erwin, Jr. (1730-aft1800) m. Mary Curry (c1735-6/30/1815)
Francis Erwin (-c1791); m. Jean Curry (-c1807)
Benjamin Erwin became the minister of Mossy Creek Presbyterian Church where he served for many years.
Frances Erwin m. William Brown; treated in her father's will in the manner one might use with an unruly child
__Erwin m. Robert Low

Edward, one of the first landowners in the Mossy Creek area, settled c1740 "up" Long Glade near what is now Tory Farm.[90] This is approximately two miles west of Bridgewater, Virginia.

Edward owned, during his years in Virginia a total of 955 acres of land

[89] *Spotsylvania County Deed Book G*, 1766-1771, p. 255.
[90] C. E. May, *Life Under Four Flags in the North River Basin of Virginia* (McClure Press), p. 118.

in the Long Glade area, apparently accumulating and holding the parcels listed below until his death:

3/5/1747- 220 acres adjoining William Brown and John Anderson, purchased for 25 shillings[91]
4/5/1748- 350 acres adjoining Widow Patterson's lands- 35 shillings[92]
no date- 141 acres- 15 shillings[93]
5/12/1770- 190 acres on the southeast of his own property[94]
5/12/1770- 54 acres on the north side of Long Glade on the North River[95]

Edward Erwin is referred to as a yeoman farmer.[96] He and others of his kind in Virginia loved the land, and owned as much as they could. Edward was still buying acreage quite late in life. As was true of the Palatine emigrants, the privilege of owning their own property, their own destiny, was an exhilarating new experience. How far they had come from troubled Scotland and Ireland where they may have numbered among the oppressed!

"The records suggest there was a lengthy feud between the (reputedly unruly) Bells and the Irwins (Erwins); but feud or not, the Bells and the Irwins became neighbors on Long Glade in the Virginia Colony between 1738 and 1750 and staunch members of Mossy Creek Presbyterian Church after 1769."[97]

"The Virginia House of Burgesses in May 1742 had authorized Orange County court to divide Augusta County into precincts, to levy a tax on all tithables and to use part of the monies raised therefrom for organizing and maintaining militia companies for protection against the Indians. . .12 companies of Rangers. . .were organized in the fall of 1742."[98] Captain John Smith's Muster Roll, c1742, included Andrew Erwine, Benjamin Erwine, Edward Erwine and John Erwine and others. All of these men reported to Colonel James Patton and County Lieutenant William Beverley.

---

[91] *Virginia Land Office Patent Book 26*, p. 212.
[92] Ibid., *Virginia Patent Book 26*, p. 315.
[93] *Virginia Patent Book 28*, p. 454.
[94] *Virginia Patent Book 39*, p. 17.
[95] *Virginia Patent Book 39*, p. 81.
[96] Defined in the *World Book Dictionary*, vol. 2, as "a man who farms his own land, especially a man of respectable standing," p. 2420.
[97] May, *Four Flags*, p. 69.
[98] May, *Four Flags*, pp. 138-139.

On 11/29/1751 Edward Erwin, Sr., "yeoman," and his wife Frances deeded to Edward Erwin, Jr., "yeoman," 206 acres. On 1/27/1757 Edward, Sr. deeded to Francis Erwin 200 pounds and 148 acres.

For an anecdote about the way of life of this period, we have C. E. May's account of the responsibilities of road-building in the Long Glade area: "May 29, 1751, Augusta County Court ordered a road from John Davies Mill (Mossy Creek) to Woods Gap to be cleared. Petitioners for this road were (twenty-two men including) Andrew Erwin, . . . John Erwin, . . . Benjamin Erwin . . . (Further,) John Davies, John Erwin and Thomas Turk were ordered to mark the route for this road; and John King with the following tithables was ordered to put up sign posts of direction, clear the right of way and keep the road in repair: Andrew Erwin, . . . John Erwin, Edward Erwin . . . (and seventeen others). These petitioners and tithables resided on North River, Long Glade, Beaver Creek and Naked Creek. August 27, 1751, John King petitioned the court for more workers and overseers for this road."[99]

In his will Edward gives to his "well beloved sons Edward Erwin and Francis Erwin all the Moveable Estate that remaineth after my decease to be divided equally betwixt them except a Bed and Bedcloaths Pewter dish & two Plates a Chest and side Saddle which I give and bequeath to Frances Brown and likewise a Black Cow and Calf which I give to said Frances Brown Provided she behaves well and Marryeth by Consent & if she behaves ill she is not to have anything . . ."[100] He mentions his son-in-law, Robert Low, and appoints his "trusty and well-beloved son(s), Edward . . . and Francis Executors . . ." In this one document he manages to spell his own last name Erving and his sons last names as Erwin and Irving.

d. 1771.

Will proved 1/13/1772 at Long Glade

G-g-g-g-g-grandfather- 8th generation

"The original name was Erenviene or Erevine . . . but in different localities and different languages it was afterwards spelled Ervin, Erwin, Irwin, Irving, Irvine, etc. Erwin was the English (form).

"The Erenvienes or Erevines were among the early Celt and Gaelic settlers of Scotland about the 3rd century A. D. For a long period their main

---

[99] May, *Four Flags*, p. 94.
[100] *Augusta County Will Book 4*, p. 480.

seat was Castle Garth, in Perthshire, then about 1000 A. D., a part of the clan moved to Ayrshire and possessed the barony of Cunninghame, where the castle, river and town bore the clan's name, Irvine. Others of the clan moved to County Dumfrieshire, near the English border, and there acquired the princely estates of Bonshaw, which, with the Tower of Bonshaw and Castle Irving, became the chief seat of the Erevine clan.

"The Scottish clans, after their banishment by the Roman invaders, in 373 A. D., went with their leader, Fergusin, to fight the Roman armies in Hungary and Gaul. In 404 they returned to their possessions in Scotland, though some of the Erevines remained in those foreigh countries. Fergusin then became King Fergus II of Scotland.

"The last of the Scottish chiefs who possessed Castle Irvine and the barony of Cunninghame, in Ayrshire, was Crynin Ervine (as spelled in the British Museum), or Crynan Irving, Abathane of Dule (a title of high honor), and this Irving or Ervine, by his marriage (1004) to Princess Beatrix, daughter of King Malcolm II, of Scotland, became the ancestor of all Scottish kings, beginning with his son, King Duncan (1034).

"Macbeth, a son of King Malcolm's second daughter, murdered King Duncan, his cousin, (1040) and usurped the throne for seventeen years. After Macbeth's death the throne was restored to the royal line of Irvings."[101] By now you recognize a familiar Shakespearian plot. You know his interpretation of the events that occurred.

Annie Elizabeth Miller continues with her revelation of Erwin family highlights to claim kinship with everyone from King Robert Bruce to Presidents Andrew Jackson, Benjamin Harrison and Theodore Roosevelt, And there are *more*! Because there has been no time to read further into this history, I will leave that job to the reader. All of this may be quite accurate; snippets of this story have been found in various other references.

C. E. May provided a less colorful and completely logical explanation of the name Erwin and further information pertaining to the family's Scottish experience, which was of long duration: "The surname Erwin (Ervine, Irwin) is a place name which derives from either Irvine, Ayrshire (Bobby Burns's 'auld Ayr') or Irving, Dumfies, where the poet was exciseman during the last years of his life. The name means, therefore, one who came from Irvine or from the Irving River or from several villages of that name in Scotland. Erwin and Irving are often confused in old records. The name appears in England in the records of Hampshire County as early as 1066, the year of the Norman Conquest, and

---

[101] Annie Elizabeth Miller, *Carolina Pioneers and their Descendants* (Macon, GA, J. W. Burke Co., 1927), pp. 17-19.

in the *Domesday Book*, begun in King Alfred's time, for the year 1086."[102]

A personal anecdote: In September 1999, the author went with her husband, Bill Hodges, her sister, Martha, and her husband, Pete Black, to Irvine in Ayrshire, a village on the Firth of Clyde in Scotland which had once been one of Scotland's main trading ports. It was a charming spot, home of the Scottish Maritime Museum. We enjoyed the village and the museum, and I enjoyed another facet of the visit. Having read that the Erwin family had likely taken its name from the Ayrshire town from which it sprang, I looked at this village as a possible home of our Erwin family. It is likely, though much more research will be needed if this possibility is proven a reality. Regardless, the accepted tradition traces the Erwins from Scotland to Ulster in Northern Ireland in the 1650's, and from there to Pennsylvania, where the family was located until their migration to the Long Glade area of Augusta and Rockingham Counties of Virginia.

Life in the North River Basin

"Farming was the chief occupation of settlers in North River Basin. The average size farm contained about 230 acres; but some were much larger, containing one thousand or more acres. The large landowners in the basin before the Revolutionary War (included) Andrew and Edwin Erwin. . . .

"The chief money crops. . .were cattle, horses and hogs. The settlers usually brought horses and cattle with them, but hogs and sheep were brought in later from Pennsylvania. Cattle were more easily raised than horses. . .(and) were driven on foot to Winchester, Fort Pitt, Philadelphia and market centers in Eastern Pennsylvania. William Crow and others drove herds of them, numbering from 100 to 150 head, to market. These cattle drives were forerunners of the great ones in the far west in the 19th century.

"Some cattle and hogs were slaughtered on the farm and the meat prepared for shipment by drying, smoking and/or salting it. Then the cured meat was packed in wooden casks which were rolled to the banks of larger streams, loaded on flatboats and rafts and floated down rivers to market. The by-products from such farm slaughtering operations were tallow and hides. These were kept for local consumption. Butter was also produced on the farms. The greater part of it was consumed locally, but some was sent through Swift Run, Browns, Jarmans and Rockfish gaps first to Fredericksburg and then to Richmond. Keeping it from becoming rancid during the journey was

[102] May, *Four Flags,* p. 68.

the problem. Wrapping it in damp leaves and cloths and immersing it en route in the relatively cold water of springs and mountain streams provided some refrigeration."[103]

Wheat was favored as a crop because it could be successfully grown in the good soils along Mossy Creek. Flax production persisted as well. An itinerant preacher, Phillip Vickers Fithian, reported after visiting Mossy Creek in 1776 that there was to be a "Scotching Frolick." This was reported to be a festival involving a large number of area families who came together to "dress" flax, and have fun.[104]

Frances__(Erwin)

b. in 1705

There is conjecture, because of the use of names in the family, that Frances's last name was Francis. It is possible, I suppose, that Edward Erwin may have married Frances Francis.

m. **Edward Erwin, Sr**. (1689/1700-1771), in Ireland, according to Irvin B. Crews.

mother of John Erwin m. Jane Williams prior to 8/16/1756
Robert Erwin (-1789) m. Ann Crockett
Andrew Erwin m. Ann/Anna__
Edward Irvine, Jr. (1730-aft1800) m. Mary Curry (c1735-6/30/1815)
Francis Erwin m. Jane/Jean Curry
Benjamin Erwin
Frances Erwin m. William Brown
__Erwin m. Robert Low/Law

G-g-g-g-g-grandmother- 8th generation

Dr. Robert A. Curry

Robert's middle name is very likely Addison, since that is the middle

---

[103] May, *Four Flags*, p. 117.
[104] James W. Wilson, "The Mossy Creek Area of Augusta County, Virginia, During the Eighteenth Century: The Land and the People," a thesis submitted to the Graduate Faculty of James Madison University (August, 1993), pp. 36-37.

name given Robert, II.

b. 11/10/1717, according to his tombstone

son of **William Curry**, b. c1690 in County Antrim, Northern Ireland and
Sarah (Sallie) **Young**[105]

Dr. Curry was a Scotch-Irishman who migrated from Londonderry, Ireland to Pennsylvania in the early 1700's. By 1748 he, with his family, was in Augusta County, in the Virginia colony.

brother of William Curry (c1719-)
James Curry (c1728-) m. Rebecca Warwick
John Curry (c1730-)
Nathan Curry (1732-)
David Curry (1734-)
Isaiah Curry (1736-)
Joseph Curry (1738-)
Sarah Curry (1740-)
Jane Curry (1742-)

m. **Ann Currie** (9/23/1723-5/15/1819)

father of Ann Curry m. __Glenn
Mary Curry (c1735-6/30/1815) m. Edward Erwin (c1730-aft1800)
Isaiah Curry
James Curry - served as captain in the Continental Line during the Revolution
Alexander Curry, who moved to Kentucky in 12/1787
Samuel Curry (4/17/1770-4/15/1845) m. Mary Glenn (11/15/1774-4/23/1863)
Joseph Curry
Margaret Curry m. __Nichol
William Curry
Robert A. Curry II

Although he had studied medicine, he became a planter. It has been reported that he had also taught fencing.

---

[105] From the research of Betsy Arndt, Venice, FL as reported to Emma Jordan, 2/2001.

Upon arriving in Virginia from Lancaster County, Pennsylvania in 1748, the Robert Currys settled in the northern part of Augusta County, near the present location of Sangerville. This area is referred to as the North River Basin.

Thomas Lewis surveyed a 135 acre tract of land lying on Naked Creek for Robert in 1/1753. This land lay "six miles northwest of Augusta Stone Presbyterian Church and five miles west of Mt. Sidney in the 'Hills of Judea.' " On 5/1780, Robert added an adjoining 50 acre tract.

Robert Curry also had 400 acres between Mossy Creek and Long Glade surveyed on 9/9/1771.[106]

Among Robert Curry's achievements, as listed on his tombstone, are his service as a militia Captain in the French and Indian War; as a Captain of the Home Guards of the Virginia Militia in the American Revolution; and as an Elder of Augusta Stone Church.

For his service in the French and Indian War Robert was granted a tract of land in Highland County, Ohio known as "Crab Bottom." It is suspected that those of his descendents who moved to Ohio lived on this land.[107]

It is recorded that Robert Curry, in support of the colonial effort in the Revolutionary War contributed 687 pounds of beef, one blanket and two bushels of wheat during the period of 1782-1785.[108]

Robert wrote his last will and testament 12/29 "the year one thousand eight hundred 03." He says he is "now far advanced in years but in perfect mind and memory."[109]

d. 6/5/1804

His will was proved on 12/26/1804.

Robert was buried in the old graveyard at Augusta Stone Church in Fort Defiance, Virginia.

G-g-g-g-g-grandfather- 8th generation

---

[106] *Augusta County Survey Book 2*, p. 195, quoted by Lyman Chalkley in *Original Court Records of Augusta County*, vol. 3, p. 564.

[107] Dona Kirk Patterson, "Curry," in *Augusta County, Virginia Heritage Book, 1732-1998* (Summersville, WV, Shirley Grose and Associates, 1999), p. 140.

[108] *Augusta County Court of Claims:* 1782-1785 quoted by James W. Wilson, p. 36.

[109] *Augusta County Will Book 9*, p. 417.

Robert's personal property, including the slave woman, "Chiny" and her child and several books was valued at 110 pounds, two shillings, six pence.[110]

In the will mentioned above he gave his wife, Ann, for her lifetime, the "dwelling house," a Negro woman named "China," and two cows and two sheep. A son, Samuel, was given use of the land as long as his mother lived, and right of purchase after her death. Samuel, who took this option, paid his brothers Alexander, James, Robert A., II, Isaiah, and William eight dollars each per acre; his sister, Margaret Nichol, five pounds English money; his sister, Ann Glenn, five pounds English money; and his sister, Mary Curry, 25 pounds English money.

". . .after having been owned for 194 years by six generations of Currys, the old homestead was sold out of the family (in 1946). The rambling log house. . .which sheltered the Curry family for almost two centuries has become a ruin."[111]

During Robert's life. . . "the English, French, Irish, Scotch-Irish and Welsh pioneers in the North River Basin staked claims and secured titles to their land, built log cabins, developed farms, helped organize a local government, laid out a network of roads, established churches and created a stratified society similar to ones in Eastern Virginia and the British Isles. At the top of the society they formed were the large landowners, at the bottom, the slaves. Sandwiched in between these two classes were the professional people, merchants, small landowners, skilled craftsmen, a few non-skilled laborers and indentured servants."[112]

"Isaiah Curry (Robert's brother) settled on War Branch in West Rockingham; one of this family, James Curry, was a captain in the Continental Line during the Revolution, and after the War, Postmaster of Harrisonburg.

". . .(T)he Currys are allied by blood and by marriage with the Stuarts, Henrys, Chestnuts, Herrings and other prominent families of Rockingham County."[113]

". . .(T)here is a place named Currie in Midlothian (Scotland) (but)

---

[110] C. E. May, *My Augusta, A Spot of Earth, Not a Woman* (Bridgewater, VA, Good Printers, Inc., 1987), p. 333.
[111] May, *My Augusta*, pp. 332-336.
[112] May, *Four Flags*, p. 128.
[113] John W. Wayland, *Virginia Valley Records: Genealogical and Historical Materials of Rockingham County, Virginia and Related Regions* (Baltimore, Genealogical Publishing Co., Inc., 1985), p. 323.

there is no evidence of its having given origin to a surname. (Among the early mentions of the name was) Philip de Curry (who) granted the lands of Dalhengun and Bargower in Kyle to the Abbey of Melrose, 1179. . . John Curry of Scotland is mentioned in an Annandale charter, 1238. . . Sir Walter Curry was appointed keeper of the castles of Wyggeton, Kirkcudbright and Dumfries by Edward I in 1291. Walter de Curry took a prominent part in the capture of Edinburgh Castle from the English and was rewarded for the same in 1342. . . John Curre held a tenement in Glasgow, 1506. . .and Robert Curray was merchant burgess of Edinburgh, 1693. The minister at Row, Dumbartonshire, 1709-19, was known as Rev. Archibald Currie or M'Currie."[114] The early name in America is sometimes given as McCurry.

C. E. May, in *My Augusta* reports that the Curry name is derived from the Scottish word "curach," which means marsh or boat. He suggests that this family came from a marshy area of Midlothian.

Ann Currie (Curry)

Most of my sources did not offer Ann's maiden name.[115] Certainly this source could be correct. I print the name Currie with uncertainty, however, and hope to find more proof of its accuracy in the future.

b. 9/23/1723 in Ulster, Ireland, according to her tombstone in the cemetery at Augusta Stone Church, Ft. Defiance, Virginia.

m. **Robert A. Curry** (11/10/1717-bef12/26/1804)

mother of Ann Curry m. __Glenn
Mary Curry (c1735-6/30/1815) m. Edward Erwin (c1730-aft1800)
Isaiah Curry
James Curry
Alexander Curry, who moved to Kentucky in 12/1787
Samuel Curry (4/17/1770-4/15/1845) m. Mary Glenn (11/15/1774-4/23/1863)
Joseph Curry
Margaret Curry m. __Nichol
William Curry

[114] George F. Black, *The Surnames of Scotland*, 4th edition (New York, New York Public Library, 1974), pp. 193-194.
[115] Patterson, p. 140.

Robert A. Curry II

d. 5/15/1819

G-g-g-g-g-grandmother- 8th generation

The tombstone of Robert and Ann states that they were "builders of this beloved country."

Chapter 2
Generation 7

During the years when the individuals in this generation were struggling to carve new homes from the American wilderness, the rest of the world continued to make history as well:[116]

- In 1709, 14,000 inhabitants emigrated from the Palatinate area of Germany to North America. A year later Thomas Waddle was born in Scotland.
- In the year of Lodowich Miller's birth, George Frederick Handel was writing operas in London. Handel, a German himself, made his decision in 1726 to become a British subject. *The Messiah*, his best known work, was composed in eighteen days in 1741.
- In 1726 *Gulliver's Travels* was written by Johnathan Swift.
- England employed the first group of Hessian mercenaries in 1727. Could John Frederick Kirshof's father have been one of these? It is conjectured.
- Thomas Gainsborough, English painter, was born in that year. Mother always said that artistic talent ran in the Gaines line, and showed up again in our uncle, Lester Miller.
- William Byrd, in Virginia, was writing the "History of the Dividing Line" between Britain and the American colonies. He founded Richmond, Virginia in 1737.
- In 1729 Johann Sebastian Bach, another German, wrote the *St. Matthew's Passion.*
- Thomas Jefferson was born in Virginia in 1743.
- In 1751 the minuet was the most fashionable dance in Europe.
- Benjamin Franklin demonstrated the conduction of lightning in 1752.
- Mozart, at the age of six, was touring Europe as a musical prodigy in 1762. Two years later he presented his own composition, a symphony.
- In 1765 the British Parliament passed the Stamp Act, taxing American colonists. The Virginia Assembly challenged Britain's right to the tax.
- Technological advancements, the expansion of international trade, and the experience of increasing individual liberty sparked a movement that we know as the Industrial Revolution.
- In the face of revolt in the American colonies in 1775, England once again hired German mercenaries, this time 29,000 of them, for war in America. The American Revolution began in 1777.

---

[116] Bernard Grun, *The Timetables of History: A Horizontal Linkage of People and Events* (New York, Simon & Schuster, 1946), pp. 324-355.

Lodowich (Ludwig) Miller

b. c1724 in Chester County, Pennsylvania

son of **(Hans) Johann "Michael" Miller** (1692-1771) and **Susanna Agnes Berchtol** (Bechtel) (1688-c1752)

brother of John Peter Miller (1715-1794)
Hans Jeremiah Miller (1717-1781)
David Miller (1719-1785)
Hans Michael Miller (1720-1784) m. Elizabeth__
George Miller (1722-1798) m. Catherine__
Philip Jacob Miller (1726-1799) m. Magdalena Rochette
Michael Miller II (1728-1792)
Barbara Miller (1733-1808) m. John H. Garber (1717-1787)
Jacob Miller (1735-1815)
Eva Elizabeth Miller m. Michael Danner (Tanner) (1696-1777); she was his second wife.
Maria Elisabeth Miller (3/19/1754-); may not have lived to maturity[117]

m. **Barbara Long** (c1727-)

father of Jacob Miller (1748-1815) m. (1) Anna Martha Wine; b. in Washington County, Maryland
Lodowich Miller (1749-) m. Barbara Ann__
Abraham Miller (1750-) m. Catherine Byerly
David Miller (1750/51-1828) m. Mary Magdalena Eickenberry; b. in Washington County, Maryland
Daniel Miller (1752-) m. Anna Garber (1762-1837); b. in Dauphin County, Pennsylvania
Susannah Miller (1754-1848) m. Michael Wine; b. in Maryland
Christian Miller (c1755-1828) m. Susannah__[118]
Nancy Miller (1756-) m. Conrad Sanger (c1765-); b. in Washington County, Maryland
John Miller (1758-1791) m. Margaret__; b. in Washington County, Maryland; owned 210 acres that had once belonged to his father

[117] Mason, *Miller Record*, p. 20.
[118] Mason, *Miller Record*, pp. 58-59.

Elizabeth Miller (1760-) m. Samuel Garber; b. in Frederick County, Maryland

Frances Miller m. John Long (1761-1838)

Roberta Miller Herbert, Miller family genealogist, says that, by tradition, Lodowich had 14 children. I have found no evidence of more than these eleven children.

Michael Miller, Lodowich's father, bought "Ash Swamp" in 1745. Within seven years he had it resurveyed and conveyed to three of his sons, who swapped sections of it around until John owned the northerly portion, Philip Jacob the southern, and Lodowich had bought additional land known as "Tom's Chance," which lay on the east side of his brothers' land.

"We believe that (Lodowich's mother, Susanna Bechtol) died in 1752 at the time that Michael had the land, 'Ash Swamp,' in Maryland resurveyed for the three sons, John, Philip Jacob, and Lodowich. This explains why there was no wife's signature on the deeds at that time and perhaps why the land was divided."[119]

Men who farmed, such as Lodowich and his brothers, might be expected to obtain an adequate acreage of good land and to settle down to use that land to make a living for themselves and their families. But Lodowich did not settle down. We can assume, in spite of his mobility, that he was a thrifty, hard-working, and successful man, for he owned, during his lifetime, a *number* of pieces of good land. But settle down he did not. Floyd and Kathryn Mason offered, from their research, a plausible explanation of the numerous land transactions of Lodowich, his brothers, and many other German Baptist families. It develops in this manner:

During the confused and lawless state of revolution, some governing body had to be charged with responsibility for order in the colonies. The Continental Congress called for every town or city to elect a "Committee of Observation" to raise funds, promote the war, provide leadership, and furnish men, horses, rifles and food for the forces. These committees had full power to act and there were no courts or other government agencies to which their decisions could be appealed.

The committee, made up of local leaders, was also charged with keeping watch on the citizens. Members were responsible for seeking out and reporting those who were not cooperating with the colonial government. "Handbills containing unfamiliar instructions from 'committees' not elected by due course of law began to appear throughout the countryside where. . .farm

[119] Mason, *Miller Record*, p. 12.

families reacted in dumb amazement." Among other things. . . "Farmers were instructed not to butcher their sheep before the wool was fully grown. . ." Small factories quickly sprang up for making gunpowder, nails, paper, and other items formerly imported for. . ."Trade with the British, or consumption of British goods were to be condemned as traitorous. Things had come to the point where American citizens were being asked. . .to spy on each other." [120]

The Palatines, a people used to fleeing oppression of all sorts, accustomed to being on the move, had been given considerable help by England. William Penn, an English Quaker, had magnanimously offered sanctuary to all oppressed peoples; and England, in need of naval stores, had encouraged emigration by transporting many of the Palatines, and providing for them until they could be safely relocated in the forests of the northeast.[121] Even though this particular plan for colonization failed to materialize, the majority of the settlers of German extraction had directly or indirectly felt the support of the English Crown and were sympathetic to the British cause at the outbreak of the Revolutionary War. The patriots were aware of this sentiment. It was easy for their committees to mistake the passive German immigrants for Tories.

Lodowich had a warrant for a fifty acre tract of land known as Dunkerstown, which he vacated in 1752.[122] Was this done because of political pressures he was experiencing?

Though they were considered "Dissenters," the principles of the Mennonites, Quakers, and German Baptist "Dunkers" had been respected early in the years of conflict. They had been required to pay additional taxes of 2 shillings, 6 pence per week to the committee, but they were free to work and worship unmolested. Later, however, in the heat of the war, the local militia groups became formalized militia companies and lists were made of those who failed to participate, whether Loyalists or members of the "Peace Churches." Once identified thus, the peaceful became the enemy. While their churches were demanding discipline and restraint and providing assistance and comfort to those members who were suffering losses, the patriot government took out its rage on those at hand. They were taxed doubly and triply; their barns were burned; their livestock killed or driven off, their crops destroyed. Some chose not to voluntarily pay the assessed taxes, but to wait to have them taken by force, according to the teachings of the church. If these were fortunate, they were allowed to walk away from their property with what they could carry, leaving the rest in the hands of the Committee of

---

[120] John L. Ruth, *'Twas Seeding Time* (Scotsdale, Herald Press, 1976), pp. 45-47.
[121] Knittle, pp. 207-226.
[122] Warrant 700, *Lancaster County Records* as reported by Gene Edwin Miller, *Some Brethren Families*, Irvine, CA, 10/1979, p. 1.

Observation to be resold or otherwise used in support of the war effort, with the blessings of the 1778 Continental Congress.

As the momentum for war grew, these war-worn, peace-loving, deeply-principled Anabaptists experienced increasing pressures. Some were required to fight, which they could not do. Failure to fight could result in punitive fines, the confiscation of lands, or mistreatments which might include being beaten, tarred and feathered or jailed. At least two of the brethren were tried for treason and hanged. Many of them eventually served the Revolutionary forces in non-combatant, supportive ways, such as in the provisioning of fighting men. Many of them moved again, out of the reach of the threatening government.

It is questionable whether Lodowich was expected to volunteer for militia duty. In all probability he would have been accepted if he had done so, for he was in his fifties during the 1770's. It is certain that he would not have chosen military service, however, and that is why he was taxed and fined heavily during the long period of military action, stretching from the French and Indian War and ensuing Indian attacks, through the American Revolution.

Of this period, *The Brethren Almanac* reported, "For the first fifty years the brethren suffered many privations on account of the French war in 1755, the Revolution 20 years later, and subsequent Indian wars together with many inconveniences incident to a newly settled country. . . .The dread of the Indian's tomahawk and scalping knife was everywhere felt. In the morning before going to the fields to work, the farmer and his sons often bid good-bye to the balance of the family, fearing they might not return, or if permitted to do so, would find their loved ones murdered by the Indians."[123]

Among the descendants of Michael Miller who were "processed" by the Committee on Observation are found the names of two sons of Lodowich Miller and Barbara Long and two sons of John Garber and his wife, Barbara Miller.

It has been suggested that Maryland law was not administered so stringently as Pennsylvania law, which might account for the movement of a number of members of the family from Pennsylvania to Catholic Maryland in the 1760's. Even so, the Committee of Observation in Maryland fined them heavily, and when the fines went unpaid, confiscated their land and sold it to pay the fines for them. Once again, the two sons of John Garber who were mentioned above, and John Garber, himself, were fined, though the penalty was forgiven on the same day. Lodowich's son-in-law, Michael Wine, was fined and his land confiscated, and Daniel Miller (I) was fined in the amount of

[123] *The Brethren Almanac*, 1879, quoted by Mallott in *Studies in Brethren History* (1954), p. 90.

4 1/2 pounds. [124]

The Masons found that Lodowich had, over the years, twelve different land transactions, but only one in which he gave land to a son or daughter. "(He) moved his family from place to place during the perilous days of the French and Indian War. Land records state that in 1763 and 1767 he was living in York County, Pennsylvania. . .at the time of the birth of Daniel he was living in Dauphin County, Pennsylvania. . . .Most of the other deeds state that he was living in Frederick County, Maryland, perhaps on "Chestnut Level," located near Woodsboro, and on his farm at Beaver Creek in what is today Washington County, Maryland."[125] From the 1770's to the time of his death Lodowich paid taxes on land at Pipes Creek, Frederick County, Maryland and on a parcel of land near Taneytown, Maryland that he had received from his father. It is said that he lived at Pipes Creek.

In Frederick, Maryland my husband and I located some transcriptions of deeds pertaining to Lodowich. One, made 11/26/1782, indicates that Lodowick Miller, farmer, of Frederick County, for 125 pounds, sold 100 acres of "Germany" to Daniel Ubry of Washington County, farmer.[126]

Another transcription found, attested to in the first person, finds "Lodewick Miller of Frederick County, farmer, but now in Washington County, and heir-at-law to Michael Miller, deceased, (selling) to brother Philip Jacob Miller, farmer, for 5 sh(illings) land which I received from my father's estate, granted originally to John George Arnold 1/16/1739 and conveyed 5/14/1745 to Michael Miller, in Prince George's County. Michael Miller left no will; I agreed that my brother Philip Jacob should resurvey the original tract Ash Swamp, which was done 4/25/1752 and patented to him for 290 acres. I convey my rights."[127] We assume that whomever transcribed these words of Lodowich into the legal books did so with some accuracy. These words, therefore, are perhaps the only remaining words of this g-g-g-g-grandfather.

In one of his deeds Lodowich was called a weaver. Almost all colonial homes had a loom, an essential, as it had been for centuries. The fact that the household weaving was traditionally the job of the housewife suggests that the work accomplished by Lodowich was beyond that which might be considered basic. Perhaps his skills were greater than those of the average housewife, who might have made cloth for bedding, toweling, rugs, and simple family clothing.

---

[124] Mason, *Miller Record*, pp. 21-25.

[125] Mason, *Miller Record*, p. 25.

[126] "Washington County Land Records, Liber C," pp. 306-309, as quoted by C. E. Scheldknecht, ed., *Monocacy and Catoctin*, vol. 4, no. 1 (Middletown, MD), Family Line Publishing, 1/1988).

[127] "Washington County Land Records," pp. 563-567, as quoted by Scheldknecht, vol. 4, no. 3, p. 137.

This house was likely the home of Lodowich Miller or one of his brothers.

Perhaps he had been especially trained in his craft, or was particularly artistic as he sat at his loom. He may have owned the designs needed to make some of the wonderful woven coverlets, or intricately woven dress fabrics; or the strength to handle the heavy woolen blankets that were sorely needed in the sparsely heated cabins and homes of his time. Certainly he was not the only male "linenweber" of his era. It is pleasant to imagine him in this context.

Lodowich was, as has been revealed, a Dunker. (In the 20th century, he would commonly have been identified as a member of the Church of the Brethren.) As he moved from one safe haven to another he probably belonged to several different congregations, among them Beaver Creek, in Maryland. Wherever he worshipped, he was undoubtedly staunch in his faith and a strong influence for his children. Floyd and Kathryn Mason report in their *Michael Miller Family Record* that 80% of the descendants of Lodowich Miller's sons, Daniel Miller and Jacob Miller, remained active members of the Church of the Brethren. Of the eight church leaders honored in their book, six are descendants of Lodowich Miller through Daniel Miller (I).[128]

He was "naturalized in 1762 with the Conocoheague Community."[129]

---

[128] Mason, *Miller Record*, p. 6.
[129] Mason, *Miller Record*, p. 26.

An attempt to explain the "naturalization" along with the documents required of the Palatines follow on page 55 of this chapter.

"...(T)he big family of Lodowich Miller moved to Virginia during the period of 1775 to 1813....There is some documentation but most of our information is handed down through family tradition."[130]

d. 1792 in Taneytown, Maryland (Frederick County, Maryland)

G-g-g-g-grandfather- 7th generation

Barbara Long

b. c1727, in Germany, probably near Solingen

daughter of **John Nicholas "Nikel" Lang** (c1702-1776) and **Anna Maria Studebaker** (bpt.10/15/1702-bef1776)

Barbara arrived in Philadelphia aboard the "Harle" with her parents and two brothers on 9/1/1736 at nine years of age.

sister of John Long (1728-) m. (1)Anna Catharina Studebaker; (2)Margaret__
Frederick Long (1732-) m. Elizabeth Studebaker (c1737-)
David Long (c1738/40-1763) m. Maria Christina Studebaker (11/9/1734-)[131]

m. **Lodowich Miller** (c1724-1792)

mother of Jacob Miller (1748-1815) m. (1)Anna Martha Wine; b. in Washington County, Maryland
Lodowich Miller (1749-) m. Barbara Ann__
Abraham Miller (1750-) m. Catherine Byerly
David Miller (1750/51-1828) m. Mary Magdalena Eickenberry; b. in Washington County, Maryland
Daniel Miller (5/13/1752-8/1820) m. Anna Garber (1762-1837)
Susannah Miller (1754-1848) m. Michael Wine; b. in Maryland
Christian Miller (c1755-1828) m. Susannah__[132]

---

[130] Mason, *Miller Record*, p. 27.
[131] Harvey Long, pp. 1-4.

Nancy Miller (1756-) m. Conrad Sanger (c1765-); b. in Washington County, Maryland

John Miller (1758-1791) m. Margaret__; b. in Frederick County, Maryland; owned 210 acres that had once belonged to his father

Elizabeth Miller (1760-) m. Samuel Garber; born in Frederick County, Maryland

Frances Miller m. John Long (1761-1838)

Barbara's mother's cousins, Peter, Clement and Heinrich Studebaker, were among those who arrived on the "Harle" with "Marie" Studebaker Langen and her husband, "Nikel" Lang. The closeness of these families continued, for three of Peter Studebaker's daughters became the wives of the three sons of Nikel Lang, and at his death, Peter Studebaker divided his estate near Hagerstown, Maryland among the four Lang/Long children.[133]

G-g-g-g-grandmother- 7th generation

Our Miller family has always known of Barbara Long, without knowing exactly how she fit into the picture. The very fact that her name persisted in family annals in this uncertain state indicates that she was revered enough to be passed on in limbo. The consensus came to be that Barbara was a first wife of Daniel Miller, son of Lodowich. It was generally accepted that she had been childless and that, after her early death, Daniel had married Anna Garber, with whom he had no fewer than eleven children.

While reading a book about the *Big Long Family* of Pennsylvania and elsewhere, I suddenly found our Barbara. The family connections were right; the dates were appropriate; there was no other Barbara Long with whom to confuse her; and she had married __Miller. On the other hand we knew that Lodowich Miller had married Barbara__. Time may allow a further search for absolute confirmation, but I am certain within all reason that Barbara Long was not Daniel's first wife, but his mother. I suspect that she may be especially remembered because she came, after the death of her husband, into Virginia with the three sons who first arrived in the Shenandoah Valley.

---

[132] Mason, *Miller Record*, pp. 58-59.

[133] Harvey Long, pp. 1-3.

The Oaths of Allegiance and Abjuration (More Problems for the German Baptists)

Swearing was not something that the German Baptists could do. Their allegiance was to their God, and there was none to be sworn to anyone else. They could not "take an oath," though it might be proper to "affirm" by way of making a statement, or to respond with a yes or no. On the other hand, refusal to take an oath of allegiance was considered by the American patriots as disloyalty or as giving aid to the enemy, and on this issue, also, the members of the "Peace Churches" were misunderstood and persecuted.

It all came about this way. Many of the landowners who had earlier come from the British Isles in response to William Penn's invitation to settlement had become nervous because of the great numbers of German immigrants who were threatening the expansion of their own estates. They expressed concern about the "forreigners" who were by that time flocking into Pennsylvania, and, to some extent, into New York. Those who had earlier established themselves comfortably, who represented this attitude, would have been happy to see William Penn's invitation to the oppressed withdrawn now that they were themselves safely settled.

On September 14, 1727 the Lieutenant Governor of the Province of Pennsylvania, called together the Provincial Council. He had just been informed that a ship loaded with 400 Palatines had arrived from Holland, and there were more to follow. It was their intent to settle in the frontier areas of the colony, and it was feared that these people "being ignorant of our Language & Laws, & settling in a body together" might cause difficulties for the colony. The Council considered the matter and determined that the newcomers should, by way of naturalization, take an "Oath of Allegiance, or some equivalent to it, to His Majesty, and promise Fidelity to the Proprietor & obedience to our Established Constitution: And therefore, until some proper Remedy can be had from Home, to prevent the Importation of such Numbers of Strangers into this or others of His Majesties Colonies."

The process was further described. " 'Tis ordered, that the Masters of the Vessells importing them shall be examined whether they have any leave granted them by the Court of Britain for the Importation of these Foreigners, and that a List shall be taken of the Names of all these People, their several Occupations, and the Places from whence they come, and shall be futher examined touching their Intentions in coming hither; And further, that a Writing be drawn up for them to sign declaring their Allegiance and Subjection to the King of Great Britain & Fidelity to the Proprietary of this Province, & that they will demean themselves peacably towards all his Majesties Subjects,

& strictly observe, and conform to the Laws of England and of this Government."[134] If this statement of intention sounds a bit wordy, the several oaths which follow will astound you with their verbiage. The first of the required oaths was this: "We Subscribers, Natives and Late Inhabitants of the Palatinate upon the Rhine & Places adjacent, having transported ourselves and Families into this Province of Pensilvania, a Colony subject to the Crown of Great Britain, in hopes and Expectation of finding a Retreat & peacable Settlement therein, Do Solemnly promise & Engage, that We will be faithful & bear true Allegiance to his present MAJESTY KING GEORGE THE SECOND, and his Successors, Kings of Great Britain, and will be faithful to the Proprietor of this Province; And that we will demean ourselves peacably to all His Majesties Subjects, and strictly observe & conform to the Laws of England and of this Province, to the utmost of our Power and best of our understanding."

The second required oath was: "I __ do solemnly & sincerely promise & declare that I will be true & faithful to King George the Second and do solemnly sincerely and truly Profess Testifie & Declare that I do from my Heart abhor, detest & renounce as impious & heretical that wicked Doctrine & Position that Princes Excommunicated or deprived by the Pope or any Authority of the See of Rome may be deposed or murthered by their Subjects or any other whatsoever. And I do declare that no Forreign Prince Person Prelate State or Potentate hath or ought to have any Power Jurisdiction Superiority Preeminence of Authority Ecclesiastical or Spiritual within the Realm of Great Britain or the Dominions thereunto belonging."

And the third: "I __ do solemnly sincerely and truly acknowledge profess testify & declare that King George the Second is lawful & rightful King of the Realm of Great Britain & of all others his Dominions & Countries thereunto belonging, And I do solemnly & sincerely declare that I do believe the Person pretending to be Prince of Wales during the Life of the late King James, and since his Decease pretending to be & taking upon himself the Stile & Title of King of England by the Name of James the third, or of Scotland by the Name of James the Eighth or the Stile & Title whatsoever to the Crown of the Realm of Great Britain, nor any other the Dominions thereunto belonging. And I do renounce & refuse any Allegiance or obedience to him & do solemnly promise that I will be true and faithful, & bear true allegiance to King George the Second & to him will be faithful against all traiterous Conspiracies & attempts whatsoever which shall be made against his Person Crown & Dignity & I will do my best Endeavours to disclose & make known to King George the Second & his Successors all Treasons and Traiterous Conspiracies which I

[134] Strassburger, p. 45.

shall Know to be made against him or any of them. And I will be true & faithful to the Succession of the Crown against him the said James & all other Persons whatsoever as the same is & stands settled by An Act Entituled An Act declaring the Rights & Liberties of the Subject & settling the Succession of the Crown to the late Queen Anne & the Heirs of her Body being Protestants, and as the same by one other Act Entituled An Act for the further Limitation of the Crown & better securing the Rights & Liberties of the subjects & stands settled & entailed after the Decease of the said late Queen, & for Default of Issue of the said late Queen, to the late Princes Sophia Electoress & Dutchess Dowager of Hanover & the Heirs of her Body being Protestants; and all these things I do plainly & sincerely acknowledge promise & declare according to these express Words by me spoken & according to the plain & common Sense and understanding of the same Words, without any Equivocation mental Evasion or secret Reservation whatsoever. And I do make this Recognition Acknowledgement Renunciation & Promise heartily willingly & truly."[135]

This immense effort was made to guarantee the loyalty of a group of individuals who did not speak English; were unlikely to have understood this barrage of words, if they had learned to speak English; and were, on principle, unable to swear. Furthermore, many of the more important of these ideas, such as that of avoiding political intrigues and being good, peaceful, and honorable citizens, were simply basic to their nature and, as a practical matter, did not need the swearing.

John H. Garber

b. 1728/1732 in Coventry Township, Chester County, Pennsylvania

son of **Hans Gerber/Garver** (1700-1748)

Floyd and Kathryn Mason believe that John H. Garber was the son of John Garber, brother of Niclous Garber, both of whom died in 1748.[136] Elsewhere I have found his father listed as Hans. I believe John and Hans (Johannes) are one and the same.

brother of Martin Garber (c1733-c1800) m. Anna (Preston?)

and possibly Niclaus Carver (1742-) moved to Virginia in 1783

[135] Strassburger, pp. 3-6.

[136] Floyd R. and Kathryn G. Mason, *John H. Garber and Barbara Miller of Pennsylvania, Maryland and Virginia* (Bridgewater, VA, 1995), p. 1088.

m. **Barbara Miller** (1733-1808) c1752[137]

father of seven sons who became ministers, and three daughters:

Elder Samuel Garber (1756-1814) m. Mollie Stoner
Elder John Garber (1758-1819) m. Barbara Zook
Abraham Garber (1760-1848) m. Elizabeth Humbert (-1838). He was the minister at Middle River, Augusta County, Virginia.
Elder Martin Garber (1761-1824) m. Rebecca Stoner
Anna Garber (c1762-c1837) m. Daniel Miller I (5/13/1752-8/1820) c1783
Jacob G. Garber (1766-1836) m. Susannah Humbert
Daniel Garber (1769-) m. (1)Susanna Miller (c1780-) c1802; (2) Elizabeth Shank 1/10/1815
Catherine Garber (1771-1835) m. John Flory (1766-1845)
Joseph Garber (1733-1854) m. Catherine Leedy (1777-1851)
Magdalena Garber (6/14/1774-7/26/1832) m. George Wine (1774-1845) c1796

John bought 200 acres in Codorus Township, York County, Pennsylvania on 1/2/1751[138] and lived there until 1761, when he moved to Bedford County, Pennsylvania. While the family lived there John served as the minister at Brothers Valley Church of the Brethren.[139]

You may recall, from an earlier account, the great difficulty the Brethren had with the government of Pennsylvania. John left there, as had others, in order to avoid the pressure exerted on him and his neighbors to fight, or to sign an oath of allegiance, or to suffer the consequences of their refusal to do either. He bought land and moved his family to Frederick County, Maryland in 1767. He called his 21 acre tract in Maryland "Garbers Good Luck."

It was in Maryland that he was ordained[140] an elder at Beaver Dam German Baptist Church where he served as an assistant to Elder Jacob Danner and Elder Daniel Leatherman. [141]

---

[137] J. Paul Glick, *A 3-Generation Genealogy of Rev. Joseph Miller of Beaver Creek Church, Rockingham County, Virginia* (Waynesboro, VA, 1966), p. ix.
[138] *York County Pennsylvania Deed Book*, Deed no. A-526 as reported by Steven R. Garber and Jerry R. Masters in "Gerber, Garber, and Garver Progenitors in Pennsylvania," *Pennsylvania Mennonite Heritage,* vol. 22, no. 3, July 1999, p. 31.
[139] H. Austin Cooper, *Two Centuries of Brothers Valley Church of the Brethren* (Brotherton, PA, Two Committees, 1962), pp. 128-129, 376-377, as reported by Garber and Masters, p. 31.
[140] "...(W)e believe the Stutsman, Garber and Miller families attended the German Baptist Brethren churches in Coventry Township, Chester County and in Manheim Township, York County, in Pennsylvania; and in Frederick County, Maryland." (Mason, *Miller Record,* p. 10).
[141] Mason, *Miller Record*, p. 26.

During these unsettled years "...the war was in progress and supporters were zealous for their cause. Dunkards and Mennonites had a difficult time remaining true to their faith. The church leaders refused to cooperate with the war cause and encouraged their people to remain true to their non-resistant principles and refrain from participation and/or paying the war taxes. In addition, Elder Jacob Danner (Donner) and other local elders were buying slaves at the auctions and giving them their freedom, which was in keeping with the church's teachings but very unpopular with owners of slaves."[142]

Elder Danner was the first elder at Beaver Dam, the second recorded Maryland German Baptist Church, and was succeeded by Daniel Seiler and his son, Daniel. "The order of eldership after the Seilers (included) John Garber..."[143] He was mentioned as having been a prominent Brethren minister in Pennsylvania and in Maryland.

"We believe that the newly appointed ministers, John H. Garber and Daniel Miller I...felt oppression both from the civil authorities and the older elders of the church and that this was the reason for their relocation to Virginia."[144] It has been said that the first four families to leave Maryland to settle in the Flat Rock community in 1782 did so because their Maryland land had been confiscated. The Masons tell that 848 acres of land, called "Spring Plain," had been purchased by Jacob Danner in 1762 and sold to Dunker families, including John H. Garber, and that this land, including "Spring Plain" and some "older tracts," was confiscated in 1781 by Captain Wood. The land lay near what is today Woodsboro Town in Maryland.

"The first of the Dunkers to settle in the Valley of Virginia was John Garber, who came with his family about the year 1777. He had probably come alone and purchased land a year or two earlier. He located in the upper part of Shenandoah County near the present village of Forestville and the site of the first church– Flat Rock...Other Dunker families, notably the Myerses, Wines, Klines, Bowmans, Millers, Kageys, Wamplers, Ziglers, and Florys, moved up from Pennsylvania and settled in the counties of Shenandoah and Rockingham. The number increased so rapidly that the annual conference of the whole brotherhood was held at Flat Rock in 1799. The original congregation there was divided and subdivided, and...now comprises Flat Rock, Linville Creek, Greenmount, Brock's Gap, Lost River, Woodstock, Frederick, Powell's Fort, and Page, – nine congregations, or districts, with a

---

[142] Mason, *Miller Record*, p. 26.
[143] Mallott, p. 93.
[144] Mason, *Miller Record*, p. 26.

membership of about 2000."[145]

John S. Flory, in an early edition of the *Gospel Messenger*, provided a pleasant image of the arrival of the Garbers in Shenandoah County: "The Garber home was established a mile or so west of a large flat rock, on a fertile tract of land. With (five) grown-up sons to help subdue nature, the family prospered and founded a good estate. John H. Garber had not only the means but also the leisure and inclination to make himself useful to his neighbors. He traveled extensively on horse-back to bring the gospel message to scattered settlers. He cobbled shoes for his neighbors and for his own family. He cultivated friendly relations with the Indians and demonstrated what intelligent industry and good management could do in building a home in the Wilderness."[146]

Of John Garber and other pioneer preachers Otho Winger said: "In the history of the Christian Church there are but few examples of greater sacrifice and courage than those of these pioneer Virginia preachers. Over the mountains and through the valleys for hundreds of miles they made their rounds to preach the Gospel. Some of them traveled thousands of miles in a single year. As a result of their labors the Brethren churches grew strong in faith and in numbers."[147]

John Garber died in 1787. "According to John S. Flory, '. . .(John Garber) was universally loved and admired, not only by those who knew him best, but by the scattered settlers and the roving Indians. . . .The legend still persists that several Indians were present to witness his death. . . .' "[148]

He made his will on 9/3/1787 and it was probated on 12/27 of that same year. In it he left 2/3 of his estate to his ten children. Samuel Bechtel, a Mennonite minister, was one of his executors.

He was interred in the family plot on his farm and a small stone with the inscription "17JHG87" is all that marks his grave.

John's sons, Samuel and Martin, along with John Glick, Jr. became leaders of the Flat Rock Brethren congregation.[149]

". . .(I)n gathering the history of the Millers it has been found interesting to study the connected families such as the Garbers, the Earlys, the

---

[145] John Walter Wayland, *The German Element in the Shenandoah Valley of Virginia* (Bridgewater, C. J. Carrier Co., 1964), pp. 125-126.
[146] John S. Flory article in the *Gospel Messenger* as quoted by Clark M. Garber, *The Garber Historical and Genealogical Record*, vol. III (Butler, Ohio, 1964), pp. 8-9.
[147] Otho Winger, *History and Doctrines of the Church of the Brethren*, pp. 68-69 as quoted by Mallott, p. 115.
[148] Sappington, pp. 30-31.
[149] Sappington, pp. 30-31.

Florys, the Wines and others who married into the Miller family. Elder John Garber, for instance, came from Maryland to the Shenandoah Valley of Virginia about 1775. His descendants have permeated practically every nook and corner of the Valley, and have spread to many other states. From him have descended practically all the Garbers and Florys in Virginia, also many of the Millers, Wines and Earlys, besides other families. It is simply impossible to study any one of these lines without studying the others." [150]

The Elder in the Early German Baptist/Brethren Church

Quite a few early Church of the Brethren forebears are referred to as elders. These men were elected for life to a position of leadership in their congregations. For generations the elder was also the minister. It is possible that there was no compensation given for the services of the elder, but it was a position of esteem. "The seniority in the ministry was very much in evidence, even to the seating behind the table. The next oldest in the ministry always sat next to the elder and was considered in authority according to his place in the pulpit. The deacons likewise recognized seniority. The oldest in office was seated directly across the table in front of the elder with the next oldest beside him, and so on to the youngest. This order continued for nearly 100 years.

"The Church was democratic in form but when the elder, after consultation with the other ministers and deacons, made any declaration, it was usually accepted by the congregation. The members, . . .being of German descent, all spoke German in the early days. The sermons were all delivered in German until about 1830 after which time both German and English were used. After 1875, only English was used in the pulpit. By 1900 very few members could even converse in German. . . ."[151]

"Only a few of the early leaders of the Dunkers in Virginia were educated men; but many of them were strong in Christian character and well furnished unto good works. . . . (They were) men who loved their fellow men and did much, often through great sacrifice, to serve them."[152]

"Many of the homes were built to meet the needs of the church. Often the partitions of adjoining rooms were made so that they could be moved. Benches were used for seats. These could easily be stored away when not in use. At very large meetings the services were held in the barn to accommodate more people who sat on the benches without backs, on the hay, or any other

---

[150] Jacob Miller, as shared by Leila Maxwell Miller, source unknown.
[151] Mallott, pp. 90-91.
[152] Wayland, *German Element*, p. 126.

available space. Services were held in the open when the occasion demanded."[153]

Barbara Miller

b. 1733, probably in Chester or Lancaster County, or near Hanover, Pennsylvania.

daughter of (Hans) **Johann "Michael" Miller** (10/5/1692-1771) and **Susanna Agnes Berchtol** (Bechtel) (1688-1752)

sister of John Peter Miller (1715-1794)
Hans Jeremiah Miller (1717-1781)
David Miller (1719-1785)
Hans Michael Miller (1720-1784) m. Elizabeth ___
George Miller (1722-1798) m. Catherine ___
Lodowich Miller (c1724-1792) m. Barbara Long (c1727-)
Philip Jacob Miller (1726-1799) m. Magdalena Rochette
Michael Miller II (1728-1792) m. Elizabeth__
Jacob Miller (1735-1815)
Eva Elizabeth Miller m. Michael Danner (Tanner) (1696-1777) She was his second wife.
Maria Elisabeth Miller (3/19/1754-)

m. **John H. Garber** c1752 in York County, Pennsylvania.

mother of seven sons who became ministers and three daughters:
Elder Samuel Garber (1756-1814) m. Mollie Stoner
Elder John Garber (1758-1819) m. Barbara Zook
Abraham Garber (1760-1848) m. Elizabeth Humbert (-1838) He was the minister at Middle River in Augusta County, Virginia.
Elder Martin Garber (1761-1824) m. Rebecca Stoner
Anna Garber (1762-1837) m. Elder Daniel Miller (I) (5/13/1752-8/1820) c1783
Jacob G. Garber (1766-1836) m. Susannah Humbert
Daniel Garber (1769-) m. (1)Susanna Miller (c1780-) c1802; (2)Elizabeth Shank 1/10/1815

[153] Mallott, p. 91.

Catherine Garber (1771-1835) m. John Flory (1766-1845)
Joseph Garber (1733-1854) m. Catherine Leedy (1777-1851)
Magdalena Garber (6/14/1774-7/26/1832) m. George Wine (1774-1845) c1796

d. 1808

G-g-g-g-grandmother- 7th generation

An anecdote pertaining to Barbara Miller Garber, and to the most convenient mode of transportation during the time in which she lived: It is reported that Barbara *walked* from Shenandoah County to Maryland and Pennsylvania and back again on two occasions.[154]

Ludwig Treiber, Sr.

b. c1728 in Hesse-Darmstadt, Germany

"Ludwig Treiber came to America aboard the ship Fayne, arriving in Philadelphia, Pennsylvania 17 Oct 1749 from Rothenstein, Germany. One source states 'the fact that it follows the Palatinate and Wurttemberg makes it probable that it was Rothenstein in Central Franconia, now Bavaria.' "[155]

In a second account, the above authors indicate that the good ship *Fayne* sailed from Rotterdam, Holland, via Cowes, England, with 595 passengers aboard. This is quite likely, for it is known that many of these German immigrants stopped over in England on their way to America.

Ludwig settled in Codorus Township, York County, Pennsylvania.

m. **Anna Barbara Sprenkle** (Sprinkle) (1737-c1781) in Pennsylvania c1752

father of Michael Driver (1754-) m. Barbara___
Anna Driver (1756-) m. John Rife
Barbara Driver (1758-)
Lewis Driver, Jr. (1760-) m. Barbara Burkhart
Anna Maria "Mary" Driver (1764-) m. Peter Acker

[154] John W. Wayland, *A History of Shenandoah County,* Virginia (Strasburg, VA, Shenandoah Publishing House, Inc., 1976), p. 172.
[155] Driver and Gassett, p. 3B

Peter Driver (11/20/1766-7/1/1850) m. Dorothy Meyer (4/15/1774-10/7/1844)
Jacob Driver (1768-) m. Elizabeth Forry (10/26/1771-)
Elizabeth Driver (1771-)[156]

Ludwig and Barbara bought 127 acres in York County, Pennsylvania on 3/21/1771 from John Kagey and his wife, Sarah.

d. bef1772 in York County, Pennsylvania

Ludwig died intestate. Barbara Treiber was made administratrix of her husband's estate 2/25/1772.[157]

Their son, Michael Driber, was later named administrator on 4/9/1781. Barbara may have died before the estate was settled and the property distributed.[158]

It is recorded in the York County *Orphan's Court Record Book* that after Anna Barbara Sprenkle's death " 'Michael Driber, Administrator De bonis Non of Ludwick Driber' appeared in court August 28,1782. On that date Mary Driber, seventeen year old daughter of Ludwick Driber, late of Manchester Township, York County, chose Jacob Heidelbaugh to be her guardian."[159]

"Deed Book C, page 428, for York County records that on August 20, 1787, Michael and Barbara Treiber of Newberry Township sold 127 acres of land to Christopher and Barbara Bower of Manchester Township. This land had been sold to Ludwick Treiber, now deceased, in 1771 by John and Sarah Kagey. The deed further explained that Ludwick had died intestate 'leaving lawful issue to wit: Michael Treiber. . .eldest son and heir at law, Anna, wife of John Reif, Peter Treiber, Jacob Treiber, Barbara Treiber, Mary Treiber and Elizabeth Treiber to whom the tract of described land with its appurtenances legally descend.' "[160] This list clearly excludes Lewis Driver, Jr., named elsewhere as a son of Ludwick and Barbara.

G-g-g-g-grandfather- 7th generation

---

[156] Driver and Gassett, p. 3B
[157] *York County, Pennsylvania Will Book C*, p. 74.
[158] *York County, Pennsylvania Will Book E*, p. 187.
[159] *York County Orphan's Court Record Book E*, p. 40.
[160] Driver and Gassett, p. 3.

Anna Barbara Sprenkle

b. 1737

daughter of **Michael Sprenkle** (-c1748), Swiss immigrant, who settled first at Conestoga Township, Lancaster, Pennsylvania; then, by 1734, along Codorus Creek in York County, Pennsylvania, and **Ann Margaretha Mueller**, his wife.

m. **Ludwig Treiber**, Sr. (Lewis Driver)(c1728-bef1772) c1752

mother of Michael Driver (1754-) m. Barbara___
Anna Driver (1756-) m. John Rife
Barbara Driver (1758-)
Lewis Driver, Jr. (1760-) m. Barbara Burkhart
Anna Maria "Mary" Driver (1764-) m. Peter Acker
Peter Driver (11/20/1766-7/1/1850) m. Dorothy Meyer (4/15/1774-10/7/1844)
Jacob Driver (1768-) m. Elizabeth Forry
Elizabeth Driver (1771-)

Anna Barbara was made administratrix of her husband's estate 2/25/1772. She was replaced as administrator on 4/9/1781 by her son, Michael Driver, presumably because she was no longer able to serve or because she had died.

Her daughter, Mary, at seventeen years of age, appeared in Orphan's Court on August 28, 1782. "On that date Mary Driber. . .daughter of Ludwick Driber, late of Manchester Township, York County, chose Jacob Heidelbaugh to be her guardian."[161]

d. c1781

G-g-g-g-grandmother- 7th generation

The Kirshof/Kiracofe Family

Who were the Kirshofs and how *did* they find their way to the American colonies?

[161] Driver and Gassett, p. 3.

Some years ago, when talking to a friend from Happurg, near Nuremberg, Germany, I mentioned the Kiracofe family. Although I had made unsuccessful attempts to find their origin in Europe, I felt that the name was German, so I asked yet again. Although my friend could make nothing of the name as a printed word, with its Anglicized spelling, the pronunciation of it immediately drew a response. She said it means churchyard or cemetery, and is definitely German in origin.

"The great majority of the Germans in the Valley of Virginia came across the Potomac above Harper's Ferry, from Maryland and Pennsylvania. (T)he counties of Lancaster, Lebanon, Berks, and York, with those surrounding Philadelphia, sent south the greatest number. . . .(T)here were a few who came from New Jersey and New York; a few from the East Virginia counties of Spotsylvania, Orange, and Madison - chiefly of the Germanna families. . . .In and following the period of the Revolutionary War, the German element in the Valley was considerably increased by Hessian soldiers who came over in the English service, and remained in America; and by others of their friends and countrymen who followed them after the establishment of peace. Some of these Hessians appear to have been skilled workmen; and a few, trained students. Most of them were a valuable addition to the growing country, despite the fact that they were looked upon for many years with much contempt and no little bitterness. In consequence, they and their descendants often tried to hide as soon as possible their origin and identity, under the new language, new forms of family names, and half-learned English manners.

"The scorn heaped upon the Hessians rested upon no good reason. . . . There was abundant reason, aside from mercenary inducements (offered by the English for soldiers) why the Hessians of the last quarter of the eighteenth century should fight with and for the English. The English had for many years been fighting with the Hessians in Germany. 'For a century and a half Hessian soldiers fought shoulder to shoulder with the English troops, mainly against France.'[162] What was more natural, therefore, than that when Frenchmen fought with Americans against Englishmen, Hessians should fight with Englishmen against Americans?"[163]

There are two theories about the arrival of Johannes. One is that Johannes Friederick Kirshof was a son of a Hessian soldier. There were, supposedly, two Johannes *Kirckhoffs/Kirchhoffs* who were Hessian soldiers. One was born in the year of 1731-1732; the other 1732-1733 (in another place

---

[162] *Palmer's Calendar of State Papers*, vol. 1, pp. 483-486 as quoted by John W. Wayland, *German Element*, pp. 20-21.
[163] Wayland, *German Element*, pp. 20-21.

1736-1737). They came from Herloz, Germany. These two were reported as probable brothers as it was customary about this period of time to give every son the first name of Johann. Either one could have been John Frederick's father. (Or, more likely, there was confusion due to faulty records and, in reality, these two were the same individual.) Of the nearly 30,000 Hessian soldiers who came as hirelings of King George, at least 5000 are said to have decided to make their homes in America. These deserted, and stayed. "They married girls of local families, secured land holdings, and their descendants remain to this day in the Valley."[164]

The other theory is that John Frederick came over on the ship *Sally* 8/13/1773. If he did, he was under the age of 16 because his name was not on the ship list, unless the name was listed as John Frederick *KuKuck*. (Cousin Josiah Andrew felt that the 1773 date was the accurate one. He was a g-g-grandson of John Frederick.[165]) [166]

Dr. Paul Glick stated that this was in all probability a Pennsylvania German family, but he did not know from whence they arrived, or when. He stated that one source said there were three *Kirkoff* brothers who came from Hessen, Germany in 1752 and were United Brethren ministers. This is unverified, but there are records of Christoph Kirchkoff arriving in 1727 and a Christopher Kirkhofe arriving in 1738.[167]

In Knittle's *Early Palatine Emigration*, there is a Francis Ludwig *Kirchofen* who was found in the first list of Palatine immigrants to London in 1709. In Rupp's *Thirty Thousand Names of German Immigrants 1727 to 1773* were found the Christopher *Kirchofe* mentioned before, and his family of five, who arrived in Philadelphia 9/27/1727 on the ship *James Goodwill*, Master David Crockett, Captain; Christopher *Kirkhofe*, who arrived 9/16/1738 aboard the *Queen Elizabeth*, Alexander Hope, Commander (These could certainly have been the same man!); Urban Perkhoff (also listed as *Kerchhoff*, with the first name shown as Abraham), arriving 9/27/1740 aboard the good ship *Lydia*, with Captain James Allen; and in 10/1753, J. Peter Kirchhofer.[168] It would be difficult to reconstruct relationships among these immigrants, or between them and Kiracofe descendants. I doubt that it will ever be accomplished.

Manfred Schlien, of Germany, submitted intriguing information to the Latter Day Saints in 1997, reporting the following lineage:

---

[164] W. P. Conrad, *From Terror to Freedom in the Cumberland Valley* (Greencastle, PA, Lilian S. Besore Memorial Library, 1976), p. 122.

[165] Josiah Andrew Kiracofe to Blanche Miller (Wilson) letter, Tuesday, October 31,__.

[166] Lula Miller, *Johannes Friederick Kirshof: Early Settler and Patriarch of Northern Augusta County*, vol. 1 (Verona, VA, McClure Printing Co., 1981), p. 6.

[167] Glick, p. 46.

[168] Lula Miller, p. 4.

Johann Guenter Kirchhoff

b. 1680 in Ostscheid, Westphalia, Prussia

son of Henrich Kirchhoff and Catharina Margaretha Mueller

m. (1)Cathrina Maria Schuette 8/5/1717 in Mennighueffen, Prussia;
(2)Christine Margaretha Sprekelmeyer

father, with Cathrina, of
Johann Jochim Henrich Kirchoff (chr. 9/30/1725-c3/7/1758) in
Mennighueffen, Westphalia, Prussia[169]

buried 1/21/1733 in Mennighueffen

No further information is available about this family. Could these be the parent, grandparents, and g-grandparents of John Frederick?

Benjamin E. Coakley

b. c1750

I am indebted to Mr. Marion Coakley, recently deceased, who was a distant cousin and a true friend of our mother, as well as those in this generation who have been trying to solve the riddle of this interesting family. Mr. Coakley took time in his busy life to visit various family members, as far away as Nova Scotia, asking questions about the Coakleys and taking copious notes. Late in his life he shared his time and his notes with us, enabling us to get a handle on a very interesting lot of relatives.

son of **James Cokeley**, immigrant (-1788) and **Margaret Antonison**

If available information is correct, Benjamin was raised to high adventure. He, as a small child, could have had a voyage on the Atlantic with his parents and his brothers. He could have wondered, under the watchful eye of his mother, at the vast ocean as he observed another ship, loaded with the family's slaves and possessions, in motion on the waves near their own vessel.

[169] Manfred Schlien submission, LDS

After the landing in the Bahamas, on Andros Island, this little boy would have seen the clearing of land for the plantation, the building of shelter, the attempts at farming, and the hurricanes. Tradition says there were three devastating hurricanes in the five years that the family was on Andros.

Benjamin would have been a bit older when his father packed the family and all that was spared on the one ship that was still seaworthy and set sail again, this time for calmer waters. We have looked at the shore of the Potomac as it is approached from the Atlantic. It is beautiful. I could imagine a wide range of reactions in the mind of a little boy when he saw this new shore, so very different from the glistening sands and turquoise waters he had seen as he left Andros Island.

It is said that we are the total of our experiences. What interesting men Benjamin and his brothers may have become.

brother of William Coakley m. Mildred Sullivan 2/4/1781
James Coakley, Jr. (bpt.1/12/1746/7-) m. 1)Nancy Wilson; 2)Susannah Dishman 1/10/1798
John Coakley (c1760-1820) m. Mary__, possibly Mary Smallwood (c1765-1835)[170], and if so 5/30/1772 in St. Michael, Barbados[171]
possibly Elizabeth Coakley

m. **Catherine__**

father of John Coakley m. Sarah (Sally) Taylor 9/1795;
Daniel James Coakley (c1769-1849) m. Sarah Eleanor Vigar (c1774/5-c1850)
Benjamin Coakley, moved to Stafford County by 1810.
Elizabeth Coakley m. Warren Songfore 7/14/1801
Sarah (Sally) Coakley m. Henry Staples 4/18/1803
William Coakley m. Mildred (Milly) Staples 1/21/1804
Several of these children were located in the King George County census.

It was said (by Mr. Coakley) that this family settled in "eastern Virginia, east of Fredericksburg, and the land was located in the counties of Spotsylvania and Caroline." Tragically, most of the Caroline County records

[170] Clark, p. 11 from the files of kd4tnq@netscape.net
[171] This John Coakley, believed to be the brother of Benjamin, was a grocer in the Fredericksburg area. He advertised "Antigua Rum, 4th proof" and New England cheese, soaps and candles in the *Virginia Herald*. Sounds to me like a man with connections! The West Indian Coakleys were shippers, among other things. Were these John's connections?

have been destroyed at one time or another by fire. Perhaps the best evidence we have that they lived in Caroline was the fact that Benjamin's great-granddaughter was named Caroline Virginia Coakley, and that she was told she was named for the "beloved" county. One would suppose then that Daniel James, her grandfather, had shared his love of his childhood home with the family in a way that made an enduring impression.

It is assumed that Benjamin(e) was a planter, although very little is known of his activity in Virginia until the time of the Revolutionary War, when he served for two years, and was wounded, and eventually died of his wounds.

The U.S. 7 June 8, 1779
"Warrant to
Benjamin Cokeley for present relief and for his Rifle and accoutr(i/e)ments taken by the enemy his being a disabled soldier of certifie.e"[172]

"Pensioners Warr to Benj e Cokeleys Estate for depreciation on paper money heretofore recd for his pension each (pound sign) 8.3.4} 16/6/8 27 June 1783 Richmond, Virginia." [173]

H. J. Eckenrode and John H. Gwathmey, both noted historians, record the fact that Benjamin was a soldier in the Revolutionary War.[174] Eckenrode cites records from the 1779 *Auditor's Account Book* and from *Auditor's Account Book XV*. It is assumed that he was in the continental army.

d. 11/21/1782 in Caroline or Spotsylvania County of wounds sustained in the American Revolution.

On the basis of the two years he had served in the military, Benjamin's wife, Catherine, claimed a pension after his death, the record of which I found in the Virginia State Archives in Richmond in 1970 and have since been unable to find. It was located in Dr. H. J. Eckenrode's *Revolutionary War Records*.

G-g-g-g-grandfather- 7th generation

---

[172] Auditor's *Account Book, 1779*, p. 177.

[173] *Revolutionary Soldiers Auditor's Account Book (XV) 1783*, p. 373.

[174] H. J. Eckenrode, *List of the Revolutionary Soldiers of Virginia: Special Report of the Department of the Archives and History for 1911* (Richmond, Davis Bottom, Superintendent of Public Printing, 1912), p. 104 and John H. Gwathmey, *Historical Register of Virginians in the Revolution: Soldiers, Sailors, Marines, 1775-1783* (Richmond, Dietz Press, Publishers, 1938), p. 165.

Catherine__ (Coakley)

m. **Benjamin(e) E. Coakley** (c1750-11/21/1782)

mother of John Coakley m. Sarah (Sally) Taylor 9/13/1795
Daniel James Coakley (c1769-1849) m. Sarah Eleanor Vigar (1774/5-c1850)
Benjamin(e) Coakley moved to Stafford County by 1810
Elizabeth Coakley m. Warren Songfore 7/14/1801
Sarah (Sally) Coakley m. Henry Staples 4/18/1803
William Coakley m. Mildred (Milly) Staples 1/21/1804

Found 30 years ago in Archives in Richmond: "Benjamine E. Coakeley served 2 years in army during Revolutionary War and died Nov. 21, 1782 from wounds that he received while in the army. His wife Catherine applied for pension or death claim and received 4 warrents of pay 6 pounds each - total 24 pounds." This was attributed in my notes to H. J. Eckenrode. The actual source has, so far, not been relocated.

d. in Caroline County, Virginia aft1782.

G-g-g-g-grandmother- 7th generation

William Vigar[175]

We know little about William Vigar. The name of his parents and the dates of his life are unknown. It could be that he is the same William Vigor/Vigour/Vignor who appears in the reconstructed census of 1760 in Westmoreland County and in St. Paul's Parish records. The only two Vigars found in the 1787 census of Virginia are William Vigar of Spotsylvania County and Sarah Vigar of Westmoreland County. This Sarah, based on the coincidence of name, might well be an aunt of Sarah Eleanor.

---

[175] In 1729 in County Carlow, Ireland, Margaret Vigors, daughter of John Beauchamp Vigors and granddaughter of Bartholomew Vigors, Bishop of Leighlin and Ferns m. Henry Colclough. The Vigors of Virginia were of a County Carlow family which, bearing a "French" name, arrived there early in the 17th century. Since the Virginia name is spelled in a variety of ways, including this one, it might be more than coincidence that Sarah Eleanor Vigar married Daniel James Coakley c1800. These families may have been acquaintances in Ireland who kept in touch in the new country. To add to the coincidence, lists of wills recorded in Barbados from 1718 to 1733 include those of four Viguers. (Edward MacLysaght, *The Surnames of Ireland*, 6th edition, Irish Academic Press, 1985, p. 294.)

m. **Ann Bridges**[176]

father of **Sarah Eleanor Vigar** (c1774-c1850) m. Daniel James Coakley (c1769-3/1849)
John Vigar (6/12/1788-c1860) m. Lucy Almond (c1798-c1865) 7/15/1816 (militia captain)
Elizabeth Vigar m. John Jarvass, both of whom had died bef3/9/1829.

William served as Executor for the estate of William Bridges, his father-in-law, along with Matthew and Thomas Bridges, sons of the deceased. Executor's bond was posted on 2/4/1794 in Spotsylvania County, Virginia.[177]

There is a "burnt" record of William's purchase of land in Rockingham County. Found in Deed Book 4 is the record of land deeded "from Frances Erwin, Executor of Thomas King, to William Vigar acknowledged the above memo made from minute book for 1818, Augusta Court under the act of the assembly approved Nov. 18, 1884."[178]

So far, the only other evidence of his life that has been found is an indenture made 3/21/1829 in which Daniel and Eleanor, "formerly the daughter of William Vigar, Deceased, of the County of Rockingham and State of Virginia," sell to John Vigar for $450 "all their interest, right, title and claim, as heirs of the said William Vigar, Deceased, to one third part of a certain undivided tract or parcel of land situate, lying in the County of Rockingham on both sides of the Briery Branch, containing by deed two hundred and forty-four acres"...bought by William Vigar 7/13/1818.[179]

d. bef3/21/1829

G-g-g-g-grandfather- 7th generation.

Ann Bridges

daughter of **William Bridges** (-11/8/1792)

sister of Matthew Bridges m. Elizabeth Jarvass; executor of his father's estate

[176] William Armstrong Crozier, *Spotsylvania Records*, p. 50.
[177] Crozier, *Spotsylvania Records*, p. 50.
[178] *Rockingham County Deed Book 4*, p. 218.
[179] *Rockingham County Burnt Deed Book 8*, pp. 540-541.

Thomas Bridges, co-executor of his father's estate, along with William Vigar
Mary Bridges

m. **William Vigar** (-bef3/21/1829)

The siblings of Ann Bridges undoubtedly held an interest in Orange/Rockingham County land that was inherited from their father. It took several legal documents[180] to dispense with the division of this inheritance.

mother of **Sarah Eleanor Vigar** (c1774-c1850) m. Daniel James Coakley (c1769-3/1849)
John Vigar (6/12/1788-between 1850 and 1860) m. Lucy Almond (c1798-between1860 and 1870) 7/15/1816. John was a captain in the militia.
Elizabeth Vigar m. John Jarvass, both of whom d. bef3/9/1829

G-g-g-g-grandmother- 7th generation

Robert Coleman Gaines

b. 1740/45 in Spotsylvania County, Virginia

This birthdate was provided by the Census of Rockingham County, Virginia for 1830. The *Virginia/West Virginia Genealogical Data from Revolutionary War Pension and Bounty Land Warrant Records*, vol. 2, compiled by Patrick G. Wardell, states that Robert was born 1748-50. Since his father died in 1744 one would assume that Robert was born in 1745, at the latest.

son of **Robert Gaines** who died in Spotsylvania County near the Orange County line c1744 and **Ursula Bridges** (-aft1776)

brother of William Gaines (-1813) probably m. Jane Robinson
Mary Gaines (given a deed of gift of goods and chattels by her mother, Ursula Gaines, as was her brother, Robert)
Alice Gaines m. John Robinson (-1811)
Ursula Gaines m. Elijah Carter
Lucy Gaines, living in 1776, unm

[180] *Rockingham Burnt Deed Book 8*, p. 540.

Robert was a witness, on 11/1/1757, to the will of Joseph Collins of Spotsylvania County. The name Gatewood appears in this document as it does in the document cited below.[181] A year later Robert, having served as a witness for Robert Bickers at the suit of Robert Duncanson, was awarded pay of "four hundred forty five pounds of tobacco for seven days attendance at this Court and coming five times out of Spotsylvania County eighteen miles and returning according to Law."[182]

This man had an uncle named Henry Gaines and sometimes called Harry. On 4/5/1762 Robert, and others, witnessed a land transaction between Harry Gaines and his wife and James Gatewood in Spotsylvania County, Virginia.[183]

m. **Elizabeth Long** (c1740-aft1831) of Culpeper County, Virginia c1770

father of Thomas Gaines (1771-) m. Mildred Rowe, daughter of
Edmund Rowe
Robert B. Gaines, (bef 12/30/1772-bef1831) m. Frances Manspile
Mary Gaines (bef12/30/1772-)
Lucy Gaines
John Long Gaines
Richard Gaines m. Frances Jolly 5/4/1789 in Culpeper County
Catherine "Kitty" or "Cathy" Gaines m. (1)Reuben Terrell 3/28/1803 in Orange County; (2)Alexander Dinwiddie 10/10/1806
Amelia Gaines- assuming this is "Milly"- m. William Rice 7/23/1806; William Rice later became the Executor for the estate of Robert Gaines (husband of Frances Manspile)
Ursula Gaines m. Luke Rice 3/7/1808; son of Mary Rice
Sarah Gaines
Reuben Gaines
Elizabeth Gaines (1793-) probably m. Henry Fisher 4/12/1801

On 12/30/1772 an indenture between Alexander Spotswood of Spotsylvania County and Robert Gaines (husband of Elizabeth Long) of Orange County "lett," or leased, to Robert 175 acres bounded by Mountain

---

[181] *Spotsylvania County Will Book B, 1749-1769*, p. 329 quoted by William Armstrong Crozier, ed., in *Virginia County Records*, vol. I, *Spotsylvania County, 1721-1800* (Baltimore, Genealogical Publishing Co., Inc., 1978), p. 15.

[182] Ruth and Sam Sparacio, *Virginia County Court Records, Orange County, Virginia: Orders 1757-1759* (McLean, VA, The Antient Press, 1998), p. 43.

[183] Crozier, *Spotsylvania Records*, pp. 224-225.

Road "during the natural lives of Robert (B.) Gains, Mary, and Thomas Gains." These were three of the children of Robert and Elizabeth Long Gaines. The rent was 500 pounds of Neat Tobacco yearly.[184] This advantageous lease, which effectively tied up 175 acres of land for 58 or more years, was recorded on 4/23/1773.

This Alexander Spotswood was undoubtedly the son of John Spotswood, grandson of the former governor, who had carefully preserved his lands and mines for the future of his family to the extent that he made it impossible for them to cover their expenses. An act of the General Assembly was required to untangle the complications. In this act are found the names of a variety of folks with whom we are familiar, most notably, the brothers-in-law Reuben Long, John Robinson, esquire, and Robert *Coleman* Gains.[185]

An interesting side note here is that Alexander Spotswood's grandfather was he who indentured the Wurttemberg group, including Jacob Mansboil, causing them to work in his iron mines in Germanna. It becomes easy to understand how Robert B., son of this Robert, met and married young Frances Manspile when one understands how closely these families must have lived to one another.

In 1776 the vestry of St. Mark's Parish in Culpeper County, Virginia met and Robert Gaines was made clerk of the Lower Church. "The leading Episcopal families who adhered to the church of their fathers through evil as well as good report. . ." included the Gaines.[186]

A considerable amount of **Bond/Long/Gaines** genealogy lies in this one deed: "To All Whom it may concern or these presents Come, Know Ye that I Reuben Long, Son of **Bromfield Long** and **Elizabeth Long**, who was **Elizabeth Bond** Daughter of **John** and **Mary Bond**, all of Culpeper County which said Reuben Long is of the one part and **Robert Gains** of Orange County of the other part. Witnesseth that Reuben Long being seized in certain Slaves now in possession of his Grandmother, Mary Bond, by Virtue of a Deed of Gift made by said John Bond bearing date the __day of 177_ duely recorded in the County aforesaid Wherein after the death of said Mary he devises certain negroes to his two Daughters, Elizabeth and Mary, (the said slaves) with their Increase and to their Children equally share and share alike the said Reuben, party to these presents, being the Eldest Son of said Elizabeth by the said Brumfield Long, being so hereof seized in Reversion and being desirous to sell and dispose of the same for and in consideration of the

---

[184] *Orange County Deed Book 16*, p. 158.

[185] Hening, *The Statutes at Large*, pp. 323-330.

[186] Green, pp. 18, 36.

sum of Seven hundred pounds good and lawfull money of the State of Virginia to him in hand paid by Robert Gains hath bargained and sold all that one fourth undevided share of the Slave or Slaves aforesaid and also all such shares as the said Reuben Long may hereafter be Intitled to by heir ship or other Right In Witness whereof I the said Reuben Long hath hereunto set my hand and Seal as my act and deed this 28th day of September 1779."[187]

This deed is witnessed by B. Johnston, Robert Long, Brumfield Long and William Long.

From the 1790 census, tax records indicate the fortunes of Robert and his family:

Gaines, Robert, 1 tithe, 15 slaves, King & Queen County, 1782
Gaines, Robert, Jr. 1 tithe, King & Queen County, 1782[188]
Gaines, Robert, 9 white males 2 slaves, Orange County, 1782
Gaines, Robert, 10 white males, 2 slaves, Orange County, 1785

One's fortunes change, and though we, at this point, recognize slavery as the unjust state that it is, from Robert's point of view and that of those by whom he was taxed, his resources in Orange County reached a high point in 1798 when he was taxed on five Blacks, five horses, and $1.50 in currency. The next year his assets included two Blacks, six horses, and $2.04.

Robert paid taxes in Orange County through 1800.

On 7/24/1797 Robert and Elizabeth, his wife, sold to William Richards 41 acres, "more or less," in Orange County, for twenty pounds, current money.

On 4/6/1799 Robert and Elizabeth bought from the same William Richards fifty acres of Orange County on both sides of Mill Run for eighty pounds current money. This purchase included "all houses orchards profits & appurtenances to the same belonging. . . "[189]

In this time when westward movement was the norm, Robert was not exceptional. After his move to King and Queen County, Virginia, prior to 1782, he moved to, or at least bought land in, Orange County by 1782, and, reportedly, proceeded to Rockingham County between 1803 and 1806.[190] It is possible that a man holding property in more than one place was listed as a

---

[187] *Culpeper County Deed Book K 1779-1781*, pp. 100-101.

[188] Augusta B. Fothergill and John Mark Naugle, *Virginia Tax Payers 1782-87 Other Than Those Published by the United States Census Bureau* (Baltimore, Genealogical Publishing Co,. 1966), p. 46.

[189] *Orange County Deed Book 21, 1795-1800*, pp. 17, 108.

[190] Sutherd, *Compilation*, 1972, pp. 348-350.

resident in each county in which he was taxed.

Family tradition disagrees with his eventual move to Rockingham. Blanche Miller Wilson reported that "Robert Gaines came to the Valley from Caroline County, buying land and slaves with it, at least two times. He made two trips over to Rockingham but never lived (there) himself.

"Grandmother Caroline said her name was given her for the old home in Caroline County"[191] We have never found records of Robert's and Elizabeth's residence in Caroline, but we know that many of the Caroline County records were destroyed. Could Robert have had his principal residence in Caroline while his daughter, Lucy, Caroline's mother, was growing up? Or was Caroline the "beloved county" of the Coakleys?

Considering Robert's documented land holdings and the numbers of slaves at each location; the fact that he was a vestryman in Culpeper County, while paying taxes in Orange, and King and Queen; that, according to family tradition, he had interests in land in Rockingham; one would conclude that he spread himself thinly, indeed. It is my conjecture that he had wealth, at least to the extent that he could take advantage of land deals wherever he found them. I further believe that he, from his earliest lease of land in 1772, had the welfare of his children in mind, for that land was leased not for the period of his own life, but for the period of the lives of three of his children, presumably the only three alive at the time of the lease. Considering Blanche Miller Wilson's "traditional" information that he visited Rockingham and bought land and slaves there, never living there himself, I suggest that this may have been his pattern, and that it was he, perhaps, and not Robert B., who bought the land in Rockingham from the Deans, but that he bought it in Robert B.'s name shortly before his own death. All of this speculation makes me want to run, not walk, to any surviving Caroline County records to see if I can find any trace of Robert there. And would it not be interesting to discover who managed those acres in King and Queen, Orange, and possibly Caroline, Counties?

d. bet1806 and 1808, probably

G-g-g-g-grandfather- 7th generation

There was another Robert Gaines, presumably the son of William and Isabella, since he is the only other recorded in Gaines family data or in Virginia tax records during this generation. This fellow worried me considerably, since

[191] Personal letter from Blanche Miller Wilson To Elisabeth Hodges, "Mon. the 24th," bef 1980.

he insisted on showing up in the court order books of Spotsylvania and Orange. There were several items on the court docket in Spotsylvania in 1749: on one occasion in Orange County (1754), the complaint pertained to "retailing Liquors;" on another (1753), trespassing, assault, and battery! The rascal continually failed to appear for his hearings and the fines against him appeared to mount. At one time it was noted that a case was dismissed because "Deft." Robert was "living out of the county." One may wonder if I am being selective in disclaiming this Robert. Might I be cleverly avoiding recording descent from a troublesome ancestor? I feel I am dealing fairly with the evidence however. The first Robert (husband of Ursula) was a vestryman in Stratton Major Parish in King and Queen County during this time and had died (befl745); the second Robert (husband of Elizabeth Long), born c1740, was a bit young to be involved in such shenanigans.

Elizabeth Long

b. c1740/1743 Culpeper County, Virginia (LDS)

daughter of **Bromfield** (Brumfield) **Long, Jr.** (c1721-1/21/1778) and
Elizabeth Bond (c1732-befl773) of Culpeper County.

sister of Reuben Long (c1748-); served in a campaign against the French and Indians in 1756
John Bond Long (1749-) m. Mary Haynes. He sold his share of the slaves left by his father on 11/27/1798 to (uncle) Benjamin Long of Culpeper County.
Benjamin Long (1750-1773)
Gabriel Long (c1752-)
Brumfield Long (c1754-)
Nancey Ann Long (c1756-) m. Richard Chism/Chisholm
Mildred "Millie" Long (c1764-) m. Benjamin Head (-1808) 7/19/1785
Richard Long (c1768-) m. Elizabeth Long, a daughter of his Uncle Benjamin
half-sister of Thomas Long (1775-) Sarah's "dutiful and affectionate son;" m. Bathsheba D. Moxley

m. **Robert Coleman Gaines** (1740-c1830)

mother of Thomas Gaines (1771-) m. Mildred Rowe, daughter of Edmund

Rowe
Robert B. Gaines, Jr. (c1773-bef1831) m. Frances Manspile
Lucy Gaines (1776-)
John Long Gaines
Mary Gaines (bef12/30/1772-)
Richard Gaines m. Frances Jolly 5/4/1789 in Culpeper County
Catherine "Kitty" or "Cathy" Gaines m. (1)Reuben Terrell 3/28/1803 in Orange County, Virginia; (2)Alexander Dinwiddie of Barren County, Kentucky 10/10/1806
Amelia Gaines probably m. William Rice 7/23/1806
Ursula Gaines m. Luke Rice 3/7/1808 (son of Mary Rice)
Sarah Gaines
Reuben Gaines
Elizabeth Gaines (1793-) probably m. Henry Fisher

Benjamin Long, uncle of Elizabeth Long Gaines, died c1804. The fact that his estate was settled by a lawsuit would suggest that there was disagreement as to the division of his property. Robert B. Gaines, Elizabeth's son, was the administrator of the estate, and was ordered by the court to sell all of the land and slaves at auction, and to divide the assets among the eleven complainants.[192]

d. aft1831

G-g-g-g-grandmother- 7th generation

Thomas Waddle

In his will Thomas's name is written as it is above, but it is signed Thomas Waddell.

b. in Scotland c1710

Jim Wooddell, a descendant, says Thomas Waddle was born "somewhere in a six-county area just south of Glasgow and Edinburgh." It is further described in his material as a place "near 'Great Wooded Dell' or the Great Glen in Scotland." The Great Glen generally refers to an area near Inverness at this time, and, in the confusion of information, since the Waddles seemed to have spread over a large area of Scotland, a more thorough search

[192] Buchanan and Owens, p. 196-197.

might find some record of him in any corner of the land.

According to a "formula" suggested by Jim Wooddell, Thomas's father might have been named James and his mother Sarah. He cites a "standard" naming pattern in which the first born of each gender is named for the father's parents, the second born of each gender for the mother's parents. If one relied on an article in *The Valley Virginian*, Thomas's father might be John and his mother, Martha. All of this is, of course, tall speculation.

The surname Waddell is derived from the name Wedale, an obsolete parish of Stow in Midlothian which lay between Gallishields and Edinburgh. The first account of the name is that of Adam de Wedale in 1204.[193] One Thomas Vadle was a merchant in Edinburgh in 1555. There are many others listed in one place or another, whose names are spelled in any number of fashions over the years.[194]

In March of 2000, my husband and I traveled to Wedale Parish, to the village of Stow- "a pretty little place of high antiquity"[195] in Edinburghshire. The drive was wonderful, characterized by rolling hills, gently flowing streams, and truly pastoral scenes. The village was the same, and quite small, with one main business street. We bought drinks at the local post office and walked the short distance from there to the skeletal remains of "The Old Church."[196] Barricades at the doors indicated that entering there would have been unsafe, so we contented ourselves with searching for Waddle tombstones, of which there were several, some old enough to be barely legible and some, later ones, which could be easily read, but late enough that they could have had little to do with our Thomas. There is, of course, some question as to whether Thomas ever saw Wedale Parish. Although it is the traditional home of the family, his ancestors may have moved on from that spot at an earlier time. As usual, more research is needed.

---

193 The Adam de Wedale of 1204 was listed as "an outlaw of the King of Scots land." Shall we assume that he was either not one of our line or that his offense was that of being out of favor politically? It is safe to assume both.

194 Black, pp. 796-797.

195 Francis H. Groome, editor, *Ordnance Gazateer of Scotland: A Survey of Scottish Topography, Statistical, Biographical and Historical* (Edinburgh, Thomas C. Jack, Grange Publishing Works, 1885), pp. 404-405.

196 The ruin of the church dates to the late 15th century, when it was built on foundations originally laid in 1242. There was rebuilding done in the 17th century. If Thomas knew the village of Stow, he would have known this church, and he, too, would have referred to it as "old."

The old parish church at Wedale, now in ruins, was consecrated on November 3, 1242.

Thomas sailed from Belfast, Northern Ireland, and landed in Philadelphia on August 3, 1746.[197] (Elisabeth Hansel Woodside's research finds Thomas arriving in Pennsylvania in 1755.)

"He was an indentured servant in the household of John Fullerton, whose wife was the g-g-granddaughter of John and Priscilla Alden, for a period of 4 years."[198]

m. **Alise**/Alese__ (c1725-1818) in Philadelphia, probably at the First Presbyterian Church[199]

Thomas moved shortly after his marriage to 700 acres which lie on Buffalo Run, two and a half miles northwest of where the village of Mt. Solon now stands, in Augusta County, Virginia. C. E. May referred to the area in which he lived as Woodell Springs, which is also the name of a spring located on the west side of Narrow Back Mountain.

"On one occasion while looking through some old papers in the loft of the house built on the Old Wooddell Homestead, Howard L. Wooddell recalls reading a contract signed by King George I, granting (the above-mentioned tract of land) to Thomas Wooddell."[200]

---

[197] Personal letter from James Wooddell to Emma and Charley Jordan, 12/31/1998.
[198] *Ibid*.
[199] Lula Miller, p. 33.
[200] Wooddell, *op. cit.*

father of James Waddle- inherited from his father the "George Kiracofe Farm"

Joseph Waddell (in his will, he makes a distinction in spelling of sons' names) Thomas left this son that part of his estate known as the "Buffer Farm."

Sarah Waddle

Elizabeth Waddle

Thomas Waddle, Jr., who served in the Revolution with his father; m. Margaret Ervin. Thomas left him that part of his estate known as the "Curry Farm."

Captain **John Waddle** (4/12/1761-8/5/1852) m. Elizabeth Erwin (c1753-1834). He was left the "Old Wooddell Homestead," where his father had lived.

Martha Waddle m. Charles Hansel of Pendleton County, Virginia

Jane Waddle m. Edward Ervin

"It is understood the early Waddles were woodsmen. . .most of them moved on toward the West."[201]

"*Deed Book 21*, p. 187: Delivered to Thomas Waddle on Dec. 1763 by Wm. Preston 147 acres on North River Shenandoah, corner of Benjamin Copeland. Wm. Preston obtained this land on Nov. 21, 1759."[202]

This deed, or indenture, grants the land, and ". . .all Houses, Buildings, Orchards, Ways, Waters, Water courses, Profits, Commodities, Heroditaments, and Appurtenances whatsoever to the said premises hereby granted, or any part thereof belonging or in anywise appurtaining; and the reversion or reversions, remainder and remainders, Rents Issued and profits thereof To have and to hold. . ." to Thomas Waddel. . ."from the Day before the Date hereof for and during the full Term and Time of whole one year, from thence next ensuing, fully to be compleat and ended, yielding and paying therefore the Rent of one pepper Corn on Sady (Saturday) next, if the same shall be lawfully demanded. . . ."[203] And so it goes, this lengthy, wordy document. I trust you understood it.

"Thomas Waddle received a land grant of 25 acres on North Fork of the Shenandoah adjoining Robert Edgar and Lampler March 6, 1771." [204]

---

201 Miller, p. 34.

202 Miller, p. 33.

203 *Augusta County Deed Book 21*, p. 187.

204 Peter Cline Kaylor, *Abstract of Land Grant Surveys, 1761-1791* (Dayton, Shenandoah Press, Jan. 1938), p. 66.

Rockingham County is thought of as an area which was settled largely by families who had originated in Germany or Switzerland. It is Rockbridge and Augusta to which the Scotch-Irish were supposed to have come. There was, however, a sizeable settlement of the Scotch-Irish in the area of Mossy Creek. They did not have to purchase their original holdings, since they settled on land patented directly to them. This was an incentive that was not shared by those of their countrymen who settled in the area immediately south of them.

These early settlers were, as were those further south, devout Presbyterians who initially traveled approximately twelve miles to worship at the Stone Meeting House (Augusta Stone Church of Ft. Defiance). Such a trip made under the conditions they experienced was found to be extremely difficult, so much so that John Davis and others petitioned the Presbytery for a pastor. Land was acquired on Linville Creek in 1770 and the first log meeting house was built near an old burying ground not far from the present church building.

Thomas Waddle (Woodal), at age 61, served as an Elder in the Mossy Creek Presbyterian Church and as a commissioner to Hanover Presbytery in 1771. He also attended the meeting of the Hanover Presbytery in 1772.

"*Deed Book 21*, p. 449: 170 acres on Thorny Branch joining the plantation where Thomas Waddle now lives, formerly possessed by William Cunningham, date Mar. 18, 1777." Lula Mae Miller believed this to be the land on which Sangerville is now located. The description in the deed indicates that it lay next to Curry land.[205]

In 1778 Thomas and Alese deeded acreage to their son, James. The same deed book reports that land was later deeded to their son Thomas.[206]

Both Thomases served in the American Revolution. Listed "in 1783, in Capt. Dickey's company: Edward Erwin, Sr. and son Francis, . . .Thos. Waddle, Sr. and son Thomas."[207]

(Notice the complexity! Thomas and his son, Thomas, fought in the same company with his son John's in-laws. The Curry land mentioned above probably belonged to the family of Mary Curry, who was Edward Erwin, Jr's wife and Thomas Waddle's son's mother-in-law.)

---

[205] Lula Miller, p. 33.
[206] *Augusta County Deed Book 21*, pp. 499, 501.
[207] Chalkley, *Chronicles*, vol. 2, p. 431.

In his will, a grateful and God-fearing Thomas comments, ". . .and considering that I am thereby in a particular manner Exposed to Death as well as of the natural Mortality of my Body . . ." I have concluded that he may have been a casualty of the Revolutionary War.

His will mentions the oldest sons to whom he has already given a share of his estate. He further gives 288 acres and "a survey adjoining James Curry" to his sons Thomas and John, and to Joseph "the land he now cuts." Other children also receive bequests.[208]

d. aft9/6/1784 and bef10/19/1784

buried in the Mossy Creek Presbyterian Cemetery. His tombstone, in part, reads:

Thomas Wooddell
Died 1785
aged 70 years

The original site of the Mossy Creek Presbyterian Church, as well as Thomas's original resting place, was about one half mile from the site at which Thomas is now buried. After the church was moved, a new cemetery was established in 1840, and Captain John Wooddell, then almost 80 years old, had his father's remains moved to the new cemetery. It may have been Captain John who erred in the date of his father's death, which was November 1784. It is recorded as 1785 on the tombstone.[209]

G-g-g-g-grandfather-7th generation

Speaking of complexity, or coincidence, or whatever you may wish to call it, there is another classic example (in that such "kinship" has been discovered over and over again in my research) of it here. In the early 1920's two young women found themselves working at the Virginia School for the Deaf and the Blind in Staunton. As it turned out, Betty Hansel and Blanche Miller had many similar interests, such as cooking, card-playing, and men, of course, and so wound up sharing an apartment. Only in their later years did

---

[208] Lyman Chalkley, *Chronicles of the Scotch-Irish Settlement in Virginia, Extracted from the Original Court Records of Augusta County 1745-1800*, vol. 3 (Baltimore, Genealogical Publishing Co., Inc., 1974), p. 171.

[209] Much of Jim Wooddell's information was derived from an article which was published on the first page of *The Valley Virginian* on January 11, 1886. This newspaper was published at Staunton, Virginia, vol. XX, no. 43, edited by S. V. Yost & Son.

their offspring begin to hear of their frivolity. These two and their friends even became involved in minor scrapes now and again! Just imagine!

Ultimately both girls married, remaining fast friends. There were frequent visits between their two families, and the youngest children, both girls, were encouraged to carry on the great friendship. In the time of graying Blanche's daughter, with encouragement, took up genealogy as a vocation. Imagine her surprise and delight when she discovered that her long time friend, Dorothy Woodside McCabe, daughter of Betty Hansel Woodside, was descended, as she herself was, from Thomas Waddle/Woodell. Small world! How it would have delighted our mothers to know that there was kinship beyond that of the mischievousness of a couple of single girls who became lifelong friends.

Alese__ (Waddle)

b. c1725

m. **Thomas Waddle** (c1710-aft9/6/1784) in Pennsylvania c1745

Jim Wooddell says they were married in Philadelphia, probably in the First Presbyterian Church.

It is said that Alese could neither read nor write. This would not have been so unusual a circumstance for a woman in her time.

Alese is named in one of the Thomas's land transactions.

mother of James Waddle who inherited what is known as the "George Kiracofe Farm"

Joseph Waddell who was willed a part of "Buffer Farm"

Sarah Waddle

Elizabeth Waddle

Thomas Waddle, Jr. m. Margaret Ervin; served in the Revolution with his father; Thomas left this son that part of his estate known as Curry farm.

Captain **John Waddle** (4/12/1761-8/5/1852) m. Elizabeth Erwin. He was left the "Old Wooddell Homestead," where his father had lived.

Martha Waddle m. Charles Hansel of Pendleton County, Virginia

Jane Waddle m. Edward Ervin

d. 1818 in Bath County, Virginia

Alese lived 34 years after her husband's death. She must have been considerably younger than Thomas, as he died at the age of seventy!

Thomas left "my widdow to have a Mare and Saddle to ride a Bed and Beding a room in the House with a fire Place and fire wood found her when She Wanted and any conveniences or necessaries in the House that She Stands in need of during her widowhood my Negro Boy Bob to work for her maintainance while She Lives and him to be kept in good subjection so that he may not Vex her. . ."

G-g-g-g-grandmother- 7th generation

Edward (I. or J.) **Erwin, Jr.**

b. c1730 in Ireland. He and his brothers emigrated with their parents.

son of **Edward Erwin** (1700-1771) and **Frances__** (1705-) of Long Glade, Augusta County, Virginia.

brother of Francis Erwin, (-c1791) who served in Capt. Dickey's Company in 1783 with Edward, Sr.; m. Jean Curry (-c1807).

John Erwin (-c1761) m. Jane Williams prior to 8/16/1756; records show he also contributed to "the cause."

Robert Erwin (-1789) m. Ann Crockett

Andrew Erwin (-c1765) m. Anna__

Benjamin Erwin became a minister at Mossy Creek

Frances Erwin m. William Brown

__Erwin m. Robert Low/Law

In 1742 Edward and three brothers, Andrew, Benjamin, and John were members of Capt. John Smith's militia company in Augusta County, then Orange County.[210]

m. **Mary Curry** (c1735-6/30/1815) of Virginia

Edward may have owned the land in the vicinity of the spot where

[210] Irvin Burkett Crews, "The Crews and the Irvin Families," 1966, p. 6.

State Route 646 crossed the Glade, an area known today as Tory Farm.

father of **Elizabeth "Betsy" Erwin** (He spells her name Irvine.) m. John Waddle 1/30/1792[211] John Waddle and Edward Irwin gave surety.

E. (probably Edward) Irvine Junior m. Jane Waddle (He attested to Betsy's father's consent for her to marry.) In the *History of the Mossy Creek Presbyterian Church*, he is said to have m. (1)Elizabeth Curry,[212] then (2)Mary Percy.

Benjamin Erwin (the Rev.) m. Sarah Brewster in Rockingham 7/1782

Margaret Ervin (possibly) m. Thomas Waddle, Jr.

On 5/29/1751 the Augusta County Court ordered a road from Mossy Creek to Woods Gap to be cleared. The petitioners included Andrew, John and Benjamin Erwin. John was directed to help mark the route, and Andrew, John, and Edward were among the many ordered to put up sign posts, clear the right of way and keep the road in repair. These men, and those with whom they worked all lived within the area of North River, Long Glade, Beaver Creek and Naked Creek.[213]

On 11/29/1751 Edward became a landowner in his own right. His father and mother gave him two pieces of land, 206 acres in all, which had been patented to his father 3/1747 and 4/5/1748. This land was situated at Long Glade, apparently bordering land belonging to his brother, John. Other brothers, Francis and Benjamin, received somewhat smaller parcels of land from their father soon thereafter.[214]

"Farming was the chief occupation of settlers in North River Basin. . .

---

211 *Augusta County Marriage Book, 1792*, pp. 92-98. In addition to the standard "marriage bond" form, in this case signed by "his Excellency Henry Lee Esquire, governor of Virginia," there was a note of instruction written by the father. "Sir," it said, "you to grant the Bearer hereof, John Wooddell, lisence According to law to marry with my Daughter Elizabeth Irvine he having obtained Consent. Januy 29th 1792. EI Erwin." The bond is attested to by E I Irvine, Junior. In this negotiation, the name Erwin is spelled in three ways, in each case hand-written, presumably by a member of the family.

212 John Wayland tells a wonderful story of Mrs. Elizabeth Irvine, and Betsy's sister-in-law may well be the subject of that story. It seems that "Shawnee Kate" appeared one autumn day and "told young Mrs. Elizabeth Irvine of an attack that the Indians were going to make upon Deerfield, Mrs. Irvine's old home. And there in the Long Glade meadows the young woman caught her horse, saddled him, and as night fell set out to carry the message of warning. Thirty miles she rode through the darkness alone, through Buffalo Gap, past Elliott's Knob, across the Calfpasture River and at daylight drew rein at her father's door in Deerfield – ahead of the Indians." (John W. Wayland, *Art Folio of the Shenandoah Valley*, Harrisonburg, John W. Wayland, 1924, n.p.)

213 May, *Four Flags*, p. 94.

214 *Augusta County Deed Book 4*, pp. 277, 281; *Deed Book 7*, p. 456.

The large landowners in the basin before the Revolutionary War were. . . Andrew and Edwin Erwin . . ."[215]

"Henry Miller and his partner bought, on 12/16/1777, from Edwin Erwine (Irvine) and his wife Mary, a tract of 134 acres lying on Mossy Creek which was patented to said Erwin 5/12/1770."[216]

Edward Erwin was one of several Revolutionary militiamen found in our family lines. An anecdote pertaining to his service survives. It seems that on 10/26/1778, "Lieutenant Edward Erwin (Irvine) of Long Glade, an officer in Captain William Henderson's militia company, was returned for not appearing at Robert McKittrick's, according to his Captain's orders of 10/25/1778. Lt. Erwin admitted the charge. Because of mitigating circumstances in his case, the court ordered the presiding officer to reprimand him in the presence of the court, which he did; whereupon, Lt. Erwin resigned his commission, and his resignation was accepted by the court."[217]

In spite of this incident Edward continued to serve the cause of the Revolution. In 1783 he was in the same company as Thomas Waddle, his daughter's father-in-law, and her brother-in-law, Thomas, and his own brother, Francis.[218] He also contributed 675 pounds of beef, one rifle and 300 pounds of flour to the Revolutionary cause in the years between 1782 and 1785.[219]

In 1787 Edward was sued by Adam Stephenson, whose property was upstream from his own, for raising the water level of Mossy Creek to a level that prevented Stephenson's mill from operating. The suit continued with testimony lasting through most of 1788. Among those who were summoned to testify (on Stephenson's behalf) was James Waddle, son of Thomas Waddle.[220]

According to the minutes of the Lexington Presbytery, Edward was an elder at Mossy Creek Presbyterian Church in 1796.

In 1797 Edward Erwin, still an elder at Mossy Creek, was charged by the Session of the church with influencing his children to swear "falsity."

---

[215] May, *Four Flags*, p. 117.

[216] May, *Four Flags*, p. 213.

[217] May, *Four Flags*, p. 199.

[218] "The silk-stockinged merchants in the North and the peruked and powdered planters in the South promoted the Revolution, but neither they not their sons rushed forward either to become officers in or to fill the ranks of Washington's army. They left that to small property owners like the majority of the settlers in North River Basin; and most of them like their compatriots in the other colonies chose service in the militia rather than in the Continental army. Still, a few of them signed up to fight with Washington." (May, *Four Flags*, pp. 198-201).

[219] *Augusta County Court of Claims: 1782-1785*, quoted by James W. Wilson, p. 36.

[220] *Augusta County Survey Book 3*, pp. 216, 220, quoted by James W. Wilson, p. 40.

There is no mention of the matter which brought about the accusation, though records indicate that several civil suits involving individuals bearing the name Erwin were filed in Augusta County Court during this period. Indeed it would be impossible for me to swear to the fact that G-g-g-g-grandfather Edward was the individual in question. The name Edward was a popular one in the family! Since his immigrant father was deceased, and his son, E. Irvine, Jr., mentioned above, would have been a relative youngster, probably somewhere between twenty and thirty years of age, logic would suggest that it was Mary's husband, Edward, who was charged.

Edward appealed the charge to the Lexington Presbytery, and a committee sent to investigate the charges found them to be false.[221]

In 1796, at the time of the settling of the estate of Silas Hart, the richest man in Rockingham County, it was revealed that in addition to having been heavily invested in military certificates, he had loans outstanding to numerous people of the North River Basin, including Edward Erwin (Irvine). Mr. Hart's 43 outstanding loans had a value of over 600 pounds.[222]

Edward owned mill property. The presumption is that this was a grain mill which was operated around the turn of the 19th century and from then until 1828 by the Edward Erwins, father and son.

d. aft1800

G-g-g-g-grandfather- 7th generation

His tombstone is to be found in the Mossy Creek Presbyterian Church cemetery. Although difficult to read, in part it says:

In
Memory of
Edward Irvin II
Born Oct. 13,17-5
Died March 2(?) 18--

William and Samuel *Curry* are bound, along with Edward Erwin's other executors, and held responsible for his will. Again we find the interreliance of these early families.

---

[221] Charles Wilson Blair, *A History of Mossy Creek Presbyterian Church* (Bridgewater, VA, Bridgewater Beacon Printing, Inc., 2000), p. 35.

[222] May, *Four Flags*, p. 231.

Mary Curry

b. c1735, probably in Pennsylvania.

daughter of **Dr. Robert A. Curry** (11/10/1717-bef12/26/1804) and **Ann Currie** (9/23/1723-5/15/1819)

sister of Ann Curry m. __Glenn
Isaiah Curry
James Curry
Alexander Curry moved to Kentucky in 12/1787
Samuel Curry (4/17/1770-4/15/1845) m. Mary Glenn (11/15/1774-4/23/1863)
Joseph Curry
Margaret Curry m. __Nichol
William Curry
Robert A. Curry II

m. **Edward Erwin, Jr.** (c1730-aft1800)

In a lawsuit of Edward Erwin vs. William Curry (trespass for diverting water, April 1800) Joseph Curry deposed on 12/13/1798 that he had come in 1761 from Ireland to Augusta County. He testified that William Curry, the defendant, was his brother and that the plaintiff, Edward Erwin, was his brother-in-law.[223]

mother of **Elizabeth Erwin** (father spells it Irvine on "marriage bond") m. John H. Waddle (4/12/1761/64-8/5/1852) 1/30/1792
E. Irvine, Jr. (bearer of Elizabeth's permission to marry, granted by father)
Benjamin Erwin (The Rev.) m. Sarah Brewster in Rockingham 7/1782, while a pastor at Mossy Creek.
Margaret Ervin (possibly) m. Thomas Waddle, Jr.

There is considerable evidence of the closeness of the Currys, Waddles and Ervins: A tract of land bought by Thomas Waddle in 1777 lay next to "the Curry land," and was probably land which had been owned by Mary's family; "There were several intermarriages between the Waddles, Currys and

[223] May, *Four Flags*, p. 69.

Ervins;"[224] and Mary's in-laws fought in the same company with Thomas Waddle and his son Thomas.[225] Closeness prevailed, one might say "in love and war."

"A committee sitting as a court in Augusta County 7/16-17/1776 convicted Alexander Miller of Cooks Creek near present Dayton of having given aid and intelligence to the Crown and sentenced him to confinement to the bounds of his plantation in Augusta County for the duration of the war, (etc.). . .Witnesses testifying in the case were. . .Mary Ewin (Erwin). . ."[226]

Interestingly enough, Mary's name also appears on several land transactions. Although we did find wives' names listed in land transactions in other family lines, it is still unusual at this time in history. And refreshing.

d., according to records at Mossy Creek Presbyterian Church, 6/30/1815.

G-g-g-g-grandmother- 7th generation

John Wacker

Only twice was the name Wacker found in a general search in Scotland. In 1694 a James Wacker was born in Kilmarnock to William Wacker and Janet Boyd (Wacker). Much later, in 1780, a Wacker family was found in the birth records of Stewarton. Neither of these facts gives much help in finding John Wacker's birthplace. Perhaps, as was the case with other early settlers of Scottish descent, he was born in Ireland.

m. **Margaret__**

father of George Adam Wacker (10/1/1791-7/12/1877)
Henry Wacker
Catherine Wacker (Bowman) (-bef1795) m. John Frederick Kirshof (-c1830) 12/30/1782
Margaret Wacker m. ___Nease
Mary Wacker m. Michael Nease
Eve Wacker m. Jacob Sheets
Barbara Wacker m. John Clem

[224] Lula Miller, p. 33.
[225] Kaylor, quoted by Lula Miller, footnote.
[226] May, *Four Flags*, p. 178.

Elizabeth Wacker to whom he willed $1 because of her disobedience to her parents.

"John Wacker received a land grant of 250 acres from the proprietor's office of Fairfax in 1777. In 1778 he purchased 139 acres from James Rinehard. This land is located at Hudson's Cross Roads in Shenandoah County."[227] John and his wife, Margaret, sold to John Frederick Kirkhove 193 acres on Mill Creek for 100 pounds. Part of this was the land that was transferred from James Rinehard and part was from John Wacker's land grant.

"Catherine (Wacker Bowman Kiracofe) died before her parents. In his will John Wacker states that a settlement had already been made with John Kirshof for Catherine's share in his estate. This was probably made when John Frederick purchased the land from him."[228]

G-g-g-g-grandfather- 7th generation

Margaret__ (Wacker)

m. **John Wacker**

mother of George Adam Wacker (10/1/1791-7/12/1877)

Henry Wacker to whom was willed his inheritance of 200 acres by his brother George with the stipulation that he provide for their mother.

Catherine Wacker (-bef1795) m.(1) ___Bowman; (2)John Frederick Kirshof (-c1830)12/30/1782

Margaret Wacker m. ___Nease

Mary Wacker m. Michael Nease

Eve Wacker m. Jacob Sheets

Barbara Wacker m. John Clem

Elizabeth Wacker- who inherited only $1 because she disobeyed her parents

G-g-g-g-grandmother- 7th generation

---

[227] Lula Miller, p. 9.

[228] Lula Miller, p. 8.

Chapter 3
Generation 6

Even as our ancestors arrived and settled in the Shenandoah Valley of Virginia, there was a busy world beyond their ken. Listed below are some of the happenings that occurred in the colonies and in the greater world during the lifetimes of the individuals found in this chapter:[229]

- The Mason-Dixon Line was drawn in 1766, marking the boundary between Pennsylvania and Maryland. This was the year Peter Driver was born.
- Britain levied taxes on tea, glass, paper, and dyes in the American colonies in 1767, arousing the ire of the taxed.
- The famed Captain James Cook began his voyage around the globe in 1768. He returned in 1771, when Daniel James Coakley was just a toddler.
- In 1773 the Massachusetts colonists held a "tea party" in Boston to protest the taxes levied against their beloved cup of tea. That year Robert Gaines, Jr. was born.
- Meantime, in Vienna, the waltz was becoming the fashionable dance.
- In 1777 the American Revolution continued, and American forces were defeated at Brandywine and at Germantown in Pennsylvania. In the next year, the colonies signed treaties with France and Holland, and the Stars and Stripes was adopted as the flag of the Continental Congress.
- The planet Uranus was discovered in 1781.
- In 1785 the seismograph was invented to measure earthquakes.
- In 1787 the Constitutional Convention convened in Philadelphia to write the Constitution which was also signed during that year.
- New York was named the capital of the United States in 1788.
- The French Revolution was on-going in 1789 as a Paris mob stormed the Bastille.
- In 1790 Philadelphia became the federal capital of the United States.
- American architect, James Hoban, began work on the White House in 1792.
- In 1794 Thomas Paine wrote "The Age of Reason."
- Edward Jenner introduced the vaccination for smallpox in 1796.
- Napoleon became the commander of the armies of France, and between 1797 and 1800, he was making his presence felt in many countries: Austria, Egypt, England, Ireland, Syria, and Turkey, to name a few.
- In 1800, the United Brethren Church was formally founded in the United States.

---

[229] Grun, pp. 354-379.

Daniel Miller (I)

b. 5/13/1752, in Dauphin County, Pennsylvania

son of **Lodowich**/Ludwig) **Miller** (c1724-1792) and **Barbara Long** (c1727-) of Lancaster County, Pennsylvania (now probably York County).

brother of Jacob Miller (1748-1815) m. (1)Anna Martha Wine; born in Washington County, Maryland.
Lodowich Miller (1749-) m. Barbara Ann ___
Abraham Miller (1750-) m. Catherine Byerly
David Miller (1750/1-1828) m. Mary Magdalena Eickenberry; born in Washington County, Maryland.
Susannah Miller (1754-1848) m. Michael Wine; born in Maryland.
Christian Miller (c1755-1828) m. Susannah ___.
Nancy Miller (1756-) m. Conrad Sanger (c1765-); born in Washington County, Maryland.
John Miller (1758-1791) m. Margaret___; born in Washington County, Maryland. He later owned about 210 acres of land, located in Frederick County, Maryland, that had formerly belonged to his father.
Frances Miller m. John Long (1761-1838)
Elizabeth Miller (1760-) m. Samuel Garber; born in Frederick County, Maryland.

There were, counting Daniel, twelve children in this family.[230] One is never named, though repeatedly acknowledged.

m. **Anna Garber** (c1762-1837) c1783.

For years Blanche Miller and other family members, including J. Paul Glick, knew that Barbara Long (wife of Lodowich Miller) somehow fit into the family picture, so they gave her as a first wife to Daniel. Dr. Glick said Daniel "probably married Barbara Long in Maryland in 1780. . . .Barbara probably died early and then Daniel married Anna Garber, his next farm neighbor, shortly after coming to the Valley in 1783. . .(T)radition in the Garber family reported that Anna and several of her older brothers were left in Maryland with her father's brother when her parents moved to Virginia in 1775. If this is true it is possible that Anna and Daniel were married in

[230] Mason, *Miller Record*, p. 64.

Maryland shortly before coming to Virginia."[231]

Thanks to material gleaned from *The Big Long Family* we know that Barbara was too old to become the wife of Daniel. Since she married an unnamed Miller, and Lodowich's wife was Barbara *Somebody*, the dates were right, and the supporting community was correct, we conclude that Daniel was the son, rather than the husband, of Barbara Long. Anna, I feel reasonably certain, was Daniel's one and only.

father of Elder Daniel Miller (II) (1/16/1784-9/9/1847) m. Anna Hoover (6/17/1785-2/27/1860) 4/4/1807

Barbara Ann Miller (1785-9/9/1861) m. Isaac Long, Sr. (1/1/1784-11/10/1849) 11/5/1805

Joseph Miller (3/23/1787-11/29/1851) m. Elizabeth "Betsy" Thomas (7/10/1792-11/21/1849) 3/24/1812

Jacob Miller (1789-1849) m. Magdelene (Matena) Sanger (9/16/1789-2/6/1849) 4/20/1815

Katie Miller m. Jacob Rife- died young

Samuel Miller (12/17/1793-9/7/1861) m. Barbara Sanger (8/27/1791-5/9/1875) 3/19/1816

Abraham Miller (3/3/1796-8/5/1862) m. (1) Salome Frantz; (2) Catherine Leedy (5/3/1802-6/8/1877) c1821; went west.

Susannah Miller (1/7/1798-5/10/1862) m. John Thomas (3/20/1798-12/31/1834) c1820

Martin Miller (7/15/1800-9/19/1872) m. (1)Nancy Sanger (12/10/1795-7/23/1849) 3/27/1821; (2)Mary Cline

Michael Miller (1807-1893) m. Mary Sanger (12/6/1807-2/10/1885) 3/17/1825

John Miller m. Susan Leedy (1783-) both died young

"The writer has read that 80% of the descendants of Lodowich Miller's sons, Daniel Miller I and Jacob Miller, remained members of the Church of the Brethren. This is confirmed as six of the eight honored (in the *Michael Miller Record*) are descendants of Lodowich Miller through Daniel Miller I."[232]

He first owned land in Frederick County, Maryland. ". . .In 1770/1771 Daniel Miller paid taxes on the following:

25 1/2 acres called 'Finis Covenant'

80 acres called 'Anchor and Hope'

---

[231] Glick, p. xi.

[232] Mason, *Miller Record*, p. 6.

4 1/2 acres called 'Anchor and Hope' (This is near
Jefferson, Frederick County, Maryland)."[233]

Daniel was a leader of the German Brethren Church from his youth. "Elder Jacob Danner was the local Elder and John H. Garber, who married Barbara Miller, Lodowich's sister, and (Lodowich's) son, Daniel Miller I, served as ministers and local church leaders under Elder Leatherman (Ruling Bishop of Maryland) and Elder Danner."[234]

"In 1778 Elder Daniel Miller was buying farms next to his father-in-law, Elder John H. Garber in Shenandoah County, Virginia.[235] In 1783 he added 107 additional acres.[236]

"He then bought land and moved to the head of Cook's Creek in Rockingham County, Virginia in 1807. At one time he was paying taxes on about 1450 acres of land in Shenandoah and Rockingham Counties. . . .(As was the case with) his father and grandfather, his land was passed on to his children."[237]

Dr. Paul Glick determined that Daniel was just one of the "great influx of Brethren people who followed in the wake of Elder John H. Garber, who arrived in 1775."[238] To avoid pressures to fight or to swear to the various loyalties required, Daniel and his peers were quite happy to come to Virginia where land was undeveloped and cheap and the government was still lax. By 1787 thirty-seven families had moved from Maryland and Pennsylvania and settled in Shenandoah and Rockingham Counties. With Daniel came two of his brothers: Jacob arriving in Shenandoah County about 1748 and Abraham settling in Rockingham in 1750.

A bit of speculation: I do think it is possible that Barbara Long (Miller)(c1727-) eventually came to be with her three sons in the Shenandoah Valley. After her husband died in 1792, it might have been quite reasonable for her to come to her sons, already settled in Virginia. I believe that the reason that Barbara is associated so strongly with Daniel could be that she is somehow remembered as being with him in Virginia.

The Masons have found that Daniel's family "lived near Greenmount,

---

[233] Mason, *Miller Record*, p. 26.
[234] Mason, *Miller Record*, p. 26.
[235] Lula Miller, in her book about Johannes Kirshof, reported that Daniel lived in the same area of Shenandoah County as the Wackers and the Bowmans.
[236] Mason, *Miller Record*, p. 26.
[237] Mason, *Miller Record*, p. 65.
[238] Glick, p. x.

The home of Daniel Miller (I) and Anna Garber, Greenmount, Virginia

Rockingham County, Virginia."[239] His name is found on the 1810 census. At that time he reported his household as one free white male aged 10-16; two free white males aged 16-26; three free white males aged 26-45; one free white male 45 and over; one free white female aged 0-10; one free white female aged 10-16; one free white female aged 16-26; one free white female aged 26-45; and one free white female 45 and up. Under "all other free except Indians" he listed one, and under slaves, none. The individual described here as "other free" had, more than likely, once been a slave or a mercenary.

d. 8/1819 or 1820 in Rockingham County, Virginia. (Roberta Miller Herbert says his death occurred in 8/1819 near Harrisonburg in the vicinity of Route 42.)

buried at the Beaver Creek Church of the Brethren in Spring Creek, Virginia.

G-g-g-grandfather- 6th generation

---

[239] Mason, *Miller of 1692*, p. 7.

While most of the land in the "lower" Valley, that which lay to the north, was originally acquired by non-German speculators or agents and then sold to German settlers, some of the German pioneers obtained their own patents as soon as the Fairfax Proprietary opened to settlement in 1749. As the "lower" Valley became more densely populated, new arrivals moved farther south.

"In 1786 Jonathan Clark made a survey of farm land that was included in the old surveys made for Jost Hite[240] and later contested by Lord Fairfax. His notes on the acreage under cultivation, the condition of the buildings and the presence of orchards, were probably prepared for the Court considering the Fairfax-Hite suit. . . . All of the farms (48 in number). . . were owned by families of German or Swiss background. . . .Most farms were from 150 to 250 acres in size and the average acreage under cultivation was 41.1 acres. This did not include land that was used for pasturage. . . .(T)he European pattern of dependence on small grain cultivation (wheat, barley, rye and oats) still prevailed. . . .Most dwelling houses. . .were built of hewn logs and the most common size was a one-and-half story building, 30 feet by 24 feet with a stone chimney. There were still a few 'old cabins' and some unfinished 'hulls.' All occupied farms had substantial log barns measuring as much as 50 or 52 feet by 30 feet, but one barn was 70 feet long. Most of the barns were roofed German style, with straw thatch. Fourteen of the farms had apple orchards, some with as many as 100 fruit bearing trees.

". . .(T)he size and sturdiness of the barns is a clue to the importance of livestock to the German farmers, who relied heavily upon a diet of pork and dairy products. The personal property tax lists give the cattle owned. . . Most German farmers had at least one milk-cow and some had sizeable herds. All in all, the farms. . .continued to reflect much of the old world lifestyle.

"There was religious diversity, but it is obvious that the Swiss and German families. . .had much in common, including an agrarian life-style which emphasized hard work, frugality, respect for nature, and religious faith. They understood the importance of community and helping one's neighbor and were able to create a coherent community in which many aspects of German culture and the German language prevailed well into the nineteenth century."[241]

By the end of the Revolution, religious persecution was no longer a concern for the Brethren settlers, due to the end of the influence of the

---

[240] In 1732 Jost Hite led a number of Pennsylvania Germans south into the Shenandoah Valley. Most of these people settled in Frederick, Rockingham, and Shenandoah Counties.

[241] Daniel W. Bly, *From the Rhine to the Shenandoah: Eighteenth Century Swiss and German Pioneer Families…*, vol. 2 (Baltimore, Gateway Press, Inc., 1996), pp. 3-4.

established church of England and to Thomas Jefferson's Statute of Religious Liberty, which served to separate church and state. They arrived in Virginia in increasing numbers and, through hard work, took advantage of the opportunities that were there for them. At last they could enjoy the religious freedom and security they had come so far to find.

Anna Garber

b. c1762

daughter of Elder **John H. Garber** (1717-1787) and **Barbara Miller** (1733-1808) c1752

Anna lived in the area of the present Moore's Store in Shenandoah County, Virginia, which was near the site of the Flat Rock Brethren Church, where her husband, after her father, was one of the early ministers.[242]

sister of Elder Samuel Garber (1756-1814) m. Molly Stoner
Elder John Garber (1758-1819) m. Barbara Zook
Abraham Garber (1760-1848) m. Elizabeth Humbert (-1838)
Elder Martin Garber (1761-1824) m. Rebecca Stoner
Jacob G. Garber (1766-1836) m. Susanna Humbert
Daniel Garber (1769-) m. (1) Susanna Miller (c1780-) c1802; (2) Elizabeth Shank 1/10/1815
Catherine Garber (1771-1835) m. John Flory (1766-1845)
Joseph Garber (1733-1854) m. Catherine Leedy (1777-1851)
Magdalene Garber (6/14/1774-7/26/1832) m. George Wine (1774-1845) c1796

m. c1783 to **Daniel Miller**[243] (5/13/1752-8/1820)

mother of Elder Daniel Miller II (1/16/1784-9/9/1847) m. Anna Hoover (6/17/1785-2/27/1860) 4/4/1807
Barbara Ann Miller (1785-9/9/1861) m. Isaac Long, Sr. (1/1/1784-11/10/1849) 11/5/1805
Joseph Miller (3/23/1787-11/29/1851) m. Elizabeth "Betsy" Thomas (7/10/1792-11/21/1849) 3/24/1812

---

[242] Notes of Roberta Miller Herbert.
[243] Glick, p. x-xiii.

Jacob Miller (1789-1849) m. Magdalene Sanger (9/16/1789-2/6/1849) 4/20/1815
Katie Miller m. Jacob Rife- may have died young
Samuel Miller (12/17/1793-9/7/1861) m. Barbara Sanger (8/27/1791-5/9/1875) 3/19/1816
Abraham Miller (3/3/1796-8/5/1862) m. (1) Salome Frantz; (2) Catherine Leedy (5/3/1802-6/8/1877) c1821; went west
Susannah Miller (1/7/1798-5/10/1862) m. John Thomas (3/20/1798-12/31/1834) c1820
Martin Miller (7/15/1800-9/19/1872) m. (1)Nancy Sanger (12/10/1795-7/23/1849) 3/27/1821; (2) Mary Cline
Michael Miller (1807-1893) m. Mary Sanger (12/6/1807-2/10/1885) 3/17/1825
John Miller m. Susan Leedy (1783-) both died young[244]

d. 1837

buried at Beaver Creek Church of the Brethren

G-g-g-grandmother- 6th generation

Peter Driver

b. 11/20/1766 in Pennsylvania

In Peter's Bible records he spelled his last name Dreiwer.

son of **Ludwig Treiber** (c1728-bef1772), immigrant, and **Anna "Barbara" Sprenkle** (1737-1781) c1752

brother of Michael Driver (1754-) m. Barbara__
Anna Driver (1756-) m. John Rife
Barbara Driver (1758-)
Lewis Driver, Jr. (1760-) m. Barbara Burkhart
Anna Maria Driver (1764-) m. Peter Acker
Jacob Driver (1768-) m. Elizabeth Forry (10/26/1771-) in York County, Pennsylvania
Elizabeth Driver (1771-)

[244] Mason, *Miller Record*, pp. 65-66.

m. **Dorothy Meyer** (4/15/1774-10/7/1844)

Peter was baptized 8/29/1836, at the age of seventy, at Greenmount in Rockingham County, Virginia along with his wife, Dorothy Meyer Driver.[245]

The Drivers lived at Singers Glen, Rockingham County, Virginia.

"Peter Driver purchased 112 1/2 acres in 1797 on the head of Muddy River. In 1828 he purchased 160 acres from Joseph Baxter. The 112 1/2 acres, and considerably more, were later owned by his son-in-law, Jonothan Funk, and the 160 acres by his son, Benjamin Driver."[246]

Peter was a blacksmith.

father of Barbara Driver (1/28/1793-5/12/1878) m. John Miller 12/14/1822
Elizabeth Driver (6/5/1795-8/25/1853) m. Daniel Shickel, Sr. (12/6/1789-7/15/1852) 4/21/1814
Peter Driver (10/21/1797-2/8/1800)
Jacob Driver (5/12/1800-12/25/1868) m. Polly Funk 4/7/1823
Nancy Driver (7/26/1803-) m. Ezekiel Bryan/Brown 7/29/1822
Mary "Maria" Driver (4/28/1806-2/4/1888) m. Jonothan Funk 12/20/1830
Salome "Sarah" Driver (1/30/1809-2/6/1909) m. Peter Zimmerman 1826
Joseph Driver (4/7/1812-11/27/1884) m. (1)Mary "Polly" Showalter 1838; (2)Margaret Campbell 1882.
Johannes "John" Driver (6/4/1815-8/9/1875) m. (1)Catherine Showalter 1837; (2)Elizabeth Coffman (a widow) 1872
Benjamin Driver (12/28/1817-4/10/1895) m. Lucinda Allen 1846

These names and dates were recorded in Peter Driver's Bible in his own handwriting, in German.

Also recorded in Peter's Bible: "This book does not contain the glitter of the world. It contains the joy and food for the soul which only pleases God, and who has chosen it."

He was a member of the Church of the Brethren.

---

[245] Driver and Gassett, p. 367.
[246] Driver and Gassett, p. 367.

d. 7/1/1850

Peter also wrote in his Bible: "Time passes by and death comes fast. He, whom God forgives his sins, is saved."[247]

Peter was buried with his wife and two of their son Benjamin's children, John and Amanda, "on the Driver farm on road #777, south of the Glen." (Singers Glen, Rockingham County, Virginia)[248]

G-g-g-grandfather- 6th generation

"The Tunker Church, now the Church of the Brethren, changed from a German speaking one to an English speaking one between 1834 and 1845, and the Mennonites made the language transition still later. Many Rockinghamites of German ancestry continued to use the German language well after 1845. For instance, Peter Driver, a Tunker blacksmith living at the head of Muddy Creek in the 1850's, was never known to speak English from choice. On one occasion an English-speaking neighbor remonstrated with him, "Mr. Driver, English speaking people have the same God as you German speaking people."

"Ja, ja, I know das," Mr. Driver replied, "but Gott speaks to us Germans in a much simpler tongue than he does to du English people."[249]

Dorothy Meyer

In the notes in his Bible, Peter, in his own hand, reported Dorothy's name as Dorodea Mairin, effectively ending all speculation that Dorothy's maiden name was Rawley.

b. 4/15/1774 in Pennsylvania

m. **Peter Driver** (11/20/1766-7/1/1850)

lived at Singers Glen, Rockingham County, Virginia

mother of Barbara Driver (1/28/1793-5/12/1878) m. John Miller 12/14/1822
Elizabeth Driver (6/5/1795-8/25/1853) m. Daniel Shickel, Sr. (12/6/1789-7/15/1852) 4/21/1814

[247] Driver and Gassett, pp. 366-367.
[248] Driver and Gassett, p. 367.
[249] May, *Four Flags*, p. 221.

Peter Driver (10/21/1797-2/8/1800)
Jacob Driver (5/12/1800-12/25/1868) m. Polly Funk 4/7/1823
Nancy Driver (7/26/1803-) m. Ezekiel Bryan/Brown 7/29/1822
Mary "Maria" Driver (4/28/1806-2/4/1888) m. Jonothon Funk 12/20/1830
Salome "Sarah" Driver (1/30/1809-2/6/1909) m. Peter Zimmerman 1826
Joseph Driver (4/7/1812-11/27/1884) m. (1)Mary "Polly" Showalter 1838; (2)Margaret Campbell 1882
Johannes "John" Driver (6/4/1815-8/9/1875) m. (1)Catherine Showalter 1837; (2)Elizabeth Coffman (widow) 1872
Benjamin Driver (12/28/1817-4/10/1895) m. Lucinda Allen 1846

baptized, with her husband, as a member of the Church of the Brethren at Greenmount, Rockingham County, Virginia 8/29/1836

d.10/7/1844

Dorothy was buried with Peter and two grandchildren on the Driver farm, on road #777, south of Singers Glen, Rockingham County, Virginia.

G-g-g-grandmother- 6th generation

Peter Shickel

b. c1755

m. **Mary__**

They were the parents of **Daniel Shickel** (12/6/1789-7/15/1852) m. Elizabeth Driver (6/5/1795-8/25/1853) 4/21/1814
Mary and Peter were possibly parents, also, of
Peter Shickel m. Margaret Rader 7/1/1811
Jacob Shickel m. Eva Gowl, widow of Adam Gowl 2/20/1819

John Frederick Kirshof
(Johannes Friederick Kirshof)[250]

b. c1757 in Germany

In a newspaper article (author and place of publication unknown) which was reprinted in the *Staunton Spectator* July 4, 1884, it is stated that John Frederick's name was Jacob and he was the son of a Hessian soldier. In the obituary of George, son of John Frederick and Catherine, John Frederick's name was also given as Jacob.[251]

We are uncertain as to why and how John Frederick arrived in America. Perhaps he was a Hessian mercenary, or the son of a Hessian mercenary, employed by the English to keep peace in their troublesome colony. Whatever the cause, Josiah Andrew Kiracofe states, in an undated letter, that John Frederick came to America in 1773. Lula Mae Miller referred to John Frederick in the title of her book as "Early Settler and Patriarch of Northern Augusta County."

m. (1) **Catherine Wacker** (Bowman) 12/30/1782; (2) Barbara Koontz in Shenandoah County 2/24/1795
". . .verified by an old marriage record book in the court house at Woodstock."[252]

Catherine and John Frederick were the parents of
John Kirshof m. Susan Waddle 8/3/1810[253]
Henry Kirshof m. Margaret Detamore 3/26/1814
George Kirshof (10/1/1791-7/12/1877) m. (1)Jane Waddle (1794-c1873) 1817; (2)Mary Ann__ (-aft1877)
Elizabeth Kirshof (1787-) m. (1) Adam Firebaugh 1808; (2) George Fifer

---

250 Manfred Schlien, an e-mail correspondent from Germany, has recently published *Familienbuch Lohne* in which he names Johann Friedrich Wilhelm Kirchof who was baptized 2/20/1757 in Mennighuffen/Westfalen and his immediate ancestry. This material sounds promising, but since the book is written in German I did not buy it. Mr. Schlien, with understanding, volunteered to copy the brief Kirchof portion for me. It has been a long while since I have been able to contact him. It is sad to lose such a good contact.

251 Jim Wooddell to Elisabeth Hodges, letter, 3/11/1999.

252 Lula Miller, p. 8.

253 John was the father of Benjamin Kiracofe who married Lucinda Gaines (1/23/1842-)4/12/1866; these were the parents of William Henry Harrison Kiracofe, "Billy Ben"; he was the father of Walter Lee Kiracofe, who was the father of Mabel Kiracofe and all "the boys," who were Blanche Miller (Wilson's) cousins and close friends.

Mary Kirshof m. Henry Wilfong 8/26/1813
Christina Kirshof m. Jacob Price 1/25/1811

John Frederick and Barbara were the parents of 8 children:

Frederick Kiracofe m. Elizabeth Heifner 6/18/1820
Jacob Kiracofe m. (1)Ann Propst 1/10/1835; (2)Matilda Collins 1850
Andrew Kiracofe m. Sarah Saunders 12/1/1831
Anna Kiracofe m. Elijah Messersmith 10/16/1818
Barbara Kiracofe m. James Fleming 11/4/1830
Susannah Kiracofe m. Jacob Huffer 4/29/1820
Catherine Kiracofe m. Samuel Huffer 1/12/1827
Hannah Kiracofe m. Peter Fifer 3/17/183-[254]

Multiple records have proven that the father of the fourteen Kirshof children was John Frederick. Most of their marriages were recorded in Augusta County, the rest in Rockingham County.

He was the first Kiracofe to settle in the area near the village of Sangerville. One of the current family homes may be the original one or on the location of the original one.[255]

"It is not known whether John Frederick and his two wives belonged to the Lutheran or Reform faith. . .Records prove that two of his sons were baptized at the Old Pine Church about two miles west of Mt. Jackson. Again records indicate that several of his children were baptized at the Emmanuel Lutheran and Reform Church. He and Barbara witnessed the baptism of some of his grandchildren at the same church."[256]

"John Frederick purchased his first tract of land in 1783 or 1786 from John Wacker, his father-in-law. (It) was on Mill Creek at present day Hudson's Cross Roads in Shenandoah County. . .(and) was sold to Abraham Hess while Catherine was still living."[257] According to the deed this tract was part of the two tracts comprising a two hundred and fifty-acre grant which was given to John Wacker in 1777. The acreage has been identified as land adjoining the "Click" land and being near a sinkhole. Since there were claims to waterways and water rights, there was undoubtedly a mill on the place.

After selling this tract of land, John Frederick purchased and moved to 203 acres at Mt. Clinton, near Mt. Jackson. At the time of these transactions,

[254] Lula Miller, p. 9.
[255] Notes of Blanche M. Wilson.
[256] Lula Miller, p. 8.
[257] Lula Miller, p. 6.

John Frederick's name was spelled *Kirkhove.*[258]

In 1809, 137 additional acres, which joined his land, were purchased for 600 pounds. This John Frederick called his plantation. He willed it to his second wife, Barbara.

"In his will John Wacker (Catherine's father) states that a settlement had already been made with John Kirshof for Catherine's share of his estate. This was probably (done) when John Frederick purchased their first land from him."[259]

"We can be sure John Frederick and (his) sons built the log houses which once were on his first purchase of 390 acres. It is also believed the grandsons built the Walter Kiracofe house, the Eavey house and the Abram Cupp house. . ."[260]

In the court records of Shenandoah County, Virginia are found a number of other land transactions in which John Frederick was involved. Among these are a sale of land to John Moor, Jr. "late from Pennsylvania" for 850 pounds on 6/11/1799; and the sale of a small piece of land on Mill Creek, for just five pounds, to Adam Wirtenberger in 1795.[261]

John Frederick lived in Shenandoah County, near Mt. Jackson, until 1799 when the family moved to the northern part of Augusta County. The deed indicates that this tract started less than one mile west of Sangerville and extended west through the Emmanuel Church Cemetery.[262]

On deeds in both Shenandoah and Augusta Counties the name is spelled *Kirkhove*. In Shenandoah County, when his marriage to Barbara Koontz was recorded, the name was *Frek Kirk.* All of his descendants by Catherine spell their names *Kiracofe*, except for the family of George, son of Henry and Margaret Detamore, who spell it "*Caracofe.*"[263]

In 1826, John Waddel, and his neighbor, John Frederick Kirkhove, sold

---

[258] To find this land, "take the road west toward Orkney Springs. About five miles out there is a place named Mt. Clifton. Mt. Clifton is on a cliff and Mill Creek runs at its base. Across the stream to the south is the tract of land…" which belonged to John Frederick. There was once a mill on the stream. The deed also said there was an orchard and vineyard at that location. (Lula Miller, pp. 7, 15.)

[259] Lula Miller, p. 8.

[260] Lula Miller, p. 8.

[261] Lula Miller, p. 15.

[262] Lula Miller, p. 7.

[263] Lula Miller, p. 5.

to the trustees of the Emmanuel Lutheran and Reform Societies, an acre of land, including a building, for $10.00. Notice the change in currency from earlier transactions in which English pounds were used.

d. c1830.

"It is believed that he is buried in an unmarked grave in the original part of the Emmanuel Cemetery along with his second wife, Barbara."[264]

The will of John Frederick *Karricaffe*, written in 1828, is quaint, and indicates a warmth of feeling for various family members, for example:

To his wife, Barberry, his plantation for her lifetime, or for as long as she bore his name; her choice of his "horse creatures," one milch cow, . . .and one hundred dollars in cash.

To his granddaughter, Patsy Snelling. . ."a fine suit of clothes when she gets married." This young lady is a puzzlement, for her name, Snelling, is not that of any of the rest of the family. One wonders if she was a ward or an adopted child of Mary and Henry Wilfong. George *Karricafe*, Executor of John Frederick's will, listed as one of his expenses "twelve yards cotton to furnish the beds of Widow (his step-mother) *vs.* (This preposition seems inappropriate in this use.) Betsy Snelling in compliance with will." Could the "fine suit of clothes" have referred to bedclothes? One would notice that George disagreed with his father's spelling of Miss Snelling's name.

John F. *Karkhoff* expressed concern and affection in the 10/1828 codicil to his will, as well. He gave his daughter, Mary Wilfong, and her children after her rights to the portion of his estate that she was to inherit, denying her husband, Henry Wilfong, the right to sell the estate. In addition, he states that Patsy Snelling, clearly a favorite, is to have an equal part with Mary's other children, "in addition to what I have already given her."[265]

"Evidently (John Frederick) had made some settlements with his older sons by Catherine Wacker Bowman before his death. This was during the time that sons were given larger portions of their father's estate than the daughters received."[266]

G-g-g-grandfather- 6th generation

---

[264] Lula Miller, p. 8.
[265] Lula Miller, p. 17.
[266] Lula Miller, p. 7.

Among the many items of business George Karricafe,[267] Ex., handled was the payment of his father's burial expenses. He paid to "Reminsnider" $4.00 for the funeral sermon.

Catherine Wacker (Bowman)

b. c1761

daughter of **John** and **Margaret Wacker** as verified by John Wacker's will[268]

sister of George Adam Wacker (10/1/1791-7/12/1877)
Henry Wacker
Margaret Wacker m. __Nease
Mary Wacker m. Michael Nease
Eve Wacker m. Jacob Sheets
Barbara Wacker m. John Clem
Elizabeth Wacker (who in her father's will was left $1 because of her disobedience to her parents).[269]

m. **John Frederick Kirshof** (-c1830) 12/30/1782 in Shenandoah County, Virginia. This is verified by an old marriage book in the court house in Woodstock.

The first land which John Frederick and Catherine owned had belonged to her father, John Wacker. Lula Mae Miller seems to suggest that John Frederick bought the land, though in his will John Wacker indicates he has made an 'earlier settlement' with J. F. and his family. Perhaps "J. F." got a special deal.

mother of John Kirshof m. Susan Waddle 8/3/1810
Henry Kirshof m. Margaret Detamore 3/26/1814
George Kirshof (10/1/1791-7/12/1877) m. (1)Jane Waddle (1794-c1873) 1817; (2)Mary Ann__ (-aft 1877)
Elizabeth Kirshof m. (1)Adam Firebaugh 1808, (2) George Fifer
Mary Kirshof m. Henry Wilfong 8/26/1813

[267] A number of the spellings of John Frederick Kirshof's last name have been italicized here. There have been others.
[268] Lula Miller, p. 8.
[269] Lula Miller, p. 9.

Christina Kirshof m. Jacob Price 1/25/1811

"The descendants by Catherine Wacker Bowman (Kiracofe) spell the name 'Kiracofe' except the descendants of George, son of Henry Kirshof and Margaret Detamore."[270] They spell it 'Caracofe.'[271]

d. before 1795, before the deaths of her parents

"It is assumed Catherine was buried in the Old Pine Church Cemetery. Both church and cemetery have been destroyed."[272] Two of John Frederick's children were buried there, also. These could have been Catherine's children, or those of the second wife, Barbara Koontz.

G-g-g-grandmother- 6th generation

John Hamilton Waddle

This man is known as Captain John Wooddell. Recalling that we do not know the maiden name of his mother, one would wonder if her maiden name was Hamilton.

b. 4/12/1761 in Augusta County, Virginia

Jim Wooddell, a family genealogist, provided this birthdate and the date of John's baptism at Cook's Creek Presbyterian Church, which was 8/1761.

son of **Thomas** (c1710-aft9/6/1784) and **Alese__** (c1725-1818) **Waddle** of Wooddell Springs, Virginia.

brother of James Waddle, who inherited the "George Kiracofe Farm"
Joseph Waddle who moved to Pocahontas County, now in West Virginia
Sarah Waddle
Elizabeth Waddle
Thomas Waddle, Jr. m. Margaret Ervin; inherited the "Curry Farm." His descendants may be found in West Virginia, near the Ohio

[270] Lula Miller, p. 6.
[271] Lula Miller, p. 5.
[272] Lula Miller, p. 8.

River.

Martha Waddle m. Charles Hansel of Pendleton County, Virginia

Jane Waddle, m. Edward Ervin, Jr. (c1730-aft1800)

John's father, Thomas, died at the age of 74, beyond the life expectancy of his time, leaving a will in which John, who was one of the two sons "yet with me," inherited Thomas's "Dwelling house with all Conveniences appertaining thereto." Thomas allowed "waggon Ploughs Horses and utensils necessary for working the Plantation to be kept here in order to work for the Support of the family while together," and he appointed John as one of the three executors.[273]

m. **Elizabeth "Betsy" Erwin** (c1753-2/11/1834); marriage bond dated 1/30/1792 (Henry Lee was governor and signed the marriage bond.)[274]

father of Susan Waddle m. John Kiracofe, George's brother

Jane "Janey" (**Christinia**) **Waddle** (1794-c1873) m. George Hendrick Kirshof (10/1/1791-7/12/1877)1817

Mary Waddle m. Jacob Bumgarner 6/28/1785[275] Some say she never married.

James Waddle m. Uriah Stanforth of Greenbrier County, now West Virginia

Elizabeth Waddle m. Richard Curry of Highland County, Virginia

John Wooddle m. Elizabeth Bodkin of Rockingham County, Virginia

William Wooddle m. Mary Curry of Highland County, Virginia

Benjamin Waddle, who died at two years

Irvine Wooddle (Jim spells it Ervin.)[276] m. Annie Michael of Augusta County

Bernard Waddle m. Lydia Michael of Augusta County, Virginia[277]

The last three of these children were found in *Will Book 32*, p. 219 on a bond certifying John Wooddle (Jr.) as administrator of the estate of John Wooddle, Sr., who died 8/5/1852.

John was a Captain in the Virginia Militia in the early 19th century.

---

[273] *Augusta County Will Book VI*, pp. 429-431.

[274] *Augusta Marriage Book 1792,* pp. 92-98a.

[275] *Augusta County Marriage Book 1, 1785-1786*, p. 21.

[276] Irvine, with John and William, were found in *Will Book 32*, p. 219 on a bond certifying John Wooddle (Jr.) as administrator of the estate of John Wooddle, Sr. who died 8/5/1852. His tombstone indicates that the date of death was 8/6/1852.

[277] Lula Miller, p. 265.

There are possible conflicting reports as to where John and his family lived. Lula Mae Miller believed that he was among the first landowners in Sangerville, after it became a community. According to other records John and his family lived with his father, Thomas, at the "Old Wooddell Homestead." Both may be true.

In 1826 John Waddel and John Frederick Kirshof sold for $10 to Henry Skyles and John Michael, trustees of the Emmanuel Lutheran and Reform Societies, an acre of land which included a building. Witnessed by: Michael Daggy, Henry Kirshof and John Orebaugh.[278] This record is unclear. If these men were neighbors, did each sell 1/2 acre to the church? Or, less likely, since court records would surely show it, did they actually own a tract of land together?

After the Mossy Creek Presbyterian Church moved to its present location in 1840, John, then in his 80th year, had his father's grave moved to the new site.

d. just north of Wood Street in Sangerville at the home of his son.

Jim Wooddell says the date of death was 8/5/1852. The *Staunton Spectator*[279] is quoted as saying John died in a house in Raymond Andrews's meadow.

G-g-g-grandfather- 6th generation

His tombstone, found at Mossy Creek Presbyterian Church Cemetery, states:

In
Memory
of
Capt. John Wooddell
Who died August the 6th
1852. Aged 85 years
3 months and 25
days

Found in a copy of the *Augusta County Historical Bulletin*, Spring 1981, this wonderful tale about John Wooddell's tombstone is assumed to be accurate:

---

[278] *Augusta County Deed Book 55*, p. 52, as cited in Lula Miller, p. 16.
[279] Reprinting from *The Staunton Spectator*, 7/4/1884, as quoted by Jim Wooddell.

"Shortly after the death of Capt. John Wooddell, his son, Ervin, while pursuing a bear on a little stream called Skidmore, near the Wooddell Spring, above the Gap in North Mountains, discovered a coffin-shaped stone, about seven feet long and three feet wide, and about six inches thick. He immediately halted and examined the stone, and decided then and there that he would use it as a mark to his deceased father's grave.

"Some time after the discovery, Ervin and Annie Wooddell removed the stone from Skidmore to the Wooddell Spring, where Ervin had the age and date of death of his father inscribed on it. Hundreds of people who visited the Wooddell Spring in the last thirty-three years, have seen this curious 'Wooddell Stone'.

"The descendants of Capt. John Wooddell had for years intended to place this stone over his grave in the Mossy Creek Church cemetery, but it was never done until the 17th day of December, 1885, when W. H. Wooddell, Benjamin Wooddell, Stuart Wooddell and J. Marshall Wooddell, of New Vienna, Ohio, John H. Kiracofe, W. F. Kiracofe, Chas. Kiracofe (son of McCutchen), Jacob Andrew, Henry Andrew, Charles Hisey and Edward Andrew, eleven in number, pursuant to a previous arrangement, proceeded to the place where the stone had long lain, to remove it to the final resting place. Before the removal of the stone, however, Mr. J. M. Wooddell, of New Vienna, Ohio, delivered the following Address:

" 'My Kindred: We have assembled here in this deep hidden mountain fastness around the gravestone of our Grandsire, to remove this stone that no Michael Angelo has ever touched with his chisel, except to letter it - a stone that Nature's God Himself has hewn - a stone upon which the date of his death was inscribed about thirty-three years ago and which has ever since rested here, at the base of these evergreen mountains, to the sacred spot in the Mossy Creek Church cemetery, in the valley below, where he sleeps so sweetly in the arms of the "World's Redeemer."

'Although for more than thirty-three years his voice has been silent as the grave, we, who knew his kind nature, with fond recollections, cherish his memory and love him still.

'This healing, invigorating chalybeate[280] water that flows at our feet from this beautiful fountain, the Wooddell Spring, has spread his fame, on literary wings, from Maine to Georgia, and from the Eastern metropolis to the "Golden State".

'The poet from Florida, the land of flowers, has stood here, and this stone has inspired to paint the traditional monument that has grown around the good name of our Grandsire, in a most beautiful poem.

---

[280] The water in these springs was flavored with salts of iron.

'But we, his lineal successors of two generations distant, in whose remembrance his acts and pleasant features still shine as an oasis - as an evergreen spot in our memory - we who have gone out from the home of our loving Grandsire to people the four quarters of this broad government of ours, love him; yes, we love him still; and we will this day cover his quiet resting place with this stone as a slight token of our love.'

"This curious stone was then conveyed from the mountain to the cemetery far down the valley, and placed on the grave for which it was originally intended by Ervin Wooddell when he halted alone from the bear hunt on Skidmore, to examine it, thirty-three years ago, and now it takes its place as the most remarkable monument, by the side of the artfully designed, highly polished and costly stones that grace the beautiful Mossy Creek Church cemetery.

"It is a noteworthy occurence that Mr. Henry Andrew, who is now 75 years old, the same man that drove the team that conveyed the remains of Capt. John Wooddell to its last resting place, drove this curious stone to the same spot, and helped to place it on his tomb, more than thirty-three years afterward.

"The many warm friends of Capt. John Wooddell who have sat on this stone, as they rested from the weary chase of the bear or deer, or while they visited the Wooddell Chalybeate Spring, when they miss the stone, need not think it stolen or destroyed.

"Be not uneasy then; the stone was removed by his kindred, and rests over your old friend at the Mossy Creek Church cemetery."

J. M. W.[281]

Elizabeth "Betsy" Erwin (Ervin)

b. in Augusta County, near Bridgewater c1753

daughter of **Edward Erwin, Jr**.(c1730-aft1800) and **Mary Curry** (c1735-6/30/1815)

sister of E. Irvine Junior m. Jane Waddle
Benjamin Erwin (The Rev.) m. Sarah Brewster in Rockingham County 7/1782, while he was a minister there.
Margaret Ervin m. Thomas Waddle, Jr.

[281] J. M. Wooddall, untitled speech, quoted by Jim Wooddell in a letter to Charles W. Jordan.

m. **John Waddle** (4/12/1761-8/5/1852)-marriage bond dated 1/30/1792

We have a copy of Betsy's marriage bond. The content is this:

"Know all men by these presents, that we John Wooddell and Edward Irwin are held and firmly bound unto his Excellency Henry Lee Esquire, governor of Virginia, and his successors, in the sum of fifty pounds current money, to the payment whereof, well and truly to be made, we do bind ourselves, our heirs, and each of our joint and several heirs, executors and administrators, jointly and severally firmly by these presents, sealed with our seals and dated the 30th day of January 1792 in the 11th year of the commonwealth.

"The condition of the above obligation is such, that whereas there is a marriage suddenly to be solemnized between the above bound John Wooddell and Elizabeth Erwin, daughter of Edward Irwin of Augusta county. If therefore there shall be no lawful cause to obstruct the said marriage, then this obligation to be void, otherwise to remain in full force and virtue.

"Witness(ed and sealed by) John Wooddell and E._ Irvine"

There was a note accompanying the delivery of the marriage bond. In it E._ Erwin says: "Sir, you (are) to grant the Bearer hereof, John Wooddell, lisence according to law to marry with my Daughter Elizabeth Irvine, he having obtained Consent. (Dated) January 29th 1792. (Attested to by) E._ Irwine Junior."[282]

C. E. May commented that "The landed aristocracy was perpetuated . . .through appointments to the vestry, to the county court, to the important offices in the militia, and through marriage. Sons and daughters of the propertied class married each other, not the offspring of the 'lower classes.' " Betsy's father had property, as did John Waddle's father, and both men served as elders in the Mossy Creek Presbyterian Church before 1796.

mother of Susan Waddle m. John Kiracofe, George's brother

Janey (Christinia) Waddell (1794-c1873) m. George Hendrick Kirshof (10/1/1791-7/12/1877)

Mary Waddle m. Jacob Bumgarner 6/28/1785[283] Some say she never married.

James Waddle m. Uriah Stanforth of Greenbriar County, now West Virginia

Elizabeth Wooddell m. Richard Curry of Highland County, Virginia

---

282 *Augusta County Marriage Book, 1792*, p. 92-98a.

283 from the marriage bond found in *Augusta County Marriage Book 1, 1785-1786*, p. 21, as quoted by Lula Miller, p. 265.

John Wooddle m. Elizabeth Bodkin of Rockingham County
William Wooddle m. Mary Curry of Highland County
Benjamin Wooddle, d. at two years of age
Irvine Wooddle m. Annie Michael of Augusta County
Bernard Wooddell m. Lydia Michael of Augusta County

Janey, their daughter, was christened at the Old Emmanuel Lutheran and Reform Church. Lula Mae Miller believes that the family may have lived in that vicinity.

Elizabeth's grandfather, uncle, father-in-law, and brother-in-law all fought in Captain Dickey's Company during the Revolution.[284]

d. "at their pleasant home on Buffalo Run," 2/11/1834 at 81 years of age.

buried at Mossy Creek Presbyterian Church

G-g-g-grandmother- 6th generation

Daniel James Coakley

b. c1769, in Caroline or Spotsylvania County

son of **Benjamin E. Coakley** (10/13/1750-1782) and **Catherine__**
I believe Benjamin's birthdate may be in error. Benjamin was probably born prior to this date. Some say that he was born before his parents arrived in America. Also, Daniel James would likely have been born when his father was more than 19 years of age, though almost anything is possible.

brother of John Coakley m. Sarah (Salley) Taylor from King George County 9/3/1795; in Spotsylvania County at the time of the 1810 census.
Benjamin(e) Coakley- listed in Stafford County in the 1810 census.
Elizabeth Coakley m. Warren Songfore from King George County 7/14/1801
Sarah (Sally) Coakley m. Henry Staples from King George County 4/18/1803
William Coakley m. Mildred (Milly) Staples from King George

[284] Chalkley, vol. 2, p. 431.

County 1/21/1804

m. **Sarah Eleanor Vigar** (c1774/5-aft1850) from Rockingham County[285] (no marriage record found)

father of 11 children:

John Clyde Coakley (c1804-) m. Susan Bradshaw (1807-1886); a blacksmith for the Confederate army; d. of typhoid

Mary Ellen Coakley m. Turner Jackson 6/8/1836. Mary's son, Dr. Brown Jackson, was buried standing up in the Dayton Cemetery!

Austin F. Coakley (bef1810 - d. before his daughter's marriage on 8/30/1860) m. Lucy Pendleton Gaines (c1810-1879) 4/13/1830

Elizabeth Coakley (-1/16/1876) unm.; d. of dropsy[286]

Susan Coakley m. Henry Cromer (-9/1833)

Daniel James Coakley, Jr. (Marion Oakley's ancestor) m. Anna Alexander (1787-) in Stafford County

Frances Coakley m. James Black 6/1/1843

Samuel Coakley m. Sarah__

William Elmer, or William Henry, Coakley; moved to Brown County, Illinois c1832; died as a result of the Civil War and pneumonia

Sarah Coakley m. James R. Manning 6/14/1851

Maria Jane Coakley (We have a snatch of a letter signed by her. On the back of it is the drawing of the Nelson B. Karicofe pump!) m. John W. Limbrick 4/3/1849.

Daniel served as a bondsman for the executors of William Hawkins, deceased, whose will was proved in Orange County, Virginia 10/28/1799. In 1801 Daniel "prayed the court to release him as security" from this bond.[287]

In 1801 Daniel served on a Jury in Orange County, Virginia.[288] Still residing in Orange County in 1805, Daniel appraised an estate.[289]

---

[285] Marion Coakley research

[286] Elizabeth Coakley made her home with her father. In 1857 she made a deed to the Trustees of the Bank Church for five acres of land that were located along the waters of Dry River, adjoining the "land of Gilmer.' This may have been the area which is used by the cemetery of that church, as suggested by Blanche Miller (Wilson). Our g-grandparents, g-g-grandparents, and others of the family are buried in that cemetery.

[287] *Orange County Order Book 9*, p. 85.

[288] *Orange County Order Book 4*, p. 341.

[289] *Ibid.*, p. 796.

The Daniel (Cokely) Coakley family was listed in the United States Census records in 1810 in Rockingham County. Males under 10 years: 3; between 10 and 16 years: 1; between 26 and 45 years: 1; Females under 10 years: 3; between 10 and 16 years: 1; between 26 and 45 years: 1. They are also listed in the county tax records in 1810.

This information conflicts with the findings of Marion Coakley, who reported that Daniel, Sarah Ellen, and ten children moved in 1817 to the Shenandoah Valley, along with their slaves, to a large tract of land located north and west of Mole Hill. Perhaps Daniel and his family were in Rockingham for a while before he purchased this property. The 1810 census could have found them elsewhere in the county. Though there is no proof because land records were destroyed during the Civil War, it is said that Daniel owned as much as 700 acres. The hand drawn map of the area around the plantation (see book jacket) was found in a handbag which his granddaughter, Caroline Coakley Kiracofe, left behind to be rediscovered approximately 177 years after the plantation was settled.

Family tradition persists that Daniel James found and bought his Valley land through the efforts of his brother, John W. Coakley. Living in the Fredericksburg area, John was one of the partners in an organization called the Fredericksburg Land Corporation. (The author believes that it is possible that this man was Daniel James's nephew.)

The name of the plantation was "Flowery Garden."[290] Daniel James Coakley operated the plantation, a blacksmith shop, a stone mill and a barrel factory on the land. Our mother remembered visiting Flowery Garden with her grandmother, who, as Daniel James's granddaughter, had lived there as a child.

In the U. S. Census of 1840, Daniel James Coakley's family is described as follows: Males between 5 and 10 years: 1; between 70 and 80 years: 1; Females between 20 and 30 years: 2; between 30 and 40 years: 2; between 60 and 70 years: 1. The young male was a grandson, Daniel James Cromer, whose mother, Susan Coakley, had married Henry Cromer. She died soon after her son's birth.

The male slaves were listed as under 10 years: 2; between 10 and 24 years: 2; Females under 10 years: 3; between 36 and 55 years: 1.[291]

At the time of his death, Daniel James owned a 320 acre plantation (part of the original tract) along with two other tracts, totaling about 500 acres of land. In 1851 the plantation was divided among his eleven children and his wife. This division of land heralded the beginning of Coakleytown. There was

---

[290] Marion Coakley letter 1/6/1967.
[291] From the research of Marion Coakley.

a sale at which the slaves were sold, and members of the family bought them.

When the property was divided, John Coakley got the blacksmith shop and land; Austin got the stone mill and barrel factory;[292] Samuel and William Henry had both left the Valley single and settled in eastern Virginia; Daniel James, Jr. (Marion's ancestor) bought out some of the other children and acquired about 150 acres of the plantation.[293] Because of the way in which the property was divided after the death of Daniel James, there are still Coakley descendants on the "plantation."[294]

d. in March 1849 in Coakleytown, Rockingham County, Virginia.

Daniel James is buried next to Sarah Eleanor in the old cemetery at Dayton, Virginia. Near them are buried Mary Ellen and Turner Jackson, Susan and Henry Cromer, and Dr. Brown Jackson, the son of Mary Ellen Coakley Jackson, whose two foot square marker at the top of the "standing up" grave he requested suggests the location of the family plot. The rest of the grave markers have vanished over the years, making it impossible to say exactly where any of the rest are buried.[295]

G-g-g-grandfather- 6th generation

A tragic note shared by Marion Coakley, who lived near Coakleytown and who had grown up with and studied the traditions of the family: There was behind the house and barns on the Daniel James Coakley plantation a pond, used for watering animals, from which ice was cut in the winter. It is likely that it was used for recreational purposes also. Every year there would be a fresh outbreak of typhoid in the community, which took many lives and caused much grief. After a long period of time, the pond was found to be the source of the typhoid fever. Mr. Coakley showed us the site of the pond.

---

[292] Skill in making barrels may have been handed down from generation to generation in the Coakley family. I have read that most of the larger estates in the British West Indies had their own barrel factories, since many of the products exported there required them. (Lewisohn, p. 18.)

[293] "Uncle" George Coakley, grandson of Daniel James, who was seven years old at the time of these recollections, had found it very difficult to see these slaves sold as they seemed part of the family. This was reported by Marion Coakley, who knew Uncle George, as did our mother.

[294] Details of Daniel James Coakley's land transactions appear in *Rockingham County Deed Book 4*.

[295] Marion Coakley letter dated 1/6/1967.

Sarah Eleanor Vigar

b. c1774/5

daughter of **William Vigar**[296](-bef 3/21/1829) of the county of Rockingham and **Ann Bridges**

sister of John Vigar (6/12/1788-c1860) m. Lucy Almond (c1798-c1865) 7/15/1816
Elizabeth Vigar m. John Jarvass

m. **Daniel James Coakley** (c1769-3/1849) c1796 [297]

mother of 11 children: John Clyde Coakley m. Susan Bradshaw
Mary Ellen Coakley m. Turner Jackson 6/8/1836
Austin F. Coakley (bef1810-c1860) m. Lucy Pendleton Gaines (c1810-1879) 4/13/1830
Elizabeth Coakley (-1/16/1876) died of "dropsy"
Susan Coakley m. Henry Cromer 9/1833
Daniel James Coakley, Jr. m. Anna Alexander (1787-) Stafford County
Frances Coakley m. James Black 6/1/1843
Samuel Coakley m. Sarah__
William Elmer Coakley, probably William Henry Coakley, (1800-) died as a result of the Civil War and pneumonia
Sarah Coakley m. James R. Manning 6/14/1851
Maria Jane Coakley m. John W. Limbrick.4/3/1849[298]

On 3/21/1829 Eleanor and Daniel sold to her brother, John Vigar, for $450, ". . .all their interest, right, title and claim, as heirs of the said William Vigar Deceased, to one third part of a certain undivided tract or parcel of land . . .on both sides of Briery Branch."[299]

In the burnt deed books of Rockingham County, there is a partial

[296] Much information was lacking about "Eleanor" Vigar, until a search in the Rockingham Historical Society files brought to light a file entitled "Vigus (Vigar)." The material dealt largely with John Vigar who was listed in the 1850 census in Rockingham County, Virginia. John Vigar, on 4/6/1829, bought land from Daniel James Coakley. In the 1860 census an elderly John and Lucy, his wife, were shown in the household of William F. Kiracofe. John's daughter, *Sarah* Caroline, had married W. F. Kiracofe, a nephew of George Kiracofe. This John is Eleanor's brother.
[297] Birthdate and marriage date calculated with the aid of census records.
[298] Part of a letter written by Maria remains, including her signature. On the back of the letter is a drawing of the Kiracofe pump. These people wasted nothing, particularly after the Civil War. Many pieces of paper are used front and back, for differing purposes.
[299] *Rockingham County Burnt Deed Book 8*, p. 540.

record of Eleanor Coakley transferring land in 1849 to her son, Samuel, and in 1850 to her son, John C. Coakley.

At some unspecified date[300] there was a "Chancery Cause" Division of the lands of Daniel Coakley, Sr. who died 1848, between his wife Eleanor *Cokely* and the nine living children, including Daniel, Maria, William, Sarah, Elizabeth, Frances, Austin, John and Samuel. The division also included Susan's son Daniel Cromer and Mary's children, Ellen, Mary, Maria and Brown H. Jackson. Apparently Susan and Mary had died before that time.

d. aft1850

buried at the public cemetery in Dayton ("because it was close"- Mr. Coakley).

We have photographs of the spot, with no markers.

G-g-g-grandmother- 6th generation

Robert B. Gaines

b. bef12/30/1772 in Spotsylvania County,Virginia

son of **Robert Coleman Gaines** (between c1740-c1808) and **Elizabeth Long** (c1740-aft1831)

brother of Thomas Gaines (1771-) m. Mildred Rowe
Lucy Gaines (1776-)
John Long Gaines
Mary Gaines
Richard Gaines m. Frances Jolly 5/4/1789 in Culpeper County; William Mason presided.
Catherine "Kitty" or "Cathy" Gaines m. (1)Reuben Terrell of Orange County, Virginia 3/28/1803; (2)Alexander Dinwiddie of Barren County, Kentucky10/10/1806
Amelia Gaines-This must be the "Milly" who married William Rice 7/23/1806.
Ursula Gaines m. Luke Rice 3/7/1808, son of Mary Rice
Sarah Gaines
Reuben Gaines

[300] From the research of Marguerite B. Priode.

Elizabeth Gaines (1793-) probably m. Henry Fisher

m. **Frances Manspile**

father of 8 children: James Gaines (8/8/1801-3/18/1852) m. Rebecca Brown 4/15/1826
Susannah Gaines m. David Chandler 4/24/1826
Lucy Pendleton Gaines (c1800-1879) m. Austin F. Coakley (c1810-c1860, before the marriage of his daughter Caroline) 4/13/1830
Elizabeth Gaines m. Anderson Ruffner 4/27/1837 (given by Hubert Gaines, in place of his deceased father, as were two other daughters)
Ursula Gaines m. George W. Frankham 8/22/1841
Sarah Gaines m. William Wolfrey 9/28/1841; (m. by Thomas Rice; given by Hubert Gaines).
John W. Gaines m. Elizabeth Cammack 5/28/1842 (signed for by William Wolfrey)
Hubert Gaines m. Cynthia Gilmer 2/19/1857

The above names are listed in the order of marriage, since we know nothing of birth order other than that James was the firstborn.[301]

In an old deed book, some of which was partly burned during the Civil War, there is a land transaction dated 9/15/1806 showing that Robert Gaines bought from John Dean 104 acres of land and the slaves.

On 3/12/1808 Robert Gains transferred to Richard and Reuben Gaines the land that had been bought from the Deans in 1806. This deed, or indenture, along with twelve others, was completely destroyed by fire during the Civil War; only an indexing line is left to prove it was once there.

On 8/5/1817 Richard and Reuben Gaines made a deed to Robert Gaines, Jr. for 104 acres of land and the Negroes "as though he had never left it." This was the land bought from the Deans in 1806.

A very good question which might be asked at this point is just why Robert, Jr. would have bought land in 1806 and deeded it to two brothers two years later for a period of nine years, after which these brothers deeded it back to Robert, Jr., as if he had never let it go.

The 1810 census records place a Robert B. Gaines and an Elizabeth Gaines in King and Queen County. This is very likely Robert B. and his mother. We do know that Robert did not accept title to his property in Rockingham until 1817. Where was he employed until that time? Could it be

[301] From the Gaines file, Rockingham Historical Society, Dayton, Virginia.

that he had received land from his father, in conjunction with his mother, in King and Queen County, and that he had lived there, in support of his mother, until he decided he had reason to claim his Shenandoah Valley land?

From the time Robert and his siblings were infants Robert Coleman Gaines, his father, had sought land with their interest in mind. You will recall that he leased a tract in the Spotswood estate for the length of the lives of Robert B. and two of his siblings. We know that his land holdings were extensive. It is my belief that Robert Coleman Gaines came to the Valley in 1806, as Blanche Miller suggested, and bought land in the name of his son, Robert B. Gaines. This was probably a part of the latter's inheritance. It was then arranged between the brothers, Richard, Reuben and Robert, that the two former would have use of the land, or at least manage it, until such time as Robert chose to move to it. Whether or not the term of nine years was specified we will never know, for that document is lost.

Robert signed daughter Lucy's marriage bond in 4/13/1830.

d. in Rockingham County prior to 1831

G-g-g-grandfather- 6th generation

Frances Manspile

I find it likely that Frances was the daughter of **Michael Manspoile** and **Ann (Nancy) Long**, who were married 12/9/1772; and the granddaughter of **John Manspoile** and Nancy's parents, **Ware Long** of Essex County, Virginia and his wife, **Sarah Robinson.**[302]

Frances was *undoubtedly* the g-granddaughter of the immigrant, Jacob Mansboil (-c1779). Jacob had, among other children, a son named John, who was involved in land transfers in Orange County in 1756. We know that he had a family, for at one juncture the courts removed several young children from his household because of poverty. There is evidence in the court records that his wife had died. There were a number of children, some of them girls, who were named in these records, but I feel certain that there were also at least two sons, presumably older than the girls, named Adam and Michael, who became productive residents of Orange County during the last half of the 18th century. Michael and his wife, Ann (Nancy) Long, owned land which adjoined Gaines land at one point. It may have been very easy for Robert Gaines and

[302] Almyrta F. Long, *The Long History*, vol. 2, n.d., pp. v-vii.

Frances Manspile to become acquainted.

One of Adam's daughters, Sarah, married Zachary Lee on 5/25/1790. Another Manspoile, Lucy, daughter of one of the brothers, married Henry Long 11/7/1785. A son, named Johny, married Sally Wood in Orange County in 1796. Frances could have been the sister of any of these. If James Gaines was her first child, with Lucy Pendleton born not too long thereafter, we could assume that Frances married Robert in the late 1790s.

m. **Robert B. Gaines** who died in Rockingham County "prior to" 1831

mother of 8 children: James Gaines (8/8/1801-3/18/1852) m. Rebecca Brown 4/15/1826
Susannah Gaines m. David Chandler 4/24/1826
Lucy Pendleton Gaines (c1800-1879) m. Austin F. Coakley (c1810-c1860) 4/13/1830
Elizabeth Gaines m. Anderson Ruffner 4/27/1837 (given by Hubert Gaines)
Ursula Gaines m. George W. Frankham 8/22/1841 (daughter of Frances; given by Hubert Gaines)
Sarah Gaines m. William Wolfrey 9/28/1841 (given by Hubert Gaines); minister, Thomas Rice
John W. Gaines m. Elizabeth Cammack 5/28/1842 (signed for by William Wolfrey)
Hubert Gaines m. Cynthia Gilmer 2/19/1857

probably died in Rockingham County

G-g-g-grandmother- 6th generation

Chapter 4
Generation 5

Again we will check the tempo of the world at large, which accelerates considerably during the lives of members of this generation:[303]

- Robert Burns, beloved Scottish poet published "Auld Lang Syne" in 1794, the same year that Janey Waddle was born.
- George Washington, refusing a third term in office, delivered his Farewell Address in 1795. Elizabeth Driver was born during that year.
- The capital of the United States was moved in 1800 from Philadelphia to Washington, D. C., which was then made up of 2464 free inhabitants and 623 slaves.
- American civil engineer, Robert Fulton, produced the first submarine, the "Nautilus."
- In 1803 President Jefferson led the United States in the purchase of a tract of land reaching from the Gulf of Mexico to the Northwest - a tract which came to be known as the Louisiana Purchase.
- Alexander Hamilton, formerly the Secretary of the Treasury, was killed in a duel with Aaron Burr in 1804.
- Simon Bolivar emerged, in 1810, as a major leader in South America.
- In 1811, William Henry Harrison, later to become President of the United States, defeated the Indians under Tecumseh at Tippecanoe, Indiana.
- Jane Austin wrote *Sense and Sensibility* that year, and the Brothers Grimm wrote their *Fairy Tales* the year after.
- Francois Appert developed the technique for preserving food by canning it.
- In 1814 the British burned Washington, D. C., and later in the same year, on 12/24, the Treaty of Ghent was signed to end that war.
- In 1815 the Sumbawa Volcano erupted in Indonesia, killing more than 50,000 people.
- The border between Canada and the United States was established in 1818, while Mary Shelley was writing *Frankenstein*.
- In Austria Franz Gruber wrote the music for Joseph Mohr's "Silent Night."
- In 1820 the United States Land Law fixed land prices at a minimum of $1.25 per acre.
- Also in 1820, the Washington Colonization Society founded Liberia for the repatriation of American Negroes.
- In 1824 the United States House of Representatives elected John Quincy

[303] Grun, *op. cit.*, pp. 371-393.

Adams as President when none of the four candidates won a majority in the national election.

- Tea roses from China were introduced into Europe in 1825.
- In 1829 Andrew Jackson was inaugurated the seventh president of the United States.
- That year Chopin made his debut in Vienna, Austria, while Louis Daguerre was developing his daguerreotype in France.
- In 1830 stiff collars became a feature of men's dress. Lucy Gaines and Austen Coakley were married that year.
- Charles Darwin, a naturalist, sailed to South America, New Zealand, and Australia aboard the "H. M. S. Beagle."
- The bestseller in literature in 1833 was Davy Crockett's autobiography; in 1834 the bestseller was Victor Hugo's *The Hunchback of Notre Dame.*
- The South Australia Act allowed for the establishment of a colony there.
- In 1836 Davy Crockett, American politician and frontiersman, was killed at the Alamo.
- Victoria became the Queen of Great Britain.
- In 1839 Edgar Allen Poe wrote "The Fall of the House of Usher."
- During the year in which Nelson Bittle Kiracofe was born, Abner Doubleday was laying out the first baseball field and conducting the first baseball game ever played.
- In 1843 Charles Dickens wrote *A Christmas Carol.*
- Brigham Young led the Mormons to the Great Salt Lake in Utah in 1846.
- In 1848 the first appendectomy was done.
- In 1850 California became a state.
- Nathaniel Hawthorne wrote *The Scarlet Letter* in 1850, *The House of Seven Gables* in 1851.
- In 1851 there were 430 million people in China, 34 million in Germany, 33 million in France, 20.8 million in Great Britain, and 23 million in the United States.
- In 1852 the United States imported sparrows from Germany as a defense against caterpillars. These immigrants adapted exceedingly well.
- That year Harriet Beacher Stowe wrote *Uncle Tom's Cabin.*
- In 1855 Walt Whitman wrote *Leaves of Grass.*
- In 1857 the British Royal Navy destroyed the Chinese fleet, and France and Britain captured Canton.
- Work began on the Suez Canal in 1859.
- Abraham Lincoln was elected the sixteenth President of the United States in 1860, as South Carolina seceded from the Union, and Nelson and Caroline were married.

- Robert W. Bunsen and a man named *Kirchoff* discovered the elements cesium and rubidium that year.

"During all this time progress was rapid in Rockingham, notwithstanding the fact that she surrendered a large part of her territory in 1787 in the formation of Pendleton County (in what is now West Virginia). The people were subduing the earth and replenishing it; they were clearing forests, building houses, laying out roads, and establishing schools, churches, and towns; they were marrying and giving in marriage. . . For the year ending April, 1798, Rev. Walsh, of the Methodist Church, . . .reported 30 marriages to the county clerk, and for the next year, ending May 13, 1799, he reported 45. . . In 1781 there were about 1500 tithables[304] in the county. Accordingly, the total population was probably about 5000. In 1790 there were about 2100 tithables, and a total population of nearly 7500. By 1810 the figures were about 3000 and 12,500, respectively. There was a variety of race elements: German, Scotch, Irish, English, Dutch, and Negro, but the negroes were remarkably few, compared with the number to be found in the adjacent counties east of the Blue Ridge. The number of negro slaves reported for 1790 was only about 10 per cent of the total. Most of the taxpayers had horses, while but a few of them had slaves. . . .A fact of special significance presents itself in this connection. In 1790 all the negroes in the county were reported as slaves; there were apparently no free negroes, but in 1810 there were 200 or more free negroes. This change was probably the result, in large measure at least, of the work done within this period by the Methodists (and Anabaptists, including the German Baptists or Brethren) on behalf of emancipation."[305]

Joseph Miller

b. 3/23/1787 in Shenandoah County, Virginia

Joseph's father's home was just northwest of the farm homestead of his grandfather, Elder John H. Garber, approximately two miles northwest of the Flat Rock Church of the Brethren in Shenandoah County, Virginia. The family moved to Rockingham County about 1811.

---

[304] A tithable was anyone subject to the payment of taxes or donations in support of the church or clergy. In colonial times, the word most commonly referred to the male head of the family, however, young men over eighteen years of age were also counted as tithables.

[305] John W. Wayland, *A History of Rockingham County Virginia* (Dayton, VA, Ruebush-Elkins Co., 1912), pp. 106-107.

The home of Joseph Miller and Betsy Thomas near Beaver Creek, Virginia

son of **Daniel Miller** I (5/13/1752-1819/20) and **Anna Garber** (c1762-c1837)

brother of Daniel Miller II (1/16/1784-9/9/1847) of the Greenmount area m. Anna Hoover (6/17/1785-2/27/1860) 4/4/1807

Barbara Ann Miller (1785-9/9/1861) m. Isaac Long, Sr. (1/1/1784-11/10/1849) 11/5/1805

Jacob Miller (1789-1849) m. Magdalene Sanger (9/16/1789-2/6/1849) 4/20/1815

Samuel Miller (12/17/1793-9/7/1861) m. Barbara Sanger (8/27/1791-5/9/1875) 3/19/1816 later went to Ohio in 1839.

Abraham Miller (3/3/1796-8/5/1862) m. (1)Salome Frantz; (2)Catherine Leedy (5/3/1802-6/8/1877) c1821, in the west; lived near Lima, Ohio.

Susanna Miller (1/7/1798-5/10/1862) m. John Thomas (3/20/1798-12/31/1834) c1820

Martin Miller (7/15/1800-9/19/1872) m. (1)Nancy Sanger (12/10/1795-7/23/1849) 3/27/1821; (2)Mary Cline

Michael Miller (1807-1893) m. Mary Sanger (12/6/1807-2/101885) 3/17/1825

John Miller died young after marrying Susan Leedy (1783-), who also died young
Katie Miller m. Jacob Rife, died young

These children grew up in the Garber's Church area on Cook's Creek. The family was doubtless very active within that congregation, which was then German Baptist and is now referred to as the Church of the Brethren.

.

Joseph's father's land in Rockingham County was purchased in 1811, at about the time Joseph and his wife-to-be probably met.[306]

m. **Elizabeth Ann "Betsy" Thomas** (7/10/1792-11/21/1849) 3/24/1812
Joseph's mother's brother, Elder Daniel Garber, solemnized this marriage, and most of the other marriages in this area.

They (Joseph and Betsy) ". . .located on a farm on Silver Creek just across the hill east of the Beaver Creek Church. . .where a copious spring issues from under one of the buildings. . . .He probably lived here the remainder of his life. . .Here he reared his large family with fourteen of his sixteen children growing to adulthood. . .From here his family has spread across the continent. . ."[307] I have read that the spring referred to above actually rose *beneath* the Miller home. The remains of a stone foundation partially surround the spring.

father of Annie Miller (1813-9/15/1897) m. Jacob Sanger (1809-1886) 6/28/1832
Susan Miller (1814-1893) m. Henry Sanger (1812-1872) 5/17/1834
Jacob Miller (1815-1883) m. Fannie Wine (1812-1852) 4/5/1837
Abraham Miller (3/1/1817-7/19/1882) m. Sarah Shickel (5/9/1818-8/7/1872) 12/1839. Ringgold ancestor. Operated, on Dry River 1 1/2 miles above Bridgewater, A. Miller & Co., a woolen mill which made flannel blankets and wool suiting. The author has one of these blankets.[308]
Regina Miller (5/4/1818-5/15/1890) m. Jacob Shickel (6/16/1816-8/28/1897) 11/5/1840
Elizabeth Miller (12/5/1819-7/1/1905) m. Joel Glick (1821-1880) 3/13/1845. J. Paul Glick ancestor.

---

[306] Glick, p. ix.
[307] Glick, p. ix.
[308] May, *Four Flags*, p. 445.

Barbara Miller (1821-1902) never married
Joseph T. Miller (2/23/1823-1/20/1862) m. Barbara Glick (1829-1912) 11/2/1848
Sarah Miller (10/16/1824-11/9/1903) m. Samuel G. Glick (1823-1884) 8/26/1847. This family operated an apple butter factory.
Daniel Miller (III) (1/21/1826-3/8/1900) m. Nancy Shickel (4/22/1832-3/6/1895) 4/13/1853
Peter Miller (2/12/1828-1/7/1904) m. (1)Elizabeth Stautamyer (1832-1880) 10/1/1857; (2)Mary C. Kanost (1844-1904) 5/18/1882
Infant, stillborn- twin 5/5/1830
John J. Miller-twin (5/5/1830-8/14/1896) m. (1)Magdalene Sanger (1836-1881) 9/3/1857; (2)Amanda L. Caricofe (1840-1904) 11/19/1885
Katherine Miller (1831-1832)
Lydia Miller (5/10/1832-3/15/1910) 2nd wife of Daniel Brower (1815-1893) 2/21/1875; moved to Ohio.
Henry Miller (3/11/1836-1/20/1890) m. Sarah Catherine Wright (1836-1913) 9/27/1860[309]

"By 1800 the Church of the Brethren was well established in Virginia, with several permanent settlements. The rich limestone soil in the mountain valleys of the state afforded them, at long last, a satisfactory background for the growth of their communities of worship.

"A strong and growing settlement gathered in the Cooks Creek area of Rockingham County. As early as 1822 this congregation built a meetinghouse on land which was given by Daniel Garber, one of the sons of John H. Garber. This is the oldest meetinghouse in continuous use in Virginia. With the success of this congregation and the arrival of new settlers to the area, Cooks Creek became a parent church to other congregations, among them, Beaver Creek.[310]

"During the 1820's the Brethren in the Cooks Creek area were numerous enough to be divided into two distinct congregations. The new group which included all of the Brethren south and west of Dry River, a branch of North River, became known as the Beaver Creek congregation."[311]

"John Brower, and Joseph and Martin Miller led in the organization and establishment of the Beaver Creek Church, located on Beaver Creek west of present Bridgewater on the road from Millers Iron Works to Brocks Gap. . .

[309] Glick, pp. xv-xvi.
[310] Beaver Creek was Joseph Miller's church and that of succeeding generations, even to my mother's generation. Many members of our family are buried there.
[311] Sappington, p. 39.

(T)his road connects the present villages of Spring Creek and Montezuma. Beaver Creek Church built its first sanctuary, a log one, in 1828 on a tract of land owned by Martin Miller, who conveyed it to the trustees of the church (of which two were other Millers, one of whom was our Joseph) November 20, 1840. John Brower was the church's first minister. Other early ministers who served it were Daniel Brower, a son of John Brower and son-in-law of Joseph, and Joseph and Martin Miller."

Joseph was ". . .one of the very earliest ministers and very probably an Elder in the Beaver Creek congregation when it was formed in 1828. . . .The records indicate he was also a trustee of this church."[312]

"All of these ministers were farmers, who earned their living by tilling the soil. They have been described as 'men of God, for they gave much of their time and energy without material compensation to the ministry of the church and to the spreading of the Gospel.' This willingness to serve without monetary compensation was an important characteristic of the leadership of the Church of the Brethren in the 18th and 19th centuries; they gave sacrificially of their ability and energy.

"It can be said with some accuracy that the first three congregations to build meetinghouses: Cooks Creek, Middle River, and Beaver Creek, all grew out of the Flat Rock congregation of Shenandoah County (John Garber's church)."[313]

And the work went on. Roger Sappington in *The Brethren in Virginia: The History. . .* reported on the work of Brethren ministers from the older settlements in the Valley who made a trip to Page County around 1850 for missionary purposes. Among them was Joseph Miller. The difficulty of travelling for many hours over mountains to reach the Brethren settlements to the east was commented upon.[314]

"Joseph and Martin Miller, drafted as privates in 1814 into Capt. Robert McGill's 58th Infantry Company of the Virginia Militia, refused to march or perform tours of duty because of their pacifist beliefs; and so they were fined at a Court-Martial June 8, 1815, which was presided over by Col. George Huston. The fine for each tour of duty missed was five dollars. Joseph was fined $56 and Martin $50." [315]

d. 11/29/1851 at 64 yrs., 8 mo., and 6 days.

---

[312] Glick, p. ix.
[313] Sappington, pp. 37-40.
[314] Sappington, p. 130.
[315] May, *Four Flags*, pp. 270-271.

buried at Beaver Creek Church Cemetery, Rockingham County, Virginia.

G-g-grandfather- 5th generation

"...(M)any of the Miller descendants in colonial days built houses with movable partitions in order to accommodate the members as they met in their homes. Some barns were built to accommodate the larger meetings. In the early to late 1800's Miller and Garber descendants gave land for the building of meeting houses, schools and cemeteries."[316]

Elizabeth Ann "Betsy" Thomas

b.7/10/1792, probably in Pennsylvania.

Elder Abram Thomas thought Betsy was a sister of his Grandfather John Thomas, who married Susannah Miller, a sister of Joseph, but Paul Glick believes she was a near relative, probably a sister or niece, of Peter Thomas (m. Regina Zigler), father of Abram's grandfather, John. Knowing how siblings intermarried between two families, I favor the former suggestion.

m. **Joseph Miller** (3/23/1787-11/29/1851) 3/24/1812

mother of Annie Miller (1813-9/15/1897) m. Jacob Sanger (1809-1886) 6/28/1832
Susan Miller (1814-1893) m. Henry Sanger (1812-1872) 5/17/1834
Jacob Miller (1815-1883) m. Fannie Wine (1812-1852) 4/5/1837
Abraham Miller (3/1/1817-7/19/1882) m. Sarah Shickel (5/9/1818-8/7/1872) 12/1839
Regina Miller (5/4/1818-5/15/1890) m. Jacob Shickel (6/16/1816-8/28/1897) 11/5/1840
Elizabeth Miller (12/5/1819-7/1/1905) m. Joel Glick (1821-1880) 3/13/1845
Barbara Miller (1821-1902) never married
Joseph T. Miller (2/23/1823-1/20/1862) m. Barbara Glick (1829-1912) 11/2/1848
Sarah Miller (10/16/1824-11/9/1903) m. Samuel G. Glick (1823-1884) 8/26/1847
Daniel Miller (III) (1/21/1826-3/8/1900) m. Nancy Shickel

[316] Mason, *Miller Record*, p. 11.

(4/22/1832-3/6/1895) 4/13/1853
Peter Miller (2/12/1828-1/7/1904) m. (1)Elizabeth Stautamyer (1832-1880) 10/1/1857; (2)Mary C. Kanost (1844-1904) 5/18/1882
Infant, stillborn - twin 5/5/1830
John J. Miller- twin (5/5/1830-8/14/1896) m. (1)Magdalene Sanger (1836-1881) 9/3/1857; (2)Amanda L. Caricofe (1840-1904) 11/19/1885
Katherine Miller (1831-1832)
Lydia Miller (5/10/1832-3/15/1910) 2nd wife of Daniel Brower (1815-1893) 2/21/1875
Henry Miller (3/11/1836-1/20/1890) m. Sarah Catherine Wright (1836-1913) 9/27/1860

"...(N)ot much is known of her life aside from being a housewife and good mother..."[317] Blanche Miller Wilson told us that Betsy was said to have often served any number of guests, as well as her extensive family, a noon meal on Sundays.

d. 11/21/1849

buried at Beaver Creek Church of the Brethren not far from the side of the church building

G-g-grandmother- 5th generation

Daniel Shickel

b. 12/6/1789

Daniel was a descendant of a Pennsylvania Dutch family of German origin. The name is sometimes spelled Shickle.

son of **Peter Shickel, Sr**. (c1755-) and **Mary**__

brother of Peter Shickel m. Margaret Rader 7/1/1811
Jacob Shickel m. Eva Gowl, widow of Adam Gowl 2/20/1819
These two brothers came with Daniel into the Shenandoah Valley at an early date, coming through Brocks Gap from Pennsylvania into Rockingham County.

[317] Glick, p. xi.

m. **Elizabeth Driver** (6/5/1795-8/25/1853) 4/21/1814 in Rockingham County, Virginia. The bondsman was Elizabeth's father, Peter Driver.

father of Jacob Shickel (6/16/1816-8/28/1897) m. Regina Miller 11/5/1840. Operated a machine shop on Dry River.
Sarah Shickel (5/9/1818-8/7/1872) m. Abraham Miller 12/12/1839
Mary "Polly" Shickel (2/5/1826-6/12/1893) m. Benjamin F. Kerlin 1846
Barbara Shickel (12/11/1828-2/25/1907) m. Samuel Long 6/12/1851
Nancy Shickel (4/22/1832-3/6/1895) m. Daniel Miller (III) (1/21/1826-3/8/1900) 4/13/1853[318]

This was a Brethren family who probably lived in the Montezuma area and attended the Beaver Creek Church. ". . .(They) must have lived near the Joseph Miller family in close social and religious connection as three of their five children married into the Miller family." [319]

Daniel had a shop in Bridgewater, probably a blacksmith shop.[320]

d. 7/15/1852.

The authors of *Descendants of Ludwig Treiber and Barbara Sprenkle in the Shenandoah Valley of Virginia, The United States of America* say "Daniel Shickel's will proved 7 Aug 1852; tombstone death date 1861."

G-g-grandfather- 5th generation

Elizabeth Driver

b. 6/5/1795 in Virginia

The daughter of **Peter Driver** (11/20/1766-7/1/1850) and **Dorothy Meyer** (4/15/1774-10/7/1844) of Singers Glen,[321] Elizabeth was raised in a Brethren family.

---

[318] Driver and Gassett, p. 368.
[319] Glick, pp. xv, 48.
[320] Interview, Miss Mary Hollen, Fall of 1994.
[321] Driver and Gassett, p. 3B.

sister of Barbara Driver (1/28/1793-5/12/1878) m. John Miller 12/14/1822
Peter Driver (10/21/1797-2/8/1800)
Jacob Driver (5/12/1800-12/25/1868) m. Polly Funk 4/7/1823
Nancy Driver (7/26/1803-) m. Ezekiel Bryan/Brown 7/29/1822
Mary "Maria" Driver (4/28/1806-2/4/1888) m. Jonothan Funk 12/20/1830
Salome "Sarah" Driver (1/30/1809-2/6/1909) m. Peter Zimmerman 1826
Joseph Driver (4/7/1812-11/27/1884) m. (1)Mary "Polly" Showalter 1838; (2)Margaret Campbell 1882
Johannes "John" Driver (6/4/1815-8/9/1875) m. (1)Catherine Showalter 1837; (2)Elizabeth Coffman (widow) 1872
Benjamin Driver (12/28/1817-4/10/1895) m. Lucinda Allen 1846
All of these children are said to have been born in Virginia.

m. **Daniel Shickel, Sr**. (12/6/1789-7/15/1852) 4/21/1814.[322] Peter Driver was the bondsman.

mother of Jacob Shickel (6/16/1816-8/28/1897) m. Regina Miller 11/5/1840
Sarah Shickel (5/9/1818-8/7/1872) m. Abraham Miller 12/12/1839
Mary "Polly" Shickel (2/5/1826-6/12/1893) m. Benjamin F. Kerlin 1846
Barbara Shickel (12/11/1828-2/25/1907) m. Samuel Long 6/12/1851
Nancy Shickel (4/22/1832-3/6/1895) m. Daniel Miller (III) (1/21/1826-3/8/1900) 4/13/1853
Note that a son and two daughters married into the Joseph Miller family.

d. 8/25/1853

buried at Beaver Creek Church Cemetery, Rockingham County, Virginia.

G-g-grandmother- 5th generation

[322] John Vogt and T. William Kethley, Jr., *Virginia Historic Marriage Register: Rockingham County Marriages, 1778-1850* (Athens, GA, Iberian Press, 1984), p. 199.

Austin F.[323] Coakley

father came to the Valley "with his 10 children."

son of **Daniel James Coakley** (c1769-3/1849) and **Sarah Ellen Viger** (c1774/5-aft1850)

brother of John Clyde Coakley married Susan Bradshaw- a blacksmith, he died in Civil War
Mary Ellen Coakley married Turner Jackson[324] 6/8/1836
Elizabeth Coakley (-1/16/1876) d. of dropsy
Susan Coakley married Henry Cromer (-9/1833)
Daniel James Coakley, Jr. (Marion Coakley's ancestor) married Anna Alexander (1787-) in Stafford County
Frances Coakley married James Black 6/1/1843
Samuel Coakley m. Sarah__
William Elmer Coakley, or William Henry, had pneumonia and died during the Civil War.
Sarah Coakley married James R. Manning 6/14/1851
Maria Jane Coakley married John W. Limbrick 4/3/1849

m. **Lucy Pendleton Gaines** (c1810-1879) 4/13/1830[325]

The *Second Marriage Record of Augusta County 1813-1850* reports the marriage date as 4/15/1830. The fact that William Hank was bondsman is also mentioned there.

This couple lived near Mole Hill.

father of Robert Gaines Coakley (2/12/1833-7/28/1903) m. Mary Elizabeth Paine (Payne); lived at "Flowery Gardens" on the plantation; buried in the cemetery of Mt. Horeb EUB Church, Hinton, VA; he was reported, by tradition, to be the Deputy Sheriff of Rockingham County during the Civil War, July 1864.
Mary Anne Coakley (4/24/1837-6/2/1889) m. John Mair/Nair
Joseph Benjamin Coakley (12/23/1838-8/10/1864) m. Caroline A.

---

[323] The name Fielding appears in the family. I have found no other likely name to account for Austin's middle initial.

[324] Mary Ellen Coakley's son is remembered as a bit of a character. He was a respected doctor who expressed his individuality by insisting that he be buried standing up! And there he is, near his family in the Dayton Cemetery, standing beneath the ground in a clearly distinguishable *square* grave.

[325] *Rockingham County Index of Marriages, A-K*, Bond 785.

Lucy Pendleton Gaines and Austin F. Coakley

Carrier 9/16/__; enlisted in Confederate army 4/1861 at Malboro Point, was assistant surgeon in Lightfoot Battalion light artillery; became sick and died; probably buried at Bank Church.

Caroline Virginia Coakley (12/25/1840-4/11/1917) m. Nelson Bittle Kiracofe (11/6/1838-1/4/1874) 8/30/1860

Mariah Coakley (1843-8/4/1870)

James Austin Coakley (1844-1864) enlisted as a Confederate soldier with "Uncle George" Coakley in Spring 1863; Lightfoot Batallion, light artillery; killed near Spotsylvania Court House in May 1864 as the Confederate army was pushed back toward Richmond; probably buried at Bank Church.

Peachy Rush Coakley (8/26/1847-3/25/1924) m. (1)Catherine V. Cline; (2)Lelia M. Good

William Henry Coakley (-7/1864) Civil War casualty

Austin was a teacher in the Thomas School, the first English-speaking school in his section of Rockingham County. The school was on his father's land, just overlooking the house site.

To my great delight, we found Austin Coakley's name in the catalog of the Virginia Historical Society. Upon requesting the material, we beheld two hand-written contracts, one for a six-month term to "commence" 4/6/1835, the other, a four-month term to commence 11/16/1835. In April he taught fourteen full-time scholars and six "half-time." (Why does the thought that the majority of these half-time students were undoubtedly female keep bothering me?) One and "one-half" of these students in the April term were of the sixteen children of G-g-grandfather Joseph Miller; in the November term, three of Joseph's children attended. Other subscribers were Allen Devier, Mrs. Speck, Joseph Shue, Jacob Miller, George Smalts, A. B. Rodgers, Benjamin Fishback (who preserved the contracts for us), Samuel Glick, John Brower, Thomas McGuill, Joseph Snett, and Abram Glick.

The wording of the two contracts is similar. "I Austin Coakley of the County of Rockingham propose teaching a school for six months (Viz) Spelling Reading, Writing and Arithmetic. I, the sd, Coakley by these presents bind myself to give due attendance excepting Saturdays. For which we the subscribers bind ourselves to pay the said Coakley five dollars for each whole schollar annexed to our names. The school to be taught in the old schoolhouse near David Franks and to commence on Monday the 6th April 1835." The penmanship is fine, though noticeably different on the two contracts. I like to think that Lucy helped Austin by penning the prettier contract. Notice that these classes are not being taught at the Coakleytown school; in this instance Austin travelled to the area in which the children lived.

In my reading I came across an additional bit of information about the Coakleytown school, and, very likely, other schools of its era. A child named Joseph Heatwole, born in 1849, was one of the scholars in the one-room building. School was in session five months of the year, and most children attended until they were twenty years old. Sometimes the students were older than the teacher. It was reported that Joseph was "well educated in the three R's." It was also reported that spelling bees, using the Webster Dictionary, and arithmetic matches were popular methods of teaching.[326]

Austin was named, along with his mother and his nine then-living brothers and sisters in a Chancery Cause Division of the lands of his father,

---

[326] Patricia Heatwole Hertzler, *The Story of Melvin Jasper Heatwole, Mollie Grace Coffman* (Powhatan, VA, 1983), p. 15.

Daniel Coakley, Sr.

Austin bought at least one of the slave women, Aunt Maria, when the Daniel Coakley plantation was broken up in 1851. At that time he inherited his father's stone mill and the barrel factory.[327]

Shortly before his death it is reported that Austin was traveling between Petersburg (West Virginia) and Romney. The weather had been uncharacteristically warm, causing him to discard his blankets. He nearly froze because of a sudden change in the weather.[328]

d. February or March, 1860 of typhoid fever

He is buried beside Lucy at the Bank Church, near Dayton, Virginia.

G-g-grandfather- 5th generation

Marion Coakley's father told him that "in the fall and winter of 1848-1849 a place was cleared in the woods and a small church was built...(It) was not yet finished when Daniel James, Sr. died. The first grave was placed here March 3, 1851 in the edge of the woods along a rail fence."[329] Austin was buried there some years later.

Cemetery at Bank Mennonite Church: (two family-related rows)[330]

Thomas Hoard, Jr.-marble
Mary Hoard-marble
Thomas Hoard, Sr.-marble
Polly Burner Hoard-marble
__sandstone, unreadable
__sandstone
__sandstone
James Austin Coakley, son of Austin, Civil War casualty
Joseph Benjamin Coakley, son of Austin
Austin F. Coakley-sandstone

---

[327] Letter from Marion Coakley, Dayton, VA, to Blanche Miller Wilson.
[328] Coakley letter. Basic information came from "Children of Daniel James Coakley" by Dr. H. J. Eckenrode (Virginia State Archives). I was told of this document, for which I am still searching, by Marion Coakley.
[329] Marion Coakley letter of 1/6/1967.
[330] From a diagram provided by Marion Coakley.

	Lucy P. Gaines Coakley-sandstone
	Joseph W. Coakley, son of Daniel J., Jr.-sandstone
	Elizabeth Coakley, Austin's sister-sandstone
Maria, slave	Nelson Kiracofe, son-in-law, delayed Civil War casualty-marble
slave	undersized grave; child?-sandstone
slave	Caroline Coakley Kiracofe, daughter-marble
slave	__sandstone
	__sandstone
	Mary Black-wooden
	Fannie Black-wooden
	John Black, son(?)-wooden
	Mr. John Black-wooden
	Frances Coakley Black-marble

William Henry Coakley, son of Austin and Lucy, was also buried at the Bank Church. The location of that grave is unknown.

Wooden grave markers had very little chance of surviving the elements for very long, but when that was the best you had, you used them. At least for a short while they served as a memorial to lives lived and loved by those who mourned their deaths. Fragments of the sandstone grave markers remain in place in some cases, but none is readable. We are fortunate that some member of the family recorded the location of these graves and that the information has been safely passed to this generation.

Lucy Pendleton Gaines

b. c1810 (estimate based on the census of 1870, coupled with recorded marriage date of 1830)

daughter of **Robert B**. **Gaines** (bef12/30/1772-bef1831) and **Frances Manspile**.

sister of James Gaines (8/8/1801-3/18/1852) m. Rebecca Brown 4/15/1826.[331]
Her father officiated.
Susannah Gaines m. David Chandler 4/24/1826
Elizabeth Gaines m. Anderson Ruffner 4/27/1837 (given by Hubert Gaines who assumed his father, Robert's, role after his death)
Ursula Gaines m. George W. Frankham 8/22/1841
Sarah Gaines m. William S. Wolfrey 9/28/1841
John W. Gaines m. Elizabeth Cammack 5/28/1842 (signed for by William Wolfrey)
Hubert Gaines m. Cynthia Gilmer 2/19/1857
These records are given in the order of their marriages since birthdates are not available.[332]

m. **Austin F.** (Fielding?) **Coakley** (bef1810-c1860) on 4/13/1830.[333]

The marriage of Austin and Lucy was the *first* legally recorded in Rockingham County. The *Second Marriage Register of Augusta County, Virginia 1813-1850* records the date as 4/15/1830 and William Hank as bondsman.

We found the Marriage Bond signed by her father 4/13/1830.

Lucy and Austin lived near Mole Hill, which I have seen as Lucy and her daughter, Caroline, must have seen it, in sunlight and in mist. It was fun to imagine Lucy's life in the figurative shadow of that little hill. (I think someone told me it was an extinct volcano. This seems improbable.)[334]

mother of Robert Gaines Coakley (2/12/1833-7/28/1903) m. Mary Elizabeth Paine; lived at "Flowery Gardens" which had been part of the plantation; buried at Mt. Horeb EUB Church in Hinton, Virginia. He was said to be the Deputy Sheriff of Rockingham County during Civil War. I have found no confirmation of this.
Mary Anne Coakley (4/24/1837-6/2/1889) m. John Mair/Nair
Joseph Benjamin Coakley (12/23/1838-8/10/1864) m. Caroline A. Carrier 9/16/__; lost in Civil War.

---

[331] This couple's daughters were Lucinda Gaines Kiracofe (Cousin Lucinda) and Catherine Gaines Heatwole. The two girls were first cousins and best friends of Caroline Coakley Kiracofe, Lucy's daughter.

[332] Gaines file, Rockingham Historical Society, Dayton, VA.

[333] *Rockingham County Index to Marriage Registers, A-K*, Bond 785.

[334] "It is said that the successful conclusion of the War of 1812 was celebrated by the people of Rockingham at a barbecue on the top of Mole Hill. An ox-roast was the chief feature, the poor beast having been spared long enough to carry his own weight to the summit." (Rev. L. J. Heatwole, as quoted by Wayland, *Rockingham County,* p. 437.)

Caroline Virginia Coakley, (12/25/1840-4/11/1917) whom she named for the beloved county the family had left; m. Nelson Bittle Kiracofe (11/6/1838-1/4/1874) 8/30/1860, who died from an infection which resulted from a war wound.

Mariah Coakley (1843-8/4/1870)

James Austin Coakley (1844-1864); lost in Civil War.

Peachy Rush Coakley (8/26/1847-3/25/1924) m. (1)Catherine V. Cline (2)Lelia M. Good

William Henry Coakley- (-7/1864) Civil War soldier who was seriously wounded and died of pneumonia

I have been told that Lucy's husband, Austin, died while serving in the Civil War. This is clearly not the case, as proven by Caroline's marriage announcement, written in 1860, in which he was said to be deceased. After his death Lucy continued to appear in later censuses. She had survived the loss of her husband, before 1860, and three sons, and at least one son-in-law as a direct result of the Civil War. What terrible tragedy!

Lucy's daughter, Caroline, was forced to sell her house and lot after the death of her husband in 1874. The acreage had already been whittled away in small parcels. Lucy, herself, had bought one five acre parcel from Caroline and Nelson for $117.00 in 1871. Caroline, with her three children, were clearly experiencing uncertain times. It seems likely that they returned to live with her mother until Lucy's death three years later.

d. when her granddaughter, Ada Florence Kiracofe, was nine years old, in 1879, in Rockingham County.

buried, with Austin, at the Bank Church (Mennonite) in a grave that has lost its marker. I have photographed the area in which these graves are located.

G-g-grandmother- 5th generation

Marion Coakley in his correspondence said someone had told him that "Lucy P. Gaines named her son Joseph after grandfathers." Joseph's middle name was Benjamin and that was Austin's grandfather's name. So far Frances Manspile's parents are unproven, but neither a Joseph nor a Benjamin Manspile has been located.

". . .(S)ome of my grandmother's Gaines family were co-owners of

Sipe and Gaines (store) at Lilly- I heard it discussed as a child. . .We always knew Mr. Will Sipe and his family at Bridgewater." [335]

George Hendrick Kirshof

b. 10/1/1791 George's baptism is noted at the Old Pine Lutheran and Reform Church, west of Mt. Jackson, now in Shenandoah County.[336]

son of **John Frederick Kirshof** (-c1830), immigrant, and **Catherine Wacker (Bowman)** (-bef1795)

brother of John Kirshof m. Susan Waddle 8/3/1810
Henry Kirshof m. Margaret Detamore 3/26/1814
Elizabeth Kirshof (1787-) m. Adam Firebaugh 1808; (2)George Fifer
Christiana Kirshof m. Jacob Price 1/25/1811
Mary Kirshof m. Henry Wilfong 8/26/1813
half-brother of Frederick Kirshof m. Elizabeth Heifner 6/18/1820
Anna Kirshof m. Elijah Messersmith 10/16/1818
Susannah Kirshof m. Jacob Huffer 4/29/1820
Catherine Kirshof m. Samuel Huffer 1/12/1827
Barbara Kirshof m. James Fleming 11/4/1830
Hannah Kirshof m. Peter Fifer 3/17/183_
Andrew Kirshof m. Sarah Saunders 12/1/1831
Jacob Kirshof m. (1)Ann Propst; (2)Matilda Collins 1850
Most of these marriages have been verified in Augusta County; the rest in Rockingham County.

During Communion on 12/29/1833 at the Mossy Creek Presbyterian Church ". . . the following persons (among others) were received on examination and profession of faith: George Kirkhoff, Henry Kirkhoff, Barbara Anne Kirkhoff, Catherine Kirkhoff and Benjamin Kirkhoff. . . ." These were members of George's family.

By 4/10/1841 George, Henry and Barbara ". . .had been removed or (were) connected with other churches." George was "connected" with the Church of the Brethren. By this time the spelling of the name had evolved into Karicofe. [337]

---

[335] Blanche Miller Wilson's notes.
[336] Arthur Pierson Kelly, *200 Years in the Shenandoah Valley*, quoted by Miller, p. 2.
[337] Blair, *Mossy Creek*, pp. 263, 274.

m. (1)**Janey Waddle** (1794-c1873) (The name **Christinia** is given in the baptismal records of the Old Emmanuel Lutheran and Reform Church) 1817; (2)Mary Ann__; according to death records in the Augusta County Courthouse, she survived George.[338]

father of Barbara Ann Kiracofe m. Silas Vance 6/27/1839
Mary Kiracofe m. Henry Andrew c1832
John H. Kiracofe m. Susannah Hisey
Elizabeth "Betty" Kiracofe m. Reuben Rawley 11/30/1846
Martha Jane Kiracofe m. George McQuaine 8/29/1844[339]
Margaret Kiracofe died in youth.
Benjamin I. Kiracofe m. Mary Blakemore
James McCutcheon Kiracofe (4/6/1832-4/4/1891) m. Annie Elizabeth Beard
Nelson Bittle Kiracofe (11/6/1838-1/4/1874) m. Caroline Virginia Coakley (12/25/1840-4/11/1917)
George Madison Kiracofe m. Margaret Armstrong

George H. Kirshof, along with his brother, Henry, was administrator of their father's estate in 1830. George's father, John Frederick Karricaffe, had left his "plantation that is now occupied by George Karricaffe" to his wife "Barberry Karricaffe," (second wife, Barbara Koontz). "The residue of my estate both real and personal, I desire to be equally divided between all my children." On 12/20/1832 it was declared that the settlement had been correctly done and "aught to be allowed."

George later owned a parcel of land (owned more recently by Roland McNett), which lay on Thorny Branch west of Sangerville.

"In the 1850 Augusta County Census Records, George was listed as worth $4,500."[340] That figure was substantial in that time.

On 1/21/1873, the fragment of a letter from 82 year old George says, ". . .to drop you a few lines to let you know how I am. I am not well and have not been for some time but hope these few lines may find you all in good health. You wish to know when my sale would be. I have not been able to do

---

[338] Miller, pp. 9-20.
[339] There is a fragment of a letter written by Martha Jane on the reverse of George Kiracofe's letter to his son, Nelson Bittle Kiracofe. A comparison of the educational achievement of the two siblings indicates that education for women was still not in vogue.
[340] Miller, pp. 16-20, 265-328.

anything nor to get anybody to do for me. I want it tended to as soon as possible. You said Andrew Kiracofe had some money for me. I should be glad to get it. You said something also about the line fence. As soon as the weather (improves) and I am able I will come down and show him all about it. No more at present but Peace. Yours, George Kiracofe." His daughter, adding a note says all are well "except father."

d. 7/12/1877 on Wetstons Draft

As an 86-year-old in 1877, he had lived a very long life.

"George is buried in a marked grave down by the ravine in the Old Emmanuel Lutheran and Reform Cemetery." His brother, Henry, had given the land on which Emmanuel Church at Sangerville was built in 1832.

"In the death records in the Augusta County Courthouse, it states George was survived by his wife Mary Ann. It also states (erroneously) that his father was Jacob Kiracofe."[341]

G-g-grandfather- 5th generation

This man's adult life spanned the period from 1820 to 1860, and more. During this period the new nation was realizing its "political independence after the Revolution, and its commercial independence after the war of 1812; it was now achieving its industrial independence through the development of manufactures, the invention of agricultural machinery, and the improvement of transportation facilities; and was preparing to realize its intellectual independence, as well, by thinking for itself and writing books that were no longer fashioned upon European models. Within this period fall the Missouri Compromise, the enunciation of the Monroe Doctrine, South Carolina nullification, the abolition movement, the economic crisis of 1837, the Mexican War, the Compromise of 1850, John Brown's Raid, and the beginning of secession.

"In Rockingham County the main currents of national movements were being felt and registered, and at the same time affairs of State and local interest were riding upon high tides. Population was increasing and being widely distributed by emigration; social institutions were being developed, law systems were being perfected, military organizations were being maintained, and natural resources were being exploited. It was a time frequently marked by sharp political agitation, the constitution of the State being rewritten twice

[341] Miller, p. 265.

within the period, once in 1829-30, again in 1850-51. Churches were being extended, and not a little attention was being directed toward general education, but the chief local movements of the time appear to have been political, social, and economic, rather than religious or literary. It was a time of 'internal improvements'-some railroads being projected, some towns perhaps being 'boomed,' several banks being established, many roads being constructed, and a large number of bridges being erected. In the decade preceding the crisis of 1837 the building of turnpikes was especially in vogue, the Valley Turnpike and the one leading from Harrisonburg to Warm Springs both being constructed within that time. The Rockingham Turnpike, leading from Harrisonburg eastward toward Swift Run Gap, was not built until some years later, but still within the period under consideration. The roads, good and bad, were being utilized, not only for neighborhood communication and transportation, but also for a great wagon trade with Scottsville, Fredericksburg, Winchester, and other markets; and the Shenandoah River at the same time was a throbbing channel of navigation between the eastern sections of the county and the cities on the Potomac."[342]

Christinia "Janey" Waddle

b. in 1794

daughter of **John Waddle** (4/12/1761-8/5/1852) and **Elizabeth Erwin** (c1753-2/11/1834)

baptized in the Old Emmanuel Lutheran and Reform Church. Her name was given as **Christinia** in the baptismal records. On 11/8/1813 Jane Waddell, and her sister Susanna, (probably the Susan listed here) proved their "knowledge of the way of salvation and their faith in Christ," and were admitted as members of Mossy Creek Presbyterian Church.[343]

sister of Susan Waddle m. John Kiracofe, her husband's brother
Mary Waddle m. Jacob Bumgarner 6/28/1785
James Waddle m. Uriah Stanforth of Greenbrier County, now West Virginia
Elizabeth Waddle m. Richard Curry of Highland County

[342] Wayland, *Rockingham County*, pp. 112-113.
[343] Charles W. Blair, *Mossy Creek*, p. 255.

John Wooddle m. Elizabeth Bodkin of Rockingham County
William Wooddle m. Mary Curry of Highland County
Benjamin Waddle who d. at two years
Irvine Wooddle m. Annie Michael of Augusta County
Bernard Waddle m. Lydia Michael of Augusta County

Elizabeth, James, and Polly (a nickname often used for the name Mary) were members of Mossy Creek, along with Susanna and Jane Woodall, at the time of the "June sacramental occasion" in May of 1817.

m. **George Hendrick Kirshof** (10/1/1791-7/12/1877) 1817, as verified by Augusta County Marriage Records

mother of Barbara Ann Kirshof m. Silas Vance 6/27/1839
Mary Kirshof m. Henry Andrew c1832
John H. Kirshof m. Susannah Hisey
Elizabeth "Betty" Kirshof m. Reuben Rawley 11/30/1846
Martha Jane Kirshof m. George McQuaine 8/29/1844
(Her father lived with her when he was elderly.)
Margaret Kirshof died in her youth.
Benjamin I. Kirshof m. Mary Blakemore
James McCutchen Kirshof (4/6/1832-4/4/1891) m. Annie Elizabeth Beard
Nelson Bittle Kirshof (11/6/1839-1/4/1874) m. Caroline Virginia Coakley (12/25/1840-4/11/1917) 8/30/1860
George Madison Kirshof m. Margaret Armstrong

d. c1873

Based on notes in a leather-bound notebook which belonged to her son, Nelson Bittle Kiracofe, she had given birth to thirteen children, nine of whom were living; she had seventy grandchildren and fifteen g-grandchildren; and she had been married for 56 years and a member of the church for fifty of those years.

It is believed that Janey was buried by George in an unmarked grave.

G-g-grandmother- 5th generation

Chapter 5
Generation 4

This is a generation whose lives should seem less remote to those of us living in the 21st Century. The names of those involved in the world's progress, as well as in the world's crises, will be more familiar. One hundred and fifty years: what is that in the history of the world?[344]

- Abraham Lincoln was just entering politics as a member of the Illinois legislature in 1834 when *The Hunchback of Notre Dame* by Victor Hugo was a best seller.
- Halley's Comet reappeared in 1835. Daniel Miller (III) was nine years old at the time.
- That year there were 1,098 miles of railroad in America, and Phineas T. Barnum was starting a career that would make good use of them.
- Davy Crockett was killed at the Alamo in 1836.
- Martin Van Buren was inaugurated as the eighth President in 1837 and Victoria became the Queen of Great Britain.
- Jenny Lind, "the Swedish nightingale" made her debut in Stockholm and Charles Dickens's *Oliver Twist* was a bestseller in 1838. And Nelson Bittle Kiracofe was born.
- The population of the world was growing: Great Britain, 18.5 million; Ireland, 8 million; America, 17 million.
- Edgar Allan Poe wrote his first detective story, "The Murders of the Rue Morgue."
- Iowa became a state in 1846 as war and negotiations continued between the United States and Mexico over New Mexico, Texas, California, Utah, Nevada and Arizona.
- In 1848 gold was discovered in California. The rush was on!
- Dickens and Poe were busy writing, as were Nathaniel Hawthorne, William Wordsworth, Robert Louis Stevenson, Guy de Maupassant, and Herman Melville.
- David Livingstone was exploring Africa in 1852.
- In New York in 1853 Heinrich E. Steinweg (Henry Steinway), with three of his sons, began manufacturing pianos.That same year vaccination against smallpox was made compulsory in Great Britain. That was also the year Daniel and Nancy Shickel Miller were married.
- Ferdinand de Lesseps was commissioned by France to build the Suez Canal in 1855.

---

[344] Grun, pp. 398-450.

- In 1857, while Great Britain was conquering India and destroying the Chinese fleet, one of her generals, Robert Baden-Powell, was founding the Boy Scout movement.
- In 1859 Charles Darwin published *On the Origin of Species by Natural Selection*. In the same year Dickens wrote *A Tale of Two Cities*; Tennyson the *Idylls of the King,* and Oliver Wendell Holmes *The Autocrat at the Breakfast Table*.
- Caroline Coakley and Nelson Kiracofe were married in 1860. The United States had by that time grown to a nation of 32 million. It was about to become embroiled in the War Between the States. Even as war loomed, Americans created: Edward Everett Hale wrote *Man Without a Country*; Ebenezer Butterick developed the first dress pattern; the National Academy of Sciences was founded in Washington, D. C.; and Congress established free city mail delivery, all in 1863.
- The Thirteenth Amendment to the Constitution abolished slavery in 1865.
- In 1867 Russia sold Alaska to the United States for $7,200,000. My! How numbers had grown! And speaking of numbers, in 1871 there were 39 million people in the United States; in Germany 41 million; in Great Britain 26 million; and in France 36 million.
- By 1872 the General Amnesty Act had pardoned most ex-Confederates.
- In 1876-77 Alexander Graham Bell invented the telephone and Edison the phonograph.
- The cathedral in Cologne, Germany, begun in 1248, was finished in 1880.
- Also in 1880, Dostoevsky wrote *The Brothers Karamazov*; Englishmen Gilbert and Sullivan wrote *The Pirates of Penzance*; Frenchman Rodin sculpted *The Thinker*; and New York City streets were first lit by electricity. And although they aren't works of art, it is notable that, for the first time, one could buy cans of fruits and meats in stores!
- In 1882 Robert Louis Stevenson completed *Treasure Island* while the first skyscraper- 10 stories high!- was being constructed in Chicago.
- In New York Harbor the Statue of Liberty was dedicated in 1886.
- In 1887 Sir Arthur Conan Doyle wrote *A Study in Scarlet*, his first Sherlock Holmes mystery. A year later "Jack the Ripper" began his reign of terror, creating a mystery which has yet to be solved in London.
- Benjamin Harrison was president in 1889 when the Dakotas, Montana, and Washington became states.
- The 1890's produced many innovations: Henry Ford's first car, Lumiere's motion-picture camera, Roentgen's x-rays, and my mother, Blanche Odessa Miller, born 11/30/1896.

Daniel Miller (III)

b. 1/21/1826

son of **Rev. Joseph Miller** (3/23/1787-11/29/1851) and **Elizabeth "Betsy" Thomas** (7/10/1792-11/21/1849)

Daniel, the tenth of Joseph's and Betsy's sixteen children, was undoubtedly born in the house that straddled a generous spring just east of the Beaver Creek Church of the Brethren. My sisters and I have visited the site and have seen the spring, though the house on Silver Creek no longer stands.

brother of Annie Miller (1813-9/15/1897) m. Jacob Sanger (1819-1886) 6/28/1832
Susan Miller (1814-1893) m. Henry Sanger (1812-1872) 5/17/1834
Jacob Miller (1815-1883) m. Fannie Wine (-8/12/1852) 4/5/1837
Abraham Miller (3/1/1817-7/19/1882) m. Sarah Shickel (5/9/1818-8/7/1872) 12/1839
Regina Miller (5/4/1818-5/15/1890) m. Jacob Shickel (6/16/1816-8/28/1897) 11/5/1840
Elizabeth Miller (12/5/1819-7/1/1905) m. Joel Glick (1821-1880) 3/13/1845
Barbara Miller (1821-1902) did not marry
Joseph T. Miller (2/23/1823-1/20/1862) m. Barbara Glick (1829-1912) 11/2/1848
Sarah Miller (10/16/1824-11/9/1903) m. Samuel G. Glick (1823-1884) 8/26/1847
Peter Miller (2/12/1828-1/7/1904) m. (1)Elizabeth Stautamyer (1832-1880) 10/1/1857; (2) Mary C. Kanost (1844-1904) 5/18/1882.
stillborn infant (twin) (5/5/1830)
John J. Miller (twin) (5/5/1830-8/14/1896) m. (1)Magdalene Sanger (1836-1881) 9/3/1857; (2)Amanda L. Caricofe (1840-1904) 11/19/1885.
Katherine Miller (1831-1832)
Lydia Miller (5/10/1832-3/15/1910) m. Daniel Brower (1815-1893) 2/21/1875
Henry Miller (3/11/1836-1/20/1890) m. Sarah Catherine Wright[345] (1836-1913) 9/27/1860

[345] Glick, pp. xv-xvi.

m. **Nancy Shickel** (4/22/1832-3/6/1895) 4/13/1853.

father of Sarah F. Miller (3/24/1854-2/7/1860)
Elizabeth Susan Miller (1/2/1856-2/7/1928) m. Elder Anthony Arnold Miller (3/13/1851-10/27/1935) 1875
Peter Shickel Miller (1/22/1858-10/13/1930) m. Maria Susan Roof (6/27/1862-2/13/1933) 10/281883
William Henry Miller (7/2/1860-1/22/1944) m. Lula McLaughlin (12/5/1869-5/11/1960) 12/25/1895 This is Uncle Will- Edna's and Janie's father.
Jacob Thomas Miller (7/31/1862-10/1/1894) m. Maude Rebecca Harnsberger (4/2/1872-9/1934) 1891
Benjamin Kerlin Miller (1/6/1865-4/15/1926) m. Ada Florence Kiracofe (8/2/1870-4/24/1943) 12/21/1893
Lydia Barbara Miller (2/17/1867-4/14/1949) m. William Lee Beard 1890
Mary Catherine Miller (3/15/1870-12/14/1920) m. William Minor Miller (8/10/1867-2/17/1944) 1892 (Roy Miller's parents; Charles's grandparents)
Nannie J. Miller (10/11/1872-11/18/1936) m. William Minor Miller (deceased sister's husband) 1922[346]
Joseph Daniel Brower Miller (12/30/1874-12/1/1911)[347] unmarried

Daniel Miller was an elder of the Brethren Church, a farmer, and perhaps a cabinetmaker. At the very least he built an impressive cherry desk which now belongs to his g-grandson, Charles Miller.

Galen Miller, first cousin of my mother, in his 90's at the time Leila Maxwell Miller and I interviewed him in 1995, remembered the Daniel Millers, who were his grandparents. He recalled that they raised strawberries and melons for sale at the market. He remembered when they sold watermelons on the courthouse "market" square in Harrisonburg, as was the custom of the time.

---

[346] Glick, pp. 30-33.
[347] Uncle Joe was the youngest of Daniel's sons and unmarried. He probably spent a bit more time with his nieces and nephews than did most of the others of Daniel's family. Whatever the case, he was definitely a favorite of Blanche Miller and her brothers. They looked forward to his visits and, as little children will do, made up a singsong rhyme with which to tease him and show their affection. It resulted from something Blanche's infant brother had said to Uncle Joe on one occasion, and Mother told us of it, more than once- a fond childhood memory surfacing for a moment's reflection. Lenford had reported to him the tragic loss of a duck, "Duckity-Do-Da-Duckity-Died." They were grief-stricken when Uncle Joe was killed in a sawmill accident when they were still young.

The Daniel Miller (III) home:
Birthplace of Benjamin Kerlin Miller and his daughter Blanche Odessa Miller

Daniel built a most impressive house for Nancy and their family. It was three stories and rises today, as then, near a spring and against a high hill between Bridgewater and Spring Creek on the farm now known as the "Jordan" place. My mother was born in that house and told of the immense kitchen on the ground floor with a comparable dining area, and of the "dormitory" arrangement on the third floor. Having been raised as one among sixteen, Daniel must have felt that a big family needed special accomodation. It seems there were two sets of stairs to the third floor, and two "sides" of that area. One was for the boys of the family, the other for girls.

The family attended Beaver Creek Church of the Brethren, a short drive by horse and buggy.

"Many elders and ministers served the Beaver Creek churches (Beaver Creek and Elk Run) from the beginning in 1828 until the present. The following is a list of these servants of God with dates as available:

Frederick Sherfy 1844-1889
Daniel Miller (Elk Run)
Peter S. Thomas 1857-1930"[348]

[348] Robert E. Houff, *One Hundred and Twenty-five Years for Christ, 1828-1953: A History of the Beaver Creek Congregation*, 1952, pp. 5-6.

Believed to be Daniel Miller (III)

Believed to be Nancy Shickel

Charles Miller with the cupboard built by
Great-grandfather Daniel Miller

The Miller family contributed significantly to the founding and establishment of the Beaver Creek Church of the Brethren. There were "Two deeds of importance (to the church), dated in the year 1876 and recorded in the Rockingham County Court House. . . . Both deeds were made on May 23, 1876. The first was. . .forty-nine square poles of land from Jacob S. Miller and wife Elizabeth to the trustees of the church, Samuel Wine, Daniel Miller and Samuel Glick, the land to be used for a burial ground and for hitching ground.[349]

"The second. . .fifty-four square poles of land from Martin P. Miller and wife Rebecca and from Samuel A. Miller and wife Catherine to the trustees. . .Samuel Wine, Daniel Miller and Samuel Glick." [350]

On pages ten and eleven of the Houff history mentioned above there are accounts of three other deeds representing land given by several people to Beaver Creek Church "for the permanent use of the church" in 1885. Daniel Miller was still among the trustees of the church at that time.

As mentioned elsewhere, the Brethren were zealous in their faith and anxious to share it with others on the frontier. They spent considerable time and energy trying to develop Brethren communities in distant areas. One such effort reached into Pocahontas County, in what is now West Virginia.

One Uriah Hevener, who had settled in the area of Arbovale, built a "large two and one-half story hewed log house, which was used for many years down to the twentieth century for religious services in the community." Many "faithful ministers rode out from the Valley of Virginia including John Kline, Abram Thomas, Joseph A. and Daniel Miller. . .three generations of Martin (Martain) Millers, and others less specifically named including. . . Garbers (and) Drivers. . ."[351]

Pacifists such as Daniel and his people do not get involved in warfare, so little needs to be said here of the War Between the States, which Daniel's life spanned. He was 35 years of age when it began.

One of the most visible issues in this war was, of course, the slavery issue. The Brethren had been sensitive to the injustice of slavery from the time they arrived in the colonies. From the earliest days they were exceedingly strict on the subject. No member of the church was allowed to own, or even to hire, slaves. One area bishop, in enforcing this rule, is said to have expelled

---

349 There were no motorized vehicles in this time. Parking was required, however, for the black buggies or surreys that brought the families to church, and for the handsome steeds that powered them. Such parking lots, though seldom seen, are a wonderful sight!

350 Houff, *ibid.*, pp. 9-10.

351 Sappington, pp. 150-151.

from the church his own father-in-law, one of the leading citizens of Augusta County.[352] Members had, over the years, been instrumental in freeing many enslaved people, although doing the right thing often created misunderstanding in the communities in which they lived.

The Lutheran Tennessee Synod, a body with whom the Dunkers of the Valley of Virginia were associated, had issued a position against slavery in 1822, in advance of other religious groups. This group decreed, "That (slavery) is to be regarded as a great evil in our land, and (this body of church leaders) desires the government, if it be possible, to devise some way by which this evil can be removed."[353] They also advised every minister "to admonish every master to treat his slaves properly, and to exercise his Christian duties towards them."[354]

"The church in Virginia had always been loyal to the general Brotherhood. This is evidenced by (the members' following of) her doctrines under the most adverse and trying conditions. The attitude on slavery gave a most difficult and perplexing problem for these churches to solve, and to uphold the principles of peace under the fearful scourge of the war in the South was an ordeal that few could have withstood. The record of what the Virginia Brethren endured during the war is one of great heroism and Christian fidelity. It reached its climax in the martyrdom of one of the state's greatest leaders, Elder John Kline."[355]

d. 3/8/1900 at age 74

buried at Beaver Creek Church near Spring Creek, Virginia.

The inscription on his tombstone says, in part:

"Dearest Father
We have laid Thee
in the peace. . ."

Daniel Miller was very even-handed in the writing of his will: each child was to be treated alike and the grandchildren whose parents had died were not to be excluded. He asked for a tombstone similar to the one at his wife's grave. "I direct," he decreed, "that my children may by mutual consent and agreement divide all my estate as aforesaid without any administration or order of court, and record such division as a final and full settlement of my estate by them. . ."

---

[352] Wayland, *German Element*, p. 181.
[353] *Henkel's History of the Tennessee Synod*, p. 52, as quoted by Wayland, *German Element*, p. 182.
[354] Wayland, *German Element*, p. 182.
[355] Winger, p. 69.

G-grandfather- 4th generation

Nancy Shickel

b. 4/22/1832

daughter of **Daniel Shickel, Sr**. (12/6/1789-7/15/1852) and **Elizabeth Driver** (6/5/1795-8/25/1853)

sister of Jacob Shickel (6/16/1816-8/28/1897)[356] m. Regina Miller 11/5/1840
Sarah Shickel (5/9/1818-8/7/1872) m. Abraham Miller 12/12/1839
Mary "Polly" Shickel (2/5/1826-6/12/1893) m. Benjamin F. Kerlin 1846
Barbara Shickel (12/11/1828-2/25/1907) m. Samuel Long 6/12/1851

m. **Daniel Miller** (1/21/1826-3/8/1900) 4/13/1853
Note that Nancy and two of her siblings, Jacob and Sarah, married members of the Joseph Miller family.

mother of Sarah F. Miller (3/24/1854-2/7/1860)
Elizabeth Susan Miller (1/2/1856-2/7/1928) m. Elder Anthony Arnold Miller (3/13/1851-10/27/1935) 1875
Peter Shickel Miller (1/22/1858-10/13/1930) m. Marie Susan Roof (6/27/1862-2/13/1933) 10/28/1883
William Henry Miller (7/2/1860-1/22/1944) m. Lula McLaughlin (12/5/1869-5/11/1960) 12/25/1895 (parents of Edna and Janie)
Jacob Thomas Miller (7/31/1862-10/1/1894) m. Maude Rebecca Harnsberger (4/2/1872-9/1934) 12/21/1893
Benjamin Kerlin Miller (1/6/1865-4/15/1926) m. Ada Florence Kiracofe (8/2/1870-4/24/1943) 12/21/1893
Lydia Barbara Miller (2/17/1867-4/14/1949) m. William Lee Beard 1890
Mary Catherine Miller (3/15/1870-12/14/1920) m. William Minor Miller in 1892
Nannie J. Miller (10/11/1872-11/18/1936) m. William Minor Miller

[356] Nancy's brother, Jacob Shickel, operated a machine shop on Dry River. In 1878 he ordered a lathe which weighed 6300 pounds from Philadelphia. It was shipped by train and had to be taken from Harrisonburg to his shop by wagon! In his shop he did lathe work and made screws and bolts. (May, *Four Flags*, p. 445.)

1922, after her sister's death
Joseph Daniel Brower Miller (12/30/1874-12/1/1911) unmarried

Galen Miller reported that Nancy smoked a pipe. Her husband, Daniel, supposedly gave her a pound of tobacco every year for Christmas. I suspect that this was most unusual behavior for the elder and his wife! I wonder if this was a fact that was known beyond the family.

d. 3/6/1895

buried at Beaver Creek Church of the Brethren near Spring Creek, Virginia.
Her tombstone reports:

Nancy
Wife of
Daniel Miller
died
March 6, 1895
aged
62 yrs., 10 mos.,
& 15 ds.
We miss the kind and. . .
Thy fond and. . .
Obscured by. . .
We miss. . .

G-grandmother- 4th generation

Nelson Bittle Kiracofe

b. 11/6/1839

son of **George Henry Kiracofe** (George Hendrick Kirshof) (10/1/1791-7/12/1877) and **Jane Waddle** (Wooddell) (1794-c1873)

brother of Barbara Ann Kirshof m. Silas Vance 6/27/1839
Mary Kirshof m. Henry Andrew 1832
John H. Kirshof m. Susannah Hisey
Elizabeth "Betty" Kirshof m. Reuben Rawley 11/30/1846
Martha Jane Kirshof m. George McQuaine 8/29/1844 (Her father lived

with her in his old age. We have a letter written by her to Nelson Bittle Kiracofe.)

Margaret Kirshof died in her youth.

Benjamin I. Kirshof m. Mary Blakemore

George Madison Kirshof m. Margaret Armstrong

James McCutcheon Kirshof (4/6/1832-4/4/1891) m. Annie Elizabeth Beard (a letter from him to Nelson is included.) "Cutch" was the father of Josiah Andrew Kiracofe, who corresponded with Blanche Miller Wilson about their family.

m. **Caroline Virginia Coakley** (12/25/1840-4/11/1917) 8/30/1860

The Rockingham Register and Advertiser reported the wedding. The announcement read:

"Near Dayton, in this county, on the 30th of August, by Rev. Geo. V. Leech, Capt. N. B. Kiracofe, of Augusta County, and Miss Caroline Virginia, daughter of Austin Coakley, dec'd, of Rockingham Co."[357]

Notice that! *CAPT.* N. B.!! Having never heard that this gentleman had attained any particular rank, I went in search of his service record. I was unable to confirm the rank of captain and was advised that the title might have been one of affection and esteem that had no other merit. Perhaps this was the equivalent of the title of colonel in Kentucky. Regardless, his service record is this:

"Kiracofe, Nelson Bittle: Pvt., Co. D. B(orn) near Sangerville, Augusta Co., 1839. Resident of Sangerville. Enl(isted) Staunton 7/16/61. Deserted 8/5/61. Wrote denial in *Rockingham Recorder* 12/13/61. 'Came home sick with measles, now sick with fever. Can be found at residence of Lucy Coakley near Mole Hill, Rockingham Co' "[358] Lucy Coakley, of course, was his mother-in-law, and this home is likely where his pregnant wife, Caroline, was staying, and where his firstborn was expected to arrive at any time.

It is far from uncommon to find soldiers during the War Between the States who were said to have deserted or to be "away without leave." They were often encamped close enough to their homes to know what transpired there, and close enough to make a quick trip home when it was time to plant the crops or handle some other business. Nelson may have needed to be on hand at the time of the birth of his first child. On the other hand, it would have been unwise to take measles home to Caroline and the unborn child, though it

---

[357] Dorothy A. Boyd-Rush, *Marriage Notices from Extant Issues of the "Rockingham Register," Harrisonburg, Virginia, 1822-1870* (Heritage Books, Inc., 1993), p. 246.

[358] Robert J. Driver, ed., *52nd Virginia Infantry* (Lynchburg, VA, H. E. Howard, 1986), p. 127.

is unlikely that the danger of that was fully understood at that time.

There were differing reactions to desertion. Stonewall Jackson placed deserters before a firing squad. Nelson seems to have suffered no ill effects, apparently as a result of his published explanation; his brother "Cutch" was fined six dollars the *second* time he deserted.

Nelson Bittle Kiracofe wrote to his parents from the battlefield, from a "Camp Near Morefield June 24, 1864:"
"Dear Father and Mother

"I take up my pen to drop you a few lines to let you know how and where I am. We reached the South Branch Valley last Saturday Night and found Lieut McNeill & his party camped near Morefield. They had had a fight with the Swamp Dragons at Petersburg that evening. He captured their train and killed eight and wounded a good many, but his victory over them cost us dearly. The Brave & gallant Lieut Dolan at the head of 25 men fell mortally wounded while gallantly leading a charge. The ball entered his cheek and lodged in the back part of his head. When he fell some of the Boys stopped to pay some attention to him but he told them not to mind him but to charge ahead after the Swamps. Franklin Davis of Petersburg was wounded through the (thigh). They were taken to a house close by and everything done that could be done for them. Lieut McNeill after taking care of his wounded fell back to Morefield. Here we joined him Saturday night or rather Sunday morning for we marched nearly all night. After graining our horses awhile we started for Petersburg Sunday morning about 7 oClock, but before we reached the place we received the sad intelligence that Lieut Dolan was dead. Determined to give his body a decent burial we went on but when we got within a half mile of the place the old Capt's keen eye discovered a party of Swamps on a high brushy hill behind the house intending to prevent us from taking the body away. But never at a loss to know what to do the Capt turned his course as though he was going to fall back but took around through the mountains and the first thing the Swamps knew we charged them in their rear killing 3 wounding several and routing the balance completely (We were dismounted and charged on foot.) Having thus taken possession of the body we started toward Morefield with it. We camped 4 miles above the town that night and the next morning just as we were about to start about 350 yankees made their appearance on the hill above Morefield on hunt of us. We of course had to leave the corpse and take to the brush. They came on up the road and went into Mr. Seymour's house where the body of Lieut Dolan was and opened the coffin and cursed the dead body and said they didn't intend to let us bury him but they left that evening and the people in the neighborhood buried him temporarily and on Wednesday we were able to get the body and take him to Morefield and we buried him in the cemetery with the honors of war in the presence of the largest crowd of people I ever saw upon such an occasion. Capt McNeill made a very beautiful and an appropriate speech at the grave. While he spoke tears rolled down his cheeks. I looked over the entire congregation and was not able to discover a dry face in the crowd. Thus I have attempted to give you a brief sketch of the death and burial of one of the Bravest and Noblest young officers that has ever fallen in defence of the south. Peace to his ashes.

Peaceful be his gentle slumber
Peaceful in the Grave so low
He no more will join our number
He no more our sorrows know

"I was quite unwell several days ago. I had the dysentery but I have got it completely checked and feel as well as ever this morning. We are having our horses shod today. That is a mighty good sign for something. I think we will turn up somewhere among the yankees before long. Don't be uneasy about me. I will try and take good care of myself. Show this to Brothers Bill and Ben and give them my best respects. If the mails are established you can send letters to Harrisonburg and I can get a letter from there any time as our Boys are frequently there. Tell Bill and Ben to write to me too and send me all the news and tell me about Cutch if you have heard anything. Nothing more but remain your affectionate son untill Death.

N.B Kiracofe

P.S. Direct to N. B. Kiracofe
McNeill's Rangers } To George & Jane Kiracofe
Harrisonburg, Va."

father of George Davis Kiracofe- "Uncle Davis" (8/29/1861-2/16/1942) m. (1)Margaret M. Kiracofe, his first cousin, known as "Aunt Mag" (12/29/1861-spring 1924); (2)Katherine Hottle of Mt. Solon- 20 years younger than he, who had been his wife's nurse. He was an ordained Methodist minister.

Virginia "Aunt Jennie" Lee Kiracofe (5/16/1864-5/19/1943) m. Clinton H. Leary 1883

Ada Florence Kiracofe (8/2/1870-4/24/1943) m. Benjamin Kerlin Miller (1/6/1865-4/15/1926) 12/21/1893

Mother told us a story about Nelson's return from war. A lady in the neighborhood who was known to read tea leaves advised the family that

Nelson would return home on a given day and that he would approach with his hands folded behind his back. The family thought it a strange forecast, but noted that this was indeed his manner as he approached. Whether this had anything to do with the fact that he had a wound in his hand I do not know, for it has only now occurred to me to ask. The seer might have gone on to prognosticate a short and difficult life for the returning man.

Nelson had ridden away on his horse to serve in the cavalry. He walked home. He had left a prosperous little community which was in turmoil because of the perceived oppression of a "foreign" power. He returned to a defeated community which had been sacked, indeed burned, as the war swept back and forth over it. Farms were barren land; livestock was rare; buildings were destroyed. The money of the South was worthless. He had an injury which would not heal and which, by his admission, sapped his strength. And life must go on.

Records indicate that Nelson was "paroled" on 5/18/1865. I believe this was a part of the repatriation process, though the dates given below are not the same. He is said to have "Enl(listed) McNeil's Rangers 3/10/1863 . . .5'11", dark complexion, dark hair, hazel eyes."[359]

On 7/18/1865, N. B. *Caricofe* signed his repatriation papers before James H. Callison, Notary Public of Augusta County. In the signing he spelled his name incorrectly. That was probably the easiest way to get the job done without a hassle, and this ceremony must have been the equivalent of a bitter pill. The document stated that he did ". . . solemnly swear (or affirm)[360] that I will uphold and defend the Government of Virginia as restored by the Convention which assembled in Wheeling on the 11th day of June, 1861."[361]

After that Nelson got busy.

He became a minister. As early as 9/8/1866 he received a certificate which stated that he, ". . .having been duly recommended by the Class of which he is a member, and examined as required by the Discipline, is, in the judgment of the Quarterly Conference of Bridgewater Circuit a proper person to be licensed, and is hereby AUTHORIZED TO PREACH THE GOSPEL." This certificate was issued at Mt. Solon, Virginia.[362]

On 3/29/1872 he received a Certificate of Licensure, not a fancy document as was the authorization to preach, but a handwritten one on lined paper, representing more accurately the resources of the South during these

---

[359] Robert J. Driver, *52nd Virginia Infantry,* Addendum for the Second Edition, n.d., p. 196.

[360] The word *affirm* was doubtless used to make the document useful for the many Anabaptist conscientious objectors who were, and are, found in the area.

[361] From the original document.

[362] From the original document.

post-war years. It said that he, "...a member of the Christian Church of Dayton in Rockingham County, State of Virginia, has been carefully examined upon the various branches of learning as required by the government of the Christian Church, and has given satisfaction, and is licensed as a probationer to preach the Gospel of the Lord Jesus Christ, wherever the providence of God may call him."

The issuing body was the Executive Committee of the Valley of Virginia Churches Conference, and this license was "...subject to its satisfaction or rejection at its next annual session."

He was apparently successful as a probationer for not long after, on a date that has been lost from the document, he was granted a Certificate of Ordination, again hand-written. It states that "...Brother N. B. Kiracofe, having proved his gifts as a licentiate, having been recommended by the churches to which he has ministered, and having passed a satisfactory examination, as required by the government of the Christian Church, has been this day set apart and ordained to the office of an Elder, by prayer and the imposition of hands and is hereby authorized to administer the ordinances of the Church..." and the second page was lost.[363]

Related to this is a document signed by the Clerk of the Rockingham County Court in November 1873, allowing Nelson to celebrate the Rites of Matrimony. This document, beautifully penned, is written on lined ledger paper.

Nelson served churches at Antioch, Dayton, Rushville, and Linville, and possibly in other locations. Every evidence would indicate that he was exceedingly active during the few years of his service. There are sermon notes, numerous letters to and from fellow pastors, and various other papers. Two pastors in the Valley wrote asking him to come to help them with services. Not a great deal of money was to be had for this job, however. In the minutes from the Antioch Church Session Meeting on 12/7/1872, it is recorded that the purpose of the meeting is "...the adoption of some plan to secure a support for Rev. N. B. Kiracofe, our Pastor." A committee was appointed.

Long after his death his service as a minister in the Christian Church was reported as follows:

"Rev. N. B. Kiracofe

"Rev. N. B. Kiracofe was recommended for ordination at Valley Conference held at Soliloquy church in Shenandoah County, Virginia, and was solemnly set apart to the gospel ministry by the presbytery on Sunday 15th of October, 1872. He was chosen to preach the annual sermon before the next Conference, and appointed on the Executive committee. At the conference at

[363] From the original document.

Linville, he was appointed on the committee on Rules of Order and By-laws. In 1873, he delivered the annual sermon, and was chosen a delegate to the General Convention to meet the following May 1874.

"His ministerial career was brief. He was distinguished for his 'meekness, piety and efficiency' as one of the highest examples of Christian virtues and usefulness. He was one of the church's most earnest workers."[364]

In a further effort to support his family, he, and someone named A. A. Hess, bought "the entire right for Brigg's Patent Atmospheric Churn in the Counties of Rockingham, Shenandoah, Page, Warren, Clarke, Frederick, Berkeley and Jefferson, (and) would respectfully inform the citizens of those counties, that they have made arrangements to supply the INCREASING DEMAND! for this superior Churn. We also wish to sell the right for the six last named Counties. Persons wishing to engage in a pleasant and at the same time GOOD PAYING BUSINESS will find it to their interest to apply to us at once. . . .All persons are cautioned against manufacturing, selling or using this Churn without authority from us or our authorized Agents within the above Counties." This flyer, professionally printed, is signed *KIRACOFF*, HESS & CO. and dated 9/1/1870. Poor Nelson! Even here the name is badly spelled![365]

Isaac A Sheppard & Co., of The Excelsior Stove Works and Hollow Ware Foundry of Baltimore courted his business before the ink was dry on the document mentioned above. On 6/11/1870, Sheppard, hearing of Nelson's acquisition of his rights to the Atmospheric Churn, wrote that "Mr. W. W. Briggs has employed us to make his churn casting and has fixed the price at .60 (cents) per set payable on delivery. When you need casting we would be pleased to have a line."[366] By 9/9/1870 Mr. Sheppard was sending a slightly longer letter, this time a complaint that he had not received payment for castings sent to Nelson.[367] In July Nelson had written to his brother James that he ". . .had expected to be up before this time but I have been busy harvesting for some time and am now trying to get my churns under way. We have ordered a lot from Baltimore which will be here this week. I also have a lot in Dayton which I will have ready for sale soon. I sold one this evening in Dayton to a Mrs. Bowman. . .for six dollars and have some 20 or 25 orders to fill at the same price. I believe its a right 'gooder' thing but the great trouble is to get started."

---

[364] P. J. Kernodle, *Lives of Christian Ministers* (Richmond, Central Publishing Co., 1909), pp. 380-381.
[365] From the original document.
[366] Letter from I. A. Sheppard to N. B. Kiracofe, Esq., June 11, 1970.
[367] Letter from I. A. Sheppard to N. B. Kiracofe, Esq., September 9, 1870.

He tried his hand at selling other things. There is a letter dated 5/28/1870 written to R. S. Bush & Co. It says, "Having seen your card in the papers in regard to your patented White Wire Clothesline and being at this time employed in selling several important inventions, I wish to know what inducements you will offer. Please send me your circular containing terms. Good references given if required. Yours respectfully, N. B. Kiracofe, Dayton, Rockingham Co., Virginia."

He was a farmer. There have been allusions to farming activity in previous paragraphs. It was customary for a householder with any land at all to, at the very least, plant a garden for the use of the family. Grocery stores as we know them did not exist. Nelson apparently had more than a garden to tend, for he refers to his *crops*. Between all of his other activities, when his health would permit, he would raise grain. There is but one indication of his purchase of land. A promissory note written by N. B. Kiracofe on 2/19/1869 declares "On or before the first day of January, 1870, I promise and bind myself & my heirs to pay unto Peachy R. Coakley on order the full sum of one hundred and eleven Dollars with interest from date, it being in payment for his interest in the Estate of Austin Coakley, Dec(eased) purchased of him by me and conveyed by deed bearing this date to me, the said interest in the said Estate being bound for the redemption of this bond. Given under my hand and seal. . ."

In a letter of 6/14/1870 he reports to his brother Benjamin Kiracofe, Esq. that . . . "the season so far has been remarkably wet. The wheat, however, is doing well, the oats promises to be very good. Corn is growing but there appears to be a Spirit of Rivalry between the corn weed and grass, each striving to outgrow the other. . . ."

At the same time he was writing about the vagaries of farming, Nelson was selling land. Recalling that the Valley was impoverished by war, and that Nelson had an ever-troubling wound in his hand, we might imagine that working large areas was difficult for him. On 3/24/1870 Nelson sold eight acres to Jacob Sanger;[368] on 9/18/1871, he sold five acres to Lucy Pendleton Gaines Coakley, widow of Austin Coakley and Caroline's mother, for $117.00;[369] on 9/18/1871, he sold nine acres of the home tract of Austin Coakley to John Paul.[370] This was undoubtedly land which he and Caroline had inherited. In a

---

[368] *Rockingham County Deed Book 5*, p. 302. For a description of this land, sold for $100, the deed suggests "lines and corners reference the Old Coakley Deed for partition." This was the land inherited by Caroline from her father.
[369] *Rockingham County Deed Book 8*, p. 112.
[370] *Ibid.*, p. 113.

final sale, 3/24/1875, Caroline, by then a widow with three small children, sold their home to her brother Peachy Coakley for $133.33.

In order to pay for a horse he had bought from Caroline's Uncle Daniel Coakley, Nelson dug a cistern ($4.00); dug a cellar ($4.00); helped him haul logs ($0.50); made fence for one day ($0.63 1/2); worked on the road for one day ($0.80); did some plowing ($0.50); and made 785 shingles ($9.28). After making 950 more shingles, he had whittled his indebtedness on the horse down to $2.99. He later cut 705 more shingles and thereafter owed only seventeen cents.

In a letter written to his brother Benjamin Kiracofe on 6/14/1870, Nelson Bittle playfully says, "I saw Robert Gains last Sunday and heard from you all. I suppose he told you that I was still trying to 'run' water up hill."

He did try that. With his brother, James M. "Cutch" Kiracofe, this enterprising man invented a pump and then corresponded with Messrs. Chipman, Hesmer & Co., 407 F Street, near Patent and Post Offices, Washington, and with William Michael, Jr. in the House of Representatives there.

There is interesting, and revealing, correspondence between "Cutch" and Nelson in 1871 and 1872: "Cutch" writes, "Dear Brother, I Rec(eive)d yours of the 26 Nov. was sorry to hear that you were complaining again; hope your health is better by this time. I was glad to hear that you are making some very important improvements in Hydraulics; I would like very much to see you at this time;. . .If you are not able to work and are able to ride come up and see me; I would like to have a long talk with you with regard to some very important improvements which I have discovered with regard to a combination of my Hydraulic Ingine and our proposed Force Pump. I have also discovered a very important feature in your self-feeding fountain for the use of Cisterns & Shallow Wells;. . ." Nelson replies on 2/17/1872 in handwriting that seems to have degenerated to a readable scrawl, "Dear Brother, I just today Recd your letter and hasten to reply. I must first state that I paid very dear for my trip up there as I took sick on Sunday night after I got home and have been sick nearly ever since. The first week I was confined entirely to the house but I am now knocking around again, but as bad as the weather is I would not like to start that far (to Mt. Solon) at present. I will come up, however, as soon as possible. I went to see Mr. Shickle and Mr. Airhart who told me that they could cast the Air vessels if they had the pattern but said it would cost a good deal to get them up. . .He says that he cast the heads on the posts of the fence around the Hospital in Staunton- they are hollow- but if we can get the one in

Mt. Solon (to do the job) we had better do that and try the thing. There are a number of persons waiting patiently for it. . .I will come up as soon as I feel able and the weather (improves). I can't stand exposure as I used to stand it. The balance are tolerable well. We have moved. Yours in haste. N. B. Kiracofe." From "Cutch": . . . "as regards our force pump, I sent to N. Y. for a circular of the submerged pump. I have recd it with drawings, specifications, the like. It is *nothing* like ours & nothing like the Scotch (pump) I sent you. I understand it now fully, so we are not beat yet. . .Very Respectfully, James M. Kiracofe."

In the letter of June 14, 1870 Nelson's outlook was unusually positive as he said of the pump business, "Well, as Wartman says, 'The skies are bright and brightening.' All the best men in the county here who have any knowledge of Hydraulics or Hydrostatics or any of the Laws of Philosophy which govern the operations of water works urge me to push the thing through and I am now making preparations to make a practical experiment with it. I am full of hope. But it is said that 'hope deferred maketh the heart sick,' so I want to push it through before I get sick of it." He goes on to say, "If Providence should favor you with a surplus of wheat this year, please remember me as I have no wheat out this year. We are well as usual. My respects to you all. Yours respectfully, N. B. Kiracofe."

Nelson did have some success with his pump. In his precisely kept suede pocket-sized notebook he notes that he made a pump costing $16.75 for William Messersmith, and in 1873, only months before he succumbed to the infection that he had brought home from the war, he noted that he had made $447.80 from the pump business.

Blanche Miller Wilson said of her mother that "She (Ada Florence, Nelson's daughter) sang beautifully and always insisted that her father taught her to sing."[371] We have evidence from original documents that Nelson Bittle organized and taught in singing schools, which provided a popular form of entertainment in those times.[372] Two of his contracts have survived, one for the Dayton School and one for the Rushville School. They are similar, reading, "N. Bittle Kiracofe respectfully proposes to teach local Church Music at

---

371 Letter from Blanche Miller Wilson, January 17, 1969.

372 "In November, 1867, a great musical convention was held in Harrisonburg, in Rev. T. D. Bell's (Presbyterian) church. The session continued for four days; 122 delegates from Harrisonburg, Dayton, McGaheysville, Bridgewater, New Erection, Singer's Glen, Cross Keys, Union church, and Edom, in Rockingham, and from Mossy Creek, Parnassus, Augusta church, and Bethel church in Augusta County, were present. A constitution was adopted and a permanent organization effected. Rev. T. D. Bell was elected president. . . .Subsequent meetings of the organization, which was known as the Valley Musical Association, were held at Mossy Creek (1868), Harrisonburg (1869), Bethel church (1870), and Tinkling Springs (1872)." (Wayland, *Rockingham*, pp. 39-40).

Dayton, Rockingham County, Va. The terms of tuition are $1.00 per Scholar or $3.00 per Family ticket for thirteen lessons to be paid at the close of the School. The Subscribers to Keep the (school)house in good order, etc. We the Subscribers do severally agree to comply with the above and pay the said Kiracofe the sums annexed to our respective names."

The more complete of the tattered contracts shows evidence of 27 scholars in the Dayton class. The lower half of the Rushville contract is missing.

Wayland, in his *History of Rockingham County*, asserts that there are "probably more people, old and young, in Rockingham who can sing, and who love music, than in any other section with the same population in America. . . Most of the people of the county are church-goers, and nearly every member of every congregation sings. Singing is a common pastime in many homes, and singing classes are frequently conducted in the churches as well as in the schools. . ."[373]

There was good reason for all of this activity on the part of this man who returned from the War Between the States with a wound that could not

Believed to be a picture of Nelson Bittle Kiracofe

[373] Wayland, *Rockingham*, p. 151.

be healed and who, with this wound, must have worked very long days to accomplish all that he did in the eight years he was given from the day he walked up the road with his hands clasped behind his back to the day of his death.

From Wayland's *History of Rockingham* we discover why Nelson Bittle may have worked so hard at so many endeavors: ". . .thousands of families were reduced to absolute want and on every hand the signs of desolation were pitiable in the extreme."[374]

d. 1/4/1874

". . .he died of blood poisoning when my mother (Ada Florence Kiracofe) was 3 years old."[375]

buried at the Bank (Mennonite) Church one mile north of Rushville (near Dayton). His tombstone says:

Nelson B. Kiracofe
Died January 4, 1874
Aged 35 yrs., 1 mo., 24 das.

G-grandfather- 4th generation

Caroline Virginia Coakley

b. 12/25/1840 in Rockingham County

daughter of **Austin F. Coakley** (bef1810-c1860) and **Lucy Pendleton Gaines** (c1810-1879)

sister of Robert Gaines Coakley (2/12/1833-7/28/1903), who lived at Flowery Gardens. Mother remembered going there when she was about five years of age, and passing by it when the family visited Great-Uncle Peachy; m. Mary Elizabeth Paine

---

[374] William Henry Harrison Kiracofe, husband of Lucinda Gaines Coakley, who was the daughter of Lucy's brother, James, experienced bankruptcy, leaving Nelson Bittle Kiracofe, Lucy's son-in-law, among many others as a creditor. It seems that a contract for the construction of a mile of the new North River Railroad was let in July of 1873 to William H. Kiracofe. Others held similar contracts. There had been great excitement as speeches were made and the oldest citizen of the town of Bridgewater threw out the first shovelful of dirt. The line was to extend westward as far as the Ohio River. Then in September came a major economic downturn. The notice that Nelson received concerning this bankruptcy was preserved in Great-grandmother Caroline's black handbag.

[375] From a letter from Blanche Miller Wilson.

Caroline Virginia Coakley (Kiracofe) and her daughter, Ada Florence Kiracofe

Mary Ann Coakley (4/24/1837-6/2/1889) m. John Mair/Nair
Joseph Benjamin Coakley (12/23/1838-8/10/1864) m. Caroline A. Carrier (9/16/_-)
Mariah Coakley (1843-8/4/1870)
James Austin Coakley (1844-1864) Confederate soldier
Peachy Rush Coakley (8/26/1847-3/25/1924) m. (1)Catherine V. Cline; (2)Lelia M. Good
William Henry Coakley (-7/1864)

m. **Nelson Bittle Kiracofe** (11/6/1838-1/4/1874) 8/30/1860[376]

The marriage announcement reported: "Near Dayton, in this county, on the 30th day of August, by Rev. Geo. V. Leech, Capt. N. B. Kiracofe, of Augusta County, and Miss Caroline Virginia, daughter of Austin Coakley,

[376] *Rockingham County Marriage Registry*, p. 182.

dec'd, of Rockingham County."[377]

mother of George Davis Kiracofe (8/29/1861-2/16/1942) m. (1)Margaret M. Kiracofe (12/29/1861-spring of 1924); (2)Katherine Hottle of Mt. Solon
Virginia Lee Kiracofe (5/16/1864-5/1943) m. Clinton H. Leary 1883
Ada Florence Kiracofe (8/2/1870-4/24/1943) m. Benjamin Kerlin Miller (1/6/1865-4/15/1926)[378] 12/21/1893

Like many other women, Caroline was left at home during the War Between the States when her husband, Nelson Bittle, went to fight. In the fall of 1864, due to an altercation resulting in the death of a member of General Sheridan's staff, Sheridan ordered that every house within 5 miles of the place where his officer was killed be burned. The people were warned of the burning, and they moved into surrounding fields, where they waited in the chill of an October night to see their homes go up in flames. Great-grandmother Caroline was one of these. Mother told us that she moved into the family's orchard to wait. But the house was not burned. For some reason the order to burn the area was withdrawn and the families were spared this particular tragedy.

One page in Nelson Bittle Kiracofe's little brown suede notebook enumerates items which he must surely have bought at the request of Caroline. Listed are: 3 1/2 yds K Jeanes *at* (25 *cents*) *equals* 87 1/2 *cents*; 3 yds Br cotton (15) 45; 3 yds Bl cotton (12 1/2) 37 1/2; 1 shirt Bosom 25; 1/2 doz buttons (15) 7 1/2; 3 1/4 yds calico (12 1/2) 41; 1 pencil (10) 10. The total cost was $2.52 1/2. I filled in the blanks for you for the first item. You must complete the rest yourself.

On 3/24/1875, one year, two months and twenty days after the death of her young husband, Caroline sold to her brother Peachy Coakley[379] a "house and lot," for which she received $133.33. It is believed that this was the home in which she lived with her three children, ranging at the time from five to fourteen years of age. It is likely that she took her children back to the home of Lucy, her mother, who lived until 1879. How she managed from 1879 until sometime after 1893, when she became part of the household of Ada Florence, her daughter, and B. K. Miller, we do not know. We do know that

---

[377] *Rockingham Register and Advertiser*, October 5, 1860 (Friday), p. 2.
[378] *Rockingham County Deed Book*, vol. 108, p. 373.
[379] *Rockingham County Deed Book 11*, p. 523.

she was very influential in the running of Ada's household and the raising of her children. Her memory was much adored by our mother.

One of the stories pertaining to Grandmother Caroline involved her baking of pies in the basement kitchen of the B. K. (former Daniel) Miller home. The children of Ben and Ada were playing as children will do when the younger brother, Lenford, became angry and chased Blanche, and, as I recall the tale, other children, around the big table on which the pies cooled. Lenford did not like the fact that other children could reach the table, perchance to pinch the goodies, and he could not. He expressed his displeasure by threatening the others with a large knife, until Grandmother Caroline rescued them.

Recalling the precariousness of the financial situation of almost everyone who survived the War Between the States in the Rockingham area, I chose to include portions of a letter that Caroline received about a year after Nelson's death.

"Dear Sister

. . .I am very much disappointed in John for not paying you your money. He wanted the (presumably Nelson's) tools and I let him have them with the understanding that he was to pay you and I am surprised that he has not paid you long ago. I am very sorry that I have no money at this time to send you. Times have been hard and I have not been able to collect anything that was coming to me. I have a job which I will commence in the morning for M. G. Harmin of Staunton which I will finish, if nothing happens, the first of the week after this next, and I expect (to receive) money from it. If John doesn't pay you before that time, I will pay you myself, as much as I can. I hope you may be able to make some arrangement until that time."

This concerned brother-in-law, James M. "Cutch" Kiracofe, invites her to ". . . come up as soon as you can. Get on the horse and ride up if your wagon is not in condition to run."[380] The letter was sent to Caroline at an address in Dale Enterprise, Virginia.

This was indeed a lean time for many, many families in Rockingham, in Virginia, in the South.

In one additional land transaction, on 3/20/1876, Caroline and her brother, Peachy, sold to Lewis Knicely land valued at $50.00.[381] Mother always spoke fondly of Uncle Peachy and recalled visiting him in the

---

[380] Letter from James McCutcheon Kiracofe/Kirshof to Caroline Virginia Coakley Kiracofe, 6/6/1875.

[381] *Rockingham County Deed Book 12*, p. 491.

Coakleytown area. It is possible that he did a great deal to enable his sister Caroline and her children to get through their difficult times.

"Grandmother (Caroline) had firsthand information on the Revolution. When speaking of hardships of the Civil War, she would invariably add 'but it wasn't nearly so bad as the other war (Revolution).' "[382] Considering her losses, it is difficult to imagine how the Revolutionary War could have had a greater impact on her life.

A small anecdote from the life of Caroline is revealed in a letter between two bubbly young cousins when Ada, the recipient, was seventeen years of age. Among the exhuberant cataloging of boys in which she is interested, Cousin Ida says, "Well I heard you all are boarding the school teacher." Just that. It doesn't take many words to suggest what Caroline did in order to make the money necessary to keep her little family going in the winter of 1887.

In August of 1915, Caroline, then in her 75th year, received a letter from her granddaughter, Blanche, then nineteen years of age. It has been stated that Caroline lived for years with Ada and Ben Miller and that she was a major influence in the lives of her grandchildren. At this moment, however, Caroline was in Wardensville, West Virginia with her son, Davis Kiracofe, and his ailing family. Blanche inquired as to their health, shared some news, and then added, "We are getting along fine and Mama said I should tell you not to worry at all about us and to stay just as long as you want to." As one reads the letter one gets the feeling that, on the contrary, Grandmother was very much missed and that Blanche would have preferred telling her to hurry home.

d. 4/11/1917 in Rockingham County.

buried at the Bank Church (Mennonite) near Dayton beside her husband.

The tombstone reports:

Caroline V.
Wife of N. B. Kiracofe
Born December 25, 1840
Died April 11, 1917

G-grandmother- 4th generation

[382] Letter from Blanche Miller Wilson.

"The Valley (had been) a highway of marching armies and an almost constant battlefield, from the beginning to the end. When the end came conditions may not have been quite so bad as some of its enemies desired: a crow could perhaps have found a few pickings here and there, especially if he had been of the vulture species; but the ruin was certainly complete enough. On October 7, 1864, Sheridan at Woodstock reported to Grant that he had destroyed over 2000 barns filled with wheat, hay, and farming implements; over 70 mills, filled with wheat and flour; that no less than 3000 sheep had been killed and issued to the troops; and that a large number of horses had been secured. Near Dayton and Harrisonburg he had burned all the houses in an area of five miles.[383]

". . .(S)ome people had to go out of the country, or from one locality to another, for a time, to keep from starving. And yet, in less than a generation afterward, a native of Rockingham, who had returned to his boyhood home, and had climbed to the top of Peaked Mountain to get a wide horizon, could write as follows:

" 'As I stood aloft gazing down on this prosperous valley, with its winding waterways and fertile meadow lands dotted thickly over with comfortable farmhouses and massive barns, with here and there a thriving town or village, I could but call up in contrast the devastated wastes left lying here on my departure in 1869. . . .Time and industry have prevailed; and, looking upon the present scenes of plenty and happy prosperity, without a knowledge of what has been, one would never dream of any time other than a thriving and peaceful one for the great Valley of Virginia.'[384]

"The remarkable and rapid recovery of the Shenandoah Valley has doubtless been due in large measure to the fact that the bulk of the losses that the people suffered during the war, aside from the long death-roll, was in property other than slaves; and to the fact that, apart from such material losses and sadly depleted numbers, they came out of the conflict much as they had entered it: taught in the habits of economy and with hands hardened to labor."[385]

It was in this remarkably restored place that Ben Miller and his wife, Ada, started their lives together. It was into this life that Blanche Odessa

---

[383] J. Lewis Peyton, *History of Augusta County, Virginia* (Bridgewater, VA, Charles R. Carrier, 1953), p. 239

[384] From the *Tuscola* (Ill.) *Review*, December 6, 1895, as quoted by Wayland, *German Element*, p. 187.

[385] Wayland, *German Element*, pp. 186-187.

Miller, and her brothers, Ted and Lenford, were born. It was one hundred years ago, more or less. Such a short time for so much change to have taken place.

Chapter 6
Generation 3

It is easy to relate to developments which occurred during the time in which our grandparents lived:[386]

- The War Between the States had just ended when, in 1865, in England, Lewis Dodgson created the fantasy we know as *Alice's Adventures in Wonderland* and Benjamin Kerlin Miller became a reality.
- Johann Strauss II had just written "The Blue Danube" when Ulysses S. Grant was elected President of the United States in 1868. That same year the Cincinnati Red Stockings became the first professional Baseball Club, and began the practice of wearing uniforms for play.
- During 1870, the year in which Ada Florence Kiracofe was born, Heinrich Schliemann began his excavation of ancient Troy.
- During that period, Jules Verne wrote *Twenty Thousand Leagues Under the Sea* and *Around the World in Eighty Days*; Verdi wrote the opera *Aida*; and P. T. Barnum opened "The Greatest Show on Earth."
- About the time Ben and Ada were wed, in 1893, there were tragedies for others around the world. There was a global influenza epidemic; a widespread famine in Russia; and an earthquake in Japan which killed as many as 10,000 people.
- In 1896, William McKinley was elected President, Utah became a state, the Klondike gold rush began, and Blanche Odessa Miller was born.
- By 1901 electricity was replacing steam as a source of energy.

Before he died in 1926, B. K. Miller had seen amazing happenings, such as

- man's first successful flight;
- the first railroad tunnel built under water;
- a successful expedition to the North Pole;
- the first broadcast of voice and music over radio;
- the first deep-sea research expedition;
- the return of Halley's comet in 1910;
- the first successful expedition to the South Pole;
- the development of jet propulsion and subsequent experiments in rocketry;
- the first farm tractor;
- the first transcontinental telephone call between New York and San Francisco, and the first wireless service between the United States and Japan.
- World War I.

---

[386] Grun, pp. 429-469.

The wedding portrait of Ada Florence Kiracofe (in white) and Benjamin Kerlin Miller

Beaver Creek Church of the Brethren: The Miller family church

Benjamin Kerlin Miller

b. 1/6/1865 at North River[387]

Blanche Miller Wilson, his daughter, reported in her notes that he was born on 1/9/1865. She really should have known, should she not? Regrettably, every issue cannot be resolved.

son of **Daniel Miller** (1/21/1826-3/8/1900) and **Nancy Shickel** (4/22/1832-3/6/1895)

brother of Sarah F. Miller (3/24/1854-2/7/1860)
Elizabeth Susan Miller (1/2/1856-2/7/1928) m. Elder Anthony Arnold Miller (3/13/1851-10/27/1935) 1875
Peter Shickel Miller (1/22/1858-10/13/1930) m. Marie Susan Roof (6/27/1862-2/13/1933) 10/28/1883
William Henry Miller (7/2/1860-1/22/1944) m. Lula McLaughlin (12/5/1869-5/11/1960) 12/25/1895 (parents of Edna Miller and Janie Meyerhoffer)
Jacob Thomas Miller (7/31/1862-10/1/1894) m. Maude Rebecca Harnsberger (4/2/1872-9/1934) 1891
Lydia Barbara Miller (2/17/1867-4/14/1949) m. William Lee Beard 1890
Mary Catherine Miller (3/15/1870-12/14/1920) m. William Minor Miller (8/10/1867-2/17/1944)(Roy Miller's parents) 1892.
Nannie J. Miller (10/11/1872-11/18/1936) m. William Minor Miller (deceased sister's husband)1922.
Joseph Daniel Brower Miller (12/30/1874-12/1/1911)

m. **Ada Florence Kiracofe** (8/2/1870-4/24/1943) 12/21/1893[388]

father of **Blanche Odessa Miller** (11/30/1896-3/27/1980) m. James Moore Wilson, Sr. (2/2/1898-3/18/1983) 6/2/1928
Lenford Patterson Miller (10/9/1900-7/1/1966) unm.
Lester Benjamin Miller (5/3/1905-7/30/1975) m. Miriam Elizabeth Neiland (11/16/1910-11/22/1970) 9/24/1949

"Mimi" and "Ted" were the proud parents of an adopted daughter, Elaine Neiland Miller (6/25/1956-) m. Thomas Bell, and the grandparents of Brittany and Justin Bell.

---

[387] *Rockingham County Register of Births 1862-1870*, p. 73.
[388] *Rockingham County Marriage Register, Book 2*, p. 89.

For some reason we don't know as much about our grandfather as we should. We know that his daughter, Blanche, loved him and remembered him fondly. She liked to tell of him trying to teach her to handle the horse and buggy, and she said that he did not want her to accept teaching positions away from home. Galen Miller told of how B. K. sent Lenford and himself one cold, snowy evening to drive Blanche back to her teaching location, possibly at McGaheysville. Galen recalled that they came back almost frozen.

On 12/15/1899 B. K. Miller, then 34 years of age and the father of a three-year-old Blanche, bought sixteen acres of land on the waters of North River, Beaver Creek, and Spring Branch from the estate of Samuel Cline. He paid $550 and committed himself to pay $150 on 3/1/1900, and a total of $400, guaranteed by bonds, at some unspecified date. He had paid off this indebtedness by 10/21/1901. He may have seen this purchase as a means to an end, however, for on 12/10/1901 B. K. exchanged this land and one dollar to Lydia Miller Beard and W. L. Beard, his sister and her husband, for their interest in the Daniel Miller place.[389]

Daniel Miller had, on 3/1/1899, sold his property to the Beards and to his son, Joseph Daniel Brower Miller, and they shared in the ownership. As of March of 1899 then, the land and home and appurtenances were owned by Uncle Joe, who was in the sawmill business in Georgia, and the Beards, who lived on the place. It is assumed that their father, Daniel Miller, also lived there with whichever child was in residence until his death in 1900.

On 9/6/1902 J. D. B. Miller sold his interest in the homeplace to B. K. for $1300 and interest, some portion thereof to be paid annually, with the full amount to be paid by 3/1/1909.[390] B. K. kept up a correspondence with his brother, and a few of those letters have somehow survived. Now and then the report on the farming operation is rosy, and Uncle Joe is urged to come home to enjoy the produce; in other instances there is apology for the money that has not been sent. It is my belief that Uncle Joe may never have seen a good part of that money.

On a snowy day in January of 1910 B. K. tells of cold weather and "I did not get any money for you. I made some inquiry but did not succeed. I think I might have got it by March, but was too late for the place. Money matters are a little close at this time." He says he went to the meeting of the stockholders of the woolen mills the former Saturday and will enclose Joseph's check which represented a two percent dividend. At the end there are

[389] *Rockingham County Deed Book 66*, p. 512.
[390] *Rockingham County Deed Book 73*, pp. 158-159.

brief notes from Blanche, then fourteen years of age, and from Lenford, who was ten. Blanche wrote, "Hello, Uncle Joe, How do you like Georgia by this time? Blanche."[391] Dear Uncle Joe, Duckity Do, was killed in Georgia in a sawmill accident the next year.

On 9/11/1910 B. K.'s report to his brother is considerably more enthusiastic, and one imagines that his financial pressures have lessened somewhat. Although the weather was too wet for wheat, it was ideal for making hay, and "apple picking is in order at this time, and a big crop, of every variety" is expected. The price he quoted was $1.00 per bushel and he expected good demand. "If you want a few apples write me and give shipping directions and I will start them that way."

In this same letter he tells of what might have been the very first car in the Miller family. "Will (is) in the automobile business. About the time I rec(eive)d your last letter he phoned and insisted that Ada and Blanche come down one Saturday. They rigged themselves up in their best and went to spend the night, not knowing, but expecting something, of course. About dusk Will(iam Henry Miller, brother) came in with his new car. They all must take a ride, so they piled in and downtown they went. Now you know that they use all the daylight before they light up the town. Down at Robson's store (Will) backed to turn around and struck the electric light pole and made it very uncomfortable for those in the back seat. The lights lit just in time for him to go back home. I went down the next day, but they did not take (the car) out on the street that day. They have been enjoying it ever since." What a nice tale, and what an agreeable memory for the fourteen-year-old Blanche to retain!

In this newsy letter, B. K. also announces that there was to be a reunion of the Miller family, descendants of Joseph Miller, in October or November of that year. If Uncle Joe couldn't come for that, he was encouraged to come earlier. "At this time we have plenty of melons and peaches and we would be glad if you were here to help devour them."[392]

Demonstrating sisterly concern, on 1/13/1911 B. K.'s sister, Lydia Beard, wrote him that "Nannie (their sister) told me that you are suffering with your back. Did you ever try Doane's kidney pills? I use them sometimes and they relieve me soon after I take them. I hope you are better by this time. Love and best wishes to all, Lydia."

Our father said that B. K. Miller lost the Daniel Miller place. Although Mother and her brothers were born there and we know that they lived there

---

[391] Letter from Benjamin Kerlin Miller to Joseph Daniel Brower Miller, 1/13/1910.
[392] Letter from Benjamin Kerlin Miller to Joseph Daniel Brower Miller, 9/11/1910.

for ten or more years, by 3/1/1912 B. K. was selling the place. G. S. Jordan bought it for a cash payment of $5000 and a commitment for $8000 more, $2000 of which was to be paid annually, beginning 3/1/1913. The entire debt was paid off by 3/22/1916. [393]

B. K.'s next purchase of land, on 9/1/1913 was from Jacob Weaver, and was undoubtedly the "Patterson place." It contained 67 acres, three of which he had sold by the time of his death in 1926. We know that the B. K. Miller family was living at the "Patterson place" near Spring Creek at the time Blanche was married there in 1928.

I believe that, as children, we had the impression that our Grandfather Miller was a farmer, and this was confirmed for me in an interview with Williette Miller Firebaugh, his cousin, who said he farmed and also rented out land to neighbors who raised melons and strawberries, among other things, on it. She said he also worked for her mother's brother, Daniel Weaver, who was a builder. She believed he had built or helped to build the house across the road from the one in which our Uncle Lenford lived, which we recall as Ruby Swecker's home. That's quite an attractive house, Grandfather!

I am told that his initials are carved on a timber in the barn of the Daniel Miller/Jordan place, though I have never had the opportunity to see them.

I believe I recall with accuracy a story Blanche Miller told her children about B. K.'s father getting angry at him for making a tilt-top table for his future bride rather than doing the job he was supposed to be doing in Daniel's shop. Mother owned that table.

Miss Mary Hollen, a cousin through the Shickel line, said during an interview in the fall of 1994, shortly before her death, that Ben farmed and had a "shop," presumably for woodworking, in Bridgewater, "where he fixed things." She also said that he "owned land next to the graveyard." Miss Hollen's health was fragile, and she was a bit vague in some of her comments that day. She was gracious to allow us to bother her at all in her nursing home in Bridgewater.

When I asked about Ben, Miss Hollen said he was a "piddler;" then, as though to save his granddaughters's feelings, she added, "I didn't mean to say that!" My sister, Emma, and I came away from the interview feeling that, at the very least, our grandfather was very likely a right-brained individual, somewhat unlike most of those destination-motivated, methodical and logical German ancestors from whom we have sprung.

When he died B. K., as he called himself, was a stockholder in two corporations. On 4/1/1918 he had bought one share of capital stock in the

---

[393] *Rockingham County Deed Book 94*, pp. 253-254.

Rockingham Farmers Co-operative for $50.00. Later, on 8/4/1924, B. K. bought one share of the Ideal Milling Company, Inc. of Bridgewater. For this share he paid $100.00. It might be interesting to attempt to cash in these two stock certificates in 2005.

After his death, on 5/3/1930, Ada Miller, his wife, and his three children sold 64 acres of land to Riley W. Evers. This land was "situated near Spring Creek, being land of which the late B. K. Miller died seized and possessed," and was surely the "Patterson place." It sold for $8000, half of which was paid at the time of sale with the other half to be paid $1000 to Blanche O. Miller Wilson, $1000 to Lester B. Miller, and in 1931, the final $2000 in two payments to Ada F. Miller.

Along with the land was sold "all of the machinery in the carpenter shop, consisting of Planing mill, Moulder and Matcher, Lathe, Shaper, etc." It seems as if much of B. K. Miller was bargained away on that day.[394]

d. 4/15/1926 in Spring Creek

Mother said her father had been a Methodist, a deviationist in this staunch Church of the Brethren family, but he was buried "back home" at the Beaver Creek Church, in the first grave in the "new" part of the cemetery. Perhaps Ada had been instrumental in his choice of a place of worship. She had, after all, been influenced by her father, who was a pastor in the Christian Church.

Grandfather- 3rd generation

During the research process, it became apparent for whom Benjamin Kerlin Miller was named. His mother, Nancy Shickel, was the sister of Mary Shickel who married Benjamin Kerlin. One might assume that this man was someone who was noted for his success, or someone of wonderful character, or hopefully, both, even if he was *not* our grandfather. What I have found is that he was on the board of directors of the North River Manufacturing Company, which was organized at Bridgewater in 1877 to make woolen goods, fertilizers, agricultural implements and castings, and to do general repair work. Repairing steam engines was the specialty of the organization. The mills and shops were located at Natural Falls on North River just above Bridgewater. Officers of the company were J. W. F. Allemong, president, and Samuel S. Miller, secretary. Other than Benjamin Kerlin, the directors were John Flory, Joel Garber, John H. Hale, Daniel W. Byerly, Daniel Kiser and

---

[394] *Rockingham County Deed Book 146*, p. 517-518.

John C. Miller.[395]

Mother would talk about the Miller woolen mill or mills and the fact that her Millers were involved with them. I always knew that the mills were in Bridgewater, and that at least some of the blankets, maybe all, were creamy white with a red border design. I have one of the Miller blankets, thanks to Leila Maxwell Miller.

The Church of the Brethren
A More Modern View

It seems appropriate, as we recognize the end of the substantial "Brethren" influence in our family, to try to understand what that denomination is that makes it different from others. That influence has been with us in every generation since the Anabaptists in Europe pushed beyond the pronouncements of Martin Luther, demanding less form and more personal participation in worship. The following is a comprehensive description of the church as written by John Wayland in 1964. One wonders how much effect our modern world has had on its practices since that relatively recent time.

"In doctrine and worship the Dunkers are orthodox and evangelical. They are neither mystics nor ascetics, as some have supposed. Yet, like the Mennonites, they are marked by certain features that are more or less distinctive and peculiar. They observe as religious ordinances the kiss of charity, feet-washing, and the apostolic love-feast (agape) in connection with the communion in the eucharist; they practice the rite of anointing with oil, in cases of severe illness, though they do not at all neglect medical and hygienic aids; they avoid the taking of oaths (holding their simple word as binding all their powers), going to law, membership in secret societies, and fashionable dress; and are unalterably opposed to war and easy divorce of husband and wife. In consequence of their non-resistant principles, they, like the Mennonites, have been accused of a lack of patriotism, and have at times suffered much in consequence of this and their refusal to bear arms. But they are not lacking in patriotism. They only believe that war is always wrong and debasing. They believe, as a thoughtful writer of history has said, that 'there are few things, if any, more important to the steady growth of a free nation than the maintenance of domestic virtues and the sanctities of family life.'[396] They believe in helping the State and the nation, not by means of war and

---

[395] May, *Four Flags*, p. 445.

[396] Frederick Seebohm, *The Era of the Protestant Revolution*, p. 223, as quoted by Wayland, *German Element*, p. 128.

great standing armies, but by the useful and productive industries of peace; by earning an honest living, paying just debts and equitable taxes, by avoiding strife and contention as far as possible, by settling peaceably, man to man or by additional counsellors, such disputes as inevitably arise; and thus making almshouses, jails, law courts, asylums, many policemen, and the expense of maintaining all these, largely unnecessary. They would apply this principle of peacable adjustment of differences upon a large scale, and have nations, as well as individuals, observe the golden rule in business and diplomacy, and settle all disputed points by honest reason and just arbitration before, rather than after, the battle.

"Neither the Dunkers nor the Mennonites have thus far sought an appreciable share in public or political life, partly because of their religious convictions in regard to formal oaths, and partly because the holding of certain offices might require them to violate their peace principles."[397]

Today, as in 1964, the membership of the Church of the Brethren is still of predominantly German extraction. In the Shenandoah Valley it is at its strongest in Rockingham and Shenandoah Counties, though there are churches in many other areas of Virginia, as well as in states that lay to the west, in any place where early members carried their faith.

Ada Florence Kiracofe

b. 8/2/1870 in Rockingham County, Virginia[398]

daughter of **Nelson Bittle Kiracofe** (11/6/1838-1/4/1874) and **Caroline Virginia Coakley** (12/25/1840-4/11/1917)

Since Ada's father, Nelson, died as a result of wounds sustained during the Civil War when she was only three years of age, Uncle Peachy Coakley, her mother's brother, was like a father to her. Blanche, her daughter, remembered him well and loved him dearly.[399]

sister of George Davis Kiracofe (8/29/1861-2/16/1942) m. (1)Margaret (Aunt Mag) M. Kiracofe (12/29/1861-spring1924), (2)Katherine Hottle of Mt. Solon

Virginia Lee Kiracofe (5/16/1864-5/1943) m. Clinton H. Leary 1883

---

[397] Wayland, *German Element*, pp. 128-130.
[398] *Rockingham County Register of Births 1862-1870*, p. 57.
[399] Letter from Blanche Miller Wilson.

The youthful Ada Florence

Ada Florence (center, standing) amidst others at a church social. Seated below her is her mother, Caroline Virginia Coakley, and next to their grandmother are Lenford Patterson Miller and little Lester Benjamin Miller

Ada Florence and the multi-generational Christmas cactus

"She (Ada Florence) sang beautifully and always insisted Grandfather (Nelson Bittle Kiracofe) taught her to sing. I'm sure it's true."[400]

m. **Benjamin Kerlin Miller** (1/6/1865-4/15/1926) 12/21/1893[401]

This couple was married until the death of B. K. 33 years later. At some moment in that period, Ada gave to B. K. a classically sculptured and flowery post card, unstamped and unmailed, offering "Best Wishes for your birthday." It declared "This is from our old girl, Ada."

mother of **Blanche Odessa Miller** (11/30/1896-3/27/1980) m. James Moore Wilson (2/2/1898-3/18/1983) 6/2/1928

Lenford Patterson Miller (10/9/1900-7/1/1966) unm.

Lester B. Miller (5/3/1905-7/30/1975) m. Miriam Elizabeth Neiland (11/16/1910-11/22/1970) 9/24/1949

"Mimi" and "Ted" were the proud parents of an adopted daughter, Elaine Neiland Miller (6/25/1956-) m. Thomas Bell, and the grandparents of Brittany and Justin Bell.

J. Moore Wilson said that Ada was "sickly" and indicated that she was a very dependent person. He recalled that Grandmother Ada often called on our mother, who lived sixty or so miles away and had four lively children needing her attention, to do for her, that she did little for herself. In one of two letters written by B. K. Miller which have survived, he notes, in 1910, that "Ada's health has been much better this summer." Her mother, Caroline, lived with Ada's family for years while they resided at the Daniel Miller place near Bridgewater. Mother often mentioned Caroline and referred to things she had learned from her.

Mother was called upon to nurse her mother during World War II. She was forced to leave my sisters and brother, who were already enrolled in school, with Grandmother Wilson in Raphine, while she spent months in Spring Creek, doing everything she could for her mother. I, being too young for school, went with Mother.

I recall visits in the sick room. The room was darkened, and I remember standing at the foot of the silent woman's bed, saying what I had been instructed to say, and leaving quietly.

To keep things quiet for her mother, Mother farmed me out to various relatives and friends from time to time. One family I visited was the Ringgolds, conscientious objectors who made Brown Betty for me and rolled my hair into

---

[400] Letter from Blanche Miller Wilson.

[401] *Rockingham County Marriage Register, Book 2*, p. 89.

curls. In return for their kindness I sang "Praise the Lord and Pass the Ammunition" for them. For some reason Mother was horrified!

I also remember spending time with Snoozy Swecker, a little girl of about my age, and her aunt, with whom she lived. There were other people who were kind enough to put up with me for the sake of my dying grandmother, as well.

One impression of that long winter, still surprising to me after all these years, resulted from that fact that Rockingham County had practice air raid drills! We never had them in Rockbridge, and I was a bit young to understand fully what was being practiced, but dark shades were drawn and lights were dimmed until the village church bell sounded an all-clear. I still puzzle over what the Germans were expected to target in that sparsely settled village.

d. 4/24/1943, on an Easter Sunday, in Spring Creek, Virginia of pneumonia. Both of her sons were then serving in WWII.

buried beside her husband at Beaver Creek Church of the Brethren in the first row of the "new" section.

Grandmother- 3rd generation

There are pictures which record our visits to Grandmother's house in Spring Creek. In one set of photographs the three older of us are playing with kittens on her porch. In some we are posed on the lawn. I have an older picture of Grandmother on her porch with a Christmas cactus- *the* cactus. It has survived and today the massive plant reminds me almost daily of a small, gray-haired lady whom I never really knew.

Chapter 7
Generation 2

Dr. John Wayland cited some of the notable events which transpired in the Harrisonburg-Rockingham area during the early childhood of Blanche Miller and Moore Wilson.[402]

- In September of 1896 there was one of a series of unusual floods in Bridgewater. The Dry River flowed across the town.
- On 10/15/1896 the cornerstone of the present-day Rockingham County Courthouse was laid. Blanche Odessa Miller was born a month later.
- In the November election of that year McKinley received 3525 votes from Rockingham citizens, beating out William Cullen Bryant and others.
- On 5/12/1898 men were leaving Harrisonburg to fight in the war in Cuba.
- In February 1899, thermometers in the county registered 23 degrees below zero and there was deep and drifted snow.
- In May 1899, experimental rural free mail delivery routes were established in the county. In June of that year the system was approved and activated.
- In 1902 the first automobile was owned in Harrisonburg. Shortly thereafter Uncle Will Miller, B. K.'s brother, bought the first one in Bridgewater.

In the greater world, there was great contrast between the activities of 1900 and those of 1980, the years which roughly encompassed our parents' lives. Here are just a few examples:[403]

- In England in 1901, Queen Victoria died, and King Edward VII succeeded her to the throne; in America in 1980, a movie star, Ronald Reagan, was elected President.
- In 1901 the Social Revolutionary Party was founded in Russia; in 1977 Communist Party leader Leonid Brezhnev was elected the first President of the rapidly changing Soviet Union.
- In 1904, a New York policeman arrested a woman for smoking a cigarette in public; in 1980, Vigdis Finnbogadottir became the first female President of Iceland.
- A hundred years ago we were bragging about Orville's and Wilbur's first powered flight, the first motor driven bicycles, the first radio broadcast of voice and music, Kipling's *Just-So Stories*, the establishment of Mother's Day, early North Pole exploration, the first practical electric self-starter for automobiles, Jim Thorpe's athletic achievements, and Madame Curie's successes, for starters!

---

[402] Wayland's *Rockingham*, p. 178.
[403] Grun, pp. 452-597.

James Moore Wilson

b. 2/2/1898 in the "house on the back of the place," his place, two miles west of Raphine in Rockbridge County,Virginia.[404]

son of **Samuel McCown Wilson** (11/13/1856-4/12/1926) and **Emma Amelia Wade** (7/15/1863-1/7/1951) 4/15/1886

brother of Ada Poague Wilson (8/16/1887-10/27/1973) unm.
Walter Scott Wilson (10/25/1890-9/6/1964) m. Margaret Smith 7/30/1889-1/23/1962) 6/28/1922
Samuel Brubeck Wilson (12/16/1893-11/4/1918) died at age 25 in France at the end of WWI
Ollie Wade Wilson (2/9/1889-5/14/1897) died at age 8 of lockjaw
Nellie Larew Wilson (10/20/1900-10/11/1992) m. James Fielden Huff 5/2/1933 From this marriage came one son, James Huff, our only first cousin.
Roy McCown Wilson (9/18/1908-10/5/1996) m. Helen H. Sherman 10/30/1951

Daddy and his sister, Ada, went to school in the schoolhouse on Gravelly Hill (in the woods below Glenn Wilson's home). Some of the young Wilsons, probably including our father, also attended school in Raphine. Because he had a number of children traveling to the village each day, Mac Wilson built a stable there in which the horses and buggy were kept while the children were busy in the schoolhouse.

Daddy did not finish high school. Both his grandfather and his father were ill and unable to tend their farms, and the older boys were serving in World War I. He was drafted, one might say, into farming, an important career that he admitted to me in his later years, he would never have elected. He did his job well, regardless.

Education was very important for this man who didn't have an opportunity to finish his. He worked hard to enable his children to get all they would of it. Only later, when I began my study of the Scotch-Irish, did I understand that this passion for learning was a part of his fiber. It was almost a cultural trait.

---

[404] This house was originally log and of two storeys. It had been covered with clapboard siding and the inside walls were plastered and painted. A large lean-to style kitchen on the back of the house featured a very large fireplace, the mantle of which was one immense hewn limestone rock, approximately seven feet long, as I recall. Moore moved that fireplace and its mantle to the sunroom off the living room of our home in his later years.

The newlyweds: Blanche and Moore

The Miller home in Springcreek, Virginia where Blanche and Moore were married on June 2, 1928

m. **Blanche Odessa Miller** (11/30/1896-3/27/1980) in Spring Creek, Virginia near Bridgewater on 6/2/1928[405] According to marriage certificate they were married by E. A. Wilcher.

After considerable study about where they might settle down, Blanche and Moore, in 1930, built a home on land purchased from Miss Betty Lockridge, a neighbor of Moore's parents. This redwood Dutch Colonial home, with an early addition, proved an adequate home for them and their four children.

father of **James Moore Wilson, Jr.** (10/10/1930-) m. Maude LaRue Fauber (4/16/1929-) 4/11/1952
Martha Miller Wilson (11/13/1932-) m. Walter Barrett Black (2/6/1932-) 8/27/1955
Emma Wade Wilson (11/13/1932-) m. Charles Willard Jordan (9/15/ 1933-) 9/13/1952
Elisabeth Anne Wilson (7/7/36-) m. (1)Martin Quinter Miller, Jr. (12/12/1930-) 1/13/1956; (2)William Long Hodges (7/22/1930-) 6/16/1972

The home farm for this family lay across the rolling hills of Rockbridge County. On the hillsides Daddy raised a sizeable flock of sheep and some cattle. On the gentler slopes he cropped, raising wheat, corn, and hay. During World War II and in subsequent years he operated a truck farm, raising many more vegetables than his family required. He also had a large family garden near the house where the best vegetables ever were raised every year he lived there, except the last one or two. Even then enough volunteer plants grew to provide him with some delightful surprises. Chickens were also raised, to be sold, to be eaten, and to provide eggs for table and market.

The sheep produced wool and lambs for market. Some of the cattle were kept for milk production; some raised for market. But they were never butchered on the place. We bought our beef. We ate our pigs.

The fenced orchard provided the pigs with spacious quarters where they grew and multiplied. Butchering day, along about Thanksgiving every year, was an event in the neighborhood. On our butchering day several men would arrive at Grandmother's farm, which Daddy also managed, with their sharpened knives. We children were kept in the house, well away from the slaughter and the mess. At the end of the day, there were freshly ground sausage, hams to be cured, great slabs of bacon and spare ribs, and the

[405] *Rockingham County Marriage Register, Book 4, p. 176.*

wonderful tenderloin which was a specialty in our home. In the early days, before freezing vast quantities of meat became a practicality, Mother canned much of it. The canned tenderloin was often a feast after church on Sunday. Daddy was known for his well-seasoned sausage and for his ponhaus and liverwurst. Yummy! No one ever thought of removing the fat. In those days food and guilt were not associated. Drink and guilt, yes; food and guilt, no.

Dad bought a second farm, "the Weaver place" when we were young. He expanded his operation until he was farming over three hundred acres.

We had a wonderful childhood and youth. We never lacked for anything, yet were taught responsibility. We helped with chores, but had far more than we realized in comparison with other children of our time.

The church - the Presbyterian church - provided for our society. We lived a good distance away, but attended every appropriate function, from Bible School to picnics. A good Scotsman wouldn't think of raising his children any other way. Regularly worshipping at Mt. Carmel, our own church, we also attended special functions at Old Providence and New Providence, both of them churches in which our ancestors were founding fathers. Everyone knew the handsome Moore Wilson, and his twin girls - and the rest of us.

Daddy was a Deacon of the church for years, then an Elder. In his later years he was named ruling Elder Emeritus of Mt. Carmel Presbyterian Church. He proudly attended services there, almost to the end, with his son, and his grandsons and their families. It was appropriate.

I remember Sunday mornings. Daddy would sit (sometimes snoozing) with his arm over the back of the pew, and, as a little girl, I would find my way inside the curve of that arm. I would manage his hymn book and enjoy the sharing of that which was so important to both of us. I was so proud of him.

There were some wonderful family activities, as well. There were the drives on Sunday afternoons, to Goshen Pass in the spring; or to Craigsville to see Pocahontas, the uniquely-marked,[406] trained horse that belonged to a member of the family; or to visit friends. There were fairs and horse shows. And there were trips: the trip to Jamestown and Williamsburg; the family visit in Charlestown, South Carolina; and the cross-country trip to California, in the big black Dodge that looked vaguely like a hearse and grew hot and short-winded when crossing the Rockies. And family visits, and Sundays with the Woodsides, and community barbecues, and trips to Miss Kathleen's store,

[406] The horse had a silhouette of the head of an Indian maiden on its shoulder!

where there were wonderful, drippy ice cream cones! What wonderful memories!

One of the tragedies that beset this man, who looms so large in the minds of those he left behind, was that he became paralyzed from the waist down when he was in his early fifties. He had taken a fall from a wagon, we were told, when he was a teen. After that time he had suffered bouts of pain that were of increasing severity, to the day he lost the use of his lower body and was hospitalized. No one knew much about spines or how to fix them in those days, but the University of Virginia Hospital tried, operating on him twice within three months before sending him home. They told him there that they were unsure whether he would ever walk again. He suffered and wept, and by brute determination, he walked. In time he went on to farm, not as he had, but with devices he had figured out that would enable him to live fully. If he wanted to catch a sheep, he fell on it. He had two tractors, twins again, and he used these in order to get around the place. He learned to fall without hurting himself; this sober man claimed to have learned to fall like a drunk.

He maintained a place of leadership in his family. Not only his wife and children, but his mother, brothers and sisters looked to him to manage family affairs, provide for the needs of those who could not do for themselves, settle estates, and lead the procession at family funerals. Dad's brothers would drive to our home and park by the road to wait for him to pull away. They would follow. He was the head of the family, and his children still love and admire him tremendously - for all that he was.

d. 3/18/1983 at 85 years of age at King's Daughters' Hospital, Staunton of congestive heart failure

buried at the top of the ridge, Mt. Carmel Presbyterian Church Cemetery, Steele's Tavern (Midway), Virginia.

Father- 2nd generation

Mrs. Via, a pleasant little lady whom I knew during the time she was residing in a nursing home I visited, had grown up near and attended Mt. Carmel Church. Clearly she had had a crush on Moore Wilson in her youth. She told me how handsome he was and how nice he was to her and others. She added that he was "such an aristocrat." Her face glowed. I think she still harbored feelings for him, after all those years.

My sisters and I have visited Mrs. Martin (Nellie) Harris on several occasions. She is a distant "Moore" cousin and has been helpful to us in our search for family information. During a visit in March of 1999, she pronounced Moore Wilson to be a gracious man. His daughters readily agreed.

Blanche Odessa Miller

Little Miss Blanche

Blanche with her brother Lenford

Blanche (left) and a friend in graduation attire

Five friends on a Rockingham County swinging bridge (Blanche at left front)

This wonderful old covered bridge, the "longest single wooden span in the world" at a length of 280 feet, was featured on the front cover of Blanche's Bridgewater High School graduation announcement.

b.11/30/1896 at her Grandfather Daniel Miller's house, now known as the Jordan place, near Spring Creek, Virginia. See page 151.

daughter of **Benjamin Kerlin Miller** (1/6/1865-4/15/1926) and **Ada Florence Kiracofe** (8/2/1870-4/24/1943).[407]

sister of Lenford Patterson Miller (10/9/1900-7/1/1966)
Lester B. Miller (5/3/1905-7/30/1975) m. Miriam Elizabeth Neiland (11/16/1910-11/22/1970) 9/24/1949; adoptive parents of Elaine Neiland Miller (6/25/1956-) m. Thomas Bell. They are the parents of Brittany and Justin Bell.

A wonderful graduation announcement and program provides more than the basic information about Blanche's graduation in 1915 from Bridgewater High School. Though water stained, it is still elegant: a double fold tied with green and gold ribbons representing the class colors. The event took place in the high school auditorium at eight o'clock on Thursday, May 13. There were only four graduates, three Millers and one Wright, and our own Blanche Odessa Miller delivered the valedictory! A floral motif and a listing of class flower, motto and colors complete this most informative announcement, which was proudly printed for the occasion by the Ruebush-Kieffer Company of Dayton, Virginia.

Blanche completed a "normal school" education at Bridgewater College and later attended that which is now known as James Madison University. She prepared herself to become a teacher. She had musical training and played the piano for groups while in high school and college. We never knew how well she played. Although she helped us a bit with our piano lessons, we never heard her play.

m. **James Moore Wilson** (Sr.) 6/2/1928 at her mother's home in Spring Creek, Virginia.[408] The service was performed by E. A. Wilcher.[409]

Mother referred to the house in which she was married as "the Patterson place." It has since been known as the Lester Wright place and is now the James Knicely place.

We visited the Knicely family on two occasions. The first time, Bill and I, absolute strangers to the nice young couple who live there, stopped by

---

[407] *Rockingham County Marriage Register, Book 4*, p. 176.
[408] *Rockingham County Marriage Register, Book 4*, p. 176.
[409] Marriage Certificate.

on a rainy day. Mrs. Knicely listened to my story and invited us in to track through her house. I was so excited by this opportunity that I returned some months later with my sisters in tow. We studied the house, trying to imagine in which room the vows had been exchanged. Thanks to this cordial young family, I have envisioned the moment.

Blanche and Moore honeymooned at Niagara Falls, as was done by "everybody" in their day. Blanche wrote to her dear friend, Betty Hansel, that they were having a huge time. I have wondered about that comment, traded between those two sillies.

Mother was a teacher. I think it is safe to say that she loved her career. She did get tired, as we all do of this or that inconvenience or some threat to the "way things are done," but teaching was as good for her as she was good for teaching. She had prepared herself for a career against her father's wishes, and she accepted positions that her parents did not want her to have, particularly if it meant that she would be living away from home. She boarded and taught at Centerville, Virginia, and at McGaheysville, where the schools were referred to by none other than Dr. John Wayland as "the best schools in the county," and at Winchester. I believe she had some experience in other schools in that part of Virginia, but my memory is vague on the details.

Her parents really got excited, we were told, when she accepted a position as a government worker in Washington, D. C. during one summer. We know that she met a number of people she enjoyed tremendously, including a couple of fellows, but, once home, she never returned to work in the big city.

She was an early special educator- before the term was coined. She moved to Staunton and taught the blind at the Virginia School for the Deaf and the Blind from 1923-1930. These may have been her most carefree, and, perhaps, her happiest years. She made many friends, and experienced real success as a teacher. We heard many stories about those times.

Nothing goes on forever, however, and these happy experiences came to an end when Blanche found another passion in life, named Moore Wilson. They met and married and she soon found herself an expectant mother on a farm in Rockbridge, an uncomfortable distance from many of her other interests.

Blanche buckled down to become a farmer's wife, a role which was not terribly satisfying for her. She didn't do farm work, mind you, but she kept house, gave birth to and raised four children, did gardening, and represented her family well in the community at large. She even got to teach a little; due to the illness of my fourth grade teacher, she substituted in that class for a major portion of the year. Perhaps that exposure to teaching roused old interests, for the next year, Mother decided that the county schools were not good enough for her children, and arranged to continue our educations in Staunton.

Jim, our brother, chose to remain at home with Daddy, but Mother bundled up three girls and installed them, with her, in an apartment in town. Early each Monday morning Daddy drove Mother to work and us to school and each Friday he picked us up at the apartment, and we went home to resume our lives there. It was a strangely successful venture, I feel, working well for all concerned. Mother took on considerable work and responsibility in order to do this, but she was once again able to teach full time. She did that from 1946 to 1967, when she was seventy years old and we finally teased her into writing her letter of resignation. It wasn't something she wanted to do. She had given twenty-nine years of her life to teaching, but she gleaned twenty-nine years of satisfaction, and pleasure, from it. Not a bad trade.

mother of **James Moore Wilson, Jr.** (10/10/1930-) m. Maude LaRue Fauber (4/16/1929-) 4/11/1952

Martha Miller Wilson (11/13/1932-) m. Walter Barrett Black (2/6/1932-) 8/27/1955

Emma Wade Wilson (11/13/1932-) m. Charles Willard Jordan (9/15/1933-) 9/13/1952

Elisabeth Anne Wilson (7/7/36-) m. (1)Martin Quinter Miller, Jr. (12/12/1930-) 1/13/1956; (2)William Long Hodges (7/22/1930-) 6/16/1972.

d. 3 /27/1980.

After many small strokes had deprived her of her health and left her confused, she finally succumbed to a fall brought on, it was felt, by a heart incident.

buried on the hilltop at Mt. Carmel Presbyterian Cemetery, Steele's Tavern, Virginia.

Mother- 2nd generation

I recall with love and pleasure this very feminine lady and her devotion to her family, her friends, and her flowers. There are many wonderful memories associated with her life.

The home of the James Moore Wilsons (Sr.) at Raphine, Virginia

The four young Wilsons, with their dog, Sport, waiting for the school bus

Chapter 8
Generation 9

Time warp! We are returning to a slower time, one in which the progress is easier to follow, and one in which life was simpler even though it lacked some of the convenience of our own lives.[410]

- In 1674 French troops ravaged the Palatinate, which clearly affected many of our ancestors.
- In 1676 Nathaniel Bacon wrote "The Declaration of the People of Virginia" which promoted rebellion.
- In 1677 William III married Princess Mary. This union resulted in the eventual naming of the second institution of higher learning on the continent William and Mary in 1692.
- In 1681 a Royal Charter was granted for Pennsylvania, "Penn's Woods."
- John Bunyan's *Pilgrim's Progress*, Part I was published in 1678, as Stradivari was making the first cello.
- In 1683 a peace treaty was signed between William Penn and the Indians, and the first German immigrants arrived in North America in search of that same peace.
- Versailles, near Paris, became a royal residence in 1682.
- The first meteorological map was drawn by Sir Edmund Halley in 1686, the year Richard Gaines was born.
- Louis XIV of France invaded the Palatinate and captured Heidelberg.
- A French explorer, Baron de La Hontan, visited the Great Salt Lake in present day Utah in 1689.
- Volume 3 of the *La Fontaine Fables* and William Penn's "Essay on the Present and Future Peace of Europe" were published in 1693, at about the same time that Johann Michael Mueller was celebrating his first birthday.
- In 1697 the Spanish devastated the last remains of the Mayan civilization.
- By 1702 many German streets were lit by oil lamps. Some of these might have been in the town where Maria Studebaker was born that same year.
- Cotton Mather, a New England clergyman, was writing "Curiosa Americana" in 1712 while George Frederick Handel was writing operas. In 1717 Handel completed his ever fresh and lovely *Water Music* which was first played on the Thames in London.
- The first innoculation against smallpox took place in England in the same year.
- In 1719 Daniel Defoe completed *Robinson Crusoe.*
- In 1721 rifles were first introduced into America by Swiss immigrants.

---

410 Grun, pp. 308-331.

Now to Then

The reader might question the organization of this history. We have started with the generation in which the largest number of immigrant ancestors came to the American colonies and have moved, generation by generation, to that of our parents. Why then the sudden jolt backward into the seventeenth century and the lives of ninth generation ancestors?

Although we have continued to discover new "grandparents," there are many, many others that are not known, and perhaps not traceable, beyond the eighth generation. There is, in most cases, less information available about those of earlier generations whom we can identify. But there *is* information, and, in the case of the Coakley and the Gaines families, there is considerable depth which can be reported. We will do our best to trace those of whom we know to the very earliest ancestor that is known, and some lived a long, long time ago.

Johann Michael Mueller

b. 1655 in Zollikofen in the Canton of Bern in Switzerland

"During the first half of the seventeenth century, Switzerland was untouched by the horrors of the Thirty Years' War and enjoyed peace and prosperity. . .During the second half of the same century a social reaction set in which was made more acute by political and religious confusion. In 1653 the peasants of the Cantons of Bern, Luzern, Solthurn and Basel revolted against the authorities. . .Since there were good opportunities for new settlers in (a Germany) depopulated (by war), many people left the Canton of Bern during this period and journeyed northward. . .This immigration into the "lowland" (*Neiderland*), as the destination of the emigrants used to be called, lasted into the eighteenth century. . ." [411]

Due to pressures suggested in Chapter One of this book, the Mueller family moved, with many others of their religious persuasion, to the Rhineland-Pfaltz area of southern Germany c1680. These Swiss families became part of the Steinwenden and Konken German Reformed churches and are to be found in the church records, as early as 1684 in the Steinwenden church.

m. (1)**Irene Charitas**; (2)Anna Loysa Regina, who raised the young Michael

[411] Mason, *Miller Record*, p. 9.

father of Johann Nichel Mueller (6/5/1685-6/6/1685)

Johann Abraham Mueller (6/9/1686-)

Samuel Mueller (4/30/1687-died at birth)

Catharine Barbara Mueller (6/7/1688-6/21/1691)

Eva Carhrine Mueller (4/29/1691-6/29/1691)

Johann Michael Mueller (10/5/1692-1771) m. (1)Susanna Agnes Berchtol [412](5/3/1688-c1752); (2)Elizabeth Garber, widow of his friend, Nicholas Garber

Note that Michael (Jr.) was the only one of the children of Irene and Michael (Sr.) to survive to maturity.

d. 1/31/1695, at the age of forty, in Steinwenden, Germany.

G-g-g-g-g-g-grandfather- 9th generation

Irene Charitas

We know very little about Irene Charitas beyond her role in her family. It can be assumed that she was born in or near Zollikofen in Switzerland within a few years of her husband, Johann Michael. In the records of the Steinwenden German Reformed Church researchers have found the tragic enumeration of the children to whom she gave birth and who died, all within three years of their births, some much earlier. Then she gave birth to Johann Michael (Jr.). How wonderful it must have been, after so much tragedy, to have a baby who grew and developed, ultimately becoming a man of great physical and moral strength, indeed, a successful world adventurer.

Irene did not live to see her son develop to maturity, however; nor did Michael (Sr). By 1696, when Michael would have been only four years of age, Michael (Sr.) had married Anna Loysa Regina, and died, leaving Anna and little Michael to fend for themselves. On 11/29/1696 Anna married Hans Jacob Stutzman (1660-), providing her step-son with a new step-father and, ultimately, with one or more step-siblings. Perhaps it was for this step-mother, who raised him, that Michael made the difficult ocean voyage back to Germany.

G-g-g-g-g-g-grandmother- 9th generation

[412] Mason, *Miller Record*, pp. 9-10.

Hans Berchtoll

This family lived in Krottelbach, Germany. There they were affiliated with the Konken German Reform Church, and it was there that researchers found Hans and his family.

m. **Anna Christina__** bef 1686

father of Hans Jacob Berchtoll (1686-1739) m. Anna Marie Glosselloss
Susanna Agnes Berchtoll (5/3/1688-c1752) m. Michael Mueller (1692-1771)
Hans Peter Berchtoll (5/1/1690-) m. Maria Elizabeth Zimmer
Hans Heinrich Berchtoll (5/1/1690-)
Barbel (Barbara) Berchtoll (c1693-)
Ursula Berchtoll (1696-)

d. 6/15/1711

G-g-g-g-g-g-grandfather- 9th generation

Anna Christina__

lived with her family in Krottelbach, Germany

m. **Hans Berchtoll** (-6/15/1711) bef1686

mother of Hans Jacob Berchtoll (1686-1739) m. Anna Marie Glosselloss
Susanna Agnes Berchtoll (Bechtol) (5/3/1688-c1752) m. Michael Mueller (10/5/1692-1771)
Hans Peter Berchtoll (5/1/1690-) m. Maria Elizabeth Zimmer
Hans Heinrich Berchtoll (5/1/1690-) Twins!
Barbel (Barbara) Berchtoll (c1693-)
Ursula Berchtoll (1696-)

G-g-g-g-g-g-grandmother- 9th generation

Casper Stutenbecker

b. c1646, probably at or near Lutteringhausen (now Remscheid)[413]

Evidence suggests that the Stutenbecker (Studebaker) family lived in the Palatinate, a region south and west of Frankfurt along the Rhine River Valley.

son of **Peter Stutenbecker** (c1600-1676)

m. (1)unknown; (2)**Gertrude von Staden** (c1670-1706); (3)Margareta von den Beyenburg

father of **Anna Maria Studebaker** (bpt. 10/15/1702 -bef1776) m. John Nicholas "Nikel" Long (Lang) (c1702-1776)

d. 1710

G-g-g-g-g-g-grandfather- 9th generation

Gertrude von Staden

b. c1670 near Hagen, Germany

second wife of **Casper Stutenbecker** (c1646-1710)

mother of **Anna Maria Stutenbecker** (bpt10/15/1702-bef1776) m. John Nicholas "Nikel" Long (Lang) (c1702- 1776)

Gertrude died as a young woman, and Casper later m. Margareta von den Beyenburg, who also bore him one or more children.

d. 1706[414]

G-g-g-g-g-g-grandmother- 9th generation

---

[413] From the research of Bernard Freter of Hagen, Germany.
[414] Freter, *ibid.*

Brumfield Long (Sr.)

b. c1695

Brumfield was born in the vicinity of present day Port Royal in that area which was then Richmond County and is now King George County, Virginia.

son of **Henry Long**, immigrant, (1650-1733) and __**Churchill** (1654-bef1707)

Buchanan feels it likely that the name Brumfield was a family name, possibly his grandmother's maiden name, since both Brumfields and Longs owned land near Mount Landing Creek in Old Rappahannock County in 1687.[415]

brother of Henry Long (c1690-bef11/8/1753)
Mary Long (c1694-) m. John Miller
Catherine Long (c1696-) m. __Brim
John Long (c1698-bef7/7/1752) m. Elizabeth__ (Harrison?)
step-brother of Martha Long (c1707-) m. John Wharton (-bef1736) 1724
Samuel Long (c1711-bef5/6/1740)
Mary Long (c1713-aft5/1/1773) m. George Tankersley [416]173_

There is registered one Richard Long of Culpeper, who witnessed the land transaction wherein "Bloomfield" (Sr.) gave 118 1/2 acres "where Bloomfield lives" to his daughters Sally Long and Molly (Mary) Long Payne 11/16/1757 or 3/7/1758.[417] Was this Richard also a brother of Bloomfield?

m. (1)**Elizabeth Reynolds** 1713 (2)Mary Stubblefield/Slaughter[418] by1736.

father, with Elizabeth, of Reuben S. Long (1716-probably bef1762) recorded as having fought in the French and Indian War
William Long (1718-bef1767) m. Ann Durrett (c1726-)

---

[415] Buchanan, pp. 9-11.

[416] "In 1757 George Tankersley was one of thirteen 'gentlemen' appointed 'By virtue of an Act of Assembly intitled an Act for granting aid to his Majeste for the better protection of this Colony.' " *King George County Virginia Deed Book, 4*, pp. 283-286, as quoted by Buchanan and Owens, p. 125.

[417] *Spotsylvania County Deed Book E,* 3/7/1758, unpaged, as reported by Crozier, *Virginia County Records*, vol. 1, p. 206.

[418] Buchanan feels that, given the association of Culpeper County Longs, Stubblefields, and Slaughters, it is likely that Brumfield's second wife was a Slaughter or a Stubblefield.

Brumfield Long, Jr. (c1721-1/21/1778) m. Elizabeth Bond (1732-bef1773)
John Long (1726-aft1762) m. Isabella__
Benjamin Long (1728-aft2/20/1804) m. Mary Bond 1748
Henry Long (c1730-)
and with Mary__, of Mary (Molly) Long (c1736-) m. John Payne, Jr.
Sarah Long (c1738-aft1757)) m. Thomas Vaughan
Martha Long (c1740-) m. __Kay
Elizabeth Long (c1742-) m. __Apperson

In 1722-1723 Bloomfield was the plaintiff in court cases. In one case he was awarded 520 pounds of tobacco; the other case appears to have been thrown out of court.

In 1724 he was paid 150 pounds of tobacco "for work done to the Prison."[419]

On 4/15/1734 he served, along with his brother John, as a witness to the will of Cornelius Reynolds, who was probably a relative of his wife.[420]

Bloomfield's name appears often in the deed books of his time. He and Elizabeth, on 10/1-2/1730, sold 136 acres to Thomas Turner, Gent., for 80 pounds sterling. Of this tract, 84 acres had formerly belonged to Elizabeth's father, William Reynolds. The other fifty acres had been conveyed to Bloomfield by his father, Henry Long, Sr. on 11/3-4/1726.[421] At about the same time Bloomfield and Elizabeth bought 200 acres in St. Anne's Parish, Essex County, where he lived after 1734. Elizabeth's date of death is not known, but her name last appears in the 1730 deeds.

On 11/2/1726 Bloomfield and Elizabeth had sold forty acres to his brother, Henry. In 1730 they bought 200 acres from his brother, John, 150 of which Bloomfield resold to John on 5/17/1737.

On 10/4/1737, Bloomfield rented 200 acres of land in Spotsylvania from Abraham Mayfield for "rent of one ear of indian corn at Feast of St. Michaels." In 1738 he and Mary, his second wife, rented to Thomas Thornton 1000 acres of their land on Gaines Swamp in Essex County.[422]

He was back in Spotsylvania by 1741, buying 150 acres from John Wells and 118 1/2 acres from Charles Pigg. This land was reported to be

---

419 *King George County Virginia Order Book 1*, pp. 56, 135; *Order Book 1723-1725*, p. 227, as reported by Buchanan and Owens, p. 120.
420 Sudie Rucker Wood, compiler, *The Rucker Family Genealogy with Their Ancestors, Descendants and Connections* (Richmond, Old Dominion Press, Inc., 1932), p. 175.
421 *King George County Virginia Deed Book 1A*, pp. 83-88, as reported by Buchanan and Owens, p. 120.
422 *Essex County Virginia Deed Book 20,* pp. 370-372, as reported by Buchanan and Owens, p. 121.

adjacent to land he already had there, and it was on this land, on the north side of the Ti River at the mouth of Stony Run/Brooke Run in St. George's Parish, that he lived until 8/1/1763.[423] The location is about eight miles from the present town of Stephensville. He and Mary sold land in St. George's Parish, Spotsylvania County on 6/29/1744.

Brumfield was a blacksmith.

"In 1746 Brumfield, the son, initiated a court suit against his father and 'infants Mary, Sarah, Martha and Elizabeth Long,' charging that his father had not transferred to him land which his father had promised if he would come from Orange County, where he lived, to help his father operate his blacksmith shop. According to several depositions in the records,[424] when Junior first came to live with Senior in 1745 he told his brother Benjamin that he had come to obtain a position of overseer, which Sr. said he would help him obtain. Jr. didn't get the position, but Sr. agreed that if Jr. would live with him, Sr. would give him some land immediately and more land after the death of Sr. and his wife. Another deponent said that Sr. planned this arrangement because Sr. had said Jr. 'was the only son that ever did anything for him.'

"Jr. moved in with Sr. and his wife, leaving his own wife at their residence in Orange County, and began work in Sr.'s shop. A Mr. Tribble deposed that in 1745 he went to Long's to have a horse shod and found Sr. helping Jr. build a house and shop of his own on the promised 50 acres across Brooke Run from Sr.'s home and shop. However, Jr.'s wife objected because she didn't want to stay home alone. Sr.'s wife also objected: while one deponent was at Sr.'s home 'the wife (of Sr.) came and told him (Jr.) to go home in which he refused whereupon she went away and afterwards (Sr.) said to deponent "You see I have no pleasure of my son now I have him with me for that woman," meaning his wife, Mary, (Bloomfield, Jr.'s step-mother) and further said that (Jr.) was the only son in whom he delighted and (he) could not enjoy him.'

"Apparently because of the tensions, Sr. conveyed the promised land and a total of 118 1/2 acres to his son Reuben.[425] Later Reuben returned the land to Sr. Asked why he made this deed, Sr. told a deponent that Jr. had not become what he had expected; he also indicated that a Capt. Johnson would have sued him if he had given the land to Jr. And Sr. told John Long, age 21,

---

[423] *Spotsylvania County Virginia Deed Book C*, p. 555; *Deed Book D*, pp. 39-41, 299, as reported by Buchanan and Owens, p. 121.

[424] *Spotsylvania County Order Book I*, p. 442; *Order Book II*, pp. 2-3, as reported by Buchanan, pp. 9-11.

[425] Crozier, *Virginia County Records*, p. 174.

and apparently Sr.'s son, that Jr.'s child had died and that if Jr.'s wife had another son he would acknowledge that land promised him.

"On 9/6/1749 the court settled the case by ordering Sr. to deed the 50 acres to Jr. immediately and to deed him the other parcel after the death of Sr. and his wife. At the time of this decree the four daughters of Sr. were minors, but it is not clear why these, and only these, of his children were defendents in the suit."[426] The court further decreed that each of these daughters could, upon coming of age, have twelve months in which to contest the decree.[427]

Some time after the court's decision, Jr. rented his new property near Sr.'s and returned to his home in Orange County.

"Later a (Capt.?) William Johnson sued Brumfield, Sr. 'in and by a scire facies'[428] and 'the jury found Long not in debt to the plaintiff.' "

And this: ". . .(B)efore Johnson and they did settle their accounts, Brumfield, Jr., told Brumfield, Sr. he understood he, Sr., was disposing of his son Benjamin to his son John (an indenture?) and said if he would agree to let him, Jr., have Benjamin he would give him 4 pounds for him. Jr. told his father he would not be concerned with the said Benjamin if he expected there would be any dispute about him. Jr. told Sr. that said Benjamin (who had been from his father some time living with his son [Jr.'s brother] William Long), had promised to live with Jr. if he would get him from his father. Defendent (father, *Sr.*) made no answer to this."[429]

On 11/16/1757, as has been mentioned in a different context, Brumfield and his wife Mary deeded to Molly Payne and her husband, John Payne, Jr. and to Molly's sister, Sarah Long, the 118 1/2 acres previously deeded to Reuben and then returned to Brumfield.[430]

Brumfield's will of 3/4/1762 said, "In the name of God, amen. I Bloomfield Long. . .give to my sons William, Bloomfield, John, Benjamin, and Henry Long each one shilling sterling as their full share of my estate. I give to my son owing [*sic*] Long, a three year's old bay horse coalt branded B and as to the rest of my estate be it of what nature or kind so ever after my just debts are paid I give to my loving wife, Mary Long, to enable her to support and

---

[426] Buchanan, pp. 9-11.

[427] *Spotsylvania County Virginia Order Book I*, pp. 422, 439; *Order Book 2*, pp. 16-22 as reported by Buchanan and Owens, p. 121.

[428] In this type of suit the sued party is required to show cause why some charge of judgment brought against him should not be annulled, executed, or vacated.

[429] *Orange County Deed Book*, 1749, p. 512.

[430] Buchanan and Owens, p. 198.

bring up my young children and I do leave her executrix of this my will. . ."[431]

d. bef8/1/1763

G-g-g-g-g-g-grandfather- 9th generation

Elizabeth Reynolds

b. in that which is now King George County, Virginia

daughter of **William Reynolds**

m. **Brumfield Long, Sr.** (1695-bef8/1/1763) by 1713

mother of Reuben S. Long (1716-probably bef1762) .
William Long (1718-bef1767) m. Ann Durrett (1726-)
Brumfield Long, Jr. (c1721-1/21/1778) m. Elizabeth Bond (1732-bef1773)
John Long (1726-aft1762) m. Isabella__
Benjamin Long (c1728-aft2/20/1804) m. Mary Bond 1748
Henry Long (c1730-)

d. c1730[432]

G-g-g-g-g-g-grandmother- 9th generation

John Bond

b. c1702 in Essex, Virginia

There are those who suggest that John's father was Thomas Bond who was thought to have been born in Wiltshire, England.

m. **Mary Parks** (1706-aft1779) 3/2/1730

father of **Elizabeth Bond** (c1732-) m. Bromfield Long (c1728-)
Mary Bond (c1734-) m. Benjamin Long (c1730-)

---

[431] *Spotsylvania County Virginia Will Book D*, p. 47, as quoted by Buchanan and Owens, p. 47.
[432] Buchanan and Owens, p. 121.

Isaac Bond m. (1)Sarah__(1744-); (2)Lydia__(10/17/1762-)
All of these were from Spotsylvania, Virginia.[433]

Spotsylvania County Deed Book B (1729-1734) shows that on 3/2/1730 John Bond paid to George Whetley 3500 pounds of tobacco for 210 acres in the fork of the Rappahannock River. The witnesses to the transaction were G. Lightfoot, La. Chew, and Edwin Hickman.

That same day Mary Parks Bond, John's wife, acknowledged her dower interest in the land.

On 11/16/1749 John Bond made gifts to his wife and to daughters Elizabeth and Mary ". . .For love and affection which John Bond hath to Mary his now wife and to his daughter Elizabeth wife of Blumfield Long the Younger and to his daughter Mary the now wife of Benjamin Long and to the intention of advancing his family, Negro slaves Hannah and her child Phyllis and all other slaves John Bond shall be possessed of. . ." and after his death. . . "the slaves to be equally divided, one half to Elizabeth and the other to Mary."[434]

d. c1760

John Bond's will was written in 4/1756 and probated 5/15/1760 in Culpeper County, Virginia.[435]

G-g-g-g-g-g-grandfather- 9th generation

There was a man named Richard Bond in Old Rappahannock County, who was presumably of age on "2 die Aprilis 1690," as he served as a witness for a transaction between William Ball and John Clarke of Old Rappa. Could he have been a relative of our John Bond? He might even have been his father! No proof, so far-

According to the *Old Rappahannock County Deed Book 8, 1688-1692*, one William Bond owned land which was used as a reference in a land transaction between Henry Bradley and Matrum and Ruth Wright on 8/6/1690. Could he be "family?"

---

[433] Computerized records of the Latter Day Saints.
[434] *Culpeper County Virginia Deed Book A*, pp. 108-109; *Will Book A*, pp. 200-201 as quoted by Buchanan and Owens, p. 192.
[435] Notes from the Bailey/Bond Genealogical Collection in the Jones Memorial Library, Lynchburg, VA.

In the Bond family collection at Jones Memorial Library, some of the contributors suggested that everything points to the fact that the immigrant ancestor was Thomas who moved to North Carolina in 1725. Some thought he had been born in Wiltshire, England; others said he was born in Baltimore, and was a descendent of Peter Bond. All agreed that the evidence was scant. "Don't know names of parents, when or where married; purchased land near Windsor, Bertie, N. C.- lived out life there. Will dated 8/10/1767."

"Had four sons: John, Thos. James, Lewis, (and a daughter named) Martha Mary. James had a son named John. John had a son and 2 dau. by his 1st wife (unidentified). His dau. Eliz. produced 9 grandchildren;" and "2nd marriage to Mrs. Anne Smith, widow."[436] These bits of evidence, too, require more work.

Whatever John's immediate ancestry, the Bonds seem in agreement about their long term history. I have seen it reported in three different locations.

It seems that the family spread into Great Britain from Norway, where the "bonder" was a freeholder who ranked second to the earl, or Jarl, and held without fee a life interest in the estate of the "Jarl." For this ownership the bonder was expected to give service to his lord.

In those times there were no surnames. Names were derived from titles, social position, rank, or occupation. The title "bonder" was shortened into the surname Bond in England in the first part of the tenth century.

"During the Middle Ages, Harold Fairhair, ruler of Norway, introduced the feudal system and, contrary to custom, assessed the land of his bonders. They, in return, refused to recognize the assessment and would not pay the fee Harold required. In protest a great migration took place from Norway to Northumberland, England, the Orkneys and Faroe Isles, and Ireland.

"An army of these restless, enterprising bonders swooped down upon France in 912 A.D., where by right of conquest they concluded a treaty of peace between King Charles 'the Simple' of France, and Rolf, chief of the Norsemen. By this treaty they gained title to a large section of land where they settled, built permanent homes, intermarried with the inhabitants, and accepted the Christian religion. The name Norseman was changed to Normans after they were Christianized, and their country (duchy) became known as Normandy. . .

"English history shows that the Normans were (also) established and well fortified in England when William the Conqueror invaded Saxony in 1066. His army of bonders overflowed and submerged the waring tribes of Britons,

[436] Bailey/Bond Genealogical Collection, Jones Memorial Library, Lynchburg, VA.

Angles and Saxons. It is claimed that the invasion of England by the bonder William infused new energy into the Saxons who had become priest-ridden drunkards. William the Conqueror united the country and formed a strong government that gave it the distinction of being the strongest, most progressive nation of Europe for the next five centuries.

"The Normans adopted English customs and manners in order to more effectively control the citizens. This probably accounts for the fact that they were eventually absorbed until no trace of them as an individual unit could be found in all of England.

"After ascending the English throne, one of the first official acts of William the Conqueror was to look to the replenishing of the royal treasury which had been depleted under the lax rule of Edward (the Confessor). He levied a national land tax and had a complete survey made listing all inhabitants and their holdings in order to prevent tax evasion.

"This survey was completed in the year 1086, and the resultant report is known as the 'Doomsday Book.' It records various estates that were held in England by Bond families in the time of Edward the Confessor. It also shows that Bonders were included under the heading 'Liberi,' which derivation indicates that the name Bond goes back to 900 A. D.

"The medieval Norman castles decided the outcome of the Norman invasion of England. The Normans had built strongly of stone while the English almost invariably built of wood. The stone castles were grim, high-walled, deep-moated (and) windowless, and towered sixty feet or more above the heads of the besiegers. Each castle was within supporting distance of others and was surrounded by homesteads of Knights and militia."

The author goes on to tell of some of the castles and estates and of their inhabitants and their connections with some of the better-known names of the time, such as the Duke of Cornwall (son of Edward III), otherwise known as "The Black Prince" and Sir Francis Drake.[437]

It will be hard to claim any of these early Bonds until such time as we can clearly establish the line, beginning with the father of John Bond.

Mary Parks

b. 1706, probably in Essex, Virginia

daughter of **Thomas Parks I** (1670/1675-BFR3/13/1761)

[437] Robert E. Johnson, *Scattered Leaves: Genealogy of the Johnson-Bond and Utermoehlen/Bredehoeft Families* (Sacramento, CA, n.d.), pp. 8-10.

sister of Martha Parks (1702-) m. __Russell

Thomas Parks II (1705-1790) of Essex, Virginia m. Priscilla Blanton (1725-)

John Parks (5/18/1706-c1793) m. Mary Sharp (8/20/1715-) of King George County, Virginia 8/20/1732

Charles Parks (c1709-c1784) m. Susannah __

Samuel Parks (1711-) m. Mary North (1715-)

Elizabeth Parks (1718-aft5/1803) m. Christopher Hutchings (1715/1720-) 1744-45

m. **John Bond** (c1702-1760) of Essex, Virginia 3/2/1730

D. L. Parks says c1728/1729

mother of **Elizabeth Bond** (c1732-bef1773) m. Bromfield Long, Jr. (c1721-1/21/1778) of Spotsylvania County, Virginia

Mary Bond (1734-) m. Benjamin Long (c1730-) of Spotsylvania County, Virginia

Isaac Bond m. (1)Sarah__ (1744-); (2)Lydia__ (10/17/1762-)

d. aft1779

G-g-g-g-g-g-grandmother- 9th generation

Richard Gaines

b. 1686, some say in Culpeper County, Virginia

Others say he was born in that part of New Kent County which became King & Queen County, Virginia in 1691.

son of **James G. Gaines** (c1630-)[438] and **Jane__** [439]

brother of Mary Gaines m. (1)John Doyle; (2)Daniel Gaines II

Roger Gaines

Richard is also said to be "the brother of President Madison's

---

[438] Calvin E. Sutherd, *Supplement to A Compilation of Gaines Family Data with Special Emphasis on the Lineage of William and Isabella (Pendleton) Gaines* (Ft. Lauderdale, FL, 1973), p. 10.

[439] LDS

grandmother."[440]

m. **Catherine Rawlins**

The story is told by L. P. Gaines that two brothers, Roger and Richard Gaines, were traveling from the town of Jamestown into the wilderness when they discovered the home of a Mr. Rawlins who had two beautiful daughters. There was interest, apparently, until the young men acted in a manner that was considered rude by the young ladies. After apologies were made, they were forgiven and before long there were marriages to celebrate.

father of William Gaines (1705-1796) m. Isabella Pendleton (1712-1775) c1730
Francis Gaines (c1708-1775) Sutherd says prior to 7/15/1776; m. Dorothy __
James Gaines (1710-1786) m. Mary Pendleton, sister of Isabella
Thomas Gaines (c1725-1795) m. Dolly Broaddus
Richard Gaines (1726-1802) m. Mildred Hollinger
John Gaines- killed, with one of his brothers, at Braddock's Defeat near Pittsburgh, Pennsylvania in 1755
Roger Gaines
Henry Gaines (1731-1796) m. Mrs. Maria Woods Stepp
Robert Gaines (-1744) m. Ursula (Bridges/Bridger) (-aft1767)

Family tradition indicates that Richard had a Negro servant named Pompey who cared for his children and was a good influence on many of his grandchildren, teaching them folklore and woodlore. Pompey is also credited with having nursed the two Gaines brothers who were killed at the ambush of General Braddock. He was much revered by the family.

d. Culpeper County, Virginia.1755/6

Richard died intestate, although there was an inventory of the settlement of his estate.[441] Among the dozen or so entries in this inventory made by his son and executor, Francis, was a 6/1/1758 payment for a Bond for Thomas Gaines, which was to be paid by the said Richard, deceased, 2 pounds, 19 shillings, 3 3/4 pence; a 3/16/1759 payment to Fees due from the Widow Gaines; a payment to the Reverend John Thompson (Rector of St.

---

[440] G. W. Petway as quoted by Lewis Pendleton Gaines, *The Gaines Genealogy: Our Line from 1620 to 1918* (Calhoun, GA, T. H. Land, 1918), p. 10.
[441] *Culpeper County Will Book A*, 7/16/1756, pp. 133-134, 205.

Mark's) for funeral sermon, 2 pounds; a payment to Richard Pollard and John Leavell for a Coffin, 6 shillings, 3 pence; and an amount paid by Henry Gaines for an old horse and Bell, 4 pounds, 12 shillings, 6 pence. Francis paid himself, also, a sum of 1 pound, 12 shillings on 2/13/1755 for an unspecified number of ". . .Daies Work in Moving Mother with Waggon." It was not explained where or under what conditions Catherine Rawlins (Gaines) was moved. Francis signed his inventory on 8/17/1759.

G-g-g-g-g-g-grandfather- 9th generation

Catherine Rawlins

It is often difficult to find information about women in the early history of our country. Catherine is a good example of that fact. Some say that Richard's wife was related to James Madison, and this could well be true, but we may never know from what family she came. We really know almost nothing about this grandmother named Catherine.

m. **Richard Gaines** (1686-1755/1756)

mother of William Gaines (1705-1796) m. Isabella Pendleton (1712-1775) c1730
Francis Gaines (c1708-1775) Sutherd says prior to 7/15/1776; m. Dorothy__
James Gaines (1710-1786) m. Mary Pendleton, sister of Isabella
Thomas Gaines (c1725-1795) m. Dolly Broaddus
Richard Gaines (1726-1802) m. Mildred Hollinger
John Gaines d. in battle against English General Braddock in 1755
Roger Gaines
Henry Gaines (1731-1796) m. Mrs. Maria Woods Stepp
Robert Gaines (-1744) m. Ursula (Bridges/Bridger) (-aft1767)
There may have been from one to three additional sons, according to Sutherd.

"In the settlement of the estate (only an inventory is available) of Richard Gaines, Culpeper County, Virginia, Francis Gaines was named administrator by the Court and in his report to the Court he mentioned his expense 'in Moving Mother.' Thus it is very evident that Francis Gaines, the administrator of the estate of Richard, was also the son of said Richard and perhaps the oldest son. The mother's name was not mentioned and to date no documentary evidence has been found to even indicate her name, even though some have stated that her maiden name was Catherine Madison."[442]

G-g-g-g-g-g-grandmother- 9th generation

William Curry

b. c1690 in County Antrim, Ireland

m. **Sarah Young**

father of **Robert Curry** (11/10/1717-6/5/1804) m. Ann Currie (9/23/1723-5/15/1819)
William Curry (c1719-)
James Curry (c1728-) m. Rebecca Warwick
John Curry (c1730-)
Nathan Curry (1732-)
David Curry (1734-)
Isaiah Curry (1736-)
Joseph Curry (1738-)
Jane Curry (1742-)

G-g-g-g-g-g-grandfather- 9th generation

Sarah Young

b. in Ireland

m. **William Curry** (1690-)

mother of **Dr. Robert A. Curry** and others listed above

G-g-g-g-g-g-grandmother- 9th generation

[442] Sutherd, *Supplement*, 1973, p. 125.

The Manspile Family
of the Second Germanna Colony

The Robert Gaineses confounded those of us seeking knowledge of that family, in part because the name Robert was used in three successive generations of our line, as well as in other lines of the family. An additional problem had to do with the identity of the wife of Robert Gaines (1773-c1831). Blanche Miller Wilson had the name Frances Manspile in her research results, but questioned it. The name Manspile, with its various spellings, is unusual in Virginia, though less so today than in earlier years. Much time was spent in the search for the Manspile history. It was finally found in the Virginia State Library, a thread in the fabric of the story of the settlement of an area that came to be known as Germanna in Spotsylvania County, Virginia.

There were three colonies established in Germanna between 1714 and 1750, but it is the second, in 1717, that concerns us here. The "settlers" in 1717 had come from the area around Neuenburg and Schwaigern, in Germany, where it is known that emigrants were actively recruited by agents who canvassed villages to find enough families to fill a ship. Those who signed on were Protestants, largely Lutheran, and they left Germany on 7/12/1717, with the understanding that the ship was taking them to "the promised land" of Pennsylvania. The trip started poorly for during the typical stopover in England the ship's captain was imprisoned for debt. During the several weeks of his imprisonment his passengers used too many of the food stores intended for the voyage at sea, resulting in the starvation of 42% of them before the landing in America.

The final destination of these beleaguered people turned out to be Virginia, rather than Pennsylvania, where the unscrupulous captain sold approximately eighty surviving passengers as indentured servants to none other than Alexander Spotswood, Governor of Virginia from 1710 to 1722.

Whereas Governor Spotswood is generally considered to have been an able administrator, kindly treated by history, and credited, among other things, with leading a band of the "cocked hat gentry" up the slopes of the Blue Ridge Mountains in 1716 for the white man's first viewing of the Shenandoah Valley, his treatment of these unfortunate immigrants provides for us a view of the greedy side of the Governor's character. Because of his desire to build the first ironworks in the colonies on his forty-five thousand acres of land holdings, a project which required skilled labor, he had sent his agents to recruit in Germany. Whether or not he succeeded in enlisting laborers with his recruitment, he wasted no time in capitalizing on the plight of this unfortunate, disillusioned boatload of immigrants. They were, of course, forced to work in his iron enterprise in Germanna. Colonel William Byrd, who visited the iron works in 1732, described their living conditions. "This famous town consists of Colonel Spottswood's enchanted castle on one side of the street and a baker's dozen of ruinous tenements on the other, where so many German families dwelt (a scant seven years before)."[443]

The hopes of those of the families from the village of Gemmingen who sailed on this 1717 voyage had been stated in this manner: They were . . ."wanting to take ship to Pennsylvania, and there in the hardship of the wilderness better their piece of bread (sic) than they could (in Gemmingen). The author of these comments continued, "Not just from here, however, but many people are leaving other villages as well, with the same intention." [444]

Among the emigrants from Wurttenberg we find Jacob Mansboil.[445] Cerny and Zimmerman indicated that he, too, worked in the ironworks.

"While Spotswood may have recognized the injustice done these (indentured) immigrants, he profited from the situation by extracting eight years of indentured labor from them. Spotswood (at the end of their indenture) sued nineteen of them in 1723 and 1724 to force them into extended service. They were not released until 1725, (having been held) a year longer than the customary seven."[446]

The German families left Germanna and the ironworks as quickly as they were able to do so. That experience had been the final chapter of a sad period in their lives, and they moved on to take up lands of their own in the form of head right grants in the forks of the Rapidan River in what is now Madison County, Virginia. Some of the history of this group can be found in the records of the Hebron Lutheran Church, which they built by 1740.

---

[443] Bishop William Meade, *Old Churches, Ministers, and Families of Virginia*, vol. 2, compiled and reprinted by Jennings Cropper Wise (Philadelphia, Lippincott Co., 1931), vol. II, pp. 75-76.
[444] Johni Cerny and Gary J. Zimmerman, *Before Germanna* (American Genealogical Lending Library, 1990), p. 10.
[445] The Manspile (Mannsbeil, Manspeil, Mansboil, Manspoile) name was uncommon in Germany as well as in Virginia. After exhaustive research by the authors in a large area in Germany, ". . . Only one Mannsbeil was found in the entire Palatinate region: 'Hans Caspar Mannsbeil, legitimate son of Hans Jacob Mannsbeil of Imsbach in Falkenstein to Catharina, daughter of deceased Johannes Zepp of Schonborn, which two were married the 28th 9br (November, 1702) at Schonborn by Pastor Hoffmann of Dihlkirchen.' " (Cerny and Zimmerman, p. 27). Hans (Johannes), a name often appended to the name of a male child in Germany, may be obscuring the identity of our own Jacob here. If so, Jacob came to America from Imsbach in Falkenstein. Certainly the date is appropriate to Jacob's life.
[446] Cerny and Zimmerman, pp. 1-3.

immigrant ancestor, arriving from Wurttenberg, Germany "somewhat after" 1717.

There is hardly any risk in naming Jacob as our immigrant ancestor. Late discovery of this family name has not allowed a thorough study of it, so no actual connection has been made between Frances Manspile and Jacob. The name was rare in Virginia, however, this being the only known incidence, and those who researched *Before Germanna* pronounced it uncommon in Germany also. Only one entry for the name was found in the Palatinate region, and *no* mention of it was found in adjoining areas. The following family sketch has a good possibility of being correct, but may not be readily provable.

m. **Anna Maria__**

father of Margaret Manspile m. William Adkins
Anna Manspile m. James Shearer
(Jacob transferred land as gifts to the two daughters listed above in 1779.)
John *Manspeil* m. Ann Pratt (-aft1745 and bef1762) John was involved in property transfers in Orange County in 1756.

On 9/28/1728 Jacob Manspoil was among twenty persons who received from the Virginia Council "livable" patents, some of them as large as 1000 acres but more characteristically about 400 acres, in the Robinson River area which is presently part of Madison County, Virginia.[447]

On 10/3/1734 Jacob Manspoil was again granted 400 acres in Spotsylvania County for importing eight individuals, including himself, into the colonies. It seems that each person coming to the colonies was entitled to a "headright" of fifty acres of land for himself and for each person he caused to emigrate during a specific period of time. The "headright" system was flawed, and many questionable claims were made, among them Jacob's claim to have brought Jacob Bryell (Broyles), who later claimed to have brought himself. Jacob Mansboil's is the first record of a Germanna colonist being given credit for importing himself and others.[448]

---

[447] Eugene M. Scheel, *A Virginia County's History Through 1920* (Culpeper, VA, Culpeper Historical Society, 1982), p. 21.
[448] *Virginia Patent Book 15*, p. 351 as quoted by Cerney and Zimmerman, pp. 14-26.

On 9/27/1739 Jacob Manspoil bought 100 acres from John Sutton of St. Mark's Parish, Orange County, Virginia. This is the land on which he and his family supposedly lived.[449] Here he was listed as the head of a household with one tithable member.

On 2/24/1742 Jacob Manspile, along with other German protestants, appeared before "Revd John Thomason of St Marks Parish and George Samuel Klugg Minister of the German Congregation, . . .received the Sacrament of ye Lords Supper, prayed that they might Partake of the benefit of. . .an Act for Naturalizing Such foreign protestants and others there in mentioned as are settled or Shall Settle in any of his Maties (Majesty's) Colonies in America." Jacob was naturalized on 10/15/1745.

In the will of Adam Hance, one of those in whose name Jacob received a "headright" of land, John Manspile is shown as providing security. This will was proved in Orange County on 6/25/1747.

In 1740 the Hebron Lutheran Church was built. It is felt that Jacob and his family were members of this church, which still serves its congregation in the 21st century. An examination of its records revealed only one mention of Jacob and Anna Maria, however, and that on Whitsunday in 1776.[450]

Still owning their first grant, Jacob and Mary, his wife, sold part of the originial 400 acre land grant to John Broyle in 1779.

Later that same year Jacob recorded deeds of gift, transferring property to William Adkins and his wife, Margaret, and to James Shearer and his wife, Anna, on condition that these two couples maintain him and his own wife, Mary, for the remainder of their lives. From this transaction it is concluded that Margaret Adkins and Anna Shearer were daughters of Jacob Manspoil.[451] From this action we might also conclude that Jacob was "retiring" or unwell and preparing for his advanced age.

d. aft1779

There was a Jacob Manspile who was listed as a tithable among Virginia taxpayers in 1783. He was living in Culpeper County and was taxed for himself and two slaves. Was our immigrant Jacob still living in 1783, or was this another son of Jacob and Anna Maria?

---

[449] *Orange County Deed Book 3*, pp. 328-330 as quoted by Cerney and Zimmerman, p. 26.

[450] George M. Smith, compiler, translator, *Hebron Church Register, 1750-1825, Madison, Virginia*, vol. 2 (Edinburgh, VA, Shenandoah History Publishers, 1981), p. 41.

[451] *Culpeper County Virginia Deed Book K*, pp. 89-91 as quoted by Cerney and Zimmerman, p. 26.

G-g-g-g-g-g-grandfather- 9th generation

Other Manspile men were found in various land transactions and tax lists. These, Adam and Michael Manspile, appear to have led their adult lives from the 1780's to the early 1800's. They are too young to be the children of Jacob or the brothers of John and the girls. It is probable that they were the grandsons of Jacob, and that Frances Manspile Gaines was the daughter of one of them and the g-granddaughter of Jacob. I have my heart set on the possiblity of Michael being Frances's father, since he lived in Orange County near the Longs and the Gaines and married Ann (Nancy) Long. Who knows?

Anna Maria__(Mansboil)

m. **Jacob Mansboil**

mother of Margaret Manspile m. William Adkins
Anna Manspile m. James Shearer
John Manspeil m. Ann Pratt (-aft 1745 and bef1762)
possibly Jacob Manspoil, 1783 taxpayer

G-g-g-g-g-g-grandmother- 9th generation

Hebron Lutheran Church: The church of the Germanna folk, including the Manspiles

Chapter 9
Generation 10

The lives of the men known to have constituted the tenth generation of the family range broadly from the earliest birth in 1600 to the latest death in 1761. Considerable history was made within that span.[452]

- At the time of the birth of Peter Stutenbecker in the beautiful Rhine River Valley in 1600, the populations of the various nations of Europe were very different from today. Germany had approximately 14.5 million; France, 16 million; England and Ireland, 5.5 million and Holland, 3 million.
- Among the fashionable of the period, wigs and dress trains became the trend.
- In 1630 John Winthrop, the English Puritan leader, sailed with the Plymouth Company expedition to Massachusetts, founded Boston, and subsequently became the first governor of the state. It was during that year that James Gaines was born.
- Frans Hals, Dutch painter who was a contemporary of Rembrandt, was busy painting the people of the time, including Sir Dudley Colclough, an English-Irish member of the family.
- During the year in which Thomas Parkes was born, an Italian scientist named Giovanni Borelli was attempting to use artificial wings in order to fly, the minute hand was added to watches and clocks for the first time, and a group of Englishmen started a settlement which became known as Charles Town (Charleston) in South Carolina.
- The year Peter Stutenbecker died, 1696, Daniel Defoe was busy writing "An Essay Upon Projects" in which he recommended the use of an income tax. In cities, the sedan chair was a popular means of transportation.
- In 1705, the young Johann Sebastian Bach was said to have walked 200 miles to Lubeck to hear the *Abendmusiken* (Night Music), directed by Buxtehude. That was also the year in which Sir Edmund Halley correctly predicted the 1758 return of the comet which had last been seen in 1682. James Gaines died during that year.
- In 1761, the year of Thomas Parks' death, the rate of settlement in the colonies was accelerating, with many of our families from almost as many nations making their homes as far west as the Shenandoah Valley. Science was advancing, also, with the new studies of "pathological anatomy" such as the one reported in Morgagni's *On the Causes of Diseases*, and the discovery by a Russian scientist and poet, Mikhail V. Lomonosov, that the planet Venus had an atmosphere.

---

[452] Grun, pp. 266-353.

Peter Stutenbecker

b. 1600

Peter was most likely born in the Palatinate, that region to the south and west of Frankfurt along the Rhine River Valley.

father of **Casper Stutenbecker** (c1646-)

d. 1676[453]

G-g-g-g-g-g-grandfather- 10th generation

Difficult Times in Old Rappahannock

In the latter part of the 17th century, life was perhaps even more difficult for the Virginia settlers than we might have imagined. In "Old Rappa" Buchanan found information which reveals that there was a drought of such severity that the secretary of the colony reported to England, "If wee make one fourth Cropps this year Ile swear it must be miricle, having the Dryest year. . ." Virginia was competing in the tobacco market with Maryland and Carolina, with Virginia planters feeling the pinch; the colonists battled against both the king and the Indians in the battle remembered as Bacon's Rebellion; because of misunderstandings and misuses on the part of the colonists, the Indians massacred 36 colonists and burned every house within ten miles of King George; their courthouse, the seat of public affairs, was destroyed; and the county government was disrupted. It was in this setting that Henry Long and other colonists tried to create new homes in the wilderness of America, and succeeded![454]

Henry Long

b. c1650 in Old Rappahannock County, Virginia[455]

christened 2/2/1652

---

[453] From the research of Bernard Freter of Hagen, Germany.
[454] Buchanan and Owens, vol. 38, p. 115.
[455] Buchanan and Owens, vol. 38, p. 115.

Henry's mother may have been a Brumfield since both Brumfields and Longs owned land near Mount Landing Creek in Old Rappahannock County in 1687 and the name Brumfield is first used as a given name in the family at this time.[456] He may have been the son of Richard Longe who was christened 2/8/1630 at Stratton on Fosse, Gloucester, England and who came to Old Rappahannock County c1674. This Richard was referred to as "a large landowner and outstanding man,"[457] and was the son of Richard Long and Eglentine Bussell who were married 4/26/1629.[458] There was also a John Long in Old Rappahannock County at about the time we first find Henry there, but no connection has been made.

A likely connection can be made, however, between Henry, Samuel and James Long. In *Will Book A* of Essex County it is recorded that one Samuel Long of St. George Parish, dying in 1739-1740, had named his brother James as his executor and had left his property to *his* son, *Bromfield* Long, and to his daughters Mary and Elizabeth Long. Evidence seems to suggest that James and Samuel are the brothers of Henry.

m. (1)__**Churchill** (1654-bef1707) of Old Rappahannock County, Virginia by 1682; (2)Christian Allen (c1661-c1730) bef1708. Christian was the daughter of Valentine Allen and Mary Page.

Henry enjoyed the favor of his in-laws, for in 1682 John Churchill of Sittingbourne Parish (in Old Rappahannock County) gave to him, "out of goodwill and affection," land where John was living at the time, and in 1684 Alice Churchill made "son in law Henry Long" her attorney."[459]

In the *Old Rappahannock County Deed Book 8*, we find that Henry bought three tracts of land, a total of 167 1/2 acres, in 1689.

He sold 9/10/1708 to Thomas Plummer land which Christian had inherited from her father.

father with __Churchill, of Henry Long (c1690-bef11/8/1753) b. in King George County, as were the rest of the children; m. Ann Wharton

Blumfield Long (c1695-bef8/1/1763) m. (1)Elizabeth Reynolds 1713; (2)Mary (Stubblefield/Slaughter) by 1736

---

456 Buchanan, pp. 6, 9-11.

457 Thomas H. Warner, *History of Old Rappahannock County, Virginia, 1656-1692* (Tappahannock, VA, 1965), p. 168 as quoted by Buchanan and Owens, p. 116.

458 *International Genealogical Index, Gloucestershire* as cited by Buchanan and Owens, vol. 38, p. 116.

459 *Old Rappahannock County Virginia Deed Book 7*, pp. 16-17; *Order Book 1683-1685*, p. 62 as reported by Buchanan and Owens, vol. 38, p. 116.

Mary Long (c1694-) m. John Miller
Catherine Long (c1696-) m. __Brim
John Long (c1698-bef7/7/1752) m. Elizabeth Harrison

and, with Christian Allen, of

Martha Long (c1707-) m. John Wharton (-bef1736) 1724
Samuel Long (c1711-bef5/6/1740)
Mary Long (c1713-aft5/1/1773)[460] m. George Tankersley

Henry was a planter who lived near Port Royal in what is now King George County, Virginia. He was also an innkeeper and a ferry operator. There was "state intervention in private enterprise" by the colonial government even in 1705, for the Virginia Assembly set his fares. He could charge ". . .from Henry Long's over the Rappahannock River to the usual place the price for a man six pence, for man and a horse one shilling."[461]

In 1721 Henry applied for a license. . ." 'to keep an ordinary at his now dwelling Plantation.' The same year his plantation was appointed a 'Rolling House for the future'- on the tobacco road, no doubt."[462]

There are various details of Henry's life to be found in the court order books. In 1726 he was called upon to testify as to whether someone had crossed the river on his ferry; he occasionally served as a juror or appraised estates; and he sued several people for debt. In one instance the court ordered him to buy new clothes for one of his servants.

Henry and Christian owned at least 548 1/2 acres to the north of the Rappahannock and 550 acres to the south. They had given at least that much land to their children by 1726.[463]

d. 1733 at King George County, Virginia

Henry's will, dated 12/23/1732, proved 9/7/1733, gave twelve pence Sterling each to children Henry, Brumfield, John, Samuel, Mary and Catherine. To Martha he gave. . . "one Negro boy named Sharper and one fether bed and furniture as I lye on. . ." and to Mary and her husband he left ". . .all my land . . .and. . .all the rest of my Estate Negroes, Goods, Chattells and all other commodities that shall be termed or called my estate and I do order and desire

---

[460] Buchanan and Owens, vol. 38, p. 118.
[461] Buchanan and Owens, vol. 38, p. 117.
[462] Buchanan and Owens, vol. 38, p. 117.
[463] Buchanan and Owens, vol. 38, p. 117.

that none of my estate should be appraised."[464]

G-g-g-g-g-g-grandfather- 10th generation

Your Tall English Ancestors

The English name, Long, dates back to very early times: an Aetheric des Langa is recorded in Northamptonshire in 972, and the *Anglo Saxon Chronicle* records a Leofwine Lange in 1070. With the limited number of given names in use in the 11th century, there were simply too many people with the same first name living in the same area, so the Norman system of adding a surname was adopted. Sometimes the father's first name was added to the given name, or the person's occupation, or the place of birth or residence, or a nickname. Long is thought to have been a nickname, from the Old English word 'lang' meaning long, or tall. In Northern England and Scotland the name Lang or Laing survives to this day.[465]

The ancient family motto was *pieux quoique preux*, meaning "pious although chivalrous."[466] It is felt that Henry was of an English family. Perhaps he knew, and hopefully lived by, this maxim.

__Churchill

b.1654

probably b. in Sittingbourne Parish of Old Rappahannock County

daughter of **John Churchill** and **Alice__** (Churchill)

m. **Henry Long** (c1650-1733) bef1682

mother of Henry Long (c1690-bef11/8/1753) b. King George County; m. Ann Wharton
Bloomfield Long (Sr.) (c1695-8/1/1763) m. (1)Elizabeth Reynolds 1713; (2)Mary (Stubblefield/Slaughter) by 1736
Mary Long (c1694-) m. John Miller

[464] Buchanan and Owens, vol. 38, p. 118.
[465] "The Origins of Your Family Name," Blue Chip Products, 1995.
[466] From an unsigned pamphlet.

Catherine Long (c1696-) m. __Brim
John Long (c1698-bef7/7/1752) m. Elizabeth Harrison

d. bef1707

G-g-g-g-g-g-grandmother- 10th generation

William Reynolds

father of **Elizabeth Reynolds** m. Bloomfield Long (Sr.) (c1695-bef8/1/1763) 1713
John Reynolds

William had conveyed to Bloomfield and Elizabeth 84 acres which lay on the north side of the Rappahannock River. They sold part of this land in 1730.

G-g-g-g-g-g-grandfather- 10th generation

Thomas Parks (I)

b. 1670/1675 in Old Rappa County, Virginia

son of **John Parks II** (c1644-) of Old Rappahannock, Virginia

brother of John Parks (c1670-) Ulster, Ireland

Thomas's wife, who is unknown, was possibly from Albemarle County, Virginia

father of Martha Parks (1702-) m. __Russell
Thomas Parks II (1705-1790) of Essex, Virginia; m. Priscilla Blanton (1725-)
Mary Parks (1706-aft1779) m. John Bond (c1702-1760) 3/2/1730
John Parks (5/18/1706-c1793) m. Mary Sharp (8/20/1715-) of King George County, Virginia 8/20/1732; d. Wilkes County, North Carolina.
Charles Parks (c1709-c1784) m. Susannah __

Samuel Parks (1711-) m. Mary North (1715-)
Elizabeth Parks (1718-aft5/1803) m. Christopher Hutchings (1715/1720-) 1744/45

It is speculated by D. L. Parks that the children were born in Essex County, Virginia.[467]

Various transactions in which Thomas Parks was involved have been reported in *The Rucker Family Genealogy with Their Ancestors, Descendants, and Connections*:

1692 Thomas is first found in the order books of Essex County when a suit between him and John Decson was recorded.[468]
1/14/1692 He bought a life interest in the Simon Miller land in Richmond County.[469]
7/6/1725 Thomas served as a witness in Spotsylvania County;
4/2/1729 "Alexander Spotswood sold 100 acres of land in St. George Parish, Spotsylvania County, in the forks of the Rappahannock River, and Hunting Run, to Thomas Parks, son John Parks, son Thomas Parks, Jr, and son Samuel Parks, for their joint lives."[470]
4/2/1729 "John Graeme, attorney of Alexander Spotswood, acknowledged a deed of conveyance to Thomas, John, Thomas, Jr., and Samuel Parks."[471]
5/18/1736 "Thomas Parks bought 380 acres of land on Muddy Creek in the great branch of the Rappahannock River, adjoining John Latham and Col. Henry Willis from John Latham and wife, Elizabeth, of Caroline County."[472]
7/7/1741 "Thomas Parks of Orange, deeded to Christopher Hutchings of same, 147 acres for 20 lbs., land in the forks of the Rappahannock River, on Muddy Run, adjoining Philemon Cavenaugh."[473]
11/13/1751 "Thomas Park's name does not appear again in the counties of Orange or Culpeper, but in 1751 he bought in Albemarle County 400 acres of land in St. Anns Parish...from John Graves of Caroline, adjoining Benjamin Stinnet."[474]

2/24/1752 Thomas's will was written in and recorded in Albemarle County, Virginia.

[467] From the research of D. L. Parks.
[468] *Essex County Order Book 1692-1695*, p. 55 as reported by Wood, p. 436.
[469] *Richmond County Deed Book, 1692, 1693*, as reported by Wood, p. 436.
[470] *Spotsylvania County Deed Book A*, p. 377.
[471] Sparacio, *Spotsylvania County*, p. 74.
[472] *Orange County Will Book I*, p. 244.
[473] *Orange County Deed Book 6*, p. 182.
[474] *Albemarle County Deed Book I*, p. 395.

d. bef3/12/1761 in Albemarle County, Virginia[475]

The will of Thomas Parks of "Ballingers Mountains, Albemarle County" leaves to his son, Thomas, his estate, and to each of his sons, John, Samuel, and Charles, and to his daughters Martha Russell, Mary Bond and Elizabeth Hutchings one shilling each.[476]

G-g-g-g-g-g-g-grandfather- 10th generation

James Gaines

Latter Day Saints' records indicate his name was James G. Gaines.

b. c1630, in Aberbran, Brecon, Wales, likely

son of **Thomas Gaines** (c1585/90-) immigrant

It is felt that James came to Old Rappahannock County, Virginia in 1658 or earlier. He is also known to have been in Essex County.

brother of Thomas Gaines (Games) (-c1699) m. (1)Margaret Johnson; (2)Katherine Morris Pettit Longe.
Robert Gaines of old Rappahannock County
Daniel Gaines (c1625-1682) m. Margaret Rowzee (widow of Ralph Rowzee)
Francis Gaines of King and Queen, Middlesex, and Lancaster Counties in Virginia
Catherine Gaines[477]

m. **Jane** (Underwood)[478]
Sutherd thinks he may have married an Underwood because of connections with Thomas Hawkins and Ralph Rowzee, both of whom m. Underwood sisters.

father of the following, among others: **Richard Gaines** (1686-1755/56)
Mary Gaines m. (1)John Doyle (2)Daniel Gaines II, who was

475 Letter from D. L. Parks of Palmer, NE, 5/19/1999.
476 Reported by Wood, p. 437.
477 From research of Mary Reid Riley and MacFarland Williams
478 Latter Day Saints

undoubtedly her first cousin.

Roger Gaines

There still exists considerable information about James Gaines. Documents found in early court records pertaining to his life include the following:

In the will of Richard Lawson, witnessed by John Catlett and Jno Payne in 1658, James Gaines was to receive a heifer. (Sweeney, *Wills of Old Rappa County, Virginia*, p. 12.)

Half of a plot of land, designated as "386-0-40," was patented by Thomas Hawkins to James Gaines of Rappa County, 9/20/1661. Daniel Gaines was a witness. (*Family Name Index, Old Rappa Co., Bk. 1656-64*, p. 276.)

On 2/28/1663 James Gaines witnessed a deed of John Catlett to Ralph Rowzee, Jr. (*Ibid., Book 1656-1664*, p. 286.)

On 5/2/1663 a deed was recorded in Rappahannock County. [479]

On 5/7/1663 a deed was recorded in Rappahannock County.[480]

On 2/14/1664 James Gaines ". . .wit. to deed all int. 660 Thomas Brown to Capt. Alex Fleming." I failed to understand this; perhaps you will do better. (*Family Name Index, Old Rappa Co., Book 1664-1673*, p. 40.)[481]

Three hundred eighty-six a(cres) on the so(uth) side river at Occupation Creek, which had been granted to Capt. Thomas Hawkins on 9/20/1661 were assigned by him to James Gaines 3/11/1667. This transaction was recorded in 1684. (*Ibid., Book 1683-1688*, p. 151.)

Will Geere paid James Gaines 3000 pounds of tobacco and one heifer 11/14/1667. John Ryman and Daniel Gaines witnessed this on "Xo die 9 bris 1668." (*Ibid., Book 3.*, p. 217.)

On 3/11/1667 a patent transferred to Thomas Hawkins on 9/20/1661 was finally assigned to the grantee. This assignment was rec(orded) 11/18/1670 and referenced 386.25 a(cres) on the "so" side of the Rappa(hannock) at the head of "Popomans branch & Occupacon creek." (*Ibid., Bk. 1668-72*, p. 384.)

On 11/14/1667 a tract which is described as "Half int. 186-0-40 mb on Popomans and Occupacia creek" was transferred from Will Geere to James Gaines. This transaction was "rec" 11/10/1668 (*Ibid., Book 1663-1668*, p. 217.)

"William Berkley (Governor) to James Gaines 519 acres so side Rappa

---

[479] Sutherd, *Ibid.*, 1972, p. 36.
[480] Sutherd, *A Compilation*, 1972, p. 34.
[481] Sutherd, 1973, p. 114.

river, Rappa Co. beginning at a red oak nigh head of branch called Popomans & extendeth inself SE 400 perches to Occupacon creek to 365 (referring to another patent) a white oak thence #146 pches to white oak N 60 pchs to Popomans branch towards head thereof extending of mentioned 400 pchs being formerly granted to Capt. Thos. Hawkins by patent 20 Sept 1661 & by him assigned to sd Gaines and 132 acres & 3/4 the residue being due the said Gaines for the transportation of 3 persons into this colony whose names are on the records underneath this patent 11 Mar 1667. (*Ibid., Book 1668-1672*, p. 192.)"[482]

Richard Cooke paid to James Gaines 3000 pounds of tobacco for 550 acres which James had bought from Henry German by 2/15/1665. This was part of a patent of 1097 acres & 27 perches of land on the south side of the Rappa four miles from the river side and on a main branch of a creek called "Uccupacy creek," north side of branch (bounds by trees) 6/19/1668. Daniel Gaines again witnesses the transaction along with Cornelius Norwell. "Rec. by John Catlett 9-8br 1668." (*Ibid., Book 1663-1668*, p. 218.)

James Gaines paid to Thomas Hawkins of the parish of Sittingbourne, Rappa, 3000 lbs tobacco for 550 acres "head of runn of water called Occupacon Run on south side Rappa river, being halfe part of land formerly taken up by Henry German, Cornelius Nowell, John Powell &Wm Coppin as by patent 15 Apr 1665 formerly sold the sd Henry German & John Powell to Richard Cooke & by him sold to sd Hawkins that at the present signing and sealing and delivering of the parts there is & remainth in me no good & lawful title to sd land. Wit: Richd Perrott, Hen. Branch. XO die 9bris 1668 (May be 10 die, Sept. or Oct. 9, 1668). (*Ibid., Book 3*, p. 215.)"[483]

On 11/7/1670 from part of the patent of 3/17/1667 to James Gaines is transferred to Abraham Steep and James Anderson (or Andrews) "519 mb so side Rappa on Possomana br." This document, witnessed again by Daniel Gaines, was recorded on 12/3/1684 (*Ibid., Book 1680-1688*, p. 151-152.)

James Gaines, on 11/7/1670, transferred "all unsold part 519 patent" of 3/11/1667 to Cornelius Noell, Abraham Steep, and James Anderson (Andrews). John Catlett and Daniel Gaines were witnesses. This transfer was recorded on 12/17/1670. (*Ibid., Book 4*, p. 192.)

In 9/1673, James Gaines witnessed to the power of attorney from Ann Short to Thomas Freshwaters. (*Ibid., Book 1671-1676*, p.134.)

On 9/1/1673 James Gaines witnessed the transfer of a deed from Ann Short to Thomas Chevy. (*Ibid., Book 1671-1676*, p. 133.)

---

[482] Here is an example of land gained by virtue of headright. (Sutherd, 1973, p. 115.)
[483] Sutherd, 1973, p. 116.

John Andrews of St. Anne's Parish sold to John Ridgdail of the same parish fifty acres which was part of a tract of land that had been granted to James Gaines and sold by him to James Anderson. This deed was dated 11/9/1704. (*Fleet's Abstracts*, vol. 29, p. 86.)

Much of this information, including dates and quotations, is attributable to Sutherd, and through him, to many other sources.[484] Several documents, found in Ruth and Sam Sparacio's *Virginia County Court Records: Deed Abstracts of (Old) Rappahannock County, Virginia, 1682-1686 Deed Books 3-7*, (McLean, VA: The Antient Press, 1990), pp. 128-130, are included.

d. c1705

G-g-g-g-g-g-g-grandfather- 10th generation

Jane (Underwood)

Here again we have little more in the records than a first name and some speculation. Because of the close relationships between the Gaines, Hawkins and Rowzee families, since Thomas Hawkins and Ralph Rowzee m. Underwood sisters, it is the best guess of historians that Jane was also born an Underwood.

m. **James Gaines** (c1630-c1705)

mother of, at the very least, **Richard Gaines** (1686-1755/1756) m. Catherine (Rawlins)
Mary Gaines m. (1)John Doyle; (2)Daniel Gaines II
Roger Gaines

G-g-g-g-g-g-g-grandmother- 10th generation

---

[484] Sutherd, 1973, pp. 114-116.

Chapter 10
Generations 11 and 12

The individuals encountered here were of the 16th and 17th centuries. Since the dates of birth, marriage and death are largely unavailable, we must simply identify them with the general period in which they lived.

At the time Thomas Gaines Esq. was born, c1590, Sir Francis Drake was riding the high seas; Shakespeare was writing *Henry VI*, and Edmund Spenser was finishing up *The Faerie Queene*; Galileo was a professor of math at the University of Pisa; and the Emperor of Morocco took Timbuctoo. (There really is a place known as Timbuctoo!)

John Churchill

m. **Alice__**

father of __**Churchill** m. Henry Long by 1682

John and Alice lived in Sittingbourne Parish of Old Rappahannock County in 1682, when he transferred his home property to his son-in-law "out of goodwill and affection."

Because his wife named Henry Long as her attorney in 1684, it is assumed that John had died by that date.

G-g-g-g-g-g-g-grandfather- 11th generation

Alice__

m. **John Churchill**

mother of __**Churchill** m. Henry Long by 1682

Alice named her son-in-law Henry Long as her attorney in 1684.

G-g-g-g-g-g-g-grandmother- 11th generation

John Parks

b. c1644

son of **John Parks** (c1620-), immigrant

father of **Thomas Parks** (1670/1675-)
John Parks (c1670-) of Ulster, Ireland

G-g-g-g-g-g-g-g-grandfather- 11th generation

Thomas Gaines, Esqr.

The title Esquire indicates that Thomas ranked just below a knight, or, as a young man, attended a knight until he attained that rank. Various members of the Games family had achieved knighthood.

b. bet1590/1600 in Wales

Thomas is reported by a number of family genealogists as a son of the house of Newton. They seem to believe that he was the son or grandson of Sir John Games and Elizabeth Games (daughter of Meredith Games) and a lineal descendant of Sir Davydd Gam. The last part of that is certainly correct.

Thomas was sometimes reported to have been the son of Edward Games, sheriff of Brecon in 1623, who married Bridget Vaughan, daughter of Sir Walter Vaughan of Fallerstone Wilts. I doubt this.

If Thomas really married Blanch Kemeys, or Kemis, as reported, he may have been a descendant of the John Games who married Elizabeth Hoo, daughter of Richard Hoo of Skerming in Norfolk. This John was a son of Sir John Games of Newton. Theophilus Jones stated that Blanch married *Hoo* Games. I have found no indication that Hoo even had a son named Thomas, though perhaps he did. Blanch might have been Thomas's mother rather than his wife. Such confusions have occurred. Unlikely, but maybe.

It is also suggested by several genealogists that Thomas was a son of the house of Aberbran, inherited through marriage by John Games of that estate, who was the g-g-grandson of Sir Davydd. Thomas of Aberbran had at least one son, one grandson and one g-grandson named Thomas. And there was a generous scattering of "Johns" in this house, also. And Williams and Richards, and a Henry. This is the more likely lineage.

Sutherd was cautious about the claim of descent from the house of Newton, made by the editor of *The Compendium of American Genealogy*[485] among others. Mentioning the possibility, he questioned it. Theophilus Jones, preeminent historian and genealogist, fails to indicate which of several Thomases might have emigrated to America. We are left with the possibilities given above. The mystery continues.

If one had enough time there is a possibility that this puzzle could be solved, for the Gameses/Gaineses have been an influential family and much has been written about early Wales. Lacking the necessary time, if I were to bet on the most likely family and "house" for Thomas, I would choose the house of Aberbran. Aberbran and "Aberdeen," obviously a mistake of spelling, have been reported by researchers and members of the Gaines family who left their notes long before Sutherd began his quest. If you inquired as to why I chose this branch of the family, I would not hesitate to state that at least seven of the given names used in Virginia in the earliest generations are used, often more than once, in this line of the Welsh family. I believe if I were to move to another continent, another life, from the bonds of a strong, influential, and presumably closely-knit family, I would be likely to make use of old family names in my new life.

The Aberbran Gameses and the Newton Gameses, and all the rest, were cousins, all descended from Sir Davydd Gam and from his son, Morgan. Perhaps it doesn't matter too much which line our Thomas represents. As "Aunt" Myra Gaines, wife of General Edmond Pendleton Gaines, once proclaimed, "One drop of Gaines blood in a man's life would make a Gentleman of him." That may be all that is really important.

Thomas came to the Virginia colony before 1641, some say as early as 1620. He patented land in Old Rappahannock County. Evidence of Thomas's land ownership is available in the following court record. "Mr. George Hardy, 500 acs., July 17, 1648, Page 147, lyeing on the E. side of Lawnes Cr., extending to the main river, along land reputed Thomas Gaynes, along the great river to a cr. dividing some land of Alice Bennet. . ."[486]

Land grant documents report that on 2/27/1665 "Thomas Gaines (had) 1030 acres on main procosin of Piscatawy above land of Hutson and Hold and

---

[485] Frederick Adams Virkus, ed., f.i.a.g., *The Compendium of American Genealogy*, vol. VI (Chicago, The Institute of American Genealogy, 1937), p. 776.
[486] Nell Marion Nugent, *Cavaliers and Pioneers, Abstracts of Land Patents and Grants 1623-1800,* vol. 1 (Richmond, Dietz Printing, 1934), p. 177.

opposite to part of land belonging to James Vaugh."[487]

father of Thomas Gaines (-c1699) m. (1)Margaret Johnson (2)Katherine (Morris) Pettit Longe, born in and lived in Wales.

Robert Gaines

Daniel Gaines (c1625-1682) m. Margaret Rowzee, widow of Ralph Rowzee

James Gaines (c1630-c1705) m. Jane (Underwood?)

The last three of the brothers emigrated to America in the company of the Catletts and the Rowzees and, because of differences in the spelling of the name and their association with these families, it is assumed that they emigrated from Sittingbourne Parish, County of Durham, England, having lived there for some time.

Other suggested offspring include: Roger Games

Edward Games

Francis Games

Catherine Games[488]

d. in Virginia [489]

G-g-g-g-g-g-g-grandfather- 11th generation

Generation 12

John Parks

b. c1620 in England[490]

father of **John Parks** (c1644-)

G-g-g-g-g-g-g-g-grandfather-12th generation

---

487 Pauline F. Warner, *History of Essex County 1607-1692* as quoted in the *Mansfield Family in England and America* collection at the DAR Library, box 4, item 2, unpaged.

488 Sutherd, *Supplement*, 1973, pp. 2-3, 5-7.

489 Latter Day Saints

490 It was in 1620, the year of John Park's birth, that the *Mayflower* set sail on the adventure which would bring the Pilgrims to North America and the founding of the Plymouth Colony. (Grun, p. 278.)

Chapter 11
The Gaineses: Beginnings in Ancient Wales

Calvin E. Sutherd researched and wrote three books about the Gaines family of Wales and Virginia. His work suggested the possibility of a fantastic family story which excited my interest, and he provided an extensive bibliography so that anyone who wished might do the research again. Having now spent many hours pouring over relevant documents, ancient and modern, I recognize the scope of the task, and know that I may never have the time or resources necessary to complete the study. Therefore I present to you the facts as discovered from Sutherd and numerous other researchers as I have sought to pull together the history of the "antient" Games family.

Although the earliest ancestor to be named in this line may be Beli Mawr, the great king of Britons from the far reaches of time, the first of "Gaines" family ancestors who has been identified by Welsh historians is Gwraldeg, King of Garthmadryn. There is some disagreement as to whether he lived c230 A.D., as suggested by some authorities, or instead, at the end of the first century, as suggested by a manuscript in the British Museum. I know nothing of that manuscript, whether it was written within one hundred years after the birth of Christ, or whether it was transcribed at some much later time from the songs of the bards, who were the historians and story tellers of many generations.

We can assume that Gwraldeg was Celtic, a descendant of the barbarians who, c600 B.C., swept over Europe, colonizing Great Britain, including England, Ireland, the Highlands of Scotland and Wales, as well as the countries of Western Europe, permanently influencing the cultures of those lands they conquered. More specifically, Gwraldeg was undoubtedly *Briton*, for this tribe of the Celts constituted the second wave of invasion, and these were persistant enough to occupy even Wales, which proved a challenge, geographically and otherwise, for the Saxons and other would-be invaders.

These Celtic Britons were warlike people who grouped themselves into clans, built forts for protection, and fought among themselves for power. The clans lived by raising sheep, cattle and pigs. They mined and made use of iron and tin. Their social organization included noblemen; Druids, who were their scholars and priests; warriors; and the common people.

The Romans invaded Great Britain at the end of the first century, and stayed for about three hundred years, and though they might not have been said to conquer the Celts, they brought changes to Wales. Two of the more important changes were the interjection of Latin into the Celtic language, and the introduction of Christianity. At some time during all of these changes

Gwraldeg ruled Garthmadryn, under the watchful eye of the Romans.

Gwraldeg, King of Garthmadryn

Theophilus Jones and Sutherd reported that Gwraldeg lived c230 A.D. in the area now known as Brecknock. Jones added, however, that a manuscript in the British Museum states that he lived "towards the latter end of the first century."[491]

m. **Scota**

father of **Morvydd** m. Teithall (Tathall)

Gwraldeg was an adventurer. At one time he raided that part of the country known as Galloway in order to gain possession of it. His wife, Scota, and a chosen band of friends accompanied him, among them his future son-in-law, Teithall.

Grandfather- 53rd generation

"Scota"

m. **Gwraldeg**, King of South Wales

mother of **Morvydd** m. Teithall

Grandmother- 53rd generation

Annion ddu. (Annwn Du or Antonius Niger)

father of **Teithall** m. Morvydd, daughter of the King of South Wales

Grandfather- 53rd generation

---

[491] Theophilus Jones, *A History of the County of Brecknock*, vol. 4 (The Brecknock Society, 1930), p. 233.

Fifty-three Generations?
An Antidote for Disbelief

It is said that. . ."the ancestry of the greatest Welsh families can be traced for a millennium."[492] You may ask *how*, and *why*. How do you know there is any truth in the research that has provided these names? And with the risk of error, why is it important to tell of any of these shadowy ancestors from the mists of time?

There are not many people whose lives are remembered from the first century, or the third, Christ being a notable exception of the former. Anyone who is remembered was very important to those whose lives he touched. Hopefully he was a hero, a giant among men. But let us recognize the significance of power. Whether "good" or "bad" the individual who had the power or the wealth to sway the lives of others ran things, whether he generated admiration or fear. His song was sung and his story repeated through the generations until someone had the interest and the ability to record them. The Gaines family contains such individuals.

Martha and I, with our husbands, traveled to Brecon, Wales. We studied the books of Theophilus Jones[493] and Edwin Poole and others who made the history of Breconshire their life's work. The results each produced and the agreement between them, indicate that this is reasonably reliable information. We are not likely to learn more on this side of the pearly gates.

Why is it important, at the risk of inaccuracy, to claim these ancients, just because someone has said they are our ancestors? On the other hand, how could we deprive ourselves of their stories? If indeed our sources are wholly, or largely, accurate, would it not be inexcusable to omit some of the more remarkable of our forebears?

Morvydd

only daughter and heiress of **Gwraldeg**, King of South Wales

lived c260 A.D.

---

[492] *The New Encyclopedia Britannica*, vol. 20 (Chicago, Encyclopaedia Britannica, 1994), p. 607.

[493] Theophilus Jones based much of his *History of Brecknockshire* on information he found in *Llewelyn the Priest's Book*, an early Welsh manuscript in the collection at Jesus College, Oxford, and in the *Golden Grove Manuscripts* found in the *Harleian Collection*. Dr. Nicholas, another early authority on the Welsh land and people, said in 1872, "Theophilus Jones produced one of the most complete and methodical county histories in the English language. . . ." (Edwin Poole, *The Illustrated History and Biography of Brecknockshire from the Earliest Times to the Present Day*, Brecknock, 1886, p. 304).

m. **Teithall**, a young foreigner in her father's court

mother of **Teithyn**

Grandmother- 52nd generation

Teithall (Tathall)

"a Greek, a Roman or of British origin" who lived c260

son of **Annion ddu**.

King Gwraldeg, Teithall's future father-in-law, was an adventurer. With a chosen band he took possession of an area called Galloway. Teithall, who was among his attendants on this expedition, attracted notice at court and thereby obtained the hand of Morvydd, only daughter of King Gwraldeg, in marriage.

father of **Teithyn**

Grandfather- 52nd generation

Teithyn (Teithin)

son of **Teithall** and **Morvydd**, only daughter of Gwraldeg, King of South Wales

father of **Irith y Blawd**

Grandfather- 51st generation

Irith y Blawd

son of **Teithyn**

father of **Teidwaldt**

Grandfather- 50th generation

Teidwaldt

son of **Irith y Blawd**

King of Garthmadryn c342

father of **Tewdrig**

All we seem to know about Teidwaldt is that he encroached upon his neighbors and was supposed to have been the first to "assume the title of King of Garthmadrin." His son succeeded him.

Grandfather- 49th generation

Tewdrig (Tydyr, Tudor)

son of **Teidwaldt,** King of Garthmadrin

father of **Marchell (Marcella)** m. Aulach, son of the King of Britains in Ireland

Grandfather- 48th generation

Ebre

known as "the Irishman"

father of **Coronawg**

Grandfather- 49th generation

Coronawg (Corinevg, Gormac, Corineog, Cormach McCarbery)

son of **Ebre,** the Irishman[494]

King of Britons in Ireland

father of **Aulach** m. Marchell, daughter of Tewdrig

Grandfather- 48th generation

Aulach

b. in Ireland in the 4th or 5th century

son of **Coronawg** (Corinevg or Connac), King of Ireland

m. **Marchell,** daughter of Tewdrig, King of Garthmadrin in the Vale of Usk

Morris explains the presence of an Irish prince in the following manner: "After the Roman withdrawal the Irish became the familiars of Wales, raiding the coastlands, settling here and there, even establishing transient kingdoms- Brycheiniog, Breconshire to the English, was named for its Irish founder, Brychan Brycheiniog." [495]

father of **Brychan**, founder of Brecon

Many believe Aulach is buried in the churchyard of the parish church of Llanspyddyd, where an ancient stone on the south side of the church is said to mark his grave. There is no inscription, ". . .but there is a rude cross within a ring, and there are also three other smaller rings. The stone is believed to be one of the oldest of its kind in the county."[496] Would that we had known of this grave at the time we visited the church!

Grandfather- 47th generation

Jones tells us that the coat of arms of Aulach is "blazoned in the Jury Room of the Town Hall of Brecon." [497]

---

[494] Jones, vol. 4, p. 234.
[495] Jan Morris, *The Matter of Wales* (Oxford, Oxford University Press, 1984), p. 321.
[496] Poole, p. 259.
[497] Jones, vol. 4, Appendix x.

Marchell (Marcella)

b. in Garthmadrun (now Breconshire) Wales in the 4th or 5th century

daughter of **Tewdrig**, King of Garthmadrun

m. Aulach, referred to both as an Irish prince and an Irish chieftain. Considering the politics of the day he might be presumed to have been an *invading* Irish chieftain.

Interestingly enough, history reports the detail of Marchell's delicate health, and that it was for that reason that her father sent her to the Irish seaside for protection. Other evidence indicates that Marchell and her handmaidens were charming, for we are told that the Irish prince and his entourage of twelve knights were smitten and married the maidens immediately. The stuff of fairy tales!

". . .In a manuscript in the library of Jesus College, Oxford, this Corinevg (the father of Aulach, Marchell's husband) gives a written account of his son's marriage to the heiress, Marchell. It is a strange story or legend, written in Latin in the Cottonian Library, entitled 'Cognacid Brychan inde Brechenac dicta est, pars Demetiae in S. Wallia.' It proceeds: One day Tewdrig addressed his daughter, Marchell, 'I am very uneasy lest your health should suffer from the pestilential disorders which at present ravage the country. Go, therefore, my daughter to Ireland and God grant you may arrive there in safety.' Her father appointed 300 men and 12 honorable maids to wait upon her and conduct her. On the first night they reached Llansemin (perhaps Llansevin in Llangadock, Carmarthenshire) where 100 of the men died, whether from cold or pestilence is not known. The English legend asserts that it was from extreme cold. On the morrow, anxious and alarmed at this event, she rose and proceeded on her journey and arrived that night at Meidrin in Carmarthenshire. Again that night she lost another hundred men. On the following morning she rose very early and the third night brought them to Porthmawr (a harbor near St. Davids on the modern map). From there with her surviving hundred men and maidens, she passed over to Ireland. Upon news of her arrival, Aulach, son of King Gormac or Corineog, met her with a most princely train and (asked that the) cause of her coming (be) explained to him. He was smitten by her beauty and pleased with her high rank so he fell in love with her and married her, making at the same time a solemn vow that if she produced him a son, he would return with her to her own country in Wales. In due time Marchell had a son whom his father named Brychan. When the child was two years old his parents took him to Wales. . . ."[498]

Grandmother- 47th generation

Brychan

b. in the 5th century, probably in Ireland

son of **Aulach**, an Irish prince, and **Marchell**, daughter of the King of Garthmadrun in the Vale of Usk[499]

Brychan, we learn, changed the name of Garthmadrin to the land of Brychan- Brycheiniog. The ruling prince there from 400 to 450 A.D., Brychan, as well as his successors in government, are said to have lived on a knoll above Aberbran, on the Eskir River, known as the Gaer.

In the parish of Llanfrynach the church is dedicated to Brychan. It is said that he founded the church and is, indeed, buried within its walls. A like tradition persists in the parish of Llanspyddid where some say Brychan was buried; others, that it is his father, Aulach, commemorated (there) by the ancient three-foot stone at the top of which is a cross within a circle.[500]

One of Brychan's castles is said to have been located in a field known as "Cairney back." According to Edwin Poole, "amongst all the rubbish that almost covers it. . .there are small pieces of brick that are scattered all over the whole, there are to be seen in several places confused heaps of stones that in some places seem to run wholly across the field like the ruins of a wall. . .The tradition is that it was one of the castles of Brychan, first prince of Brecon, and that ever since it hath paternally descended in his race till this age, which is nearly 1400 years ago: and this tradition is generally credited. . . ."[501]

m. three wives, names unknown

Brychan was the father of 50 children, by the account of some authorities, including 24 daughters. Many of his descendants were recognized as saints and credited with propagating the Gospel among the Britons, who

---

[498] Sutherd, Reprint, 1972, pp. 8-9.
[499] *The Oxford Companion to British History* (Oxford, Oxford University Press, 1997), p. 136.
[500] Jones, vol. 4, p. 148.
[501] Edwin Poole, *The Illustrated History and Biography of Brecknockshire from the Earliest Times to the Present Day* (Brecknock, 1886), pp. 149-150.

had relapsed into Paganism."[502] A number of churches in Wales are dedicated to them.[503] His daughters include:

Gwen, his 16th daughter who m. Llyr Morini, Lord of Gloucester (mother of Cradoc and ancestor of the Gaines line)

Melari, the grandmother of St. David, patron saint of Wales

Goleuddydd (which translated is "the dawn of the day") who m. Tutwawl-beper, a Scottish prince

Brecon's sons included: Rhain and Clydwyn, between whom was divided the kingdom of Brecknock at his death.

Sutherd instructs us that "It is well to keep in mind that the tradition respecting the sanctity of Brychan's family is not a creature of the dark ages; it was current in Brecon and believed in the churches in the 12th century when Giraldus de Bari traveled through those parts. As stated in his *Itinerary,* 'Brychan had 20 and 4 daughters, all of whom, dedicated from their youth to religious observances, happily ended their days in sanctity.'"[504]

Other notable descendants of Brychan were Roderick the Great, from whom descended King George V of England; Howel the Good, who developed the first system of civil law in the British Realm; Cradoc the historian, who was a knight in the court of King Arthur; David ap Gwillam, father of Welsh poetry; Llewellyn the Great (1194-1240), the last and greatest of the Welsh kings; and you, if you number yourself in the descendants of the Thomas Gaines family of Virginia or Blanche Odessa Miller Wilson.

d. c450 A.D. As previously mentioned, he is said to be buried within the Parish church of Llanfrynach, which he reportedly founded.

Grandfather- 46th generation

The Time of the Celtic Kingdoms

The Romans legions began to evacuate Wales c383. Without the protection of the departing Romans the Welsh not only experienced attacks and raids by the Celts of Ireland, but also by the Picts from Scotland. In the 6th century the Angles and Saxons also invaded from northern Europe. The Celts found their safety in banding together and the resulting alliances

---

502 Jones, vol. 4, Appendix x.
503 Jones, vol. 4, p. 233.
504 Sutherd, Reprint, 1972, pp. 8-9.

developed into kingdoms led by early tribal princes. These kingdoms and the growth of Christianity during the 6th century are credited with the preservation of a distinctly Celtic language, as well as arts and traditions.

"The years after the Roman withdrawal were confused years for Wales, as for every other country of western Europe; but whereas almost everywhere else they were to be known as the Dark Ages, the Welsh were always to remember them, or idealize them perhaps, as years of golden glory. These were the years when the Christians, setting up their austere hermitages and monasteries all over Wales, made it a passionate enclave of their faith at a time when almost all Europe was pagan. These were the years of the *tywysogion*, the princes, and the *uchelwyr*, the noblemen, whose glittering figures were to beguile the Welsh memory ever after- aristocrats who lived in the collective consciousness as aristocrats always should, with poetry and music all around them, with wine and fine meats, with beautiful horses and beautiful women, with friends who would follow them to the ends of the earth, and bards who would sing their praises to the end of time. . . .

"Perhaps it was not much like that really, during the centuries in which the tribes of Wales became princedoms and kingdoms, and then fitfully emerged as a Welsh nation. It was doubtless squalid enough in many ways, and was certainly so confused that by now all is inextricably tangled in myth, historical theory, misreporting and propaganda. The few annals and chronicles of the day are a bewilderment of recondite claims and genealogies, and modern Welsh historians, when they get into the thick of their medievalism, are hardly more intelligible. . .

"The tales of the oral tradition, written down at last, became in time that resplendent body of folklore which delights Welsh people still. . .The princely heritage of merriment and high spirits survives to cheer us. . .The bond of family is strong still in Wales, fanciful pedigrees continue to be cherished."[505]

All of this pomp and civility, if it was indeed a civil time, should not lull us into thoughts of happily-ever-after. These kingdoms were made up of warriors who battled against one another when there was no outside force to battle. There was much disorder.

Gwen of Talgarth

16th daughter of **Brychan-** one among a reported 50 siblings

[505] Morris, pp. 58-61.

sister of Melari, the grandmother of St. David, patron saint of Wales
Goleuddydd m. Tutwawl-beper, a Scottish prince
Rhain who inherited part of his father's kingdom
Clydwyn who inherited the rest of Brecon's kingdom

m. **Llyr Morini** or Molwynen, Lord of Gloucester

mother of **Cradoc Fraich Fras**, Knight of the Round Table

Grandmother- 45th generation

Llyr Morini/Merini or Molwynen

Lord of Gloucester

m. **Gwen**, Brychan's 16th daughter

father of **Cradoc Fraich Fras**, knight of King Arthur's Court

Grandfather- 45th generation

Cradoc Fraich Fras (Caradog Frais-Fras)
Cradoc of the Strong Arm

son of **Gwen**, 16th daughter of Brychan and **Llyr Morini** or Molwynen[506]

m. **Tegawr Vron**, daughter of King Pelynor (Pyll Mawr)

father of **Cawrdaff**, who became King of Ferreg and Brecon after the death of Cradoc.
Hyfaidd, Lord of Radnor
Cadfarch Sant.
Tangwn Sant.
Maethiu neu Amaethlu Sant.

Lord of Gloucester, Cradoc was one of the knights of the Round Table

[506] "Cradoc traced his descent to Doel Codebog in the line of Beli Mawr, " an illusive and very early Briton king. This is the stuff of legends! (Jones, vol. 4, Appendix x.)

of King Arthur, according to Welsh history. He was the Lord Keeper of y Castell Dolorous, the Dolorus Tower, a dungeon where prisoners and traitors were confined. One of the three beloved chiefs of King Arthur's Court, it is said that Arthur sang of him:

"These are my three Kings of Battle, Mael, and Lludd,
Clad in armor, and the pillar of Wales, Cradoc. . ."

In the legend of King Arthur, Cradoc was the only one who could carve the boar's head perfectly, or "drink from a bowl without spilling."[507] With these two questionable examples, I feel that the bards were trying to tell us that Cradoc demonstrated perfection.

killed in 546 A.D.

From a monument at Llanfrynach the following is quoted:

"Some rival Cradoc, who with dauntless power
From base usurpers did his country save,
Yet felt, like all, the inevitable hour
When paths of glory lead but to the grave."[508]

Cradoc's descendents became rulers of Breconshire and Wales. At his death, he was succeeded by Cawrdaff, who[509] ". . .became the King of Ferreg and Brecon. After his reign there followed a succession of many, all in the blood line, who became rulers of Breconshire, North Wales, and South Wales. But what should concern anyone in the Gaines family is that the succession through Cradoc is a matter of recorded history and continued until the fall of Breconshire in 1092-3."[510]

Grandfather- 44th generation

Tegawr Vron (Tegaurfron)

daughter of **King Pelynor**

m. **Cradoc Fraich Fras**

---

[507] Anthony S. Mercatante, *The Facts on File Encyclopedia of World Mythology and Legend* (New York, Facts on File, 1988), p. 189.
[508] Poole, p. 150.
[509] Poole, p. 92.
[510] Sutherd, Reprint, 1972, p. 10.

mother of **Cawrdaff**, who became King of Ferreg and Brecon after the death of Cradoc

Hyfaidd, Lord of Radnor
Cadfarch Sant.
Tangwn Sant.
Maethiu neu Amaethlu Sant.

"Tegawr Vron. . .was celebrated by the Bards as (one of) the *three* chaste women of Britain, who possessed three valuable ornaments, of which she alone was reputed worthy. . . ."[511] One of these was a knife, undoubtedly a very special one; the rest as yet I have not discovered.

Grandmother- 44th generation

King Pelynor (Pyll Mawr)

He is also referred to as Knight of Monmouth and as Traharne, Knight of Pelenor in Monmouthshire.

father of **Tegawr Vron**

Grandfather- 45th generation

Cawrdaff

son of **Cradoc** and **Tegawr Vron**

Cawrdaff became King of Ferreg and Brecon, and was referred to by one author as "one of the seven blessed first cousins of Britain!"[512]

father of **Caw ap Cawrdaf**
Cadarch ap Cawrdaf
Cathan ap Cawrdaf
Clydawc ap Cawrdaf
Medrod ap Cawrdaf

[511] Jones, vol. 4, Appendix x-xi.
[512] Poole, p. 7.

At this juncture Sutherd and his researchers take a 273-year break, saying that we, "the Gaines family," should be satisfied to know that "the succession through Cradoc is a matter of recorded history and continued until the fall of Breconshire in 1092-3."

Theophilus Jones takes a different view, continuing to knit the family together. Unfortunately the deeds of numerous generations of individuals have ". . .neither been preserved in tradition nor celebrated in history. . . ."[513] Some grandchild in our future with even more access to Welsh history, and Wales itself, than we have today will find more of the details of their lives for us. I believe, based on the availability of information I have experienced, that more information is there to be found by the diligent researcher.

Grandfather- 43rd generation

Caw ap Cawrdaf

son of **Cawrdaff** King of Ferreg and Brecon

became King of Ferreg and Brecon

father of **Gloyw**

Grandfather- 42nd generation

Gloyw

son of **Caw ap Cawrdaf**, King of Ferreg and Brecon

became King of Ferreg and Brecon

father of **Hoyw**

Grandfather- 41st generation

Hoyw

[513] Poole, p. 7.

son of **Gloyw**

became King of Ferreg and Brecon

father of **Cynvarch ap Hoyw**
Nest
Rhywallon Rhwth y Valeg, or the Miser

Grandfather- 40th generation

Cynvarch ap Hoyw

son of **Hoyw**, King of Ferreg and Brecon

I have found little information about this man. Indeed it is remarkable that his and other of these early names have survived. Whether or not he became the ruler of Ferreg and Brecon is not stated. One would expect that, in the absence of evidence, this honor and responsibility did not fall to him.

father of **Cyndeg ap Cynvarch**

Grandfather- 39th generation

Cyndeg ap Cynvarch

son of **Cynvarch ap Hoyw**

father of **Teithwalch ap Cyndeg**

Grandfather- 38th generation

During This Period of Sparse Information

In these centuries there were as many as eighteen separate kingdoms in Wales. As previously mentioned these kingdoms were constantly engaged in warfare. "Between 949 and 1045, according to the thirteenth-century *Brut y Tywysogyon*, The Chronicle of the Princes, thirty-five of their rulers died by violence and four more were forcibly blinded."[514] The Roman roads and structures were neglected and in decay. The 8000 square miles of Wales were largely inaccessible due to the remoteness, the rugged topography, and finally the earthen "dike," a wall built in the 8th century by King Offa, the Saxon leader of Mercia, to separate his kingdom from the troublesome Welsh.

The *wealh*, the foreigners beyond the dike, whom we call the Welsh, were in a weakened state, but a distinctive culture was slowly developing. And just as slowly the many little princedoms were being consolidated into four major kingdoms. The destructive wars decreased in number, due in large part to the fact that there was much intermarriage between the kingdoms. Sharing a common language, a code of law, and the acknowledgement on the part of the rulers that most of them shared a common ancestry, the factionalized little country was destined to become the Welsh nation.

Teithwalch ap Cyndeg

son of **Cyndeg ap Cynvarch**

father of **Tegyd ap Teithwalch**

Grandfather- 37th generation

Erthil

father of **Merfyn-Frych**

Grandfather- 37th generation

Merfyn-Frych (Vrych)

son of **Erthil**

Merfyn is a "direct descendant of the ancient ruling line. . .from Maelgwn. In fact, his ancestry could not be better. His male line presumably goes back, apparently through the Isle of Man, to the men of the North, to Llywarch Hen, a first cousin of Urbgen (Urien) of Rheged, the highest in

[514] Morris, p. 59.

prestige of them all, a direct descendant of Coel Hen.

Merfyn's court seems to have been cosmopolitan. It is called an *arx* (citadel), and we have a letter from him relating to some Irishmen who paused at his court on their way from Ireland to the Continent. At Merfyn's court they were subjected to an intelligence test and had to show their credentials, and we have reason to suspect that Merfyn's court was a regular port of call for people going from Ireland to the court of Charles the Bald at Liege. In a letter which is still extant Merfyn 'greets Concenn' - and we know that Merfyn married the sister of Concenn, prince of Powys, who died at Rome. . . (H)e seems to have lifted North Wales out of the isolation in which it had lain since the death of Cadwallon into the world of the Continent. . . .His capital lay on the north coast."[515]

m. **Essyllt**

Chadwick says Merfyn owed his throne to a royal marriage, and that he substituted reason and policy for warfare in enlarging his realm. Governing North Wales about 819 A.D., he added the territory of Powys to Gwynedd.

father of **Rhodri Mawr** (Roderick the Great)

It is known that Merfyn's court was literate, and it is probable that "legends and genealogies in Wales" were written during the time of Merfyn and his son Roderick.

Grandfather- 36th generation

Essyllt

sister of **Concenn**, ruler of domains which she is thought to have inherited

m. **Merfyn-Frych**

governed North Wales with her husband about 819 A.D.

mother of **Rhodri Mawr** (Roderick the Great)

Grandmother- 36th generation

---

[515] Nora Chadwick, *The Celts* (London, Penguin, 1971), p. 100.

Tegyd ap Teithwalch

son of **Teithwalch ap Cyndeg**

King of South Wales

father of **Anharawd ap Tegyd**

Grandfather- 36th generation

Rhodri Mawr (Roderick the Great)

King of Gwynedd

eldest son of **Merfyn-Frych** and **Essyllt**

m. **Anharawd** (Angharad), heiress of South Wales

father of Cadell, who was the father of the most famous of early Welsh kings, Howel Dda

Gwendt (Gwendy) ap Angharad (-877)

Anarawd (-916) submitted the Welsh kingdom to King Alfred of Great Britain

Sutherd points to the fact that "Roderick the Great married Anharawd (Angharad), heiress of South Wales. . . .Gwendt (Gwendydd) ap Angharad was the next Lord of Brecon. . . ." Gwendt's "last name" shows him to be the son of his mother, not necessarily the son of Roderick.[516]

succeeded his father, Merfyn-Frych, in governing North Wales in 843 A.D.

"Through marriages and battles, Rhodri Mawr (Rhodri the Great), king of Gwynedd, gained power in central and northern Wales. By the middle of the ninth century, only southern realms remained beyond his authority. The king successfully fought the Vikings- raiders from Denmark- who made sweeping attacks on the coastal settlements on Anglesey."[517] By the time of

---

[516] Sutherd, *Compilation*, p. 10.
[517] *Wales in Pictures* (Minneapolis, Lerner Publications Co., 1990), p.21.

his death a Welsh state had emerged, for the moment.

In Llyswen there is known to have been a mansion for which the parish is named. The name meant "Fair Palace" and it was to this place that Roderick, the unifier of princedoms, sent the princes of Cardigan and Powis to meet and settle their disputes. The palace, reported by Edwin Poole to have been "gorgeous," has disappeared, but when the field was drained and cleared in the 19th century it was noticed that there was a stile "constructed out of carved and beaded oak, and it was supposed that this had once been a portion of the woodwork of the palace."[518]

"Rhodri's court must have been a brilliant one if we are right in thinking that the writing down of the lore of the *Gwyr y Gogledd* is ultimately due to him. The fact that the pedigrees of the Welsh kings are traced to him in the Welsh manuscripts certainly bears this out. But he was also a warrior, and is named in the *Annals of Ulster* as having slain Horm (Norse Gormr), the Danish chief, off the coast of Anglesey. This was an outstanding victory, which in all probability would reach the ears of Charles the Bald at his court of Liege where he was seriously threatened by the Danes encamped in strength on the River Seine. At his court was an Irishman, Sedulius Scotus, who about this time composed an ode on a victory over the Danes, which was almost certainly Rhodri's.

"In 876 the *Annals of Wales* record a 'Sunday Battle' in Anglesey, fought no doubt against the Danes, and this is doubtless the explanation of Annal 876 (recte 877) in the *Annals of Ulster* recording how Ruaidri (Rhodri) son of Muirmenn (Merfyn), 'king of the Britons,' came to Ireland fleeing before the Black Foreigners (i. e. the Danes). The following year (877) Rhodri's death and also that of his son Gwriad (Gwendy) at the hands of the Saxons is noted in the *Annals of Wales*."[519]

d. in battle against the Anglo-Saxons in 877 A. D.

". . .Rhodri. . .had been forced to fight on two fronts, and his death was a heavy blow to the Welsh. On the west the Danes were an increasing threat. In the east the English in Wessex and Mercia were an ever-increasing menace. By (his) inheritance of Powys he had inherited the 'garden of Wales,' but he had also inherited the feud along its borders which is witnessed by Offa's Dyke. . . .

---

[518] Poole, p. 177.
[519] Chadwick, pp. 101-102.

"With the death of Rhodri we come to the end of the old order. The brilliant Celtic heroic age had always seen Wales as the champion who would hurl the Saxons back across the North Sea. . . .Rhodri had found Wales a collection of small states and left it to his sons almost a united realm. . . .I have no doubt that it was a part of his dream of a united Celtic realm[520] that he caused to be put together. . ."[521]

Roderick's grandson, Hywel Dda (Hywel the Good) in the time of his reign in the 10th century, regained control of most of the country. In order to govern his large realm, he organized the laws of Wales into a single legal code.

Roderick the Great's descendants also include King George V of England and you, if you count yourself among the descendants of Blanche Odessa Miller Wilson, or her Gaines forebears.

Grandfather- 35th generation

Anharawd (Angharad)

daughter of **Tegyd ap Teithwalch**, King of South Wales

sister of Gwgon, the drowned king of Cardigan[522]

heiress of South Wales

m. **Roderick the Great**

mother of Cadell

Gwendy (Gwendydd) ap Anharawd[523]

Anarawd (-916) submitted the Welsh kingdom to King Alfred of Great Britain

Grandmother- 35th generation

Gwendy (Gwendydd) ap Anharawd

520 Chadwick goes on to describe his dreams as those of "heroic isolation."

521 Chadwick, pp. 102-103.

522 Chadwick, p. 101.

523 Many Welsh names were formed by using the father's given name as the son's surname. The prefix "ap," sometimes "ab," meaning of, would precede the surname.

Lord of Brecon

son of **Anharawd** (Angharad), heiress of South Wales, and presumably, of **Rhodri**

father of **Gwngy**

Grandfather- 34th generation

Gwngy

son of **Gwendy** (Gwendydd) ap Anharawd, Lord of Brecon

father of **Huganus** (Hydd, Hwgan)
Einon, from whom descended Rhys Goch

Grandfather- 33rd generation

Huganus

(also known as Hydd Hwgan, Kydd, Ky, Gy, Guy, or Hudd in different pedigrees)

son of **Gwngy**

brother of Einon ap Gwngy

from West Wales

Prince or Lord of Brecknock

father of **Dryffin** (Sir Driffin) m. Crusilla (ap Idwal ap Meuric)

For more than a hundred years the Saxons had encroached upon the Welsh countryside from the east, and matters did not improve when the Danes renewed their assaults on the Welsh coast. Huganus, ". . .by way of paying out his double enemies. . . perceiving Edward, king of England, extremely busy in the Danish wars, gathered a large army, entered England, and 'cruelly harrassed and destroyed' the king's country. . . ."[524] These acts did not go without notice.

"In the year 910 Ethelfleda or Elfleda, Queen of Mercia and daughter of Alfred the Great, sent her army into Breconshire and took the castle of Huganus; his queen and 34 of his attendants were sent as prisoners to Mercia."[525] Poole reports that "Hwgan (Huganus), smarting under his defeat, 'rather than submit to a woman,' made an unsuccessful attempt to procure the liberty of his countrymen but was slain."

d. as a result of wounds sustained in battle in 910 A. D.

Grandfather- 32nd generation

A Quick Look at Four Hundred Years
Centuries 9 through 13

After Rhodri, Huganus's g-grandfather, had lost his life in battle against the Saxons, the kingdoms of Wales had again experienced division. By the middle of the 10th century, however, Rhodri's descendant, a first cousin of Huganus, Hywel Dda (Hywel the Good) became King of Deheubarth and once again unified most of Wales.

"When Rhodri, Hywel, and Gruffydd governed Wales, the country was made up of remote (and secure) rural settlements. Farmers planted crops where the soil was fertile, but most farms raised livestock. Although small in size, the main Welsh kingdoms had a strong cultural life. Bards, or singer-poets, recorded the history of the realms in song and verse. The kings spent large sums of money to support monasteries, which acted as centers of education.

"In other parts of Wales, less powerful kingdoms rose and fell in the tenth and eleventh centuries. War broke out continually between kings and nobles and between brothers or cousins seeking power. In search of military protection, some of these kingdoms allied with the Anglo-Saxons, who were now molded into a single, strong realm called England."[526]

The Saxons had failed in efforts to conquer Wales, and had only gained access through these peaceful alliances. When the Normans arrived in England in 1066, however, they were quick and thorough in the accomplishment of

---

[524] Poole, p. 7.
[525] Sutherd, Reprint, 1972, pp. 10-11.
[526] *Wales in Pictures*, p. 22.

their objectives there. Norman law, language, government, and king replaced the English counterpart. They then started on Wales, the conquest of which took more time. The Welsh offered stiff resistance but in time the Marcher lords (as the Norman noblemen were called) took over eastern and southern Wales.

"For 200 years after the Norman Conquest, Welsh kings avoided further invasions through marriages, alliances, battles, and oaths of loyalty. These efforts allowed the Welsh to maintain their own laws, language, and arts amid Norman culture. During the twelfth and thirteenth centuries the kingdom of Gwynedd- protected by the mountains of northwestern Wales- became a stronghold of Welsh self-rule."[527]

Dryffin ap Hwgan (Sir Driffin)

son of **Hydd Hwgan** or **Huganus**

m. **Crusilla**, daughter of Idwal ap Meuric

father of **Maenarch ap Griffn** m. Elinor (ap Einon ap Selyff)
Drymbenog, ancestor of the Vaughans, m. Gwenllian, daughter of Jestin ap Gwrgan
Madoc
Rhywallon

Dryffin succeeded to the government of his father in West Wales some time after the year 910. By that time Huganus had died as a result of wounds received in the battle with Ethelfleda (Elfleda), the daughter of Alfred the Great. Dryffin's mother, the queen, and 34 of her attendants had been sent as prisoners to Mercia. Little was left for Dryffin to govern in Breconshire.

To worsen matters, ". . .Brecon and South Wales were invaded by Athelstan Glodri, who thought he had a fair opportunity of making himself master of the situation in all Ferregs; 'nor did he fail in his purpose, and ever after Dryffin is only called Prince of Brecon.' "[528]

In the period between 930-933 A. D., after he came to power, Dryffin experienced misfortunes similar to those of his father. He ultimately lost Brecknock altogether. It was only the good fortune of his son Maenarch's marriage to Elinor, daughter of Einon ap Selyff, that enabled the kingdom of

[527] *Ibid.*, p. 23.
[528] Poole, p. 7.

Breconshire to unite under the rule of the family, more specifically Maenarch, again, for a time.[529]

Grandfather- 31st generation

Crusilla

daughter of **Idwal ap Meuric**

m. **Sir Dryffin ap Hwgan**

mother of **Maenarch ap Griffn** m. Elinor, daughter of Einon ap Selyff
Drymbenog, progenitor of the Vaughans m. Gwenllian, daughter of Jestin ap Gwrgan
Madoc
Rhywallon

Grandmother- 31st generation

Idwal ap Meuric

father of **Crusilla** m. Sir Dryffin ap Hwgan

Grandfather- 32nd generation

Maenarch ap Dryffin (Griffn)

Prince of Brecknock

son and successor to that which was left of the lands and government of his father Sir **Dryffin ap Hwgan (Huganus)** and his wife, **Crusilla**

brother of **Drymbenog**, ancestor of the Vaughans
Madoc
Rhywallon

---

[529] Sutherd, Reprint, 1972, p. 10-11.

Having learned from the misfortunes of his forefathers, ". . . (Maenarch) lived peacably in his principality of Brecon, and strove to repair and improve his possessions. . . "[530]

m. **Elinor**, daughter and sole heiress of Einon ap Selyff

Because of the political position of his wife's family, as well as that of his own, Maenarch succeeded in unifying and controlling Breconshire, creating more stability than had existed for nearly 600 years. Regrettably, the tranquility did not long endure.

father of **Bleddyn ap Maenarch** (-1092) m. Elinor, daughter of Tewdwr, King of South Wales

Grandfather- 30th generation

Elinor (Elew, Elen)

daughter of **Einon ap Selyff**, Lord of Cwmwd

sister of Trahaern Fawr ap Einon, last lord of the complete territory of Cwmwd

Elinor was sixteen generations removed from Brychan, the man for whom Brecon and Breconshire were named. She was also descended, through sixteen generations of her father's line, from Cradoc, Knight of the Round Table.

m. **Maenarch ap Griffin** (Note the change; his father was called Dryffin!)

mother of **Bleddyn ap Maenarch** m. Elinor

Grandmother- 30th generation

Einon ap Selyff

son of **Griffith** who was in turn the son of Elisse

[530] Poole, p. 7.

Lord of Cwmwd and Cantre Selyff

m. **Jane,** the daughter of Meredyth ap Rhys Grug, Lord of Ystradwy

15th generation from Cradoc, Knight of the Round Table

father of **Elinor** m. Maenarch ap Dryffin (Griffn)
Trahaern Fawr ap Einon, last Lord of the whole territory of Cwmwd

Grandfather- 31st generation

Griffith

son of **Elisse**

father of **Einon ap Selyff**, Lord of Cwmwd and Cantre Selyff m. Jane (ap Meredyth ap Rhys Grug)

Grandfather- 32nd generation

Elisse

father of **Griffith**

Grandfather- 33rd generation

Jane (ap Meredyth ap Rhys Grug)

daughter of **Meredyth ap Rhys Grug**, Lord of Ystradwy

m. **Einon ap Selyff**

mother of **Elinor** m. Maenarch ap Dryffin (Griffin)
Trahaern Fawr ap Einon, Lord of Cwmwd

Grandmother- 31st generation

Meredyth ap Rhys Grug

Lord of Ystradwy

father of **Jane** m. Einon ap Selyff

Grandfather- 32nd generation

Bleddyn (Blethin) ap Maenarch, Lord of Brecknock

Edwin Poole refers to this man as "the last native prince of Brecknockshire."

son of **Maenarch ap Griffin** and **Elinor (ap Einon ap Selyff)**
Bleddyn's father gave him the principality of Brecon, which was then called Garthmadryn.

m. **Elinor**, daughter of Tewdwr mawr, the King of South Wales

father of **Gwgan** m. Gwenllian, daughter of Philip Gwys, Lord of Wiston
__ m. Idio

The princes of South Wales had long been denied their royal rights by their conquerers. In frustration, Bleddyn's brother-in-law, Rhys ap Tewdwr, put in his claim to rule and was elected prince of South Wales by the voice of the people. It was not long, however, before other princes plotted against him and, although Tewdwr put down the insurrection at first, he was later overpowered by these same claimants, with the help of a number of Norman chieftans. During a terrible battle in 1091 Rhys ap Tewdwr's lands were devastated, and the following year, in continuing battle, though the Welsh were said to have surprised and rushed the Normans, ". . .the better discipline of the Normans stood firm against the furious onslaught, and in the end won them the field."[531] Both Bleddyn and Rhys ap Tewdwr were killed. With these two Welsh noblemen fell the independence of Breconshire.[532]

[531] Poole, p. 9.
[532] Sutherd, Reprint, 1972, pp. 11-12.

The Norman conquerer, Bernard Newmarch, thought to have been half-brother of William the Conqueror, took Bleddyn's castle, stone by stone, to Aberhonddu in order to fortify his own castle. He also became the owner, through whatever means, of "Tal-y-Llyn," an old manor said to have been taken from Bleddyn by Newmarch and made his own country house. This mansion, located in the parish of Llangasty-Talyllyn, was still in use at the end of the 19th century. The conquered land was said to have been divided among the Norman knights who were Newmarch's companions.

Bleddyn bequeathed to his grandson, Trahaern, the lands of Llanphangel (Llangorse).[533]

d. 1092 in battle in Wales

"Thus fell Blethin ab Maenarch, the last although not the greatest, yet one of the bravest princes of the British blood, a man of singular virtues and by no means deserving so hard a fate; he was buried among the princes of South Wales at Strata Fflorida Abbey."[534]

Grandfather- 29th generation

Elinor

daughter of **Tewdwr** mawr

sister of Rhys ap Tewdwr mawr, King of South Wales

m. **Bleddyn ap Maenarch**

mother of **Gwgan** m. Gwenllian, daughter of Philip Gwys, Lord of Wiston
__ m. Idio

Grandmother- 29th generation

". . .resistance to the Normans never ended - (The Normans) were never able permanently to seize much more than their originally conquered

[533] On the road between Castlemadoc and Builth is Baili-brith, a dwelling which is said to have belonged to Bleddin ap Maenarch and to have remained a possession of his descendants until the beginning of the 17th century. (Jones, vol. 2, p. 192.)
[534] Poole, p. 9.

territory, and even there guerilla fighting was incessant. Successive kings of England brought expeditions into Wales, in support of the Marcher Lords, and bold tales were told by the Welsh of the long conflict - the snatching of princesses from duress in Norman castles, the kidnapping of extortionate barons, and sometimes a smashing set-piece victory, like the one in the Berwyn hills in 1167 when the princes of Gwynedd, Powys and Deheubarth combined to beat an army drawn from Normandy, Scotland, France and England, supported by a Danish fleet and financed by the merchants of London. Heroic leaders with heroic names- Rhys ap Tudur[535] (brother of Elinor), and Owain Gwynedd, the great Lord Rhys of Dinefwr - burnt their reputations forever into the Welsh memory, and there are many places still hallowed, or haunted, by legends of the Norman wars."[536]

Tewdwr mawr, King of South Wales

father of **Elinor** m. Bleddyn ap Maenarch
Rhys ap Tewdwr
Nest, mother of Angharad

Grandfather- 30th generation

Gwgan (ap Bleddyn ap Maenarch)

eldest son of **Bleddyn ap Maenarch**

brother of __ m. Idio

m. **Gwenllian**, daughter and heiress of Philip Gwys

father of Sir Walter Gwgan (Wogan)
Trahaern fychan (-1197) m. Joan, daughter of Bleddyn, Lord of Cilsant
Cadifor (had a lordship in Breconshire)
Howel
Madoc

[535] In the 19th century a man named Morris found the crown of Rhys ap Tewdwr in a rock cleft of the Rhondda. It was kept in the possession of this man and, presumably, his family. It would be interesting to see it. (Morris, p. 218.)
[536] Morris, p. 65.

Gwgan/Gwrgan tried, after the death of his father, to recover his lost "dominions," but he did not succeed. Attempts to avenge his father's death resulted in imprisonment for the rest of his life in the Brecknock Castle. Edwin Poole quotes Hugh Thomas, early genealogist and historian of the area, who said, "Gwrgan. . .succeeded to but little more than his father's misfortunes."

"Cathedine (the prisoner's or bondsman's lands) was so called from the fact of it having been assigned by Bernard Newmarch (on his completing the conquest of this portion of the principality) for the support of Gwrgan, son of Bleddyn, the deposed sovereign, whom at the same time he kept in confinement in Brecknock Castle."[537] Cathedine, said to be the only "gentleman's residence" in the parish, was still occupied during Poole's lifetime.

Grandfather- 28th generation

Gwenllian (ap Gwys)

daughter and heiress of **Philip Gwys**, Lord of Gwyston, since called "Wiston," in Pembrokeshire

m. **Gwgan (ap Bleddyn ap Maenarch)**

mother of Sir Walter Gwgan (Wogan)
Trahaern fychan (-1197) m. Joan, daughter of Bleddyn of Cilsant
Cadifor, had a lordship in Breconshire
Howel
Madoc

Grandmother- 28th generation

Philip Gwys, Lord of Gwyston[538]

[537] Poole, p. 196.
[538] The ruins of Gwyston, since called "Wiston" are found in Pembrokeshire, four and one-half miles east of Haverfordwest. The dwelling was earlier called Castell Gwis or Gwys. Built on a mound (motte) of rubble, the outside wall was polygonal. The outline of the structure, probably dating to the late 12th century, is still visible and there is a doorway which still shows the evidence of a draw bar.

father of **Gwenllian (ap Gwys)** m. Gwrgan (ap Bleddyn ap Maenarch)
Gwenllian may well have been Philip Gwys's only child- perhaps just the eldest daughter- for she was his heiress.

d. 1130

Grandfather- 29th generation

Trahaern Fychan

Lord of Llangorse, and, according to Poole "a man of great power in Brecknockshire."

"Tref Traherne," his home, the site of which is about two miles from Brecon on the Hay road, is listed by Poole as one of the historic dwellings in Brecknockshire. Poole says the property was "a part of the possessions and one of the mansions of Trehaern Fychan."[539]

son of **Gwgan** and **Gwenllian**, daughter and heiress of Philip Gwys

m. **Joan**, daughter of Bleddyn, Lord of Cilsant

father of Maud m. Howel ap Sitsyllt
Howel m. Gwenllian, daughter of Griffith ap Ivor, Lord of Sanghenith
Rees
Ellyw m. Rhys Vychan neu Mechyll
Joan m. Madoc ap Trahaern

His grandfather, Bleddyn ap Maenarch, left Llanphangel (Llangorse) to him.

d. 1197, murdered by William de Breos
Edwin Poole tells the tragic details of this event. He reports, "William de Breos was likewise a monster and a master of artfulness: on one occasion we read how he entrapped a chieftain of Brecknockshire, against whom he

---

" 'Castellum Wiz' was mentioned as being captured in 1147, although the man who probably founded it, Wizo (or Gwys) died in 1130. After it was captured once more in 1220 there were apparently plans to rebuild it, but Wiston Castle does not figure in the records again." (Alan Reid, *The Castles of Wales,* London, George Philip, 1973, p. 138.)
[539] Poole, p. 126.

entertained a secret grudge. The chieftain's name was Trahaern Vychan (or 'the little'), lord of Llangorse; he was invited to meet William de Breos, ostensibly to confer on business; unsuspicious of treachery and unprepared for defence, this descendant of Blethin determined to attend to the request; he was met by De Breos not far from Brecknock, when the latter ordered his blood-hounds to seize him, tied him to a horse's tail, and in that situation ignominiously and cruelly dragged him through the streets of the town, after which he was beheaded, and his body suspended upon a gallows for three days."[540]

Grandfather- 27th generation

Joan

daughter of **Bleddyn**, Lord of Cilsant

m. **Trahaern fychan**, Lord of Llangorse (-1197)

mother of Maud m. Howel ap Sitsyllt
    Howel m. Gwenllian, daughter of Griffith ap Ivor, Lord of Sanghenith
    Rees
    Ellyw m. Rhys Vychan neu Mechyll
    Joan m. Madoc ap Trahaern

Grandmother- 27th generation

Bleddyn, Lord of Cilsant

father of **Joan** m. Trahaern

Grandfather- 28th generation

Howel

son of **Trahaern**, Lord of Llangorse, and **Joan**, daughter of Bleddyn, Lord of

[540] Poole, p. 11.

Cilsant

m. **Gwenllian**, daughter of Griffith ap Ivor, Lord of Sanghenith

father of **Rhys ap Howel of Aberllyfni** m. Catherine ap Griffith Gwyr
Reynallt
Gwenllian m. Griffith ap Ednyfed Vychan

Grandfather- 26th generation

Gwenllian

daughter of **Griffith ap Ivor**, Lord of Sanghenith

m. **Howel**, son of Trahaern fychan

mother of **Rhys ap Howel of Aberllyfni**
Reynallt
Gwenllian m. Griffith ap Ednyfed Vychan

Grandmother- 26th generation

Griffith ap Ivor

Lord of Sanghenith

father of **Gwenllian** m. Howel

Grandfather- 27th generation

Rhys ap Howel of Aberllyfni

son of **Howel** and **Gwenllian**, daughter of Griffith ap Ivor

m. **Catherine**, daughter of Griffith Gwyr (Gower)

father of David ap Rhys y ddimau

Einion Sais m. (1)Joan, daughter of Howel, Lord of Miscin;
(2)Gwenllian, daughter of Howel ap Rhys Grug
Howel Morganwg

G-g-g-g-g-g-g-g-g-g-g-g-g-g-g-g-g-g-g-g-g-g-grandfather- 25th generation

Catherine

daughter of **Griffith Gwyr** or Gower

m. Rhys ap Howel of Aberllyfni

mother of David ap Rhys y ddimau
Einion Sais m. (1)Joan, daughter of Howel, Lord of Miscin;
(2)Gwenllian, daughter of Howel ap Rhys Grug
Howel Morganwg

G-g-g-g-g-g-g-g-g-g-g-g-g-g-g-g-g-g-g-g-g-g-grandmother- 25th generation

Griffith Gwyr (Gower)

father of **Catherine** m. Rhys ap Howel of Aberllyfni

Grandfather- 26th generation

Einion Sais

son of **Rhys ap Howel of Aberllyfni** and **Catherine**, daughter of Griffith Gwyr

Sais is a word for Saxon, and was apparently used, at least in some cases, in a derogatory manner. "Einion embraced a military life and served our third Edward in the memorable battles of Cressy (Crecy) in 1346, and Poitiers in 1356; after a long residence in England he returned to his native country with considerable opulence, and married the rich heiress of Howel. . . .(H)e became possessed by purchase of nearly the whole of what is now called the hundred of Devynnock, from Llywel on the borders of Carmarthenshire to the river Tarell near Brecon. He built a castellated mansion for his residence in the parish of Llanspyddid. . .on the fall of a small brook into the Usk, near Bettws or Penpont chapel (lately called castle field); there is still an unevenness in the surface of the ground, though there are not now the smallest vestiges of buildings remaining; Hugh Thomas, who wrote in 1698, recollects to have seen the ruins, and there are others living who remember the rubbish being removed and the soil cleared of the stones and materials of the walls. It was called from its owner Castell Einion Sais, or Einion the Englishman's castle, an appellation by which the Welsh to this day sometimes distinguish not only the English settlers among them, but also their own countrymen, who have been brought up and educated in England."[541]

Einion is said to have had another residence, in Llwel, and to have owned Aberbran during the reign of Edward III. Jones referred to him as a "territorial monopolist." Elsewhere Jones said that Einion, like his ancestors, "frequently indulged in a roving disposition." There is some question as to what was meant by this.

m. (1)**Joan** (Ioan), a rich heiress, daughter of Howel, Lord of Miscin in
Glamorganshire; (2)Gwenllian, daughter of Howel ap Rhys Grug

father in his first marriage **of Howel ap Einon Sais** m. Lettice, daughter of
Cadwaladr ap Griffith, Lord of Upper Gwent
Rees (Rhys), ancestor of Sir John Price of the Priory
Trahaern
Einion
and in his marriage with Gwenllian:
Meredith
Lleici

d. and buried in Llwel at a place called Craig Einion.

G-g-g-g-g-g-g-g-g-g-g-g-g-g-g-g-g-g-g-g-g-grandfather- 24th generation

Joan

daughter of **Howel**, Lord of Miscin

[541] Theophilus Jones, *History of Brecknockshire* (London, Edwin Davies, 1898 ed.), p. 80. Much general information has been found, or validated, on pp. 79-129 and 245-253 of this volume.

m. **Einion Sais**

mother of **Howel ap Einon Sais** m. Lettice, daughter of Cadwaladr ap Griffith, Lord of Upper Gwent
Rees, progenitor of Sir John Price of the Priory
Trahaern
Einon

G-g-g-g-g-g-g-g-g-g-g-g-g-g-g-g-g-g-g-g-g-grandmother- 24th generation

Howel ap Einon Sais

son of **Einion Sais** and **Joan**

brother of Rees ap Einon Sais
Trahaern
Einon

m. **Lettice** the daughter of Cadwaladr ap Griffith, Lord of Upper Gwent

father of **Howel Fychan** m. a daughter of Llewelyn ap Howel hen
David Llwyd, ancestor of the Skulls of Monington
Gwilym, ancestor of Griffith of Blancrai
Bleddin

G-g-g-g-g-g-g-g-g-g-g-g-g-g-g-g-g-g-g-g-grandfather- 23rd generation

Lettice

daughter of **Cadwaladr ap Griffith**, Lord of Upper Gwent

m. **Howel ap Einon Sais**

mother of **Howel Fychan** m. a daughter of Llewelyn ap Howel hen
David Llwyd
Gwilym
Bleddin

G-g-g-g-g-g-g-g-g-g-g-g-g-g-g-g-g-g-g-grandmother- 23rd generation

Cadwaladr ap Griffith

Lord of Upper Gwent

son of **Griffith**, Lord of Upper Gwent (-1084)

father of **Lettice** m. Howel ap Einon Sais

G-g-g-g-g-g-g-g-g-g-g-g-g-g-g-g-g-g-g-g-grandfather- 24th generation

Howel Fychan

son of **Howel ap Einon Sais** and **Lettice**

brother of David Llwyd, ancestor of the Skulls of Monington
Gwilym, ancestor of Griffith of Blancrai
Bleddin

m. a daughter of Llewelyn ap Howel hen

father of David, progenitor of Williams of Park Lettice near Abergavenny
Jeuan
Llewelyn m. Malt, daughter of Jeuan ap Rhys ap Ivor

G-g-g-g-g-g-g-g-g-g-g-g-g-g-g-g-g-g-grandfather- 22nd generation

Llewelyn ap Howel hen

father of a daughter who m. Howel Fychan

G-g-g-g-g-g-g-g-g-g-g-g-g-g-g-g-g-g-grandfather- 23rd generation

Llewelyn

son of **Howel Fychan** and a daughter of Llewelyn ap Howel hen.

m. **Malt**, daughter of Jevan ap Rhys ap Ivor.

father of **Dafydd ap Llewelyn** (Sir Davydd Gam)
Pfelis m. Rees David Thomas
Helen m. Griffith ap Owen
Howel ap Llewelyn (progenitor of the Powels of Castlemadoc)
Roger ap Llewelyn
Griffith (progenitor of the Bowens of Llywel) of Trecastle
Richard ap Llewelyn
Gwilyn ap Llewelyn (progenitor of the Vaughans of Peytin Gwyn)
Morgan ap Llewelyn- presumed to have been the Dominican friar whose pilgrimage to the Holy Land is a matter of record

"The whole of Garthbrengy (or Galltbrengy) at one time or other, and indeed the whole of the county has been in the possession of the family of the Gams, but the mansion and principal residence of the valorous ancestor, from whom they derive their name, was at Peytyn Gwin, in this parish, although upon his being obliged to quit Breconshire (presumably when he went to France with King Henry V) it is probable that (Sir Davydd's) younger brother Gwilym purchased it from him and his descendants. . . .This tenement, together with two others adjoining, called Peytyn du and Peytyn glas were purchased, say our heralds, by Llewelyn, the father of Sir David Gam, for three hundred marks. . . ."[542]

At Christ's College Church of Brecon there is a monument dedicated to Llewelyn ap Howel. In 1809 it was reported to be the most ancient seen in the church. Located at the entrance, the stone is inscribed "Hic jacet Llewelinus ap Howell cujus animae propicietur Deus, amen." It is believed that Llewelyn is buried here, though the date of his death, which is supposed to have occurred during the reign of Henry V, is unknown. There is a stone for Morgan, Llewelyn's son, also, and a stone on which there is a female figure which is thought to represent either the mother, wife, or daughter of Sir David Gam.[543]

". . .(F)requently. . .benefactors (of the various churches) stipulated that they and their wives should be buried within the walls of the monastery

[542] Jones, 1898, p. 245.
[543] Poole, p. 65.

or convent. . . ." This church is known as the burial place of the Games family and, more specifically, it is known that the family vault, containing the remains of most of the descendants of Llewelyn and his son Davydd who died in the vicinity of Brecon, lies beneath the stones at the doorway. As suggested previously, the Welsh honor their ancestors.

G-g-g-g-g-g-g-g-g-g-g-g-g-g-g-g-g-grandfather- 21st generation

Malt

daughter of **Jeuan ap Rhys ap Ivor**

m. **Llewelyn ap Howel hen**

mother of **Dafydd ap Llewelyn** (Sir David)
  Pfelis m. Rees David Thomas
  Helen m. Griffith ap Owen
  Howel ap Llewelyn
  Roger ap Llewelyn
  Griffith
  Richard ap Llewelyn
  Gwilyn ap Llewelyn
  Morgan ap Llewelyn

G-g-g-g-g-g-g-g-g-g-g-g-g-g-g-g-g-grandmother- 21st generation

Jeuan ap Rhys ap Ivor

father of **Malt** m. Llewelyn

G-g-g-g-g-g-g-g-g-g-g-g-g-g-g-g-g-g-grandfather- 22nd generation

Davydd ap Llewelyn (Sir Dafydd Gam)

3rd son of **Llewellyn ap Howel** and **Malt**

brother of Pfelis m. Rees David Thomas

Howel, progenitor of the Powels of Castlemadoc
Helen m. Griffith ap Owen
Roger ap Llewelyn
Griffith ap Llewelyn of Trecastle, from whom are descended the Bowens of Llywel
Richard ap Llewelyn
Gwilyn ap Llewelyn, from whom the Vaughans of Peytin Gwyn descend[544]
Morgan ap Llewelyn, a Dominican friar recorded to have made a pilgrimage to the Holy Land

This man was a colorful figure, personally, politically, and in his appearance. It is popular tradition that Sir Dafydd was "athletic" in his build and that he had red hair. His rival, Owain Glyn Dwr, described him thus in the poem quoted below. He also had a distinctive flaw, hence the name Games. It is said that he was either one-eyed or that he squinted. ". . .(T)he influence of this chieftain (was) irresistible in this country; the turbulence of his disposition instead of being an objection was a recommendation to him with many in these boisterous days, and the violence of his passions created no enemies but those against whom his resentment was directed: upon his death . . . ."(H)e was idolized, and it is not without apprehension even at this distance of time that I venture, though compelled by historical justice, to charge him with some of the worst crimes which have disgraced humanity."[545]

As to the name, Gam or Games, Poole assures us that he was known, "to his face" and on the battlefield as Dafydd ap Llewelyn, "and not Gam or squinting, by which epithet, though it was afterwards assumed by his family, he would probably have knocked down any man who dared to address him."[546]

Over the fireplace at Newton, an impressive 12th century farmhouse built by Sir Dafydd's g-g-grandson, Sir John Games (1559-1606), there is carved on the face of a ten foot wide, six foot high stone mantle an inscription which traces the ancestral line from Sir David Gam to Sir John Games and shows the Games coat of arms with the motto *Ar. Duw. Y Gyd.* (All depends on God.) This house is maintained by the English government as a public monument.

---

[544] "Family" properties, including the three Peytyns, were probably purchased by Dafydd's younger brother Gwilym when Dafydd left for France. These continued in the Gaines family "for some generations." (Poole, p. 248.)
[545] Jones, 1898, p. 510.
[546] Poole, p. 81.

Peityn gwyn was the home of Dafydd's father, bought by him from a Norman family for three hundred marks along with Peityn du and Peityn glas in the parishes of Garthbrengy and Llanddew. Peityn gwyn has also been shown as an early residence of Sir Dafydd Gam and is said to be the place from which he set off to kill Owain Glyn Dwr. At his father's death, Sir Dafydd inherited the three properties as well as Castell Einon Sais, his g-grandfather's mansion, where he lived until it was destroyed by Glyn Dwr. The latter property is now called "Castell Field."

m. **Gwenllian**, daughter of Gwilym and granddaughter of Hywel y Grach

father of many children including **Morgan Gam**, who became the ancestor of the Games of Breconshire m. (1)Tanglwst Llewelyn; (2)Margaret Lloyd

Thomas Gam

Gwladis Gam (-1454) m. (1)Sir Roger Vaughan; and who by her second marriage to (2)Sir William ab Thomas of Raglan, became the mother of William, the first Herbert, Earl of Pembroke.[547] (Gwladis, hence all of her ancestors, are also part of my husband's lineage.)

Ann Stripe, a genealogist my husband visited in Raglan, Wales, said that there were a great many other children, legitimate and otherwise. She stated that if all of Dafydd's children, legitimate and illegitimate, held hands, the resulting line would stretch from his home to the church, a distance of about three hundred yards.

We visited the church at Llantillio Pertholey and the site of Dafydd's home, according to road markers there. "Castell Field" was an unspectacular field of some four or five acres located between a road and a stream. On its perimeter there was a shallow moat, doubtless filled in considerably in the 600 plus years since Sir Dafydd lived there. Bill said it was *at least* three hundred yards to the church from the house site. I believe this site was the location of Castell Einion Sais.

According to Theophilus Jones, "During the four first years of the

[547] Gwladis's first husband and the father of her first eight children, Grandfather Sir Roger Vaughan of Bredwardine in Herefordshire, was killed with Sir Dafydd at Agincourt. He was presumably one of the three foot-archers from Brecon. Sir Watkin Llwyd, the representative of another ancient family of Brecon, was also killed with Sir Dafydd and Sir Roger at Agincourt. My husband's family, the Raglands, traces its ancestry to Gwladus, hence to Sir Dafydd.

reign of Henry the fourth, the territory of Brecknock was greatly harrassed by the incursions of that bold and enterprizing chieftain Owen Glyndwr. . .who, exclusive of the enmity which he inveterately bore to the house of Lancaster, had a personal quarrel with the well known David Gam, a native of that county and a warm supporter of the Lancastrian interest; irritable as these chiefs and indeed all Welshmen are supposed to be, they were fired by the madness of party rage and opposing factions, insomuch that their resentment against each other became as violent as it was implacable."[548]

As stated, David ap Llewelyn had been faithful to his king throughout the successful revolt of Owain Glyn Dwr against the king. He was rewarded for his services by a large share in the South Welsh lands confiscated from rebels in 1401. There is a story that David plotted against the life of Owain when they were attending the Welsh parliament at Machynlleth. But it rests on no authority, misdates the year of the Machynlleth parliament, which was 1402, and incorrectly makes David a brother-in-law of Owain.

"That this foul plot was discovered no one will lament: David was seized, imprisoned, and would have met with the fate he deserved, if he had not been saved by the intercession of some of Owen's best friends: he continued in confinement until 1412; upon the 14th June, in which year, a commission issued from the crown, directed to the king's well beloved esquire, Llewelyn ap Howel, father of his majesty's well beloved esquire, 'David Gamme, . . .'reciting his having been taken prisoner,' by Owen de Glendourdy, rebel and traitor; empowering them. . .to treat for his ransom and to exchange for him any Welshmen, adherents, favourers, succourers or assistants of the said Owen;[549] The commissioners, it appears, succeeded in releasing the king's well beloved esquire, David Gamme, upon his engaging (as it is said) not to bear arms or oppose the measures of Owen; for this favour he shewed the same sense of gratitude as criminals frequently entertain for those who have saved their lives; attacking the partizans of that chieftain wherever he met them, and betraying his designs to the English monarch whenever he could discover them; this conduct drew down upon him the vengeance of his insulted and abused adversary, who entering Breconshire with a body of his troops would probably have prevented David Gam from molesting him in future if he had met him; fortunately for the lord of Peytyn gwin he was not at home when the enemy arrived: as a punishment for repeated injuries received from him, Owen burnt his house (Castell Einion Sais) to the ground. After which, meeting with one of David's tenants on the road in his return, he tauntingly told him:

---

[548] Jones, 1898, p. 80.
[549] Rymer. Faed. tom. VIII. fo. 753 as quoted by Jones, 1898, p. 247.

"O' weli di wr coch cam,
Yn 'mofyn ei gyrnigwen,
D'wed y bod hi dan y lan,
A nod y glo ar ei phen."

which, translated, says:

"If a squinting red hair'd knave,
Meet thee and perchance should crave
To know what fate his house befell,
Say that the cinder-mark will tell."[550]

Crest of Sir Davydd Gam with arms and motto

[550] Jones, 1898, p. 247.

It must be said at this point that Sir Dafydd's loyalty to the King does not endear him to many of Welsh descent. In the library in Brecon, Wales, my sister, Martha, my husband and I found several references to the fact that there was competition between Sir Dafydd and Owain ap Griffith Fychan, Lord of Glyndyfrdwy, known to the Welsh as Owain Glyn Dwr (and to Shakespeare as Glendower). Some Welsh historians have suggested that Dafydd was cunning, perhaps deceptive, on that occasion when he was said to have plotted to kill their beloved Glyn Dwr, a leader of the Welsh people in their fight against the English.

I have provided for you reports of both sides of the issue of Sir Dafydd's behavior; you may judge for yourself.

Sir Dafydd is said to have been a "Welsh warrior." History suggests that this was the occupation of the typical male at that time in history, regardless of nationality or socio-economic standing.

If you reach back into your memory, you will remember the name of the French village, Agincourt, and if you have a truly wonderful knowledge of history, you may know that a battle was fought near there in the north of France in 1415 that is said to have brought about the decline of feudal warfare. Armed with long bows, some 13,000 English archers killed or routed more than 50,000 Frenchmen who were thought to have been better armed than they.

Theophilus Jones suggested that Dafydd was probably 55 or 60 years of age when he fought at Agincourt, since he left both children and grand-children behind at his home in Brecknockshire. He could, of course, have been younger. Regardless, he became involved, along with three foot archers from Brecon, by following King Henry V of England when he invaded France. There were, undoubtedly, at least two motivating factors that caused him to choose to leave his home at a mature age to engage in such adventure. Theophilus Jones stated that Sir Davydd held property which the king had awarded him, which would further indicate the loyalty felt between the two men;[551] and Sir Leslie Stephen and Sir Sidney Lee in *The Dictionary of Historical Biography,* Vol. VII, reported that it was said that during the year 1413 Dafydd "got into trouble by killing a kinsman (Ritsiart fawr o'r Slwch) in an affray on High Street in Brecon town." Shortly thereafter he left for France.

"It was at Agincourt that David Gam won the accolade of knighthood - at the cost of his life. In a furious action, in which with personal daring he saved the life of the king who was hemmed in and about to be overpowered, he received wounds from which he died, either on the field of battle or soon after.

---

[551] Jones, vol. 2, p. 170.

At any rate, the king there and then knighted him 'Sir Davydd Gam.' "

Theophilus Jones reported that Dafydd's valor was recognized before this one last, well-documented feat. He said that Dafydd was already rated an "esquire" (ranking next below a knight) in the service of his king before the invasion of France.[552] He was said to have "lived like a wolf and died like a lion."[553]

"Henry the fifth, following the narrow policy of his father, in the first year of his reign, passed, or at least sanctioned a very severe law against the Welsh, though from the support he received from our countrymen, Sir David Gam, Sir Roger Vaughan,[554] and their adherents at Agincourt, his sentiments were considerably altered in their favour before he died. . . ."[555]

It is reported that on the eve of the Battle of Agincourt King Henry had asked Dafydd ap Llewelyn about the number of the enemy and that he replied, ". . .enough to be slain, enough to be taken prisoners, and enough to run away." This story was first reported by Sir Walter Raleigh in his *History of the World*. Even in that time in England Raleigh was familiar with Sir Dafydd's story and delivered "an eulogium upon his bravery and exploits in the field of Agincourt, in which he prefers his greatness of soul to that of Mago, and compares him to Hannibal; while his countrymen, in consideration of this day's good services, have unanimously determined to forget his treachery towards Glyndwr, and to pardon the murder of Richard fawr."[556]

"Whether Henry the fifth rewarded the family of Sir David Gam with something more substantial than this title, which fled almost as soon as it was conferred, does not appear; it is however probable that the king did not forget his obligations to his gallant subject and defender, and that he either granted his descendants territorial possessions or bestowed a sum of money upon them adequate to their wants; for they are immediately seen rising in importance, increasing opulence, and numbers for several succeeding centuries. . . ."[557]

d. 10/25/1415, mortally wounded on the field of battle at Agincourt, while defending the life of King Henry V.

G-g-g-g-g-g-g-g-g-g-g-g-g-g-g-g-g-grandfather- 20th generation

---

[552] L. P. Gaines, *History of the Gaines Family: Our Line from 1620 to the Present Time, 1918* (Calhoun, GA, T. H. Land, 1918), pp. 1-19.
[553] Jones, vol. 1, 1909, p. 98.
[554] The alliance between the Gam/Games family and the Vaughan family is said to have endured for nine generations. (Poole, p. 228.)
[555] Jones, 1898, p. 126.
[556] Jones, 1898, p. 247.
[557] Jones, 1898, p. 248.

Theophilus Jones, Welsh genealogist (1758-1812), declared ". . .From this David Gam, all ye Games of Brecknockshire, all ye Vaughns, and all ye Herberts of South Wales are descended and ye most part of all the nobility of England."[558]

Sir David's coat of arms is described as a black shield bearing a silver chevron on which there are five drops of blood. Above the chevron there are two silver spearheads and below it one silver spearhead. These weapons of war are tipped with blood, alluding to the cause and manner of his death. The crest is a rampant lion, signifying a "raging, ferocious" leader of armies and denoting strength.

Due to the seemingly complex "unfixed" naming system of the time, so unfamiliar to us, Sir Dafydd was known in the army as Llewellyn, which was his father's name. It is assumed by historians, Theophilus Jones among them, that it was Dafydd that Shakespeare was writing about in his play *Henry V* when he wrote of the exploits of Fluellin, who saved the king's life, even as Dafydd had done at the end of his own life. Jones said in *The History of Brecknockshire*, ". . .there was no other person of that country in the English army who could have been supposed to have been upon such terms of familiarity with the King; and it must be observed that Llewellyn was the name by which he was known in that army. . . ."

"It has been argued. . .that Shakespeare was a Welshman himself, so well did he know the foibles of the people, and there are several places in Wales which he is claimed to have visited."[559]

Gwenllian

daughter of **Gwilym (Gwylym) ap Howel y Grach**

m. **Sir David Gam**, or Dafydd ap Llewelyn

mother of numerous children including **Morgan**, who became the ancestor of the Games of Breconshire

Thomas Gam

Gwladis Gam, (-1454) m. (1)Sir Roger Vaughan, and after his death (2) Sir William ap Thomas of Raglan, who became the father of

[558] Jones, vol. 1, pp. 160-161.
[559] Morris, pp. 380-381.

William, the first Herbert, Earl of Pembroke (my husband's line).

G-g-g-g-g-g-g-g-g-g-g-g-g-g-g-g-g-grandmother- 20th generation

Gwilym ap Howel y Grach

son of Hywel y Grach

father of **Gwenllian** m. Sir Dafydd Gam

G-g-g-g-g-g-g-g-g-g-g-g-g-g-g-g-g-g-grandfather- 21st generation

Morgan Gam

son of **Davydd ap Llewellyn ap Howell (Sir Davydd Gam)** and **Gwellian**

brother of Thomas Gam
Gwladis Gam m. (1)Sir Roger Vaughan of Bredwardine; (2)Sir William Thomas of Raglan

m. (1)Tanglwst Llewelyn (2)**Margaret Lloyd**

father, with Tanglwst, of Maud m. Owen Griffith ap Owen Gethin
father, with **Margaret Lloyd**, of Alice m. Jenkin Stradling
Gwenllian m. Morgan Prees Gwilym
Gwallter ap Morgan of Porthgwyn
Meredith ap Morgan
Jeuan or Edward ap Morgan m. Anne Lloyd
Gwilym ap Morgan
Thomas ap Morgan
Llewelyn ap Morgan of Penfathrin m. Jennet Rhaglan
Jeuan hir, ancestor of the Gwyns of Bodwigad
David ap Morgan

G-g-g-g-g-g-g-g-g-g-g-g-g-g-g-g-grandfather- 19th generation

Margaret Lloyd

daughter of **Llewelyn Gwilym Rees Lloyd ap Adam** and **Golewdydd Vychan**

sister of Gwilym Lloyd
Lewis ap Gwilym Llwyd of Castel Hywel

m. **Morgan Gam**

mother of Alice Gam m. Jenkin Stradling
Gwenllian Gam m. Morgan Prees Gwilym
Gwallter ap Morgan of Porthgwyn
Meredith ap Morgan
Jeuan or Edward ap Morgan m. Anne Lloyd
Gwilym ap Morgan
Thomas ap Morgan
Llewelyn ap Morgan of Penfathrin m. Jennet Rhaglan
Jeuan hir from whom the Gwyns of Bodwigad descend
David ap Morgan

G-g-g-g-g-g-g-g-g-g-g-g-g-g-g-grandmother- 19th generation

Llewelyn Gwilym Rhys Lloyd ap Adam

m. **Golewdydd Vychan**[560]

father of **Margaret Lloyd** m. Morgan Gam
Gwilyn Lloyd
Lewis ap Gwilym Llwyd of Castell Hywel

G-g-g-g-g-g-g-g-g-g-g-g-g-g-g-g-grandfather- 20th generation

Golewdydd Vychan

m. **Llewelyn Gwilym Rhys Lloyd ap Adam**

---

[560] Vychan is another spelling for and, normally, interchangeable with, the name Vaughan.

mother of **Margaret Lloyd** m. Morgan Gam
Gwilyn Lloyd
Lewis ap Gwilym Llwyd of Castell Hywel

G-g-g-g-g-g-g-g-g-g-g-g-g-g-g-g-g-grandmother- 20th generation

Llewelyn (Llen) of Penfathrin

son of **Morgan ap Sir Dafydd Gam** and **Margaret**, daughter of Llewelyn Gwilym Rhys Lloyd ap Adam

brother of Alice Gam m. Jenkin Stradling
Gwenllian Gam m. Morgan Prees Gwilym
Gwallter Gam
Meredith Gam of Porthgwyn
Jeuan or Edward Gam m. Anne, daughter of Gwilym Lloyd
Gwilym Gam
Thomas Gam
Jeuan hir Gam, from whom the Gwyns of Bodwigad are descended
David Gam
step-brother of Maud Gam m. Owen Griffith ap Owen Gethin

m. **Jennet Rhaglan**

father of Catharine Games m. Matthew Goch of Cedewin
Anne Games m. Llewelyn Morgan of Ffrwdgrech
Jennet Games m. Philip John of Marchogtir
__Games m. Trahaern Morgan tew.
John Games m. Jennet Havard of Aberbran
William Games m. Jane Skull
David Games, a natural son
Hopkin Games, a natural son

Henry VIII of England, concerned about the lawlessness of the Welsh when the Norman barons were no longer there to maintain order ". . . appointed fourteen persons, amongst whom were his secretary Thomas Cromwell. . .and Llewelyn ap Morgan ap Sir David Gam, empowering them or any two of them to act as justices itinerant within the town and lordship of Brecknock, to hear and determine all complaints and suits. . . according to the laws and customs there used and known."[561]

G-g-g-g-g-g-g-g-g-g-g-g-g-g-g-grandfather- 18th generation

Jennet Rhaglan

daughter of **Lewis Rhaglan**

m. **Llewelyn Games of Penfathrin**

mother of Catharine Games m. Matthew Goch of Cedewin
Anne Games m. Llewelyn Morgan of Ffrwdgrech
Jennet Games m. Philip John of Marchogtir
__Games m. Trahaern Morgan tew.
John Games m. Jennet Havard of Aberbran
William Games m. Jane Skull

G-g-g-g-g-g-g-g-g-g-g-g-g-g-g-grandmother- 18th generation

Lewis Rhaglan

father of **Jennet Rhaglan**

G-g-g-g-g-g-g-g-g-g-g-g-g-g-g-g-grandfather- 19th generation

Sais Gwalter

son of **Rhosser Fychan** and __ **Baskerville** (granddaughter of Sir Miles Pitcher)

m. **Florence de Bredwardine**

father of **Rhosser hen (Roger) of Bredwardine**

G-g-g-g-g-g-g-g-g-g-g-g-g-g-g-g-g-g-g-grandfather- 22nd generation

[561] Jones, vol. 4, p. 128.

Continued Struggle Against Norman England

When William the Conquerer succeeded in overpowering Saxon England in the years after 1066, he declared himself lord of Wales as well. He gave land along the border between England and Wales to strong Norman lords who established fortresses and commenced attacks on the Welsh. They had some success, claiming at one time most of central and southern Wales. Sometimes the Welsh chieftains were allowed to remain on their lands; some declared their loyalty to English overlords; and some of them continued to fight bitterly for their independence. By 1230 a Welsh prince by the name Llewelyn the Great, through diplomacy, marriage and battle, was able to draw much of the country together again. By 1262 his grandson, Llewelyn II, had driven out most of the Normans and was acknowledged as the Prince of Wales by the Norman king of England, Henry III. These were not permanent gains, however, for Llewelyn II was killed in battle against Edward I, and the Welsh revolt collapsed. Wales then came under the rule of the English king or his sheriffs or barons. And so it went for another 200 years.

During the time in which the Norman "Lord Marchers" ruled Brecknockshire, these victors demanded complete servitude. "As showing the state of bondage of 'the people' during the reign of these very autocratic 'Lords' this was the sort of obedience that was exacted by the Lord of Crickhowell from his tenants: 'All the tenants that helde their land of the saide prince ought to acknowledge the lords by the words followinge, that is to saie, first he ought to come before the lord kneelinge, and acknowledge to hould of the lord of Crughowell such rents and lands by service of homage, and ought to close his handes within the lorde's, deposeinge truly, on his faith by God and the holy Evangelists, that with his whole heart and soul above all things he shall love his lord, and in all places of any dread, shall stand up by his lord, him to defend, and his bodie well and truly, and without fraude and guile against his enemyes keep. And this done the lord shall command him to stand upp from his kneelinge, and shall kisse him, and after that all the tenants (are) soe sworn, they shall give the lord or his officer by him appoynted, the sum of 5 poundes of lawful money of England immediately after the oathes and homages made. . . .The Welsh tenants shall give to the lord at his making knight reasonable ayde, that is to witte, eight pence for to buy him a horse. The saide tenants shall give unto the lord at his first cominge to his lordshippe 100 shillings; and to the marryinge of his first begotten daughter 100 shillings; and to the son of the saide lord when he is made knight, five poundes. . .;" they shall come to pay their rents on specified days; they should bring their oxen to plough for the lord on certain days; keep the property of the lord in good repair; but, "If any man enters the saide parke (the lord's demesne) and there be founde, he ought to be attached by the Keeper of the Parke, and to be kept in the stocks, without the gate of the said parke, till he pay up, or else to loose his right foot, if the parke be closed round about." It would appear that a duty was required for every act but the breathing of those subjugated.[562]

The Welsh continued to revolt throughout the 1300's and by 1402 Owain Glyndwr, considered a national hero by many Welshmen to this day, had actually driven the English out. Henry IV, however, in spite of civil war in England, raised an army and again subdued Wales by 1410.

Henry Tudor, of Welsh descendency, combined his forces with those of the House of Lancaster of England and defeated the House of York, ending the war which had plagued England for many years. Because of his victory in 1485 the English Parliament proclaimed him King Henry VII of England. Until the 1600s when the Stuarts of Scotland became the royal family of England the Tudors, a dynasty of Welsh origin,[563] ruled England, and the citizens of Wales slowly gained their rightful place as English citizens.

Roger (Rhosser hen) of Bredwardine

son of **Sais Gwalter** and **Florence de Bredwardine**

m. **Anne**, a daughter of Sir Walter Devereux, Lord Ferrars of Chartley[564]

father of **Sir Roger Vaughan of Bredwardine** m. Gwladis, daughter of Sir Davydd Gam

G-g-g-g-g-g-g-g-g-g-g-g-g-g-g-g-g-grandfather- 21st generation

Anne Devereux

---

[562] Poole, p. 19.

[563] Unfortunately, if we would "claim" the Tudors, we must claim King Henry VIII as he is one of them. Referred to by Theophilus Jones as the *dread* sovereign, his great vanity and his misdeeds are known to all. Through his Acts of Union of 1536 and 1543 he united Wales and England, however, removing some of the worst of the restrictions that had earlier been placed against the rebellious Welshmen. And his shenanigans provided the opportunity for the Welsh to finally have a *Bible* and *The Book of Common Prayer* printed in their own language. For the first time, those attending church in Wales could hear the sermon in the language for which they had fought for generations.

[564] Poole, p. 94.

daughter of **Sir Walter Devereux**, Lord Ferrars of Chartley

m. **Roger (Rhosser hen) of Bredwardine**

mother of **Sir Roger Vaughan of Bredwardine**

G-g-g-g-g-g-g-g-g-g-g-g-g-g-g-g-g-g-grandmother- 21st generation

Sir Walter Devereux

Lord of Ferrars of Chartley

father of **Anne Devereux** m. Roger Vaughan of Bredwardine

G-g-g-g-g-g-g-g-g-g-g-g-g-g-g-g-g-g-g-grandfather- 22nd generation

The Vaughan Connection

At this juncture we will meet several generations of Vaughan ancestors. Being unaware that their pedigree would literally fall into my hands, I did not spend time with this illustrious family. Time spent would be richly rewarded, however, for they, like the Gams/Gaineses, have their roots in ancient Briton. These were among those who came very early into Wales, after which time they and their descendants became men of power and fit subjects for those who collected, and often sang, the earliest of Welsh history. Upon examination you will discover that this family is descended from a number of the individuals we have previously encountered, starting with 31st generation grandfather Dryffin, Prince of Brecon, and his wife, Crusilla, and moving backward down Dryffin's ancestral line. The following listing will take us from Sais Gwalter and Florence of generation 22 to Dryffin in the early 10th century.

Sais Gwalter[565]

son of **Rhosser Fychan** and **__Baskerville,** daughter of Sir Ralph Baskerville

565 This Vaughan pedigree was provided by Jones, vol. 3, Appendix.

m. **Florence Bredwardine**, daughter of Sir Walter de Bredwardine

father of **Rhosser hen of Bredwardine** m. Anne Devereux

G-g-g-g-g-g-g-g-g-g-g-g-g-g-g-g-g-g-grandfather- 22nd generation

Florence Bredwardine

daughter of **Sir Walter de Bredwardine**

m. **Sais Gwalter**

mother of **Rhosser hen of Bredwardine** m. Anne Devereux

G-g-g-g-g-g-g-g-g-g-g-g-g-g-g-g-g-g-grandmother- 22nd generation

Sir Walter Bredwardine or de Bredwardine

father of **Florence Bredwardine** m. Sais Gwalter

G-g-g-g-g-g-g-g-g-g-g-g-g-g-g-g-g-g-g-grandfather- 23rd generation

Rhosser Fychan

son of **Rhosser Fawr of Llechryd** and **Joice Walbieffe**

m. **__Baskerville**, daughter of Sir Ralph Baskerville

father of **Sais Gwalter** m. Florence de Bredwardine

G-g-g-g-g-g-g-g-g-g-g-g-g-g-g-g-g-g-g-grandfather- 23rd generation

__Baskerville

daughter of **Sir Ralph Baskerville**

m. **Rhosser Fychan**

mother of **Sais Gwalter** m. Florence de Bredwardine

G-g-g-g-g-g-g-g-g-g-g-g-g-g-g-g-g-g-g-g-grandmother- 23rd generation

Sir Ralph Baskerville

m. __**Pitcher**, daughter of Sir Miles Pitcher

father of __**Baskerville** m. Rhosser Fychan

G-g-g-g-g-g-g-g-g-g-g-g-g-g-g-g-g-g-g-g-g-greatfather- 24th generation

Sir Miles Pitcher

father of __**Pitcher** m. Sir Ralph Baskerville

G-g-g-g-g-g-g-g-g-g-g-g-g-g-g-g-g-g-g-g-g-g-grandfather- 25th generation

Rhosser Fawr of Llechryd

son of **Einon/Jeuan** and **Jennet**, daughter of Rhys Grug of Cwmdu

m. **Joice Walbieffe**

father of **Rhosser Fychan** m. __ Baskerville

G-g-g-g-g-g-g-g-g-g-g-g-g-g-g-g-g-g-g-g-g-grandfather- 24th generation

Joice Walbieffe

daughter of **Sir William Walbieffe**

m. **Rhosser Fawr of Llechryd**

mother of **Rhosser Fychan** m. __Baskerville

G-g-g-g-g-g-g-g-g-g-g-g-g-g-g-g-g-g-g-g-g-grandmother- 24th generation

Sir William Walbieffe

father of **Joice Walbieffe** m. Rhosser Fawr of Llechryd

G-g-g-g-g-g-g-g-g-g-g-g-g-g-g-g-g-g-g-g-g-g-grandfather- 25th generation

Einon or Jeuan

son of **Howel** and **Gwladis**, daughter of Morgan Fychan, Lord of Aeron

m. **Jennet**, daughter of Rhys Grug of Cwmdu

father of **Rhosser Fawr of Llechryd** m. Joice Walbieffe

G-g-g-g-g-g-g-g-g-g-g-g-g-g-g-g-g-g-g-g-g-g-grandfather- 25th generation

Jennet

daughter of **Rhys Grug of Cwmdu**

m. **Einon** or **Jeuan**

mother of **Rhosser Fawr of Llechryd** m. Joice Walbieffe

G-g-g-g-g-g-g-g-g-g-g-g-g-g-g-g-g-g-g-g-g-g-grandmother- 25th generation

Rhys Grug of Cwmdu

father of **Jennet** m. Einon/Jeuan

Grandfather- 26th generation

Howel

son of **Sitsyllt/Cecil** and **Lleici/Lydia**, daughter of Griffith ap Madoc ap Cadrod

m. **Gwladis**, daughter of Morgan Fychan, Lord of Aeron

father of **Einon/Jeuan** m. Jennet, daughter of Rhys Grug of Cwmdu

Grandfather- 26th generation

Gwladis (ap Morgan Fychan)

daughter of **Morgan Fychan**, Lord of Aeron

m. **Howel**, son of Sitsyllt/Cecil and Lleici/Lydia

mother of **Einon/Jeuan** m. Jennet, daughter of Rhys Grug of Cwmdu

Grandmother- 26th generation

Morgan Fychan

Lord of Aeron

father of **Gwladis** m. Howel

Grandfather- 27th generation

Sitsyllt/Cecil

son of **Llewellin** and Joan, a daughter of Cynhyllin, Lord of Ystradwy

m. **Lleici/Lydia**, daughter of Griffith ap Madoc ap Cadrod

father of **Howel** m. Gwladis, daughter of Morgan Fychan, Lord of Aeron

Grandfather- 27th generation

Lleici or Lydia

daughter of **Griffith ap Madoc ap Cadrod**

m. **Sitsyllt/Cecil ap Llewellin**

mother of **Howel** m. Gwladis, daughter of Morgan Fychan, Lord of Aeron

Grandmother- 27th generation

Griffith ap Madoc ap Cadrod

father of **Lleici/Lydia** m. **Sitsyllt/Cecil ap Llewellin**

Grandfather- 28th generation

Llewellin

son of **Moreiddig Warwyn** and **Elinor**, daughter of Lord Rhys, Prince of South Wales

m. **Joan**, daughter of Cynhyllin, Lord of Ystradwy

father of **Sitsyllt/Cecil** m. Lleici/Lydia

Grandfather- 28th generation

Joan

daughter of **Cynhyllin**, Lord of Ystradwy

m. **Llewellin ap Moreiddig Warwyn**

mother of **Sitsyllt/Cecil** m. Lleici/Lydia, daughter of Griffith ap Madoc ap Cadrod

Grandmother- 28th generation

Cynhyllin

Lord of Ystradwy

father of **Joan** m. Llewellin ap Moreiddig Warwyn

Grandfather- 29th generation

Moreiddig Warwyn

son of **Drymbenog**, Lord of Cantref Selyff and **Gwenllian**, daughter of Jestin ap Gwrgan

m. **Elinor**, daughter of Lord Rhys, Prince of South Wales

father of **Llewellin** m. Joan, daughter of Cynhyllin, Lord of Ystradwy

Grandfather- 29th generation

Elinor

daughter of **Lord Rhys**, Prince of South Wales

m. **Moreiddig Warwyn**

mother of **Llewellin** m. Joan, daughter of Cynhyllin, lord of Ystradwy

Grandmother- 29th generation

Lord Rhys

Prince of South Wales

father of **Elinor** m. Moreiddig Warwyn

Grandfather- 30th generation

Drymbenog

Lord of Cantref Selyff

son of **Sir Dryffin,**[566] Prince of Brecon, and **Crusilla**, daughter of Idwal ap Meuric

m. **Gwenllian**, daughter of Jestin ap Gwrgan

father of **Moreiddig Warwyn** m. Elinor, daughter of Lord Rhys, Prince of South Wales

Grandfather- 31st generation

Having Made the Vaughan/Gaines Ancestral Connection
We Return to the Gaines Pedigree We Left on Page 287

Sir Roger Vaughan of Bredwardine

son of **"Roger (Rhosser hen) of Bredwardine"** and **Anne**, a daughter of Sir Walter Devereux, Lord Ferrars of Chartley

Poole reported that Sir Roger was a native of Bredwardine in Herefordshire. His ancestry was closely intertwined with the ancestry of the Gaines family.

m. **Gwladis**, daughter of Sir Dafydd Gam

father of eight children, including "three legitimate and one natural son," among whom were: **Sir Roger Vaughan of Tretower**, third son m.

---

[566] Here once again are Sir Dryffin and his wife, Crusilla, ancestors of the Vaughans, who have been introduced on pages 257-258 of this document as ancestors of the Gaineses! Both the Gaines and the Vaughan lines stretch far back into Welsh history, and one can tell from the success of my research that the Welsh are thorough historians!

Gwladis Gam
Lewis Vaughan (said to be "natural") m. Anne (ap Jenkin Cradoc of Gower)

d. 10/25/1415 on the field of battle at Agincourt

G-g-g-g-g-g-g-g-g-g-g-g-g-g-g-g-g-grandfather- 20th generation

Jones referred to him as the *gallant* Sir Roger.

A young woman named Gwladis lost a great deal at Agincourt, for her husband and her father were among those who died there. It is thought by historians that her small son, who was to become Sir Roger Vaughan of Tretower, was also in attendance at Agincourt, and survived. Another Welshman who accompanied Sir Dafydd on this mission was Sir William ap Thomas of Raglan, whom Gwladis later married.

Gwladis

daughter of **Dafydd ap Llewelyn** and **Gwenllian**, daughter of Gwilym ap Howel y Grach

sister of **Morgan** m. (1)Tanglwst, daughter of Meredith Bwl Gwalter Gwillim Llewelyn; (2)Margaret, daughter of Llewelyn Gwilym Rees Lloyd ap Adam
Thomas ap Dafydd Gam

m. (1)**Sir Roger Vaughan of Bredwardine** (-10/25/1415); (2)Sir William ap Thomas of Raglan aft1415

mother, while m. to Sir Roger Vaughan of Bredwardine of
Sir Roger Vaughan of Tretower
Lewis Vaughan of Merthyr Tydfil m. Anne, daughter of Jenkin Cradoc
and five other siblings
While m. to Sir William ap Thomas, mother of seven children

I have read and reported of the considerable wealth of the descendants of Sir Dafydd Gam. There has been some speculation as to how the wealth came into the family. Now I will report on where some of it went.

Effigy of Gwladis, daughter of Sir Davydd Gam and wife of Sir Roger Vaughan of Bredwardine in St. Mary's Church, Abergavenny, Wales. The figure next to her is an effigy of her second husband, Sir William ap Thomas. Sir Roger, her first husband, had been killed on the field at Agincourt.

In my office in the early hours of a morning, I discovered that my husband's Raglans had married into "my" Gams (which, of course, means that the Gams are *his*, also.) On a subsequent visit to Raglan Castle, we discovered that the curators there had created an interesting self-guided tour, which told much of the story of the castle and the family. I made a considerable point of showing Bill that the information there indicated that Sir William Thomas, after marrying Gwladis Gam, used Gam money to refurbish *his* castle. There was even a wee bit of teasing about this detail. While visiting Anne Stripe, the Raglan genealogist, he checked the facts with her and she agreed that indeed this was so. She, like Bill, is descended from both families, as indeed are we, through Gwladis and the Vaughans, rather than the Thomases.

". . .(T)he poet, Lewis Glyn Cothi, called (Gwladis) 'the star of Abergavenny, the strength and support of Gwent and the land of Brychan.'"[567]

"Lady Gwladys. . .the ancestor of all the noble families of the Herberts and Somersets. . .(is buried) in Saint Mary's Church, Abergavenny, (in) an alabaster altar tomb, richly wrought, and supporting effigies of Sir William (who died in 1446) and of Lady Gwladys (who died in 1454)."[568]

These effigies, called the finest in Wales, were likely carved between 1450 and 1460, the armour of Sir William being typical of that in use then. "On the Lady Gwladys' effigy is the contemporary long veil, the close under-garment and tight sleeves, and the gown close round the neck and falling fuller and fuller covering the feet. Over all is the mantle fastened with a double cord and tassel."[569]

d. 1454

G-g-g-g-g-g-g-g-g-g-g-g-g-g-g-g-g-grandmother- 20th generation

Raglan Castle

Gwladis, the only documented daughter of Sir David Gam, lost both her first husband and her father in the fighting at Agincourt in 1415 and at some later time married Sir William ap Thomas of Raglana (Raglan). She thereby became the mistress of Raglan Castle, which is in the 21st century an

---

[567] Horatia Durant, *Raglan Castle* (Risca, Great Britain, Starling Press, Ltd., 1980), p. 25.
[568] Poole, p. 14.
[569] Durant, pp. 25-26.

Views of Raglan Castle.
Home of Gwladis,
daughter of Sir Davydd Gam,
and her second husband.

impressive ruin in Monmouthshire, Wales. Located almost 10 miles north-east of Pontypool it has been referred to as "the most perfect decorated stronghold of which this country can boast. . . ." The castle covers approximately four acres and is surrounded by a wall on which there are the remains of three large and two small defensive towers. The dominant feature of the castle is the hexagonal keep,[570] called the Yellow Tower of Gwent, which is five storeys high, and was in its day the tallest structure in Wales.[571] A moat surrounds the tower.

The construction of Raglan, which we have visited on two occasions, is presumed to have been begun c1430, on the foundation of a 12th century fortification. There is some question as to the original owner, but William ap Thomas, the second husband of Gwladis Gam, who may have started the construction, certainly owned the castle from a very early date. Very soon after the completion of Raglan, Henry Tudor became king and effectively merged the houses of York and Lancaster, ending the Wars of the Roses and the medieval period in England and Wales, causing Raglan to be ". . .one of the last true castles ever to have been built. . ."[572] in those countries. Nothing so elaborate would have been required after that time.

It is elaborate, and though in ruins, there is enough of it in place that one may indulge in fantasy about Raglan in its heyday. We saw large rooms, very much intact and thought to be porters's lodges, which suggested how cold life in the castle might have been in the worst of weather; we saw the courtyards; the great hall, now open to the sky, with the remains of ornate fireplaces on two levels; the kitchen tower with its immense fireplaces; and the grand stair, surrounded by intricately carved stonework (I could imagine descending those stairs in my elegant gown, attended, of course, by a handsome knight that might have been Bill.); and the *loos*! One could look right down into the *loos* from the outer wall and imagine how cold attending one's personal needs might have been. We saw a *stone* seat on one of the openings!

I mentioned that Bill might well have been the knight in attendance. Well, he might, for the first time we visited Raglan we knew nothing of Gwladis, and not very much about Sir Davydd. We went there because Bill had been raised with a picture of the castle on the wall of his bedroom, and told that this was the Ragland family castle. After solving the confusion caused by the "unfixed" naming system, he finally figured how his Ragland family was associated with the castle. It was later that I found the connection

---

[570] The keep was the strongest part of a castle or fortress.
[571] Reid, pp. 124-126.
[572] John R. Kenyon, BA, ALA, FSA, FRHistS, *Raglan Castle* (Cardiff, Cadw: Welsh Historical Monuments, 1994), p. 3.

between the Gams/Gaineses and the Raglands/Longs that proved us cousins, and only when we returned with Martha and Pete, years later, did we find that Gwladis, with the help of Sir Davydd, had provided much of the money which allowed this "most perfect decorated stronghold" to be built.

Sir Roger Vaughan of Tretower

son of **Sir Roger Vaughan of Bredwardine** and **Gwladis**, daughter of Dafydd ap Llewelyn (Gam)

half-brother of Lewis Vaughan of Merthyr Tydfil m. Anne, daughter of Jenkin Cradoc of Gower

It is suggested by Theophilus Jones that Roger, though very young at the time, accompanied his father to France, for ". . .he alone, of all the children, received the honour of knighthood. . .(and) his connexions in life shew him to have associated with the heroes of Agincourt, for he married for his second wife Margaret, daughter of James Lord Audley. . . ."[573]

m. (1)**Denis Vychan**, daughter of Thomas Vychan of Tyleglas; (2)Margaret, daughter of James Lord Audley

father of **Watkin Vaughan of Talgarth**
Sir Roger Vaughan of Porthamal, knighted in 1546, m. (1)Lady Eleanor Somerset; (2)Jane Whitney; several times a Member of Parliament
Sir Thomas Vaughan of Tretower, the last Vaughan to be knighted

Tretower Castle was the inheritance of William, son of William ap Thomas, Roger's step-father. William was so devoted to his half-brother, Roger, that he gave Tretower to him, though he retained the lordship of the manor and castle. About 1459 Roger made many improvements to the castle, adding a west range of apartments, a hall and a solar, perhaps with his mother's comfort in mind. It is conjectured that Gwladis lived with him after the death of William ap Thomas.[574]

". . .(Sir Roger's) issue by different women, whether wives or

[573] Jones, vol. 2, p. 172.
[574] Durant, p. 25.

concubines is by no means clear, nor does it seem to have been very material in his time; they were so numerous that they are with difficulty followed.

"Although his father and his father's companion-at-arms, Sir Dafydd Gam, were enthusiastic Lancastrians, fighting and giving their lives for King Henry V, this Sir Roger became, for some unapparent reason, a violent Yorkist, and consequently, after the manner of those times, 'lost his head.' "[575]

At one time Roger Vaughan of Tretower and his half-brother, Richard (Herbert), also Yorkist, had been sent by the Chief Justice of South Wales to demand the surrender of Carreg Cennen Castle in Carmarthenshire. In 4/1462 they captured it, though the fortress was practically impregnable. In order to keep it from being inhabited by enemies again they decided to destroy it. "Five hundred men were ordered to bring bars and picks and other instruments of iron to accomplish its destruction. But as the formidable remains of Carreg Cennan testify, they were only partially successful and the outer walls still present a splendid example of 13th and 14th century castle-building."[576]

"Sir Roger Vaughan. . .was the richest commoner in Brecknockshire. Several members of the family were, at varying periods, high sheriffs of the county. . . ."[577]

G-g-g-g-g-g-g-g-g-g-g-g-g-g-g-grandfather- 19th generation

Tretower Castle

We walked past the manor house and through a field in which there was left no doubt that many sheep had spent much time in and around the ruins of Tretower. The ruins are located conveniently, on A479 between Abergavenny and Brecon, and, though without my notes, I knew someone in the family had owned this castle. That family member was Sir Roger Vaughan and, since the 15th century, others through successive generations to the time when Charles Vaughan sold it in 1786.

The castle was first founded by a Norman knight named Picard. Although he is known to have been in the Breconshire region by 1106, the actual date of this construction is unknown. It is a motte-and-bailey type castle, meaning that it was built on an artificial knoll or "tump" and that there was a curtain wall surrounding the outside courtyard. It was intended to protect Picard's lands in the Usk Valley from assaults by the dreaded Welsh

---

[575] Poole, p. 228.
[576] Durant, p. 33.
[577] Poole, p. 324.

Tretower Castle. Home of Sir Roger Vaughan
and Denis Vychan

rebels. The first structure was undoubtedly wooden, though the present stone ruins show that the structure was made more defensible as time went by.

Tretower is the only Norman keep known to have been rectangular. After having been severely damaged, however, it was replaced by an English-style round tower. This round tower-keep was three stories high with walls eight feet thick. The great hall is thought to have been on the second floor and the lord's quarters on the third. The shell wall was one story high with three towers. From the upper levels of the castle, there was a visible and defensible field of fire, and during peaceful times, there was a good view of the beautiful Welsh countryside.

Tretower was captured by the Welsh in 1233 and again in 1322. Listed as a defensible stronghold in the time of Henry IV, it was defended, though damaged, in the attack of Owain Glyn Dwr and his Welsh forces in 1403. Soon thereafter it became the property of the Vaughan family. The castle today is a ruin, a shell, having never been restored after the last of many onslaughts. What we saw inside the largely destroyed circular interior was some carved stonework on fireplaces, stone window seats, and the remains of stairways. There was just enough there to fire the imagination.

Late in their tenure the Picards built a fortified manor house in which they and later residents lived in times of peace. The Vaughans were said to have greatly improved that structure, which we did not visit.

Denis Vychan

b. at Tyleglas, presumably

daughter of **Thomas Vychan**

m. **Sir Roger Vaughan of Tretower**

mother of **Watkin Vaughan of Talgarth**
Sir Roger Vaughan of Porthamal, knighted in 1546, m. (1)Lady Eleanor Somerset; (2)Jane Whitney; several times a member of Parliament.
Sir Thomas Vaughan of Tretower, the last Vaughan to be knighted

G-g-g-g-g-g-g-g-g-g-g-g-g-g-grandmother- 19th generation

Thomas Vychan of Tyleglas

father of **Denis Vychan** m. Sir Roger Vaughan of Tretower

G-g-g-g-g-g-g-g-g-g-g-g-g-g-g-grandfather- 20th generation

John Games

son of **Llewelyn of Penfathrin** and **Jennet Rhaglan**

brother of Catharine Games m. Matthew Goch of Cedewin
Anne Games m. Llewelyn Morgan of Ffrwdgrech
Jennet Games m. Philip John of Marchogtir
__Games m. Trahaern Morgan Tew
William Games m. Jane Skull
David Games
Hopkin Games
The last two sons are referred to as "natural" sons, as opposed to "legitimate" sons, unless I am mistaken.

m. **Jennet Anne Havard** of Aberbran

It was through this marriage that Aberbran, an estate which had once belonged to their ancestors, came back into the Games family.

father of **John Games of Aberbran** m. Anne Vaughan, daughter of Sir William Vaughan

G-g-g-g-g-g-g-g-g-g-g-g-g-grandfather- 17th generation

Jennet Anne Havard

b. at Aberbran

daughter of **William Havard** of Aberbran

m. **John Games**

mother of **John Games of Aberbran** m. Anne Vaughan, daughter of Sir William Vaughan

G-g-g-g-g-g-g-g-g-g-g-g-g-grandmother- 17th generation

William Havard of Aberbran

The Havards were descended from the Norman conquerors. Their ancestor was one of those awarded extensive Welsh lands at Pontwilym by the actions of Bernard Newmarch, thought to be the brother-in-law of William the Conqueror. The family name was said to be derived from Havre de Grace, the place in Normandy from which they came.

William's home, Aberbran, was a fortified manor house which may have been quite old at the time of his arrival there.[578]

father of **Jennet Anne Havard**

G-g-g-g-g-g-g-g-g-g-g-g-g-g-grandfather- 18th generation

[578] Llyfrgellydd, *The National Library of Wales Journal,* vol. xxiv, Aberystwyth, 1885-1886, pp. 214, 221.

Watkin Vaughan of Talgarth

son of **Sir Roger Vaughan of Tretower** and **Denis Vychan**

brother of Sir Roger Vaughan of Porthamal m. (1)Lady Eleanor Somerset; (2)Jane Whitney; several times an MP
Sir Thomas Vaughan of Tretower- last Vaughan to be knighted

father of **Sir William Vaughan** m. Katherine Havard
Roger Vaughan of Talgarth (-1625) m. Jannet Llewelyn of Garregvawr

Watkin Vaughan's Talgarth was quite near his son William's Porthamal, and the church at Talgarth is within one half mile of the ruins of the wall there. Watkin Vaughan and his son, Sir William, were also neighbors.

G-g-g-g-g-g-g-g-g-g-g-g-g-g-grandfather- 18th generation

The motto on the Vaughan coat of arms, which reflects their kinship with ancients who are also ancestors of the Gaines, is *Asgre lan dio gel ei pherchen*, translated "Rich is the possessor of a good conscience."

John Games of Aberbran

son of **John Games** and **Jennet Havard** of Aberbran

m. **Anne Vaughan**, daughter of Sir William Vaughan

father of nine daughters and three sons, including:
Catherine Games m. William Walbieffe
Joan Games m. (1)David Gwyn of Glanbran; (2)Roger Williams of Park-ar-Irvon; High Sheriff in 1602.
Margaret Games m. Sir David Williams of Gwernyfed
Elizabeth Games m. (1)Ievon Rhys of Buallt; (2)John Price of the Priory, Brecon
Joan Games m. John Gwilym John Vaughan of Ystradfellte
Maud (natural daughter) m. Ieuan Rhys John Vaughan of Porthyrogof
William Games m. (1)Elizabeth Morgan of Newton; (2)__Bodenham of Rotherwas; High Sheriff of Brecon in 1562 and 1576

Thomas Games m. Elinor Morgan of Pen-y-crug;[579] High Sheriff in 1578.

Richard Games m. Mary Pritchard[580]

John Games was the High Sheriff of County Brecon in 1559 and in 1608.

A wooden memorial, carved to depict John Games and his wife, Anne Vaughan (Games), and four other family members, was placed in the Church of St. John the Evangelist in Brecon by their son, Thomas. Descriptions of it in 1587 and three hundred years later are found in the footnotes on this page.

G-g-g-g-g-g-g-g-g-g-g-g-g-grandfather- 16th generation

Anne Vaughan

daughter of **Sir William Vaughan** and **Katherine Havard**

---

[579] Edwin Poole reports to the reader of a tomb which dates to the 16th century which was determined to be the burial place of some of the Games of Aberbran. Since it had been described when it was a relatively new monument, Poole tells of it in that state and as a ruin in the 1880's: "One of the six wooden figures belonging to this tomb is still in the Priory Church; it is the effigy of a lady in the dress of the 16th century, and is now placed near the font. The following is Mr. Bloxom's (1555) description of it: 'Lying loose in the nave, but removed from its original position, is the recumbent effigy, carved in wood, of a lady, temp. Mary, circa 1555. The head is represented as reposing on a square double cushion – on the head is worn the close-fitting cap of the period, with the partlet on the top, and round the neck is a ruff. Over the petticoat is a double chain, worn over the shoulders and in front of the breast; the petticoat is stiff in front, and hanging by a chain reaching nearly to the feet is a pendant ornament, pomander or perfume box. Over the petticoat is worn an open robe or gown tied round about the waist with a scarf: this gown is in numerous folds, and is open in front up to the shoulders. The middle portions of the arms are gone, about the wrists are ruffs, and the hands are conjoined in prayer. The face is somewhat mutilated. This is the latest instance I have met with of a recumbent sepulchral effigy carved in wood.' " (Poole, pp. 43-44.)
"Churchyarde, who visited Brecon in 1587, described (in a poem called 'The Worthiness of Wales') the monument as he found it soon after its erection.

'Three couple lyes, one ore the others head,
Along in tomb, and all one race and lyne…
All Fleshe and blood must yield to mortall fate.
These are indeede the auncient race of Gams,
And house and blood that long rich armes doth give
And now in Wales are many of their names
That keepe great trayne and doth full bravely live.' "

Five of the six figures on the tomb were said to have been burned by the "Usurper's (Cromwell's) soldiers." It is suggested that the remaining figure represents either Anne Vaughan, wife of John Games of Aberbran; __Bodenham, wife of William Games; or Elinor Morgan, wife of Thomas Games, as these men and their wives were commemorated here. It is known that Thomas Games caused the monument to be erected. (Mansfield papers, item 2, unpaged.)

[580] Poole, p. 93.

m. **John Games of Aberbran**

mother of Catherine Games m. William Walbieffe
Joan Games m. (1)David Gwyn of Glanbran; (2)Roger Williams of Park-ar-Irvon; High Sheriff in 1602
Margaret Games m. Sir David Williams of Gwernyfed
Elizabeth Games m. (1)Ievon Rhys of Buallt; (2)John Price of the Priory, Brecon
Joan Games m. John Gwilym John Vaughan of Ystradfellte
William Games m. (1)Elizabeth Morgan of Newton; (2)__Bodenham of Rotherwas; High Sheriff of Brecon in 1562 and 1576.
Thomas Games m. Elinor Morgan of Pen-y-crug; High Sheriff in 1578
Richard Games m. Mary Pritchard

It is generally assumed that the effigy described above is Anne's. It alone remains of the massive monument, originally depicting six members of the Games family, which her son Thomas caused to be placed at the Church of St. John the Evangelist in Brecon. It was there that it was found and largely burned by Cromwell's soldiers.

G-g-g-g-g-g-g-g-g-g-g-g-grandmother- 16th generation

Sir William Vaughan of Porthamal[581]

son of **Watkin Vaughan**; g-grandson of Sir Roger Vaughan, who died with Sir Davydd at Agincourt.

m. **Katherine Havard**

father of Elizabeth Vaughan (1513-) (LDS) m. Edward Games of Newton (-1564)
Sir Roger Vaughan of Porthamal m. Catherine Herbert. High Sheriff in 1550; Member of Parliament 1547-1563. From 1558-1563 his son Rowland Vaughan served with him in Parliament.
Watkin Vaughan

[581] All that remains of Porthamal today are the gateway and part of the wall which surrounded the courtyard. It is thought that it was built in the 15th century, and was probably a walled enclosure topped with battlements rather than a true castle. It is located in Talgarth, eight miles north-east of Brecon. (Reid, p. 121.)

William Vaughan of Tretower- High Sheriff in 1590
Thomas Vaughan
Anne Vaughan m. John Games of Aberbran

This knight was the first High Sheriff of Brecknockshire in 1539. His son William was High Sheriff in 1590.

Among the court records reported in *The History of Brecknockshire* by Theophilus Jones, we find notes which indicate some of the activities of William Vaughan. In one instance, "The township of Mara and Blanllyfni demised to William Vaughan and Roger Vaughan, gent. . ."(and others) payment for 21 years service as High Sheriff at 16 pounds, 8 shillings and 4 pence. (Roger was probably Anne Vaughan's brother.) This Roger later rented four pigeon houses for 8 pence.

And again, "Manerial rights, herbage and pannage in New park, fishery in Brecknock mere let to William Vaughan at 103 shillings, 4 pence."[582]

MS 1555

G-g-g-g-g-g-g-g-g-g-g-g-g-grandfather- 17th generation

Katherine Havard

daughter of **Jenkin Havard**

m. **Sir William Vaughan of Porthamal**, Knight

mother of Elizabeth Vaughan (c1513-) m. Edward Games of Newton (-1564)
Sir Roger Vaughan
Watkin Vaugh
William Vaughan of Tretower; High Sheriff in 1590
Thomas Vaughan
Anne Vaughan m. John Games of Aberbran

G-g-g-g-g-g-g-g-g-g-g-g-g-grandfather- 17th generation[583]

[582] Jones, vol. 4, p. 229.
[583] LDS

Jenkin Havard

father of **Katherine Havard** m. Sir William Vaughan

G-g-g-g-g-g-g-g-g-g-g-g-g-g-grandfather- 18th generation

Thomas Gaines of Aberbran

son of **John Games of Aberbran** and **Anne Vaughan**

brother of Catherine Games m. William Walbieffe
Joan Games m. (1)David Gwyn of Glanbran; (2)Roger Williams of Park-ar-Irvon; High Sheriff in 1602
Margaret Games m. Sir David Williams of Gwernyfed
Elizabeth Games m. (1)Ievon Rhys of Buallt; (2) John Price of the Priory, Brecon
Joan Games m. John Gwilym John Vaughan of Ystradfellte
Maud (John Games's natural daughter) m. Ieuan Rhys John Vaughan Of Porthyrogof
William Games m. (1)Elizabeth Morgan of Newton; (2)__Bodenham of Rotherwas; High Sheriff of Brecon in 1562 and 1576.
Richard Games m. Mary Pritchard

m. **Elinor Morgan**, daughter of John Morgan of Pen y crug

father of Catharine Games m. Rees Awbrey of Coedmawr
Elizabeth Games
Margaret Games m. (1)Richard Thomas William; (2)__; (3)Morgan Awbrey of Yniscedwin; (4)__
John Games m. Wilgiford Awbrey of Tredomen, daughter of Sir Edward Awbrey. (Their children were Mary Games m. Josias Morgan, rector of Vainor in 1609; Catherine Games m. Thomas Morgan John of Llanerch Bledri; and **Thomas** Games[584] m. a widow of Sir __ Price of the Priory. Thomas and the widow were known to have had sons named John and William Games, The latter m. a widow of Thomas Madocks of Llanfrynach.)
William Games m. a daughter of Roger Williams of Park who was a

[584] The highlighted names on this page are those that I consider the most likely to be of our lineage.

widow of John Lloyd of Tawy. (This couple had a son, Thomas Games, who m. Joan Prichard, daughter of Richard Prichard of Llandovery.)

Richard Games m. Mary Prichard, daughter of Thomas Prichard. (This couple had a daughter who m. a Major Herbert, and three known sons: Richard Games of Llanelly and Penderin m. Elizabeth Deere, daughter of Piers Deere of Glamorganshire; William Games m. Mary Basset, daughter of Sir Richard Basset; and Henry Games.)

Thomas caused to be carved a funerary monument depicting his father and mother, his brother William and his second wife, and he and his own wife, Elinor. Verses were written or painted around the effigies. Those quoted refer to Thomas himself:

"This Thomas he of godlie seale
Upon this monie spente
To shew their race from whence they came
By thys thyr monument.

Oh Thomas Games, God graunte thee grace
To judge of good and evil
Thy daughters wise to serve God daylye
To fight against the devil

I wish thyself as rich to be
As ever Cressus was
In power to pass octavian
To bring all things to passe. . . ."[585]

Only the carving thought to represent his mother, Anne Vaughan, remains, the rest having been burned during the Cromwellian incursions.

High Sheriff in 1578

G-g-g-g-g-g-g-g-g-g-g-grandfather- 15th generation

Elinor Morgan

daughter of **John Morgan**

---

[585] Jones, vol. 4, p. 69.

sister of Elizabeth Morgan m. William Games of Aberbran

m. **Thomas Games of Aberbran**

mother of Catharine Games m. Rees Aubrey of Coedmawr
Elizabeth Games
Margaret Games m. (1)Richard Thomas William; (2)__; (3)Morgan Awbrey of Yniscedwin;(4)__
John Games m. Wilgiford Awbrey of Tredomen, daughter of Sir Edward Awbrey. (John and Wilgiford had two daughters: Mary Games m. Josias Morgan, rector of Vainor in 1609; and Catherine Games m. Thomas Morgan John of Llanerch Bledri. They also had two sons: Thomas Games m. a widow of Sir __Price of the Priory, and this couple was known to have had sons named John Games and William Games, who m. a widow of Thomas Madocks of Llanfrynach.)
William Games m. a daughter of Roger Williams of Park. (Their son, Thomas m. Joan Prichard of Llandovery, daughter of Richard Prichard.)
Richard Games[586] m. Mary Prichard, daughter of Thomas Prichard. (Of their four children: a daughter m. Major Herbert; Richard Games of Llanelly and Penderin m. Elizabeth Deere, daughter of Piers Deere of Glamorganshire; William Games m. Mary Basset, daughter of Sir Richard Basset; Henry Games.)

G-g-g-g-g-g-g-g-g-g-g-grandmother- 15th generation

John Morgan

father of **Elinor Morgan** m. Thomas Games of Aberbran

G-g-g-g-g-g-g-g-g-g-g-g-grandfather- 16th generation

The Problem and the Possible Answers

As previously stated, there is no concrete proof of the parentage of

[586] High Sheriff of Brecon in 1625 (Poole, p. 382.)

Thomas Gaines, immigrant to the American colonies. He could have come from any of the branches of the closely-related Games family of Breconshire. One would wish that one of the several genealogists or historians of the area would have commented on those who moved to the New World; there must have been a considerable number of residents who did so for one still finds Welsh names generously spread throughout the eastern states of the nation. Until conclusive information solves our problem, however, we must rely on the various American genealogists who have made claims to one branch or the other of the Gaines family, and exercise judgment in deciding which is the best of those claims.

L. P. Gaines in his book entitled *The History of the Gaines Family* provides the Gaines lineage which I prefer, and which is agreed upon by a number of early researchers. This line becomes the house of Aberbran. Starting with:

a. Sir Dafydd Gam

b. Morgan and Margaret Lloyd

c. Llewelyn of Penfathrin and Jennet Rhaglan

d. John Games and Jennet Anne Havard of Aberbran, daughter of William Havard of Aberbran - High Sheriff in 1559.

e. John Games of Aberbran and Anne Vaughan - High Sheriff in 1608. Two of his sons were Members of Parliament.

f. Thomas Games and Elinor Morgan - Member of Parliament from 1572 to 1587.[587]

g. John Games and Wilgiford Awbrey of Tredomen and perhaps, though there are other possibilities:

h. Thomas Games and the widow of Sir __Price of the Priory

i. John Games, about whom nothing is known, or perhaps one of his siblings, also unknown.

This family is shown by Theophilus Jones to use the given names Mary, Catherine, Henry, William, Roger, Richard, and Thomas, as did the family that settled in Virginia.

Aberbran, we learn from Jones, is a very ancient family seat. It is situated, along with Penpont and other estates on land which once belonged to Einion Sais. Although it had earlier left the Games family, John Games, g-g-grandson of Sir Davydd Gam, married Jennet Havard and regained the land of his g-g-g-g-g-grandfather.

Edwin Poole comments in 1886 on the absence of the Aberbran family from Wales, "It is strange that a family which played such a conspicuous part

[587] Jones, vol. 4, pp. 271-278.

in the history of the county and supplied several parliamentary representatives, should have become extinct in the year 1700."[588]

We also have another choice, the house of Newton, described more thoroughly in Appendix A. Mentioned by Sutherd and others, and starting with Sir Davy, it includes:

a. Sir Davydd Gam
b. Morgan and Margaret Lloyd
c. Jeuan/Edward ap Morgan and Anne Lloyd
d. Morgan and Gwladis Bloet
e. John of Newton and Margaret Morgan
f. Edward Games and Elizabeth Vaughan
g. Sir John Games and Elizabeth Games, daughter of Meredith Games of Buckland
h. John Games and Elizabeth Hoo, daughter of Richard Hoo of Skerning in Norfolk

In this listing the next generation, also living at the right time in history, is given as Hoo Games, who m. Blanch Kemeys, daughter of Harry Kemeys. Blanch has traditionally been reported as Thomas's wife. Could Hoo be our Thomas? I feel that there are errors here.

These are wonderful pedigrees, either of which justifies pride. They are full of knights, sheriffs, and members of Parliament (and unreported rapscallions, to be sure). There are prominent citizens among the other possible branches which have been mentioned, also. The Games family was clearly an important one.

As much information as is known has been provided about most of the individuals in these two branches. Worrisome to me is the fact that the Newton branch, the latter, presented in Appendix A, made little use of the names that came to be used in Virginia.

Poole's comments as to those who still carry "Games" blood or that of other "old British families" in their veins is that they, ". . .along with the ancestors of still surviving families, for many hundred years held sway in the county of Brecknock, some of them right through the perils and changes of the Norman times, others grown into importance since that period ended, but all holding to a line of pedigree which, like the sub-ocean cable, holds communication with the world beyond the flood. They, however, in time also decayed and gave place to others of as good quality by nature as themselves,

---

[588] Poole, p. 43.

and by favour of changeful fortune more successful in 'the struggle for life.'

"That many of the descendants of these old and 'extinct' families of Brecknockshire, cast like skiffs upon the unsteady tide, through marriage of female branches, re-emergence of forgotten scions, and the persistence of others in obscure nooks who have never emerged, are still in existence, if only known, is highly probable. Indeed, there is scarcely a neighbourhood where tradition does not speak of such. Not to speak of illegitimate offspring, of which, in a state of society now happily past, there was too great an abundance, it is probable enough that in reality, though not perhaps in name, there are some still in the land possessing the genuine blood of the old post-Norman houses."[589]

There are some Games/Gaines in Wales; I have spoken with them. And there are many, many in the "world beyond the flood," whatever the surname happens to be at this time. Sutherd did us a great favor by searching out and identifying thousands of us. The old, old Briton blood endures.

[589] Poole, p. 91.

Chapter 12
The Coakleys

"The family name, in all its variations and misspellings, is that of the parish of Cookley in Suffolk, some ten miles inland of Southwold. Cookley is the current spelling of the parish name but in the past it has been variously known as Kokli and for many centuries as Colcleghe which was the spelling used by the family until the sixteenth century when all of them throughout the country adopted the spelling Colclough while retaining the pronunciation Colcleghe. Whether the family took their name from the parish with its three manors, of one of which they were the lords for a time or gave their name to the parish is not recorded. They were almost certainly not Normans, though if Saxons they were evidently of some status for Gilbert, son and heir of Robert le Blund, one of William's barons, to whom the Manor of Ixworth had been granted, in 1100 married Alice de Colkyoke from the nearby Manor of Colcleghe of which her father was possibly lord. The earliest surviving record of the manor, apart from the not very helpful reference in Doomsday, dates only from 1456 when a Colclough was involved in a dispute over the title to one of the manors into which the parish was divided.

"By the end of the twelfth century they had spread into Norfolk where in 1224 William claimed that land at Eccles had been owned by his ancestors for many generations. By 1200 they were already in Kent, at 'Ylding,' and in Lincolnshire. Between 1205 and 1212 Sir Robert Colclough appears continuously in the public records as a litigant defending his title to the lordship of four Yorkshire manors, to land at 'Cretingham' in Suffolk and to an estate in Hampshire, where his wife Constance also owned land in her own right. He was a Grand Juror for the counties of Suffolk, Hampshire, Oxford, Berkshire, Gloucester and Hereford and at some of these assizes seems to have acted in a capacity similar to that of the Lord Lieutenant. In 1225 Colcloughs were to be found in Middlesex, Surrey, Oxfordshire and Herefordshire, and later in the century they arrived in Shropshire. They were still in York at the end of the century when one William de Coldcle got himself murdered. The families of Cockel and Cockle who are still to be found in Yorkshire, Lincolnshire, Essex, Kent, Hampshire and Devon are all distinct groups whose ancestry can generally be traced to the 16th century, but whose roots all probably lie in Suffolk.

"The first to go to Ireland was Gregory who had moved to London where he became a Freeman of the City in 1260 and was still living in 1268. The date of his move to Ireland is not recorded but between 1280 and 1285 he received a number of payments for building work at Roscommon Castle and for the pay of the troops under his command there.

"The earliest reference to a Colclough presence in Staffordshire is in 1240 when one Selwyn was involved in litigation with the Abbot of Glastonbury and the Prior of Trentham over the ownership of land in Cocknage which remained Colclough property for many centuries after Trentham ceased to have an Abbot. Nicholas Cokel, whose house in Tutbury was recorded in the inquisition of 1297 as being worth 75s(hillings) yearly, seems to have been the first of the family to have resided exclusively in Staffordshire."[590]

Get out your maps and your walking shoes at this point, for John Colclough continues with a travelogue of Colclough territory: "Burslem, where the family settled, is three miles north west of Newcastle. Just to the North, overlooking the Cheshire Plain, is Goldenhill. The Colcloughs lived in the valley to the East of Goldenhill. It is now approached from the Turnstall-Goldenhill Road by taking the right turn into Colclough Lane, and it lies on the left as one descends the valley. To the South across the Goldendale Valley can be seen the spire of St. Margaret's Church Wolstanton. One of the oldest churches in the potteries, the arms of Sneyd and Colclough can be seen on a shield on the joint of one of the hammer beams."

Thank you, John Colclough, for interesting background information which lays a foundation for our study of generations of Coakleys, some of whom are possible ancestors, most of whom are probable ancestors, and quite a few about whom we are at least reasonably certain.

Thomas Colclough

Again, when it comes to the Colcloughs, I am indebted to John Colclough of Dublin for information he has shared through the internet. We are the beneficiaries of the extensive research he and his father have done. Some of his work will be presented to you as it was found for I can not improve upon it.

This Thomas may well be one of those early ancestors: "When Edward I, the English Justinian, decided on his programme of statute law and on the reorganisation of the whole system of courts he appointed as 'King's Serjeant' and his technical legal adviser and draftsman Thomas Colclough, one of the Serjeants-at-Law. Until Edward's death in 1307 Thomas was completely submerged in the production of statutes such as the Statute of Mortmain, *De*

---

[590] John Colclough, *A Chronological Index*, as published on the internet: http://www.tourismresources.ie/colclough/pref.htm, Preface, p. 5.

Donis Conditionalibus, *Quia Emptores*, and the Statute of Winchester, and the designing and organisation of the system of courts based on King's Bench, Common Pleas, and Exchequer which remained substantially unchanged for nearly six hundred years. With the accession of Edward II in 1307 Thomas's work was complete, but he remained an unhappy member of the Royal household for the next thirteen years. To the somewhat dour lawyer the personality of the youthful king and the frivolities of the Court were uncongenial whilst his opinions on such matters as the legality of the killing of Piers Gaveston were unacceptable to the King. He was happiest when travelling to France or the Vatican on 'the King's business' even though such journeys hardly fell within the sphere of the King's Serjeant. When in 1322 his appointment ceased - whether as the result of dismissal or resignation is not recorded - he was awarded a derisory pension of '4d daily at the Exchequer for life for his long service to the King's progenitor and to the King.' He did not bother to collect this and on the accession of Edward III in 1327 it was increased to a more reasonable sum and provision made for it to be despatched to him, together with the accumulated arrears of the 4d a day, instead of (his) being required to collect (it) daily. Incidentally, in the Patent Rolls his name is spelled Cokelico or Coklico."[591]

Thomas Colclough

son of Thomas Colclough the "King's Serjeant"

brother of John Cockyleye

Thomas and his brother concentrated on the consolidation of family estates.

m. Margery__

father of William Colclough- Aide de Camp of the Black Prince at the Battle of Crecy and in the siege of Calais
Richard Colclough

Thomas is recorded as having *acquired* "a messuage[592] and 1/3 of a

[591] J. Colclough, Preface, p. 8.
[592] Defined by *The World Book Dictionary* as "a dwelling house with its adjacent buildings and the land assigned to the use of those who live in it."

bovate in Wolvedale in Rushton Jamys from Thomas de Fernyhalgh" and, in 1347, he was "granted the bailiwicks of 'Ryngelddie and Raglotie of Turkelin' in Wales. In that year, too, he was somewhat mysteriously granted letters of attorney from the Black Prince. . . ."[593]

This Thomas and his son Richard were felt by Charles Coakley of Nova Scotia to be ancestors of the Colclough family which ultimately made its way to Rockingham County, Virginia.

Richard Colclough

The king's heralds kept touch with the knights and with other men of influence in the kingdom through periodic visitation. The calls made to the estates of these men, as well as details of their lineage were carefully recorded in many instances. Burke and others have made these records available for us. It is interesting to know the exact dates of the heralds's arrivals at the estates of the Colcloughs.

Richard, reported to have been living in Bluerton in Staffordshire in 1367,[594] was the first member of the family named by Burke. The king's heralds visited him during that year and duly recorded the event.

son of Thomas (Cokelico) Colclough and Margery

brother of William Colclough[595]

m. Mary DeAstley of Warwickshire, daughter of Baron Thomas who was killed at the Battle of Evesham in 1365.[596]
Or did he marry Coralie de Gray, daughter of Lord Gray de Ruthin, as

---

[593] Eldest son of King Edward III of England, he wore black armor, and as a teenager assisted his father (1312-1377) in the Battle of Crecy (1346) and in the siege of Calais (1347) (*World Book Encyclopedia*, vol. 5, pp. 2211-2213.)
[594] Sir Bernard Burke, *Burke's Irish Family Records* (London, Burke's Peerage Ltd., 1976), p. 254.
[595] A note, courtesy of John Colclough, about "Uncle William:" "In 1342 William was appointed Escheator of Salop. . . in 1346 he was fighting. . .in France. He was a member of the King's suite but at the battle of Crecy was attached as ADC to the Black Prince with whom he remained through the Siege of Calais and for some years after and to whom, when in trouble – which was not infrequently – he never appealed for help in vain. . .(O)n his return from France in 1348 he became involved in a dispute with William Ollostone, Lord of the Manor of Harewood, and drawing his sword sliced off his head. For this he was condemned to death but the Black Prince intervened to secure a reprieve for him on account of his good services in the French wars. . .In 1361 (and once again at a later date) he was again condemned to death. . .and again was reprieved…" (J. Colclough, Preface, p. 8.)
[596] Research of Charles Colclough.

suggested by Charles Coakley? Or both? Or were there two Richards living at this time?

father of Richard Colclough

John Colclough (1355-) Richard's administrator (who also was father of a John Colclough)

William Colclough

Hugh Colclough

Richard "acquired the Lordship of the Manor of Hanley from Sir Richard de Peshale who had bought it from Nicholas de Kynnardsley, but subsequently had a considerable amount of litigation about it as did his grandson John who inherited it."[597] This property remained in the Colclough family for over 300 years.

He served as MP for Newcastle under Lyme in 1360-1371; bailiff in 1373-1374; and Mayor of Newcastle-under-Lyme 18th of Edward III.[598]

Richard was the ancestor of the ancient Colclough family who lived for generations in the vicinity of Wolstanton in Staffordshire, England as far back as the reign of Edward III (1327-1377). He was said by John Colclough to have been the recipient of the coat of arms still used by the family.

d. 1395

Wedgwood: The Pottery Connection

I have a dainty teacup and saucer decorated with stems of blue flowers and a few green leaves. On the back each piece is marked *Colclough, Longton, England*, and *Bone China*. The pattern appears to be *Royal Vale*.

Staffordshire and the surrounding area is referred to as the "Potteries." The manufacture of china and pottery early became an industry there, and the Colcloughs were among the manufacturers. It is said, in fact, that this family gave the now famous Wedgwood potteries their start. John Colclough has included this account in his informative work on the family:

"*The Wedgwood Family History* by Josiah Wedgwood MP records that 'at Trinity Term 1456 Geoffrey Middleton was suing John Richard

[597] J. Colclough, Preface, p. 8.
[598] Research of Anthony Kent, Kilmore Quay, Ireland.

Colclow of Chelle, gentleman, Thomas Keelyng, John Robynson and John *Weggyvode*, all yeomen of Wulstynton, for breaking into his close at Chatterle and taking 21 steers, 10 heifers, 6 horses and 5 mares worth 40 pounds.' The defendants did not appear and the sheriff was ordered to arrest them. This Richard Colclough appears to have been a typical swashbuckler of the time, leading bands of 'malefactors' or 'patriots' on one side or the other during the Wars of the Roses; lying in wait to murder 'malefactors' or 'patriots' on the other side and evading arrest with uniform success. The Wars of the Roses began with Warwick's victory at St. Albans on 22 May 1455 and Yorkists were still dominant in 1456. Both Richard and Thomas Colclough, who was MP for Newcastle in the Yorkist Parliament of 1450 and in the Lancastrian of 1453, were probably bailiffs of Sir Richard Bagot, Sheriff of Staffordshire in 1452/3, for in 1455 and 1456 Bagot as ex-sheriff is suing each of them for five marks. The evidence leads us to suppose that Richard Colclough, at any rate, considered the Red Rose to be the right colour. He died, or was killed, in 1473." John Colclough adds, "With John Wedgwood of Blackwood in 1474 we begin the consecutive (Wedgwood) pedigree. It may be that he is the same as that boisterous follower of Richard Colclough who broke in and lifted cattle at Chatterley in 1456."[599]

The designation "Master Potter" first appeared c1617, but John Colclough says, ". . .it is one which could have been claimed by many of the Colcloughs from the time of their arrival in Staffordshire in the 14th century, potting having been one of the major industries pioneered by the younger sons of the family, and it was their Colclough connections which resulted in the Wedgwoods becoming potters. In his will in 1656 John Colclough. . . who was William's half-brother, left to the Wedgwoods all his potting equipment and it was at the Oberhouse, for a time a Colclough residence, that the Wedgwoods established the Overhouse Pottery."[600]

Other Colcloughs, Other Endeavors

"The Colcloughs were the first to exploit the Staffordshire coal mines which involved them in constant litigation from the middle of the fourteenth to the beginning of the eighteenth centuries. By the beginning of the 17th century the North Staffordshire coalfield was already being worked commercially and the Potteries were showing the first signs of the conditions which even in the Industrial Revolution were to make them a reproach to civilization. . . .The

[599] Josiah C. Wedgwood, *The Wedgwood Family History* as quoted by J. Colclough, Preface, p. 9.
[600] J. Colclough, Preface, p. 12.

chief causes of litigation seem to have been overlapping titles due to faulty surveying. . . .

"The case of Bayley v. Wedgewood which was before the court continuously for twenty years started in 1679. . .arose from a 99 year lease to William (Colclough) which on his death had passed to his son John and thence to the Wedgewoods. The plaintiffs claimed that 'They deny that John Colclough was ever seised of the mines in fee. . . .John Colclough did get coals but the defendants believe and doubt not that though he, John Colclough, was a great & rich man & very wise & had many friends & great friends & converted a great part of the coal so gained to his own use yet he compounded for the same with the owners of the land where the coals were.' In another case it was said of John that he was 'a great commercial arbitrator and (was) accounted a very able and honest gentleman.' There were many other cases some of which went on for fifteen years or more. John's father, William, was also highly regarded; in the case of Hargraves v. Wedgwood, re Churchyard House, in 1679, seventeen years after his death, it was said 'William Colclough, gent, who was coroner of the County and a person of great parts and integrity and was feoffee to uses in both the earlier indentures if he had taken the premises to be church land would not have been a feoffee to the prejudice of the Church.' "[601]

A Gap in Colclough History

The pieces of the family picture fail to fit at this juncture. There appear to be two, possibly three, generations for whom we have no names. Undoubtedly one of Richard's sons represents the first of those generations, but which son? According to Burke, Richard is the ancestor, not the father, of: Thomas Colclough, below.

Anthony Kent of Kilmore Quay, Ireland, whom I employed to do research, offered the following list as known ancestors of Sir Anthony:

John Colclough, living in 1444, father of
Norman Colclough,[602] living in 1433, father of
Richard Colclough, and only here do the various sources I have studied arrive at some agreement.

---

[601] J. Colclough, p. 11.
[602] Norman may have been a brother of Thomas of Warwickshire.

Thomas Colclough[603]

of Warwickshire, England

We have evidence that Thomas lived 11 (1481) and 22 years (1492) into the reign of Henry VI.

son of **John Colclough**[604]

m. **Mabal Langrishe**

father of John Colclough, Esq., of Bluerton
Richard Colclough of Wolstanton (Yolverton)

G-g-g-g-g-g-g-g-g-g-g-g-g-grandfather- 17th generation

Mabal Langrishe

daughter of the Baron of Langrishe Manor, Hants County, England

m. **Thomas Colclough** of Warwickshire 1298

mother of John Colclough, Esq. of Bluerton m. Margaret of Loraine
Richard Colclough m. Blanche Davenport

G-g-g-g-g-g-g-g-g-g-g-g-g-grandmother- 17th generation

Baron of Langrishe Manor

lived in Hants County, England

father of **Mabal Langrishe** m. Thomas Colclough of Warwickshire

G-g-g-g-g-g-g-g-g-g-g-g-g-g-grandfather- 18th generation

---

603 Thomas was reported by those who did research for Charles Coakley several decades ago as well as by *Burke's Irish*, p. 254.
604 *Burke's Irish*, p. 254.

Richard Colclough

son of **Thomas Colclough** (John Colclough says this name should be Norman Colclough) and **Mabal Langrishe**

m. **Blanche Davenport** of Davenport, Cheshire

Mayor of Newcastle-under-Lyme in 1479

father of **John Colclough** m. Agnes Lockwood

G-g-g-g-g-g-g-g-g-g-g-g-g-grandfather- 16th generation

Blanche Davenport

daughter of **William Davenport** of Davenport, Cheshire

m. **Richard Colclough**

mother of **John Colclough** m. Agnes Lockwood

G-g-g-g-g-g-g-g-g-g-g-g-g-grandmother- 16th generation

William Davenport

reportedly of the family of Bromley-Davenport of Capesthorne[605]

lived in Davenport, Cheshire

father of **Blanche Davenport** m. Richard Colclough

G-g-g-g-g-g-g-g-g-g-g-g-g-g-grandfather- 17th generation

---

[605] *Burke's Irish*, p. 254.

John Colclough

son of **Richard Colclough** of Newcastle-under-Lyme and **Blanche Davenport**

m. **Agnes Lockwood**

father of **Richard Colclough** m. Eleanor Draycote of Paynesley in Staffordshire
Thomas Colclough (Anthony Kent reports that his name was Norman); received Delph House as a gift from his father in 1523

lived at Bluerton in Staffordshire, England

G-g-g-g-g-g-g-g-g-g-g-g-grandfather- 15th generation

Agnes Lockwood

inherited Lockwood, referred to as "an heiress"

m. **John Colclough** of Bluerton, Staffordshire 1483

mother of **Richard Colclough** m. Eleanor Draycote
Thomas (or Norman) who received Delph House from his father

G-g-g-g-g-g-g-g-g-g-g-g-grandmother- 15th generation

Richard Colclough

son of **John Colclough** of Bluerton and **Agnes Lockwood**

brother of Thomas (or Norman) Colclough

lived at Wolstanton (or Yolverton), Staffordshire, England

m. **Eleanor Draycote** of Paynesley

father of John Colclough, a citizen of London in 1566

Anthony Colclough of Bluerton and Tintern Abbey, Ireland; m. Clare Agard of Derbyshire
Matthew Colclough of London, a draper
Richard Colclough

Richard had the prestigious position of commander of the Gentlemen at Arms to Henry VIII. A man of means, his fortune was divided according to the custom of the day. It was understood that the eldest son, John, would inherit his father's estates, as it was expected that the next eldest, who was Anthony, would succeed his father in his position at Court. Other children were expected to make their own fortunes.[606]

G-g-g-g-g-g-g-g-g-g-g-grandfather- 14th generation

Eleanor Draycote

daughter of **Sir Thomas Draycote**, Knight of Paynesley in Staffordshire

m. **Richard Colclough** of Woolstanton, Staffordshire

mother of **Anthony Colclough** m. Clare Agard
John Colclough, a citizen of London
Mathew Colclough of London, a draper
Richard Colclough

G-g-g-g-g-g-g-g-g-g-g-grandmother- 14th generation

Sir Thomas Draycote

lived at Paynesley in Staffordshire

father of **Eleanor Draycote** m. Richard Colclough of Woolstanton, Staffordshire

G-g-g-g-g-g-g-g-g-g-g-g-grandfather- 15th generation

[606] J. Colclough, ch. 2, p. 4.

Sir Anthony Colclough, Knight

b. 1501 in Staffordshire, England

son of **Richard Colclough** of Wolstanton, Staffordshire and **Eleanor Draycote** of Paynesley. It is elsewhere stated that he was a native of Bluerton and Wolstanton in Staffordshire in England.[607]

"The Colcloughs were descended from a very ancient and noble family of Staffordshire, whose descendant Sir Anthony Colclough came to Ireland during the reign of King Henry VIII. (Anthony) was a beneficiary of the policy of Monastic Dissolution."[608]

brother of John Colclough, citizen of London, 1566
Mathew Colclough, of the London family; a draper
Richard Colclough

Schooled for battle, Anthony became bored with peacetime military duties and considered becoming a wool merchant, as had his brother, Mathew. The position would have brought him wealth and prestige, but he would have had to apprentice himself for seven years, which was distasteful to him. He figured the way to get into the Worshipful Company of Drapers, as the guild was called, was to study in Calais, France. When duties allowed he would go to Calais, and there he met, and subsequently married a stapler's [609]daughter, Thomasina Sutton. Much later, in 1572, he was invited to join the Drapers, in an honorary capacity, as a member of the Queen's Household instead of as a wool merchant.[610]

m. (1) Thomasina Sutton (He divorced her 3/30/1547.); (2)**Clare Agard** (-1590) 1562; daughter of Right Hon. Thomas Agard, Privy Councillor of Foston, Derby, Ireland, and sister of Francis Agard of Foston, Derbyshire, who was the Queen's chief steward in County Wexford

Anthony's first wife, Thomasina Sutton, was Catholic, as was he at the time they were married. Some time later, after a child was born to them, he

---

[607] Kevin Whelan, *Wexford: History and Society* (Dublin, Geography Publications, 1987), p. 131.
[608] Art Kavanagh and Rory Murphy, *The Wexford Gentry*, vol. 1 (Bunclody, Ireland, Irish Family Names, 1994), pp. 79-80.
[609] A stapler is one who sorts grades and fibers, such as cotton or wool.
[610] J. Colclough, Ch. 5, p. 1.

"espoused the cause of Her Majesty," declaring himself a Protestant, which was ". . .befitting a mercenary." Thomasina feared that her son would be reared a Protestant, as well he might have been, so she fled with him. Because of her departure the marriage was declared void by the statutes of Kilkenny and this son was a son no more. He is completely lost to family records.

John Colclough reports that the properties of Clare Agard's family in Staffordshire were near to those of the Colcloughs. When the Agards left for Ireland, three years before Anthony was asked by the throne to make the move, they vainly urged him to join them.[611] It was not long, however, before the call of duty outweighed his resolve to remain in Staffordshire.

England was constantly at war, and Henry VIII, in the face of continuing and costly problems in France and Scotland, decided on a policy of pacification in Ireland. He appointed Sir Anthony St. Leger as Lord Deputy of Ireland. St. Leger was an able administrator as well as a soldier, and he knew the Irish well, since he had previously spent considerable time among them. When he left for Ireland in 1540 he took Anthony Colclough with him as a member of his staff.[612]

Anthony "settled in Ireland 34(th year of) Henry VIII, 1542"[613] His first home in Ireland was the Black Castle, where he lived in the 1540's. While at this location he served as Constable of the Marches with the duty of keeping the powerful Irish family, the Kavanaghs, from causing trouble. (As recently as the 1990's his home there, the "Garrisson in Leighlinbridge, a 5 bedroomed Georgian house with riverside gardens incorporating the Black Castle" was available for purchase at a suggested price of 160,000 Irish pounds.)[614]

"The Secretary of Lord Deputy Bellingham wrote to Anthony Colclough who was by then at Leighlin to prepare Leighlin Castle of that place for the reception of the Lord Deputy, 'for his lordship knoweth of no other place to resort unto this winter.' " He also told him to "send away Mr. Rogers horse if he be recovered the disease."

Anthony Colclough replied, "Sir: I have sent away the horse for heyre I cane not gett no mele for hym, for I am glad to lede my hey frome Karlagh

---

[611] J. Colclough, Ch. 5, p. 1.
[612] J. Colclough, Ch. 5, p. 1.
[613] Sir Bernard Burke, *The General Armory of England, Scotland, Ireland and Wales; Comprising a Registry of Armorial Bearings from the Earliest to the Present Time* (London: Harrison, 59, Pall Mall, 1884), p. 213.
[614] J. Colclough, Dublin, from an announcement of a Colclough Family Rally.

(Carlow) to serve growbe wiche commys here upon Munday next to care teymer. Sir, you shall hauve the fairest casull here that shal be within all Ireland and I trust a pray tye hansume logine for your selft."

Not all of us can spell, and Anthony, himself, reported a "lak of lernyng" on his part when he apologised to Lord Deputy Bellingham in a letter dated May 1548 which has made its way to the Public Records Office in London. He had been raised to be a soldier and poor spelling did not hamper him "in military or civil administration, in the performance of magisterial functions, or in his membership in the Royal Household[615] as commander of the Gentlemen at Arms during four reigns."[616]

"In a second letter (Anthony) says he has begun to work a very good quarry of slate which will be useful to Carlow as well as Leighlin, and desires to be sent six pick-axes, twenty shovels, some ordinance powder and money to carry on the works. He further says the county will be glad to show the utmost of their powers in furthering the works."[617]

Anthony also lived for a time in Old Ross Castle and the manor house at Old Ross, at Ferns Castle where he was Constable, and at other places in Wexford or Carlow for which he had military responsibility. Only after his appointment as Military Governor in Wexford in 1559 did he direct military operations from a fixed headquarters, usually from Ballyknocken in Queen's County (demolished by Cromwell's forces in 1649).

Receiving his commission on 3/21/1559, he was named Captain (commander) of Pensioners,[618] who were Queen Elizabeth I's Band of Puritans in Ireland,[619] as well as Military Governor, responsible for executing martial law throughout County Wexford.[620]

"Anthony was not particularly interested in property dealing (which was the chief consideration of most of his compatriots in Ireland) for he was more concerned with the consolidation of the Staffordshire estates which had come to him on the death of his brother John, though there is no record of his having made any further acquisitions there after 1577 when he and Clare jointly purchased 'a toft (a knoll or hillock), a dovecote, a garden, 80 acres of

---

[615] Anthony "had the ear of the Queen and could act as a kind of liaison officer between her and the City – a role which he assiduously fulfilled during the remaining twelve years of his life." (J. Coclough Ch. 5, p. 1.)

[616] Correspondence as reported by J. Colclough, Ch. 5, p. 1.

[617] George Dewey Colclough, *Information Concerning the Colclough Family in the United States of America, England, and Ireland* (Burlington, NC, Burlington Letter Shop, 1969), unp.

[618] *The American Heritage Dictionary* defines a pensioner as a mercenary, "due a pension by way of patronage."

[619] Burke, *General Armory*, p. 213.

[620] *Burke's Irish*, p. 254.

meadow, 80 acres of deer park and 80 acres of land' in the neighborhood of Wolstanton. He had houses in Endon, Blurton, Wolstanton and Newcastle-under-Lyme and with his marriage to Clare became possessed of the Agard London mansion in Hackney. . . .

"The extent of the estates which he had inherited on his brother's death - the list of them reads like a gazetteer of North Staffordshire - made Anthony a person of great wealth and not requiring 'entertainment', i.e. pay and expenses. This made his employment popular with the authorities who were trying to run the government of Ireland on a shoe-string with only a few thousand pounds a year to pay for the army and the civil administration. On his inheriting the estates he was reluctant to leave Ireland and the company of the Agards so he arranged that his cousin George Draycott should take over the management of them on his behalf. Draycott's administration caused some anxiety and in 1576 there is a record of an appeal to the Chancery Court by tenants of the estate for protection against his 'sly practices.' Apart from his Court duties as commander of the Gentlemen at Arms, his estates also called for frequent visits to England and in Irish records he is constantly mentioned as being 'absent in England' and many documents which had to be submitted to the Queen or the Privy Council were carried by him personally. Equally, of course, we find that where he should appear in English records he is noted as 'absent in Ireland on the Queen's service.' Considering the difficulties and discomforts of present-day travel between Ireland and England this mobility of Anthony and his family is bewildering. Their normal means of transport seems to have been a ship from Waterford, Wexford or Bannow Bay to Bristol which took rather more than 24 hours, and then by relays of horses to London or Wolstanton which would take another day and a half. Travel to Dublin too involved a 24-hour sea trip and this was considered safer and quicker than travel by road."[621]

Rosegarland had served as Clare's residence in Ireland and was a gift from her brother at the time of her marriage to Anthony. The transfer of property to Anthony was made in a document of "reversion of the lease granted to (Francis) Agarde" in 1556-1557.

According to Sir Nicholas White, Master of the Rolls, Colclough sold his interest in the Manors of Kilcowan and Rosegarland for 1000 pounds.

When Anthony and Clare first took up their lease to Tintern, shortly after their marriage in 1562, they inherited the simple but comfortable dwellings of the monks, whose order did not demand the Spartan existence of

---

[621] J. Colclough, Ch. 5, pp. 2-3.

the cloister. These dwellings were apart from the abbey itself.

Within weeks the Keatings, one of the Irish tribe-families, attacked and burned the abbey, resulting in Anthony and his household taking refuge in the tower, which was all that remained. "This proved an impregnable fortress with its only approach by means of a narrow staircase, its first flight straight and then spiralling clockwise upwards, on which a single swordsman could hold up an army; the stone vaulting of its lower floor making it safe from any attempt by the attackers to burn out the defenders."[622]

The Colclough family immediately set about to make the tower their home, but found it miserably crowded, causing them to look to Rosegarland, the estate given as a marriage settlement to Clare by her brother. It was at that time a "grim-looking Norman castle" which had already proven its value as a fortress, having turned away numerous Kavanagh attacks.[623] "In (1570) we find Anthony Colclough, Esq. in possession and residing at Rosegarland."[624]

But Rosegarland also proved to be uncomfortable, according to John Colclough. Although secure, it afforded little more living space than had the tower of Tintern. Anthony petitioned the Queen for a fee-farm grant to the Tintern Abbey, "in consideration of his 28 years of unpaid service to the Crown." This grant would make the expense of remodeling Tintern for the satisfactory use of his family reasonable. On 10/10/1566 his petition was granted.

"The records state that on the 10th day of October 1565 Queen Elizabeth addressed a letter to Sir Henry Sidney, the Lord Deputy, ordering a lease in reversion to be made to Sir Anthony Colclough, of the dissolved monastery and lands of Tintern, upon the expiration of a lease formerly made to James Croft, Knight of Crofts, County Hereford, the interest of which Sir Anthony had purchased 18th May, 1557, and by patent dated 27th August, 1575. The Queen granted the said monastery and lands to Sir Anthony and his heirs in Fee."[625]

Apparently the title to Tintern was not satisfactory and Anthony and his friends felt it was not what the Queen had intended. Here is the story as told by John Colclough of Dublin from research done by his father and himself:

"His friends at Court were so numerous and powerful that they were even able to intimidate the most senior of civil servants - John Thomas, Chief

---

[622] J. Colclough, Ch. 1, p. 1.

[623] "It was in the form of a square courtyard with massive crenelated towers at the four corners, the largest being the residence which the Colcloughs occupied for some eight years. . .the tower still stands. . . ." (J. Colclough, Ch. 1, p. 1.)

[624] Phillip Herbert Hore, ed., *History of the Town and County of Wexford from the Earliest Times to the Rebellion of 1798* (London, E. Stock, 1901), pp. 181-183.

[625] Notes of Charles Colclough.

Rembrancer to Cecil - into reversing his own decision after he had declared that the file was closed and the matter could not be discussed further. The circumstances were that after Anthony's petition to the Queen for the grant of the fee farm of Tintern Abbey instructions were issued to Thomas to have the necessary deed of grant prepared for the Queen's signature. When the document duly signed was handed to Anthony he saw that it was a grant of the Abbey buildings only and not even of the land on which they stood, let alone the surrounding estate possession of which was essential for defensive purposes in excluding the Kavanaghs and Keatings as well as for the support and maintenance of the Abbey and its occupants. Anthony refused to accept the grant whereupon Thomas asserted that to reject a gift from the Queen amounted to High Treason and Lese Majeste and a furious row ensued. The outcome was that in a report to Burley dated 12 August 1567 Thomas, having tried to justify his action, went on '. . .sythens (since then) which time I understand some of Mr. *Coughlers* friends of good callyng and reputation in this realm have muche myslyked of me for not passing of the same leace and have also (as it is said) written some words of discredite unto your Honor againste me. Wherefore I thought it my duty to advertise your Honor of the causes that moved me to stay the making of the leace, least upon their suggestion yo honor might conceive an evill opinion of me without desert. And of H. M.'s (Her Majesty's), the coppy of the old leace whereby Coughler now enjoyeth it and the causes that moved me to take exception unto the warrant.'

"Ten days later the Lord Deputy wrote of Thomas to Lord Burghley, 'I come more to judge of him the better for his parts sence his trust to the office of the Exchequer, and that in two points, the one for Sir Edward Butler's lease, the other for *Cockells*, whose lease had passed I beleve a great way from the Queen's meaning, if he had not more syrcomspectly consyderyd thereof then some of good credit in Ireland wold have had as by serten nots which I required him to mack upon his refusing to draw a grante ther forther inclosed maye to your Lordship appere, the gyvft as it is in *Cocles* leace and lying in so good quarters and parts as it doth is a matter of no small vallu, and such a gyvft as wold ryght well content for a ryght good service. I had heard that some of *Cocles* new frynds greatly stomack Mr Thomas for refusing to passe the lease as it was receyved and that they had or wold write to you in mattewr against him.

Fro Thomas Court beside Dublin, August 22, 1567.

s. W. FitzWILLIAMS'

"After this Thomas had to get a further grant prepared giving

Colclough the whole estate for which he had asked."[626] This grant was made "subject to obligation to fortify the Abbey within three years and to maintain there three English horsemen and four archers or arquebusiers and to pay a rent of 22 pounds, 2 shillings and 8d. (British penny or pence)."[627]

By 1576 there was another document "(under the Queen's letter, July 16) to Anthony Colclough, gentleman, of the site of the Abbey of Tintern and other lands. To hold *forever* by the service of 1/20 part of a knight's fee, rent 26 pounds 4 shillings."[628] As we suspected, rents have always gone up. Here we have proof.

When Anthony finally obtained a clear title to the Abbey, he erected, in response to the terms of the grant, fortifications which are still there today. Walls are still rimmed with battlements from which armed men could defend the abbey and a small defensive tower stands on either side of the road approaching it.

When Anthony's renovations at Tintern were complete "it was adequate to afford suitable hospitality to a succession of Lords Deputy in their vice-regal progresses round the country. In 1579 guests at Tintern included not only the Lord Deputy Drury but also the Lord Justice Sir William Pelham and the whole military force which he was leading against The Earl of Desmond."[629]

"Lands in County Carlow, including the old Celtic monastic site of St. Mullins, were also granted to Colclough, but his peaceful use of them was considerably disturbed by the local Kavanaghs who regarded that territory as theirs. Eventually the Kavanaghs and Anthony Colclough came to an understanding and some years later Elinor Colclough, daughter of Sir Thomas and a granddaughter of Sir Anthony, married Brian Kavanagh of Poulmounty, a place on the Wexford-Carlow border, not far from St. Mullins."[630]

In *Analecta Hibernica*, No. 20, Colclough family documents pertain to Sir Anthony and his properties:

> 1579. "Feoffment by Anthony Colcoghe of Tyntern, esq., to Thomas Siggins of Sigginstown, gent., and Walter Roche of New Ross, gent., of the site of the Abbey of Tyntern, and lands and tenements of Tynterne, Lenash, Downaghmayne, Rathnegearagh, Baly(*sic*), Dowdoine alias Owenduffe, Tabbarnaffe, Ballygartie, Gainestowne,

---

[626] J. Colclough, "The Abbey," p. 4.
[627] J. Colclough, Ch. 1, p. 1.
[628] From a compilation provided by those who meet and guide at the newly reopened Tintern.
[629] J. Colclough, Ch. 1, p. 2.
[630] Kevin Whelan, ed., *Tintern Abbey County Wexford: Cistercians and Colcloughs Eight Centuries of Occupation* (Saltmills, County Wexford, Friends of Tintern, n.d.), p. 21.

Ballyfarnsye, Clomyne, St. Brandan, Kilmore, Ballybaight, C(*sic*)town, Co. Wexford; in trust for himself, with successive remainder to Clare Colclogh alias Agard, his wife; Thomas Colclogh, his son, Leonard Colclogh, his son, John Colclogh, his son, Jacquetta, Frances(?), Mary, and Clare Colclough, his daughters."[631]

Another interesting document, found among the unpublished Coakley paper and reported in *Analecta Hibernica* was the following:

1576. "'Instructions for Anthony Colclogh Esquier howe to execute to proceade in marshall lawe in the county of Wexford.' He is given instructions for dealing with 'idle persons or vagabones: persons suspected of harbouring malefactors, and persons travelling by night or not having in his Companie some honest *(sic)* in English aparrell.' He may take meat and drink for horse and man provided they are not taken for more than one night in each barony and may proceed against those who cess themselves on the Queen's loyal subjects as soldiers. His authority is not to extend over any gentleman or freeholder having 40/- worth of land yearly or. . . goods. The constable of each parish is to give warning to the parish priest or curate 'to publish & declare the premisses openlie in the Churche to thintent (the intent?) the people maie not be ignorant of the same.' "

father of **Sir Thomas Colclough**, Knight of Tintern (4/1/1564-8/23/1624) m. (1)Martha Loftus; (2)Eleanor Bagenal (-11/1682)

Frances Colclough (a son)

Ratlife Colclough

Anthony Colclough- m. __Walsh; killed in service to Ireland in 1598

Lenard Colclough- High Sheriff of Queen's County, 1596; m. Honora Walshe; lived at Ballyknocken until his death; d. in battle during the Nine Years War 5/29/1597

John Colclough (1565-)

Mathew Coclough (1566-)

Jacquetta (Jacquet) m. Rt. Hon. Sir Nicholas Walshe, Esquier, Lord Chief Justice of the Common Pleas in Ireland

Fraunc Colclough m. William Smethwicke

Mary Colclough- not mentioned on the memorial; m. John Cots of Woodcots, Salop.

Clare Colclough m. (1)William Snead (Sneyd) of Bradwell,

---

[631] John F. Ainsworth and Edward MacLysaght, "Survey of Documents in Private Keeping," 2nd series, *Analecta Hibernica*, no. 20 (Dublin, Stationery Office, 1958), p. 6.

Staffordshire, Esquier; (2) Sir Hugh Wrottesley of Staffords
Elinor Colclough d. "junge"[632]

King Henry VIII's policy of pacification was a very successful one. The human efforts of the English/Irish and the Irish were coincident, except in the region called the Pale,[633] which lay in the area for which Sir Anthony was responsible. "Simmering unrest would boil up into insurrection unpredictably. . . .He quickly developed a sympathy for the Irish and an understanding of their problems and grievances which enabled him to anticipate fairly accurately why, when and where trouble would break out. The peasantry did not have to beat their spades and plough-shares into swords and pikes. They kept their weapons hidden in the thatch (of their roofs) immediately available when the grape-vine summoned them, but as often as not the grape-vine also reached Sir Anthony, and when they came to the mustering area they found him already there with his troops, so they would quietly disperse and return their weapons to the thatch until next time. When fighting did occur he used the minimun of force required to restore peace and did not attempt to pursue or punish a defeated enemy. Once the pikes and swords were back in the thatch they were again his friends and neighbours and in consequence on three separate occasions Anthony was charged with treason."[634]

The Crown and its representatives kept him busy. He was justice of the peace, High Sheriff in 1581, member of a commission to execute martial law in 1558, of a commission to assess Wexford's obligation for the provision of horses and footsoldiers in 1572, of a commission for dealing with Desmond's revolt in Munster in 1579, and of a commission to examine Etchyngham over Dunbrody lands in 1580. John Colclough, inveterate family researcher, adds, "Of his energy and ability much is said in Hore's *History of the Town and County of Wexford*. His wealth and his influence with the Lord Deputy and the Court made him the target of the jealousy of many of the penniless adventurers who were hoping to make their fortunes in Ireland by speculation and questionable land-dealings, and up to the time of his death he was the subject of continual allegations of treasonable activities, of embezzlement of public funds, of extortion, and from time to time there were conspiracies to defraud him."[635]

---

[632] Memorial for Sir Anthony found in the ruins of the small church at Tintern. The spellings are those found on the memorial.
[633] The Pale was the territory around Dublin, Ireland within which most of the English authorities lived, as if behind a barrier, during the time of the Irish uprisings.
[634] J. Colclough, Ch. 1, p. 2.
[635] J. Colclough, Ch. 1, p. 3.

He was an exceedingly active and capable man and was rewarded for his service eventually by a fee-farm grant of the Abbey and a knighthood. As "Captain of the Pensioners, in which part and others of great charge, he continued a most faithful servant during the reigns of monarchs from Edward VI to Elizabeth I."[636]

He was generous of spirit. In 1575 it was noted that he had given the site of the ancient Celtic Abbey of St. Molyns (St Mullins) "to one Brian McCahir (a Cavanagh/Kavanagh). . .so that the said Brian shall thereby not only be a good subject and in obedience but pay 40 pounds a year rent." John Coakley reported a knowledge of other instances of Sir Anthony awarding land to former rebels.

The Kavanagh family, as well as the Keatings, who had burned the bride and bridegroom out of Tintern Abbey, were like saddle burrs for much of Anthony's time in office in the Wexford area, but he seemed to manage their problems without malice. The eventual marriage of Sir Anthony's granddaughter, Elinor, to Brian Kavanagh of County Wexford and County Carlow, grandson of the Brian McCahir mentioned in the previous paragraph, provides concrete evidence of the lessening of tensions between the Colcloughs and the Irish.

Because of his good management Lord Burghley recommended that he be ". . . known to be of good service and to have builded in a rebellious country and to have maynteyned it (and that he) should be given land to the valewe of 19 pounds 5 shillings next adjoyning to his house in fee farm."[637]

Once again we will hear from the opposing team, represented by a letter from Nicholas White, of whom Queen Elizabeth reportedly said that he never had a good word to say for anybody. He reported on 5/15/1571, "I understand that one Anthony Cockley which hath profitable farms of her Ma(jesty) in this County of Wexford is gone into England. I must report him as an unprofitable man to H(er) M(ajesty) and a great bearer with the Irishry of this County against the administration of Lawe for his own private gayne, whose friendshipp with them dothe greatly disadvantage Her Highness. I writ this not of purpose to hinder him, but rather to prove it his disposition to hinder others. He had the lands of two principall gentilmen of this Cuntrey (named Ketyng and Nevell) in farme of H.M. and hath sold his interest in them for 1,000 pounds ster(ling) whereof he caryed over now with him a greate porcon, and yet upon all this scope of ground he kept not 3 serviceable men for the defence of the Cuntrey, but relied wholy to the practises of the

[636] From material distributed upon a visit to Tintern Abbey, County Wexford, Ireland.
[637] Letter from Lord Burghley, 1575, as reported by J. Colclough, Ch. 1, p. 2.

Irishry procuring favor for them with the higher powers."[638]

Sir Henry Wallop commended Anthony in a letter written in 3/1581 to Secretary of State Lord Walsingham in which he said, "The Counte off Wexford and dyvers partes adjoyning ys(is) farre oute of order, the Cavenaghs in rebellyon in great nombers, dissentyon between Mr. Masterson, Seneschall there, and Mr. Cokleye, an Inglishe man, the best of that Contrye, with the gretest septe of the Cavynaughes, the said Mr. Cokley having auctoryte (authority) from my Lord Deputy hath made peace untyll Mayedaye and ys now tretyng with the other septe of Arteboye. Although I hould yt(it) not honorabell forr a prynce to make peace with rebells, yet the myscheffe (mischief) off this time considered I take yt good pollicy." [639]

knighted 9/7/1582 by Queen Elizabeth I

There is a story, told in *The Twilight Lords*, by Richard Berleth, about Sir Edmund Spenser. You remember, he was the English poet (1552?-1599) you studied in your junior year of high school who wrote "The Faerie Queene." He became, in the year 1580, the secretary to Lord Grey of Wilton who had been appointed Lord Deputy of Ireland. He was one of the titled Englishmen who, like Sir Anthony Colclough, was granted extensive Irish lands in return for moving to Ireland, taking over and ruling the land, and subduing or driving out the Irish. In 1581 Sir Edmund Spenser was granted a lease for property at Enniscorthy.[640] The gift included a friary, with mill and orchard; a manor, ruined castle, an old weir; and farmlands. Spenser held the property for only three days and cashed it in, selling the lease for silver to one Richard Synnot, an English gentleman of some consequence in the neighborhood. It is recorded that Spenser bought land at New Ross, further south of Wexford, a few days later from Lord Mountgarret, an impoverished Irish nobleman. This property he held until 1584, when he sold the lease to "Sir Anthony Colclough, another English settler."

This property at New Ross almost immediately became the "dower house" of Sir Anthony's widow. [641]

---

[638] J. Colclough, Ch. 1, p. 3.
[639] J. Colclough, Ch, 1, pp. 3-4.
[640] To quote Berleth, ". . .Elizabeth and her advisors (understood). . .that life in Her Majesty's Irish provinces was so brutal, so uncertain, that good and loyal men had to be bribed to stay. (These men) were not given the lands of rebels merely. . .to bankrupt the Crown or humiliate Irish families. By no other means (would these Englishmen stay)." (Richard Berleth, *The Twilight Lords*, New York, Alfred A. Knopf, 1978, p. 185.)
[641] J. Colclough, Ch. 5, p. 3.

d. 12/9/1584

The little ruined church which stands across from the main gate of the abbey is the site of Sir Anthony's grave. Capella ante Portas, or possibly an earlier church which it may have replaced, was built by monks around the 14th century. It was intended to serve the local Irish, who, by decree, were not allowed to enter any monastery. It is believed that Sir Thomas, Anthony's eldest son, renovated the chapel at the same time he established a memorial to his father there.[642]

The memorial is set in a wall of the little church. The stone into which the inscription is carved is well preserved to the extent that the letters, though small, are still remarkably distinct after four hundred years. The first part of the inscription is in Latin and, according to Sean Cloney, "speaks in general laudatory terms of the patriotic qualities of men such as one with the ancient and lofty lineage of the soldier Anthony Colclough." The part that is written in English reads: "Here lieth the body Syr Anthony Colcloughe Knight, eldest sune of Richard Colcloughe of Wolstanton in Stafordshire Esquier who came first into this land the 34 yere of Henry the 8 and then was Captayn of the Pensioners in which place and others of greater charge he continued a most faythful serviter during the life of Edward the VI and Queen Mary and until the XXVII uer of our most noble Queen Elizabeth and then died the IX of December 1584. He left his wife, Clare Agare, daughter of Thomas Agare Esquier 7 sonns, Frances, Ratlife, Anthony, Syr Thomas Colclough, Knight, John, Mathew, Lenard and 5 doghters, Jaqnet who married to Nicholas Walshe Esquier of the Priveie Counsayle and one of the Justice of the Kings Bench in Ireland; Fraunc married to William Smethwike of Smethwik in Chesier; Clare married to William Snead of Brodwal in Stafordshire Esquier; Elinor died junge."

G-g-g-g-g-g-g-g-g-g-grandfather- 13th generation

". . .ancestor of the Irish family of Colclough of Tintern Abbey and Duffry Hall, and the branches formerly living in Carlow, Queen's County, etc."[643]

Tintern

"Lucy Wilmot Maria Colclough of Tintern Abbey, was born in 1890.

---

[642] Whelan, *Tintern*, pp. 21-22.
[643] Burke, *General Armory*, p. 213.

She lived in the Colclough Family Castle of Tintern until 1958 when she presented Tintern Abbey to the nation. She retained the lands remaining to her following the Land Acts of the 1890s.

"She was the last of the Tintern Colcloughs and prior to presenting the Castle to the nation she had the rooms cleared and the rubbish burned. The 'rubbish' that was destroyed, except for a few items saved by a curious workman, consisted of all the estate records and other documents dating from the 16th century. And so a priceless collection of manuscripts and documents of importance to the Nation was inadvertently destroyed."[644] One author suggested with some authority that the parchment on which they were written had come to be lampshades. How badly we need those documents now!

"A charming story is associated with the founding of the abbey. William Marshal, Earl of Pembroke, and his wife, were crossing over to Wexford from Britain when their ship was overwhelmed in a storm. He vowed that if they survived the voyage he would found an abbey wherever the ship safely touched land. Miraculously avoiding the treacherous rocks the ship finally beached herself at the creek where William built Tintern Abbey in thanksgiving for his deliverance. . . .

"Called after its more famous counterpart in Wales which supplied its first monks, the abbey was built about 1200 and was occupied by the Cistercians for about 300 years."[645]

During this era of relative peace at Tintern Abbey, the Pope granted to Henry II of England[646] permission to annex Ireland. Thus began centuries of problems for Ireland. Henry invaded with his Norman armies, to whom he gave huge chunks of land. The Irish, however, did not succumb to their losses. During the generations of warfare which followed many of the new settlers intermarried with the Irish and became disloyal to the king. In this way the Irish regained control of their lands. By 1400 those who remained loyal to the crown had retreated into a region around Dublin which became known as the Pale, and from which they technically "ruled" Ireland. This area was said to be "defended by a stone and wood equivalent of the Iron Curtain."[647]

Various monarchs, fifteen of them in fact, had, in the period between the rule of Henry II and the rule of Henry VIII (1509-1547) continued in their efforts to subdue the Irish, with Henry VII, among others, tightening control and increasing pressure on the situation. Henry VIII, busy with other mischief

---

[644] Kavanagh and Murphy, vol. 1, p. 78.

[645] Brian Fox, *Wexford: A Touring Guide* (Wexford County, Ireland, South East Tourism, n.d.), pp. 47-48.

[646] Henry II ruled England from 1154-1189.

[647] Derula Murphy, *Ireland* (Salem, New Hampshire, Salem House, 1985), pp. 33-34.

and not wanting war with the Irish, decided on a policy of allowing the Irish to keep their own culture and institutions and govern themselves. This worked admirably until Henry declared himself the head of the church and, in 1536, dissolved and destroyed everything Catholic, including Tintern. Many of the bishops of the Catholic Church were murdered in the dissolution process, but John Power, the last Abbot of Tintern, surrendered "in the 31st year of Henry VIII" (1547) and records seem to indicate that he was allowed to remain at the destroyed abbey.

After the dissolution Tintern Abbey, which was to mean so much to the Colclough family and the Irish nation, was first granted by King Henry VIII to a William St. Lo in 1539. Four years later it was granted to Anthony Colclough, an officer in the army, who was at that time fighting in other parts of the country. During Anthony's absence the ruined abbey was leased to one Thomas Wood in 1552, and, finally, ten years later, in 1562, Anthony claimed his grant. That was also the year in which the Gaelic forces, in revolt against the "invaders," burned what was left after Henry's destruction of the property. Five years later Anthony established his title to Tintern and set about converting the tower of the abbey, which was all that survived, into a fortified residence. Of the stones that came from areas of the ruined structure that would not be rebuilt, he constructed a unique fortified bridge across the Bannow River at some distance from the residence and two round defensive towers at the head of the road leading to the tower. The Colclough family did not occupy the fortified abbey until 1576. They lived there from that time until 1959, almost 400 years.[648]

"For a period of about twenty years, from when the church was despoiled c1540 to the time when Anthony Colclough came on the scene in 1562, the local people of the district, men, women and children, were buried either within the church walls or immediately outside them." One could imagine the reasons for these outlawed Catholics to seek the sanctuary of their ruined Abbey as a resting place for those they loved. "All local memory of those burials was lost, but when over one hundred human skeletons were discovered during archaeological excavations in 1982-83, it was realised that the Colclough family had lived on top of a cemetery."[649]

We first visited Tintern 7/3/1998. Six of us arrived only weeks after the newly refurbished abbey had been opened to the public. I was delighted to find that I was the first Colclough descendant to return after the reopening.

---

[648] Sean Cloney, "The Colcloughs," *Tintern Abbey County Wexford: Cistercians and Colcloughs, Eight Centuries of Occupation* (Saltmills, County Wexford, Ireland, Friends of Tintern, n.d.), pp. 19-22.
[649] Whelan, *Tintern*, p. 21.

Tintern as seen from its gates

The fortified bridge built by Sir Anthony Colclough

The chapel outside the gates of Tintern: Burial place of generations of Colcloughs. The memorial to Sir Anthony is studied by the author and her sister, Martha Black

Tintern (Minor) Abbey, the home of the Colclough family for 400 years

The vaulted ceiling of the Lady Chapel, now a museum.

The tower of Tintern. Note doorways and fireplaces installed by Sir Anthony. Corbels suggest where floors were suspended in order to make the monastery into a home.

Michael Buggy spent a great deal of time guiding us around the ruins, explaining every detail and answering every question. Long-suffering traveling companions toured the grounds more quickly and waited with remarkable patience as Bill and I absorbed Michael's every word. Michael has since that time provided corrections and further explanations when they were requested. Thank you, Michael.

The massive stone structure, "in extreme length, 175 feet and 54 in width," was built in the shape of a cross.[650] The height of the tower, which was the home of the Colcloughs after the Kavanaghs destroyed the rest of the abbey buildings, was divided into five stories and fortifications were added.

We were told of the great east window in the chancel as we stood there, on the foundation of an area that had once been a very elegant banquet hall for Colclough families and, looking up, saw the stone corbels which, securely mounted in the walls, had supported the various floors placed above us by Sir Anthony or by his son, Sir Thomas. Access doorways and fireplaces to warm the damp Irish air, now suspended uselessly above our heads, had known generations of use. Visible lines on the walls which gave evidence to the installation of earlier roofs proved that the roof had been "raised," creating additional space in which the family had lived.

The nave, in Anthony's time, was walled off from the residence in the tower, though in the 1700's, in less threatening times, it too was converted into dwelling space by John Colclough. There are photographs which show the results of this development.

We were invited into an undercroft, not customarily seen by visitors, in which tools and the like were stored along with some Colclough items. One was a large screen, which had been used as a partition between rooms. Although there was no mention of restoring part of the Colclough dwelling at the time of this or a subsequent visit, I am now told that this is a part of the plan for the abbey's future.

Tintern as a Colclough residence.

The north transept was developed into a "lady chapel," by John Colclough, the son of "Sir" Vesey and eventually, during the lifetime of Lucy Marie, the last Colclough resident, it became a kitchen. "(A) large room above it was designed as a library, with a beautiful though massive

[650] G. D. Colclough, unp.

Gothic window facing the sea."[651] When we visited the lady chapel it was in use as a small museum.

The stones remaining from the destruction of some of the original areas, such as the monk's cloister, were not only used in the building of the fortified bridge across the Bannow, and the round defensive towers on the access road to the abbey, but also in an ornate castle-style wall which hid the presence of the lime kiln and the ancient Lady Well, dedicated to St. Brigid, near the gate. The well, "a beautiful spring of pure fresh water. . .may date back to times preceding even the monks' first arrival in Tintern."[652]

The roofless ruins of the small church, Capella ante Portas, in or near which Sir Anthony and many other family members are buried, are located a few hundred metres southeast of the abbey. It is thought that Sir Thomas, Sir Anthony's son, may have ordered the renovation of the chapel around the time he had the memorial to his father erected. A vault for members of the Colclough family was later constructed underneath the church. During World War II the vault was sealed, however, to prevent theft of the lead coffins. Most of the tombstones in the chapel and in the graveyard are quite old and it is obvious that the weather and the natural vegetation of the place are all that disturb them.[653]

"The family was still in possession of Tintern Abbey at the end of the (19th) century when they owned 13,000 acres of land in County Wexford."[654] "Lucy Marie, the last Colclough resident, left in 1959. . . .The abbey is now a National Monument and the Heritage Division of the Department of Arts, Culture and the Gaeltacht has just completed an extensive restoration programme."[655] It is open to the public much of the year.

"The Colclough family over many generations were of immense benefit to the ordinary people of the district. Good landlords ensured a contented people. There was considerable employment not only on the Abbey farm which was extensive but in the flour mill, and also making bricks, burning lime, dock work at St. Kierans, transporting limestone, coal, grain, flour, sand and gravel on land and water, maintaining roadways, building and construction work which rarely ceased year in year out, gardening, tree planting and felling, carpentry work, smithwork and all the other activities necessary to ensure the smooth and profitable running of a large estate.

"The Colcloughs were deeply committed to the promotion of

---

[651] Whelan, *Tintern*, p. 27.
[652] Whelan, *ibid.*, p. 36.
[653] Whelan, *Tintern*, pp. 21-22.
[654] G. D. Colclough, unp.
[655] Fox, *Wexford,* no. 627.

knowledge: as well as establishing a classical school for boys in the mid 1700s, they were responsible for a boy's school operating in Saltmills in the early 1880s. A new school-cum-teachers' residence was built for both sexes at Saltmills in 1839 (now the Colclough Memorial Hall). Caesar, writing from London in July 1839, informed his Tintern agent Jacob Goff (to whom the overall responsibility for running the school was delegated) that: 'I expect there will be no meddling in sectarian proselitizing nor any difference made between Protestant, Catholic, Quaker, Jew or other and that Mr. Archdale (the Rector) and the Parish Priest coincide in the conducting (of) the school - or I shall abolish it.' This is an excellent example of Colclough liberal thinking and sentiments."[656]

Michael Buggy called Tintern one of Ireland's most important historical sites. He indicated that in this time of trying to bring the two major political/religious factions together in Ireland, the contributions of the Colclough family would be rediscovered. Among the examples that we heard of behaviors which generated the love and respect that the Irish feel for the Colclough family are these: In the savage time of Cromwell, the Protestant Colcloughs were known to hide Catholic clergy by dressing them in the blue and yellow livery worn by their own servants, which allowed them to continue to work with the dispossessed Catholics in the area; in 1798 the Colcloughs worked toward understanding and cooperation between Protestants and Catholics as people were trying to do two hundred years later in 1998; an early Caesar, known as the "Great Caesar" was quite a sportsman-in football, boxing, you name it! He challenged or was challenged by all up and coming athletes and he generously entertained the townspeople after sporting matches; and one of the later Caesars, as previously stated, had, though Protestant, given the land for a Catholic church, and had built an interdenominational school, before such an ecumenical movement was thought of! Kathleen Kinsella, another guide at Tintern when we were visiting there reported with enthusiasm of seeing Lucy "standing at that door" once when the former was a small child. Michael said the locals still tout the family, and brag about knowing Lucy Maria, who allowed each family to cut a tree from the place for firewood each year. Michael said the community revered the family, as he obviously did.

A proclamation, presented to Miss Colclough in honor of the St. Leonard's Christmas tree in 1929 says:

"United with the timeless, we, the children, heartily welcome you to our school, and thank you for your great kindness in giving us this beautiful

[656] Cloney, p. 36.

XMAS Tree.

"Down the ages, the name Colclough has stood for bravery, nobility, and generosity.

"We are proud of the lustre your noble name has shed, not only on our immediate district, but on the history of our native county.

"We rejoice that you have again taken up your residence amongst us, and pray that God may leave you many years to carry on the noble traditions of your illustrious predecessors of Tintern Abbey."[657]

Clare Agard

daughter of **Rt. Hon. Thomas Agard** (-1549) of Staffordshire, England, who became Controller of the Treasury; a member of the Privy Council of Ireland; treasurer of the Irish Mint; Farmer of the Customs for the Ports, and Governor of Wexford.[658]

sister of Francis Agard, who was the Queen's chief steward in County Wexford and who became a Privy Councillor, Governor of Wexford, Receiver of the Irish Revenue and . . ."very wealthy and prominent"[659]

m. (1)**Sir Anthony Colclough**, Knight (1501-12/9/1584); (2)Sir Thomas Williams, of Wales[660]

Clare's very successful brother gave her the Agard Hackney mansion and the lease of Rosegarland as a marriage settlement.[661]

mother of **Sir Thomas Colclough**, Knight of Tintern (4/1/1564-1591) m. (1)Martha Loftus (-3/19/1609); (2)Eleanor Bagenal (-11/1632)

Frances Colclough

Ratlife Colclough

Anthony Cloclough m. __Walsh of County Kilkenny; killed in Ireland in 1598

[657] Whelan, *Tintern*, p. 37.

[658] Kavanagh and Murphy, vol. 1, pp. 79-80.

[659] James Johnston Abraham, *John Coakley Lettsom, His Life, Times, Friends, and Descendants* (London, William Heinemann Medical Books, Ltd., 1933), p. 12.

[660] Clare's second husband died three years after the marriage in the Tower of London after disagreement and ensuing litigation involving his stepson, Sir Thomas Colclough. John Colclough said there were problems "from the day of his wedding to that of his death." (J. Colclough, Ch. 5, p. 1.)

[661] J. Colclough, Ch. 5, p. 2.

Lenard Colclough High Sheriff Queen's County 1596; m. Honora Walshe; d. in battle (-5/29/1597) during the Nine Years War
John Colclough (1565-)
Mathew Colclough (1566-)
and 5 daughters: (See information from the memorial to Sir Anthony.)
Jacquetta (Jaquet) Colclough m. Sir Nicholas Walshe, Esquier, Chief Justice of Queen's Bench in Ireland
Fraunc Colclough m. William Smethwicke of Smethwick, Cheshire, England
Mary Colclough m. John Cots of Woodcots, Salop, England
Clare Colclough m. (1)William Sneyd, Esquier, of Sneyd, Staffordshire; (2)Sir Hugh Wrottesley
Elinor Colclough d. "junge"

The children of Clare and Anthony were largely brought up in England, which was considered a safer place for them than Ireland. Four of their daughters married men from the Staffordshire area.

Clare had joined her husband in Ireland.

Clare, as well as her brother, Francis, inherited their father's extensive estates in Derbyshire and Staffordshire. From a cousin she had also inherited property in Calais in 1534.

d. 1590

G-g-g-g-g-g-g-g-g-g-grandmother-13th generation

Rt. Hon. Thomas Agard

of Foston, County Derby, England

father of **Clare Agard** m. Sir Anthony Colclough, Knight (1501-1584) 1562
Francis Agard (1529-) the Queen's chief steward in County Wexford, Privy Councillor, Governor of Wexford, Ireland, Receiver of Irish Revenues

Thomas Agard was sent, with others, by King Henry VIII to Ireland to establish a government in Dublin and to gain the confidence of the Irish. His particular responsibility involved, further, the surveying of the countryside and the assessment of its mineral resources. There was a particular interest in the development of lead mines.

During his lifetime Thomas Agard also served as Controller of the Treasury, a member of the Privy Council of Ireland, treasurer of the Irish Mint, and, for four years, Farmer of the Customs for the Ports.[662]

In Staffordshire, Agard lands adjoined the Colclough properties. The two families were neighbors and friends. When the Agards relocated in Ireland, as part of Henry VIII's retinue, Anthony Colclough was encouraged to join their family there. John Colclough has reason to believe that Thomas Agard was much respected by Anthony, and, when Sir Anthony St. Leger, newly appointed Lord Deputy of Ireland beckoned, Anthony Colclough followed.[663]

d. at his Hackney mansion in England in 1549

"The Lord Deputy Grey had described him as a 'sour and honest puritan inclined to Protestantism' and disliked him so much that he contrived to see that he got no pay for his services, but St. Leger in 1553 managed to get for him a posthumous payment of 150 pounds."[664]

G-g-g-g-g-g-g-g-g-g-g-grandfather- 14th generation

Sir Thomas Colclough, Knight of Tintern

b. 4/1/1564 at Rosegarland[665]

son of **Sir Anthony Colclough** and **Clare Agard**

Thomas's family first arrived in Ireland in 1542, eventually taking up residence at Tintern in 1576 after extensive renovations were made to the abandoned Cistercian abbey. Sir Thomas continued the work begun by his father of developing it into a family stronghold.

brother of Frances Colclough
Ratlife Colclough
Anthony Colclough m. __Walsh; killed on service in Ireland
John Colclough lived in Staffordshire and served as steward of the family estates

[662] J. Colclough, Ch. 5, p. 1.
[663] J. Colclough, Ch. 5, p. 1.
[664] J. Colclough, Ch. 5, p. 1.
[665] J. Colclough, Ch. 6, p. 1.

Mathew Colclough
Lenard Colclough m. Honora Walsh of the Walsh Mountains; High Sheriff of County Wexford 1596; killed in 5/29/1597 during the Nine Years War
and 5 girls: Jacquet Colclough m. Rt. Hon. Sir Nicholas Walsh, Justice of Queen's Bench in Ireland
Frances Colclough m. William Smethwicke
Mary Colclough m. John Cots of Woodcots, Salop
Clare Colclough m. (1)William Sneyd of Bradwell, Staffordshire; (2)Sir Hugh Wrottesley of Staffordshire
Elinor Colclough died young

In 12/1589 Hugh Allen, Bishop, and the Chapter of Ferns leased to Thomas Colcloughe of Rathnerny in County Wexford the town and manor of Kinneighe, and the lands of Conbroc, Ballerowane, Ballecollane, and Donraghte in the parish of Kinneighe for 61 years at 27 pounds yearly.[666]

m. (1)Martha Loftus (-3/19/1609) the daughter of the Most Rev. Adam Loftus, the Archbishop of Armagh, Lord Primate of All Ireland and 1st Provost of Trinity College, Dublin in 1591; (2)**Eleanor Bagenal** of Dunleckney (-11/1632)1612

Though these two ladies are never mentioned in the Coakley papers, the names Loftus and Bagenal are prominent ones in the area.

Due to the fact that Thomas married twice ". . .his descendants became embroiled in the Wars of the 17th century on opposing sides."[667] Martha Loftus, the first wife of Sir Thomas, and his children who were born to her were Protestant. His second wife, and their children, however, were of the Catholic faith. When Sir Thomas died in 1624 the property of Tintern was passed on to the Protestant family, represented by his son Sir Adam, and then on to his grandson Sir Caesar. The estates in the Duffry which Sir Thomas had inherited from his father descended to the Catholic children, Dudley, Anthony and John. The line between the Protestant and the Catholic descendants was not clearly drawn, however, a condition which contributed to all sorts of interesting situations, as described below.

Often the religious/political divisions in the family were between generations of the same family and members of the same generation within the same family. The Great Caesar, born in 1694, was said to have had two

[666] Ainsworth and McLysaght, p. 7.
[667] Kavanagh and Murphy, vol. 1, p. 80.

Catholic brothers and three Protestant ones. "During the operation of the Penal Laws sectarian land-grabbers trying to get hold of the Colclough estates on the ground that they were held by Papists constantly found themselves defeated because, though the occupant might be a Papist, the legal owner was his Protestant son. When the Duffry was seized from the Papist Dudley it had to be returned to his Protestant son Patrick. The Protestant-owned Tintern Abbey was a place where Catholic priests unlawfully serving the local community could take refuge from priest-hunters, disguising themselves in the blue and yellow livery of the Colcloughs. The Protestant Colcloughs also maintained the Catholic teachers who educated the local children in defiance of the law. In a case before the Wexford Assizes in 1763 resulting from the marriage in 1753 of Adam Colclough of Duffry Hall, a Protestant, and the Catholic Mary Anne Byrne of Cabinteely, both of whom had thereafter constantly changed their religion, it was observed that . . .'indeed it was not free from doubt as to what religion Adam Colclough professed; as a race the Colcloughs were reckless and regardless of religion; sometimes they were Catholics and sometimes Protestants. . . .' "[668]

father of (1st marriage) Sir Adam Colclough (-4/14/1637) 2nd born and heir,
High Sheriff 1630, 1st Baronet of Tintern Abbey (created 1628); m. Alice Riche[669] 3/26/1623
Norman Colclough (-bef3/1606)
John Colclough of Pouldarrig m. Katherine Synnott in 1642
Richard Colclough (-1624)
Leonard Colclough killed in 1588 serving against the Spanish Armada
Anthony Colclough d. young
Anne Colclough m. (1)Nicholas Bagenal of Dunleckney; (2) Sir Thomas Butler 1st Baronet, Member of Parliament of Cloughgrenan
Jane Colclough m. John Wogan of Woxton Hall, Pembrokeshire, Wales[670]
Martha Colclough m. Major John Piggot of Dysart, Queen's County
Elinor Colclough m. Brian Kavanagh of Poulmonty (-1662), County Wexford
Mary Colclough m. Sir Nicholas Walshe, Knight of Ballycarrigmore, County Wexford

---

[668] J. Colclough, Ch. 6, p. 2.
[669] Her grandfather had been Lord Chancellor to Henry VIII. (J. Colclough, Ch. 6, p. 3.)
[670] Herein lies one of life's lovely coincidences. Wogan of Woxton appears as well in the Gaines family. Gwenllian, daughter of Philip Gwys of Pembrokeshire, and Bleddyn ap Maenarch were the proud parents of Sir Walter Gwrgan, who was perhaps the originator of the Wogan line.

Thomas Colclough (-1609) possibly with his mother at childbirth
and (2nd marriage) **Dudley of Monart** (1613-1663) m. (1)Katherine
Esmonde; (2)Mary Barnewell
Anthony Colclough of Rathlan, County Wexford m. Mary Esmonde of
Johnstown; MP for Wexford 1634
John Colclough living in 1642; brought the Rosegarland estates into the
family
Mabal Colclough d. unm.

In 1584 Sir Thomas inherited Tintern. Records indicate that his inheritance and ownership of the estate were the source of ill feelings between him and his neighbor, Masterson, who was reported to have been "at loggerheads with Thomas Colclough, the other most prominent representative of the New English in County Wexford. . . .In May 1557 (Masterson) had purchased the lease of Tintern Abbey and in August 1576 the queen had granted the lands to (Anthony) Colclough in fee."[671]

In 1584 Thomas was also arranging for the acquisition of extensive tracts between Enniscorthy and the Blackstairs Mountains in a region known as the Duffry.[672]

In the *Colclough Papers* we find considerable evidence of Sir Thomas's land dealings:

"8 Dec. 1589. Lease by Hugh Allen, Bishop, and the Chapter of Ferns; to Thomas Colcloughe of Rathnerny, Co. Wexford, esq.; for 61 years. . . 27/- yearly; of the town and manor of Kinneighe, and of the lands of Conbroc, Ballerowane, Ballecollane, and Donraghte, containing 5 (*sic*)cates, in the parish of Kinneighe, Co. Wexford. . . ."

Documents bearing the signature of Sir Thomas still exist, including this notification of the surrender of property by Allexander Dewrox (Devereux) and others to Sir Thos Coclough 1596:

"17 Apr. 1596. Bond of Allexander Dewrox of Maglasse, Co. Wexford, gent. and Michael Keatinge of Baldwinstowne, Co. Wexford, gent., to Thomas Colclaughe of Tyntyrne, Kt., of 200 pounds; for conveyance of messuages and lands in the upper Garderums (?), Kennegh, Dowro(*sic*), Dromdraugan, Ballyroshin, Ballmolrick, Laynestown, Baller(*sic*), Ballecullan, Ballyellick, Ballycause, Prestistowne, Co(l)marshe, C(*sic*), and Daltonis place, Co. Wexford.

"1 May 38 Eliz. (1596). Conveyance by Allexander Cosbye to Thomas

---

671 *Fiants, Ireland, Elizabeth*, no. 2890, as quoted by Whelan, *Wexford*, p. 131.
672 Cloney, p. 22.

Colclough, Kt., for 600 pounds, of the villages messuages, and lands of Caishel, Kil(*sic)*, Ballehela, Capiclough, Cloughpooke, Ballecilla, Tomclana, Ballyknockan, Kilcolmanbane, Kepowle alias Kilpowlye, Clonecrick, Ballegormil, Ballekerock alias Ballekero, and the advowsons of the rectory and vicarage of Kilcolmanbane and the rectory and vicarage of Ballequilla, all in Queens Co. . . ."[673]

In the year 1596, at the beginning of the Nine Years War Donal Spainneach and his kinsmen "took up arms against the queen" with the Kavanaghs and O'Byrnes and others of the Irish and Anglo-Irish. . . .(J)ust outside Enniscorthy on 19 May 1598[674]. . . Wallop, Masterson and Colclough joined forces, amounting to about 400 soldiers and were opposed by the previously named group. . . .The New English forces were heavily defeated and 'there were slain of the queen's soldiers 309 persons and the rest put to flight.'. . .Among those slain was. . .Leonard Colclough, brother of Sir Thomas Colclough."[675]

Ultimately the New English regained the lands and their hold over the Irish and Anglo-Irish and. . . "lands confiscated from the Irish because of complicity in the rebellion were granted to patentee officers of the crown. Most of the Duffry area was granted to George Carew. . .in 1604 and he sold (it) to Sir Thomas Colclough of Tintern. . . ."[676]

From the *Colclough Papers*, futher land transactions:

"(c.1600). Particulars of a grant to be passed to Sir Thomas Colclough of escheated lands in Co. Wexford: the towns and lands of Ballyell(*sic*), Ballyconeran, Ballyrickard, Askenmore, Askebeg, Monney alias Monneyslewboy (?), in the territory called Farrenhammon; and 100a. wood and pasture in Killoghill, Clonemoroghmore (?), Bally(ci)neran, Ballyrickard, containing altogether 1000a. land, worth yearly above . . .6 pounds 18s. 4d.

"20 Oct. 1601. Feoffment by Alex(ander) Deveroux of Maglasse, Co. Wexford, gent., to Thomas Colclough of Tyntyrne, Kt., of messuages and Kynnegh and other denominations (as in bond of 17 Apr. 1596).

"14 June 2 Jas. I, 1604. Feoffment by George Carewe, Kt., one of the King's Chamberlains, to Thomas Colclough, Kt.; of the following lands in le

673 Ainsworth and MacLysaght, pp. 4, 7-8.

674 There is disagreement among sources about this date.

675 Whelan, *Wexford*, pp. 133-134.

676 *Cal. Patent Rolls Ireland, James I*, pp. 55-58 as quoted by Whelan, *Wexford*, p. 134.

Duffrie, which had been granted him by letters patent, 3 Apr. 2 Jas. I. (1604): Corgraige, Comlecarny, (sic)Whylaghgeis, (*sic*)lanrostie, Ballyarrell, Ballyowen, and the fourth part of Kilallegane, containing 216a. arable and pasture, being parcel of the possession of John fitz James of Corgraige, attainted, worth 18/- Irish a year; Corcanroe and Killchollinge, containing 60a. land, wood, and pasture, being parcel of the possessions of Donat mcTeige, killed in rebellion, worth 5/-Irish a year.

"18 June 1606. Feoffment of Morrogh mac Donill Dorroch of the Retlanmore in the Duffrey, Co. Wexford, 'yoman,' and Teige mac Donill Dorroch of the same, to Sir Thomas Colclough of Tinterne, for 'the just some' of 20 pounds 10s.; of one-third of the towns and fields of Reylanmore and Kilmashell in the Duffrey.

"20 Dec. 1610. Deed of exchange of Arte mc Hugh Oge of Tombrucke, Co. Wexford gent., with Sir Thomas Colclough; of 60a. in Moynarte parish of Templeshanboghe, in the Duffry, formerly of Owen Bane mc Calloghe, attainted; in part exchange for the lands of Moynebeg, Moniemore, Farranangea, Tombrucke, Tomfarna, Cloheby, and the fourth part of Killalegan."[677]

The English crown tried to make the plantations in which the Colcloughs played such a large role accord to a code of law, and in 1611 the king issued a writ of resumption to the sheriff of Wexford, "directing him to seize for the king's use all the lands from the river of Slaney (South) to the Blackwater of Arklow (North) and from the sea (East) to the bounds of Carlow and Kildare (West)." This writ was based on two claims, one from 1/7/1395 to Richard II, and the other from Poyning's parliament of 1494-5. "The next step in the legal process of confiscation was to empanel a local jury in county Wexford to find the title for the crown.

"At first the local jury brought in a verdict of *ignoramus* on December 1611. Five recalcitrant jurors were censured. Walter Bryan (and others) were condemned to pay fines of 30 pounds English apiece and to be imprisoned during pleasure. A new jury was assembled consisting of the eleven who had found for the king and these were joined by Sir Thomas Colclough, a member of the commission. . . .Not surprisingly, this new jury found that the king's title to the lands was valid."[678]

[677] Ainsworth and MacLysaght, pp. 8-11. (Translated from Latin.)
[678] Whelan, *Wexford*, pp. 137-138.

Thomas was said to have been cool, calculating and long sighted.[679] "Sir Thomas spent a great deal of time in England but had no concern with the Court or the City of London. . . .His activities concentrated on raising as much money as possible from the Staffordshire estates, not only selling but buying on 'bull' speculations, for the purpose of investment in Irish land, of which by the end of his life he had acquired over 25,000 acres." In 1615 he sold 10 separate tracts in Staffordshire and another 500 acres there in 1616. In 1618 he bought 610 acres. In 1623, when his eldest son and heir, Adam, was married to Alice Riche, he gave the young couple 1090 acres as Alice's marriage settlement.[680]

Thomas's father's job assignment had been to take and control Irish lands for England. That was Thomas's job, as well, and it appears that he did it well. John Colclough reports that he was a shrewd land-grabber and forecloser. He would lend money to "improvident" land owners and demand repayment without mercy. The land he took from the indebted was often worth more than the amount of the loan. He also controlled certain church properties, and was the recipient of the tithes. In 1623 he received 900 pounds from this source. Faced with such facts one wonders how the family came to be so revered by the Irish.

"The plantation of north Wexford. . .was in many respects a disappointment to those who had initiated the scheme." James and his advisors found that less than one half of the "undertakers," the men given land after the rebellion of 1598, had taken possession of their lands. Many had sold them to each other, some had leased them to the original Irish owners who remained restless and problematical. Among the "New English" who were established in the barony of Scarawalsh before the plantation scheme "was Sir Thomas Colclough of Tintern. All of Colclough's lands at that time were situated in western Scarawalsh, an area that was not affected by the plantation. Colclough was not resident in the barony at the time, being based at Tintern, but there was a great deal of acrimony between Colclough and (Thomas) Masterson, who had replaced him as constable of Ferns Castle. Wallop wrote about the 'dissention between Mr Masterson, seneschal there and Mr Colclough, an English man, the best of that country.' Given the prominent part played by Masterson in the allocation of the lands under the scheme of plantation, it is hardly surprising that Colclough was not a beneficiary. He concentrated his energies instead on acquiring lands directly by

---

[679] J. Colclough, Ch. 6, p. 1.
[680] J. Colclough, Ch. 6, p. 1.

purchase from the Irish, which he did with considerable success."[681]

"When (his deceased brother) Leonard's son Anthony married Ismay Browne of New Ross Sir Thomas gave them the title to Ross Castle as part of the marriage settlement."[682]

Back at Tintern, it is thought that Sir Thomas renovated the little ruined church just outside the main gates of Tintern Abbey in 1615, at the time he established a memorial to his father therein. The memorial, set in the wall of the church, is still quite legible after 400 years, most of which time it has been subjected to weathering. No tombstone in the chapel has survived the elements as this memorial has.

He was reported by Burke to have been Justice of the Peace for Wexford at some time in his career, but he was a soldier as his father had been before him, and there were always problems for Ireland or for England and no scarcity of battles to be fought. His arm was wounded in two places and his horse was shot from under him in a 1597 battle of the rebellion in County Wicklow in which his brother, Leonard, was killed;[683] in 1588 he served against the Spanish Armada; and much of his working life was spent, as had been Sir Anthony's, in fighting with and trying to placate the Kavanaghs. The fact that one of his daughters, Elinor, married Brian Kavanagh of Polmonty may have been one indication of his success.[684]

He ". . .received the honor of Knighthood from Sir William Fitzwilliam, Lord Deputy of Ireland 10/24/1591."[685]

d. 8/23/1624.

buried at Tintern "with Heraldic honours"[686]

G-g-g-g-g-g-g-g-g-grandfather- 12th generation

As mentioned above, Sir Thomas had a Protestant family and a Catholic family. Given the politics of the era, it is understandable that these

[681] Whelan, *Wexford*, pp. 140-142.
[682] J. Colclough, Ch. 6, p. 2.
[683] At this time Thomas was living with his family in Ross Castle, but he moved to Ballyknocken and gave Ross Castle to Leonard's wife.
[684] Kavanagh and Murphy, vol. 1, p. 80.
[685] G. D. Colclough, unp.
[686] Kavanagh and Murphy, vol. 1, p. 81.

two families matured with different philosophies and allegiances. The Catholic descendents, forinstance, supported the Civil War of 1641-1649. Because of their support of the losing side, they came to be in deep financial trouble. A plot was therefore devised by Dudley of Monart and his brothers, Anthony and John, to seize the estate of Tintern, which was then the property of the Protestant descendents. Their plan succeeded and for a short time Tintern was held by the Catholic brothers. Cromwell was afield, however, and no friend of Catholics. After his brutal suppression of the rebellion, Cromwell awarded the property to its rightful owner, Sir Caesar.

Dudley, Anthony and John, having been in league with the rebels, paid a price for their participation. Dudley of Monart, forinstance, forfeited about 14,000 acres in Scarawalsh and Shelmalier. (His son, Patrick of Duffry, later managed to regain more than half of the land lost by his father.)

From the *Colclough Papers*, pertaining to Sir Thomas's property:
"1635-6. Replication of the Bishop of Ferns to the answer of Sir Adam Colclough. He alleges that Alexander (Devereux) was not the lawful (owner) in 1560, and so could not make leases; and that the manor of K(*sic)* was leased by him to his son, James Devereux without the consent of the Dean and Chapter. He also states that Sir Thomas Colclough, Sir Adam's father, knew the grant to be 'both illegall, unjust and unconscionable and ought not to bee of any force. . . .' "[687]

After studying a person for a while, one comes to take a personal interest in his comings and goings. Little details become important in rounding out the shape of the character. It is arguable whether this anecdote reveals one of the major achievements of Sir Thomas's Irish experience, but there are those today who would likely consider it so, for he is credited with bringing oysters from Milford Haven in Wales and establishing beds on the southwest shore of Bannow Bay near a place still known as Oyster Point.[688]

Eleanor Bagenal

b. 1586 in Ballymoon, Carlow, Ireland

daughter of **Dudley Bagenal**, Esquire of Dunleckney, County Carlow and **Mabell Fitzgerald**

---

[687] Ainsworth and MacLysaght, p. 12.
[688] Whelan, *Tintern*, p. 22.

m. (1)**Sir Thomas Colclough**, Knight of Tintern (1564-1624) in 1612;
(2)Lucas (Luke) More, 1st Earl of Fingall (-3/29/1627/1637)
Eleanor Bagenal was Sir Thomas's Catholic wife.

mother of Mabal Colclough d. unm.
Dudley of Monart m. (1)Katherine Esmonde; (2)Mary Barnewell
Anthony Colclough
John Colclough

survived Sir Thomas

d. 11/1632

G-g-g-g-g-g-g-g-g-grandmother- 12th generation

"Feb. 1702. Order on the rehearing of the case of James Butler, Duke of Ormond, v. John Pigott Colclough, esq., and Margt. his wife. The case originated in a mortgage of the Saltee Islands, made in 1615 for 40 pounds by Walter, Earl of Ormond, to Sir Thomas Colclough, whose widow (Eleanor) refused redemption unless she was allowed a year's profit of the island. (The mortgage is said to have been lost during the rebellion of 1641.) "Ordered that the plaintiff, if he will redeem the mortgaged premises, pay the defendants 270 pounds 12s. 6d.; but that if he pays them 100 pounds by next Mayday, they shall assign to him their interest in the premises. (Summary of a fourteen page document.)"[689]

Dudley Bagenal

of Dunleckney, County Carlow

b. 1558 at Newry Castle, County Down, Northern Ireland

son of **Sir Nicholas Bagenall** (1530-) and **Eleanor Griffith** (1534-)

brother of Sir Henry Bagenall (1556-8/14/1598) of Stoke
Ambrose Bagenal (c1560-)
Frances Bagenal (c1562-)

[689] Ainsworth and MacLysaght, p. 13.

Mary Bagenal (c1564-)
Margaret Bagenal (c1566-)
Isabel Bagenal (c1568-)
Mabel Bagenal (1571-12/1595)

m. **Mabell Fitzgerald**

father of **Eleanor Bagenal** (1586-11/1632) m. Sir Thomas, Knight of Tintern aft1609
George Bagnall of Ballymoney and Dunleckney

d. Idvone, Carlow, Ireland

G-g-g-g-g-g-g-g-g-g-grandfather- 13th generation

Mabell Fitzgerald

m. **Dudley Bagenal** (1558-) of Dunleckney, County Carlow

mother of **Eleanor Bagenal** (1586-11/1632) m. Sir Thomas Colclough, Knight of Tintern aft1609

G-g-g-g-g-g-g-g-g-g-grandmother- 13th generation

Sir Nicholas Bagenall, Knight

b. c1530 in Newcastle Under Lyme, Staffordshire, England

It is said that Nicholas arrived in Ireland in 1539, being the first of his family to emigrate. The dates may then be questionable, since it is unlikely that he would have come by himself at the tender age of nine. It is also reported that, regardless of the fact that he was a member of an influential Staffordshire family, he left home in disgrace. Pardoned by King Henry VIII, he was later to become a privy councillor and marshall of the English army.[690]

son of **John Bagenhall** of Newcastle, Staffordshire and **Ellen Whittingham**

---

[690] Edward MacLysaght, D. Litt., M.R.I.A., *More Irish Families* (Galway, O'Gorman Ltd., 1960), p. 25.

brother of Mabel Bagenal m. Hugh O'Neill, his "bitter foe"[691]
half-brother of Sir Samuel Bagenal, regimental commander in the Munster campaign

m. **Eleanora Griffith** (c1534-) of Pentherne, North Wales

father of Sir Henry Bagenall (1556-8/14/1598) of Stoke; killed at the battle of the Yellow Ford
Dudley Bagnall (c1558-) m. Mabell Fitzgerald
Ambrose Bagenal (c1560-)
Frances Bagenal (c1562-)
Mary Bagenal (c1564-)
Margaret Bagenal (c1566-)
Isabel Bagenal (c1568-)
Mabel Bagenal (c1571-12/1595)

He bought estates in the area of Newry, County Down in Northern Ireland, where he wrote a description of Ulster in 1586.

On 12/18/1573 Nicholas Bagnoll, Kt., who was at that time serving as a Marshall in her majesty's forces in Ireland, was commissioned, along with many other men of the area, to "enquire into felonies, robberies, and trespasses; to admit (in the Lord Deputy's absence) persons to the Queen's peace; to determine all controversies; to array troops, and generally to carry on the administration of Ulster; and to treat, parley with, and when necessary to punish rebels there."[692]

d. 1590 Newry Castle in County Down[693]

G-g-g-g-g-g-g-g-g-g-g-grandfather- 14th generation

Eleanor Griffith

b. c1534 at Penrhyn (Pentherne) Castle, Caernarvonshire, North Wales

[691] MacLysaght, *ibid*., p. 25.
[692] Ainsworth and MacLysaght, p. 259.
[693] LDS

daughter and co-heir of **Edward Griffith**

m. **Sir Nicholas Bagenal** (c1530-1590)

mother of Sir Henry Bagenall (1556-8/14/1598) of Stoke
Dudley Bagnall (c1558-) m. Mabell Fitzgerald
Ambrose Bagenal (c1560-)
Frances Bagenal (c1562-)
Mary Bagenal (c1564-)
Margaret Bagenal (c1566-)
Isabel Bagenal (c1568-)
Mabel Bagenal (1571-12/1595)

d. 1573 at Newry Castle, County Down, Northern Ireland

G-g-g-g-g-g-g-g-g-g-g-grandmother- 14th generation

Edward Griffith

of Pentherne (Penrhyn), North Wales

father and co-heir of **Eleanor Griffith**[694]

G-g-g-g-g-g-g-g-g-g-g-g-grandfather- 15th generation

John Bagenhall

John is the first of the family to be registered at the College of Arms.[695]

of Newcastle, Staffordshire

m. **Ellen Whittingham**

father of **Sir Nicholas Bagenall** of Newry, County Down m. Eleanor

---

[694] Sir Bernard Burke, C.B., LL.D. (Ulster King of Arms), *Burke's Genealogical and Heraldic History of the Landed Gentry of Ireland* (London, Burke's Peerage Ltd., 1958), p. 44.
[695] Burke, *ibid.*, p. 44.

Griffith

Mayor of Newcastle in 1519, 1522, 1526, 1531, and 1538

G-g-g-g-g-g-g-g-g-g-g-grandfather- 15th generation

Ellen Whittingham

daughter of **Thomas Whittingham**

m. **John Bagenhall** of Newcastle, Staffordshire who lived in the first half of the 16th century

mother of **Sir Nicholas Bagenall** of Newry, County Down m. Eleanor Griffith

G-g-g-g-g-g-g-g-g-g-g-grandmother- 15th generation

Thomas Whittingham

father of **Ellen Whittingham** m. John Bagenhall

G-g-g-g-g-g-g-g-g-g-g-g-grandfather- 16th generation

Dudley Colclough of Monart

b. 1613

son of **Sir Thomas Colclough**, Knight of Tintern (aft1547-1624) and his second wife, **Eleanor Bagenal** (1586-1632), daughter of Dudley Bagenal

step-brother of: Sir Adam Colclough, heir of Tintern, created a baronet in 1628; m. Alice Riche, daughter of Sir Robert Riche, Master of the Chancery in England, Chamberlain to the Marquis of Wellesley, and Lord Lieutenant of London in 1629. . .
Norman Colclough (-bef3/1606)

John of Pouldarrig- m. Katherine Synnott in 1642
Richard Colclough (-1624)
Lenard Colclough I (-1588)
Anthony Colclough
Anne Colclough m. (1)Nicholas Bagenal of Dunlickney; (2)Sir Thomas Butler, 1st Baronet; MP of Cloughgrenan
Jane Colclough m. John Wogan of Woxton Hall
Martha Colclough m. John Piggot of Dysat, Queen's County
Elinor Colclough m. Brian Kavanagh of Poulmonty
Mary Colclough m. Sir Nicholas Walshe of Ballycarigmore
Thomas Colclough (-1609)

and brother of: Mabal Colclough d. unm.
Anthony Colclough of Rathlin m. Mary Esmonde of Johnstown Castle; Captain of Confederate force in Wexford in 1642; MP for Wexford in 1634
John Colclough living in 1642; brought Rosegarland estates back into the family.

From the *Colclough Papers*:
"22 Mar. 1625. Feoffment by Morrish mc Donell Ower of . . ., Co. Wexford, and Cahire mcDonell Ower of Tomechorry, Co. Wexford, freeholder; to Dudley Colclough of Monart, gent. . .; of part of the lands of Tintubber in the Duffrey." (Dudley was 12 years of age here!)[696]

Sir Thomas Colclough, Dudley's father, had two wives, the first Protestant, the second Catholic. He had children as a result of both marriages. Upon his death in 1624 he left Tintern and its lands to the children of his Protestant wife and the vast lands in the Scarawalsh to his Catholic children. Dudley, the firstborn of this union, had immense holdings.

"Dudley got a patent (from his father's estate) for the castle, town and lands of Monart in 1627."[697] "The Scarawalsh lands were conveyed to Dudley Colclough in 1628 when he was 15 years of age. Dudley went to live in Monart which was situated on his lands in the Duffry area of Scarawalsh."[698]

m. (1)**Katherine Esmonde** (-11/6/1700), daughter of Robert Esmonde of the Johnstown Castle in 1633; (2)Mary Barnewell, daughter of Sir Patrick Barnewell of Crickstown

[696] Ainsworth and MacLysaght, p. 11.
[697] Kavanagh and Murphy, vol. 1, p. 82.
[698] Whelan, *Wexford*, p. 142.

"Because of his marriage to Katherine. . .(Dudley) acquired further lands in northern Scarawalsh including the townlands of Ballyshonock, Ballynastragh and Garryhasten in the parish of Moyacomb.

father of :(1st marriage) Patrick of Duffry (1633-1691) m. Katherine Bagenal in 1671; inherited Duffry and built Duffry Hall; High Sheriff of Wexford, 1688; MP for Enniscorthy 1689; sentenced to death for helping in the escape of Charles I of England; died in the Tower before his execution.

Lawrence of Monart (sentenced to the Tower of London by Cromwell- from the court of Maidstone; was one of the judges who refused to grant a summons against clergymen who would not give up their "prayer book".)

Thomas of Currach (Captain of a cavalry regiment) m. Mary Pomeroy

"By 1640 the number of Irish people owning land was only one third of what it had been a mere twenty years earlier. In the western portion of the barony of Scarawalsh, Henry Wallop and Thomas Colclough bought up quite an amount of Irish land. Colclough, in particular, acquired a great deal of land from the Irish and from a grant of 1,000 acres received from the crown in 1604. He built up his holding mainly by purchase but also by mortgage foreclosure, until in 1640 his son (Dudley) owned 11,885 acres. . . .Through inheritance, purchase and further mortgage foreclosure, and marriage alliances Dudley at this time possessed the biggest landholding in the barony.[699]

"An inquisition taken in 1617 showed 'the town and lands of Glanderick, Monglass, Kiltrea, half of Caim, and the woods of Aughrim are in the possession of Edward Butler and his heirs.' In 1640, Butler was still in possession of most of these lands extending in all to 1470 acres but part of them had been lost to Dudley Colclough."[700]

According to Hore, in his *History of the Town of Wexford*, Bellevue was the property of Dudley Colclough prior to the Cromwellian Confiscations. It was then called Ballycheoge.[701]

Obviously Dudley of Monart, like his father, was skilled at land procurement. It was said that he held as many as 14,000 acres in Scarawalsh and Shelmalier in his prime. He got into trouble, however, by siding with the losing forces during the Civil War of 1641-1649.

---

[699] Whelan, *Wexford*, p. 142.
[700] Whelan, *Wexford*, p. 144.
[701] Kavanagh and Murphy, vol. 1, p. 71.

"In the 1641 rebellion Tintern, then home of one of Sir Adam's sons, Sir Caesar Colclough, was garrisoned by a small force of thirty (of the Queen's) soldiers from Duncannon. It became home to some 200 refugees in the winter of 1641, but in the summer of 1642 it was taken over by the rebels. The rebel forces were led by Dudley (of Monart), John and Anthony Colclough,[702] half uncles of Sir Caesar. They had refrained from besieging the castle while Caesar's mother, Lady Colclough, still resided there, but she had left Tintern in the late Spring and it was then they decided to take it for the Confederates.[703] As an added inducement the Colcloughs were promised 400 pounds if they captured the stronghold."[704] For a short time they actually held Tintern, but eventually lost it to Cromwell's forces. After the rebellion, Tintern was returned by Cromwell to Caesar.

"As a result of his participation in the rebellion (Dudley) forfeited all his land,[705] totalling 14,614 acres, and was banished to Connaught. Before leaving he was permitted to gather the remains of his harvest, sell off his stock and fell 100 pounds worth of timber which he sold to (Francis Harvey) a Wexford merchant. An inquisition of 1653 when he left described him as of Monart with a household of 13 persons, 6 cows, 3 garrans and 6 swine."[706]

After the suppression of the Rebellion in 1653 Dudley and his brothers did surrender their lands but they were able to effect a modification of the order to transplant into Connaught. ". . .(F)ollowing numerous lengthy appeals the order to transplant was ignored or forgotten, probably due to behind the scenes diplomacy. During the Cromwellian epoch Dudley and his family went to live in Huntingdon Castle, in Clonegal, County Carlow, which had been built by Lord Esmonde of Johnstown in 1625. Lord Esmonde was a Protestant and an uncle of Dudley's wife. They remained in Huntingdon

---

[702] A further complication: John and Anthony were both Protestants!

[703] "The attacks on the Abbey started in February 1642 with the arrival of a small group of men who led away the plough-horses. When Major Aston led a party in pursuit to recover the horses he ran straight into an ambush. One of his party was killed and another wounded and the Major himself had an unnerving experience when a gun pointed at his head by one of the ambush misfired six times in succession. Following a certain amount of desultory fighting round about the Abbey for some months the High Sheriff, Hugh Rochfort, and the Wexford County Council, all of whom were now Royalists, for the Civil War had now started in England, offered Dudley Colclough of Monart, John of Pouldarrig and Anthony of Rathlin together with Colonel Devereux and William Sutton 400 pounds if they could seize the Abbey from the English troops. After some months of attacks and sieges by the Colcloughs with a force of 300 rebels Major Aston surrendered at the end of the summer subject to a proviso that his men might go freely into Munster and this was agreed...The motives of the Colcloughs in leading the attack on the Abbey were probably to ensure that it did not get out of hand and to prevent the sacking of their ancestral home." (Kavanagh and Murphy, vol. 1, p. 81.)

[704] Kavanagh and Murphy, vol. 1, p. 81.

[705] According to the research of Mr. George H. S. King, Virginia genealogist, . . ."no less than 14 Colcloughs suffered under the Williamite confiscation of the lands of Irish Papists." Reported by George Dewey Colclough, *Information*, unp.

[706] A garran is a small, hardy horse bred in Ireland. (John Colclough, Ch. 6, p. 4.)

during the upheavals of the period, theoretically occupying the castle as a military station." After Dudley's death in 1663 his family remained at Huntingdon until 1674, when it is probable that they moved back to Duffry Hall. . . ."Dudley's son Patrick (a Protestant) was in fact a grantee of much of his father's confiscated estates. After prolonged legal wrangling he eventually succeeded in wresting back much of the lands."[707]

A syndicate of Adventurers who had bought over 5000 acres from a number of County Wexford residents, including one Thomas Colclough, established an iron works there. "In 1661 the Iron Works (which) appear to have been working as the syndicate petitioned the King to restrain Dudley Colclough from preventing them obtaining timber (as fuel for their smelters). They pointed out that they had brought in many hundreds of English workmen and their families to colonise the countryside around which formerly had been a 'nursery and refuge' for rebels.

"Again in 1664 the syndicate petitioned that the lands they had developed be exempted from the grant made to Dudley Colclough and his son Patrick by the King. The petition was sanctioned by an Act of Parliament in 1665 in the name of John Morris and Robert Clayton." By this time Dudley was dead, leaving his heirs the headaches of his deeds and misdeeds.[708]

d. 1663, killed in battle in France, probably while serving Charles II abroad.

G-g-g-g-g-g-g-g-grandfather- 11th generation

Johnstown Castle, home of the William Esmonde family

---

[707] Kavanagh and Murphy, vol. 1, p. 82.

[708] Art Kavanagh and Rory Murphy, *The Wexford Gentry*, vol. 2 (Bunclody, Ireland, Irish Family Names, 1996), pp. 135-136.

Huntingdon Castle, home of the Esmonde family and sanctuary for Sir Dudley of Monart during his exile.

With the attack of Cromwell on seemingly everything Irish, a great deal of land was confiscated. We have no way of knowing exactly what was lost to Cromwell of Dudley's vast holdings. Some of the lost lands were "parcelled out to Cromwellian soldiers in lieu of wages." Many families who lost their land never regained it, despite their allegiance to Charles II. "A 1666 list of dispossessed landowners included (William Browne) as a person who had continued to serve the king abroad and who was therefore to be restored to 600 acres of (the land he lost). Only two other landowners in Wexford (James Devereux of Ballymagir and Dudley Colclough of Monart) were to be assigned such large estates."[709]

Katherine Esmonde

daughter of **Patrick Esmonde** of Johnstown Castle

m. **Dudley Colclough of Monart** 1633

mother of Patrick Colclough of Duffrey Hall (-c1690) m. Katherine Bagenal of Dunleckney (-11/6/1700)

Lawrence Colclough

[709] Whelan, *Wexford*, p. 471.

Thomas Colclough m. Mary Pomeroy of Pallace, County Cork

G-g-g-g-g-g-g-g-grandmother- 11th generation

Patrick Esmonde

son of **William Esmonde** and **Margaret Furlong** of Johnstown Castle

brother of six boys, including Robert Esmonde
Lawrence Esmonde
and of four sisters

father of **Katherine Esmonde** m. Sir Dudley Colclough of Monat (1613-)

G-g-g-g-g-g-g-g-grandfather- 12th generation

William Esmonde

son and heir of **Lawrence Esmonde** and **Eleanor Walsh**

m. **Margaret Furlong** of Horetown

father of 7 sons, including Robert Esmonde
Sir Lawrence Esmonde- appointed Major General of all the King's forces in Ireland[710]
Patrick Esmonde
and four daughters

William was killed in 1599 in a battle fought between the King's men in

[710] There is more to be known about "Uncle Lawrence. " After surviving the battle in which his father, William, was killed, he announced in 1602 to Lord Shrewsbury, the Lord Deputy of Ireland, that he had ". . .broken the Kavanagh faction and had caused Donal Spainigh Kavanagh etc. to submit upon their knees." He proceeded to build a castle and a church near Killinerin, and soon was appointed Governor of Duncannon Fort. He was said to be "an expert, prudent, and resolute Commander, of a sedate and composed spirit. . .of sanguin Complexion, of an indifferent tall stature, compact, solid, corpulent body with robustious Limms. . ." He owned vast estates in various areas of Ireland; was MP in the Irish Parliament for County Wicklow in 1613; Commissioner for the Queen's Plantations; named Baron of Lymbrick in 1622; and on and on. He was also known to have been a bigamist, proving once again that nobody's perfect. (Kavanagh and Murphy, vol. 1, pp. 101-103.)

Essex and the Kavanagh/Byrne alliance near Arklow.[711]

G-g-g-g-g-g-g-g-g-grandfather- 13th generation

Margaret Furlong

daughter of **Michael Furlong** of Horetown

m. **William Esmonde** of Johnstown

mother of seven sons, including Robert Esmonde
Sir Lawrence Esmonde- appointed the Major General of all the King's forces in Ireland
Patrick Esmonde
and four daughters

G-g-g-g-g-g-g-g-g-grandmother- 13th generation

Michael Furlong

lived at Horetown

father of **Margaret Furlong** m. William Esmonde of Johnstown Castle

G-g-g-g-g-g-g-g-g-g-grandfather- 14th generation

Lawrence Esmonde

son of **James Esmonde** (lived c1520) and **Isabel Rossiter** of Rathmacknee Castle[712]

m. **Eleanor Walsh**, daughter of Walter Walsh

father of **William Esmonde** of Johnstown m. Margaret Furlong of Horetown

---

[711] Kavanagh and Murphy, vol. 1, pp. 101-102.
[712] Kavanagh and Murphy, vol. 1, pp. 100-101.

G-g-g-g-g-g-g-g-g-g-grandfather- 14th generation

Eleanor Walsh

daughter of **Walter Walsh** of the Mountain

m. **Lawrence Esmonde**

mother of **William Esmonde** m. Margaret Furlong of Horetown

G-g-g-g-g-g-g-g-g-g-grandmother- 14th generation

Walter Walsh

said to be "of the Mountain" meaning an area called Walsh Mountain in County Kilkenny[713]

father of **Eleanor Walsh** m. Lawrence Esmonde

G-g-g-g-g-g-g-g-g-g-g-grandfather- 15th generation

James Esmonde

lived c1520

m. **Isabel Rossiter** of Rathmacknee Castle

father **of Lawrence Esmonde** m. Eleanor Walsh

G-g-g-g-g-g-g-g-g-g-g-grandfather- 15th generation

[713] The history of this family, like that of the Fitzgeralds and others, is long. The name Walsh simply means Welshman, and the first to be so called was said to have been Haylen Brenach, son of "Philip the Welshman," an invader in 1172. Leading members of the family settled at Castlehowel in County Kilkenny, and in other areas. (Edward MacLysaght, *Irish Families: Their Names, Arms and Origins*, Dublin, Hodges Figgis & Co. Ltd., 1957, p. 281.)

Isabel Rossiter

daughter of **Thomas Rossiter** of Rathmacknee Castle

m. **James Esmonde** (lived c1520)

mother of **Lawrence Esmonde** m. Eleanor Walsh

G-g-g-g-g-g-g-g-g-g-g-g-grandmother- 15th generation

Thomas Rossiter[714]

father of **Isabel Rossiter** m. James Esmonde[715]

lived at Rathmacknee Castle

G-g-g-g-g-g-g-g-g-g-g-g-g-grandfather- 16th generation

Thomas Coakely
Thomas of Currach

b. c1640

second son of **Dudley of Monart** (1613-1663) and **Katherine Esmonde** of the House of Johnson

m. **Mary Pomeroy** of Pallace, County Cork

lived at Currach/Curragh in County Wexford

father of Caleb Coakley of Currach m. Ellen Travers

---

[714] "The Rossiters were one of the earliest families from England to be established in Ireland after the Anglo-Norman invasion; they first landed in fact in 1170. They came from Rawcester or Rocester in Lincolnshire. . .and from that time to the present day they have been identified with County Wexford. . .In 1357 Robert Rowcester made good his claim to the advowson of Rathmacree, County Wexford, claiming that the church had been built by his forbears, as was the castle of Bargy. The family was dispossessed of Rathmacree in 1653, but the name was among the most numerous in the barony of Forth, County Wexford, in 1659." (MacLysaght, *More Irish Families*, p. 209.)

[715] *Burke's Pedigree* as cited by Kavanagh and Murphy, vol. 1, pp. 100-101.

Mary Coakley
Isabella Coakley
Martha Coakley
Thomas Coakley

What other children might Mary and Thomas have had? This is the most likely to be our genealogical line, as I now understand the situation, but as members of this and other Coakley families emigrated to the Virgin Islands at about this time, we may not easily find names and connections.

Thomas ". . .was a Captain in a regiment of cavalry, serving under King William in Ireland. He acted as a guide during the march of the army from Dundalk to the Boyne, there taking part in the battle 7/1/1690. He afterward accompanied his regiment, with King William, to Dunleek. Because of his attachment to King William much of his property was destroyed, supposedly burned by the retreating army of James II.

"He was also one of the gentlemen under arms at Nottingham, under the command of Dr. Compton, Bishop of London, who formed themselves into a troop to provide escort and to guard Princess Anne when she went to meet the Prince of Orange."[716]

"Uncle" Sir Patrick Colclough, brother of Thomas of Currach, as painted by Frans Hals

"Thomas Cokly of Currach," may very well have been the grandfather of James Cokeley. If so he is our g-g-g-g-g-g-g-grandfather- 10th generation.

[716] "Old Roll Call of Gentlemen at Arms," Genealogical Office (Office of Arms), Dublin Castle, Ref. F.52, G.O.

The following inventory of the possessions of Thomas of Currach in 4/1682 was shared with Charles Colclough of Nova Scotia when he traveled to Tintern in the 1960's. Whether this list enumerated items of his "estate" or whether it was made for some other purpose we know not, for we have no information as to the time of Thomas's death. The items include ". . .one fforme and chaires; one certaine cheese; one brase candlesticke, one brase pot; one beedsteed, one feather beed, and all thereunto belonging; one joyend cupbord; one table bord; one carte, one lantern; one fflocke beed, one beedsteed; one chaire; foure dishes peuter; ffoure fliches of baccon; two barrils; one billet hatchet; one kiver; two horses and the harness thereunto belonging; two cows, and one yearling bullock; three score pigs; ffive score sheep; certain barley, oats, wheat and pease thrashed; upon the ground wheat, corne, and vetches, by estimate ffive accors."[717]

The arms of Colclough,
descended from Sir Anthony Colclough of Staffordshire

[717] Charles Colclough, notes, as shared by Esther Lancaster of Nova Scotia.

Mary Pomeroy

daughter of **Samuel Pomeroy** of Pallace, County Cork

m. **Thomas Coakley/Colclough** of Currach

mother of Caleb Coakley
Mary Coakley
Isabella Coakley
Martha Coakley
Thomas Coakley

G-g-g-g-g-g-grandmother- 10th generation

Samuel Pomeroy

of Pallace, County Cork

father of **Mary Pomeroy** m. Thomas Coakley of Currach

In his will, which was proved 1/23/1703-4, Samuel mentions his grandchildren, Mary, Isabella, Martha and Thomas Coakley.[718]

G-g-g-g-g-g-g-grandfather- 11th generation

The Causes of the "Scattering"

As has been reported, Irish history has been an extended saga of rebellion against the English. At the time of the dissolution of the Irish monasteries and the killing of Catholic officials by Henry VIII, the fortunes of Protestant Colcloughs were advanced because of Sir Anthony's favored position with the throne. He was among those who served to suppress the Irish, as was his son, Sir Thomas, and they were richly rewarded for their efforts. As generations lived and died, many members of this branch of the family remained loyal to the king, but with Sir Thomas's second marriage, potential for another loyalty was created, for this time Thomas had married a Catholic.

[718] Genealogical Office, Ref. F.52.

Catholics were very much out of favor with the English church and throne, in fact, many of England's efforts against the Irish were pointedly against the church which had been the centerpiece of Irish "civilization" since the Dark Ages. There was reason for resentment on the part of the Catholic Colclough family, who had become "more Irish than the Irish," when the Irish people were subdued, *again*, after Cromwell's victory in 1649. Cromwell's Irish policy was punitive and rigidly enforced. Dudley's loss of his vast holdings was only a part of the picture. "Soon nine tenths of the land was held by Protestants, though most of the Irish people remained Catholic. It became illegal for Catholics to buy land in Ireland. Ireland had its own Parliament, but only Protestants held office in it. When the English people forced James II to abdicate, he found enthusiastic support in Ireland, for he was a Catholic. But his army was beaten in the Battle of the Boyne in 1690, and Ireland was subdued once more. A treaty had promised the Catholics land and civil rights, but the Parliaments of England and Ireland refused to keep the terms of the treaty. Laws were passed which crushed Irish trade. The first half of the 1700's was the darkest period in Irish history."

Further notes on Ireland, from *World Book Encyclopedia*, state: "According to the laws of Ireland after 1702-1715, landowners were forbidden to acquire land other than by inheritance, or to take a lease of more than 31 years and at a crushing rental; by the Gavelling Act, if the eldest son conformed, he succeeded to the estate, otherwise it was divided, and this more than anything else served to extinguish the wealthy classes of Ireland, who were usually impoverished by high taxes or high rental; Roman Catholics were barred from all trade professions, education, jury duty, electoral vote, public office, great or small, or the right to own a horse or weapon of any kind.

"Irish Protestants. . .also were barred from public office, . . . or the ruling of their country. Their lot was much the same as their Roman Catholic neighbor's. Thus it is not to be wondered at that Irishmen, Protestant and Roman Catholic alike, soon grew to detest British Rule, and during the reign of Kings George I and II (1714-1760) Ireland was in a state of oppression, despair and decay, as a great exodus of the gentry and adventurous types left the country forever; ruined by high taxes, rentals, and various commercial acts, the Irish emigrated from Ireland as fast as their circumstances would permit, and by 1780, laws, rentals and taxes had completely crushed the upper classes. History records it as the most unjust, and perhaps the worst land system anywhere in Europe."[719]

"In the southwest of the country. . .several of the landowning families which had been established before 1700 were still present in 1850. . .(but) the

---

[719] "Eire," *World Book Encyclopedia*, 1959 ed., vol. 5, pp. 2239-2240.

Colclough family. . . had almost disappeared from the ranks of Wexford's landed class, although branches of the family still held a few small scattered properties elsewhere in the county. . . ."[720]

About the scattering of the Colclough family, English and Irish, John Colclough of Dublin says: "It is not to the geneticist but to the student of human mobility - social, economic, geographical - that the book to be written will be of greatest value with its record of the bewildering movements of this small and readily-identifiable group. So long as there was a family seat occupied by a recognised head of the family commanding an income beyond his own spending capacity such as at Tintern Abbey, Wexford, with its rent-roll from 25,000 acres, or the Delph House at Cheadle (England) with its coal and iron mines, potteries and foundries, the group remained immobile. The social back-ground provided by the family seat facilitated marriages which brought in further wealth and established the economic independence of the cadet branches. The head of the family provided loans for the purchase of commissions and sinecures and gave leases at low rents of subsidiary mansions with sufficient farm-land to support them and allow the tenants to serve as Members of Parliament, J.P.'s, town councillors and aldermen. In times of agricultural depression the rents could remain unpaid and the loans be forgotten. The dependent circle extended to sons, grandsons, nephews and cousins.

"In the case of the Blurton and Endon Colcloughs withdrawal of support was a process which went on progressively for over two centuries following the departure of Anthony to Ireland in 1540 and his brother Matthew to London and Calais and the gradual running down of the Colclough Staffordshire estates. With the Cheadle Colcloughs it came when the conditions created by the Industrial Revolution and by their own prosperity made the Delph House no longer habitable and they dispersed to London and the colonies. In Wexford it resulted from the marriage of the 50-year-old Caesar to a young woman whose chief motivation was hatred of all Colcloughs including her husband and who devoted 40 years of her life to waging a war on them which is now part of English legal history.[721]

"The political factors which led to the break-up of other ancient families were not significant in the case of the Colcloughs. In the Wars of the Roses they fought on both sides. During the Civil War they avoided identification with either side. In Ireland when a Papist was dispossessed of

---

[720] Whelan, *Wexford, p. 217.*

[721] This case, dragging on in the courts of Ireland for years, finally ended when a purported will was found behind some old furniture at Tintern. The widow, about whom it was whispered that she caused Caesar's death by tampering with his medicine, lost her case. Much of the Colclough money was lost in the expense of the process. (Kavanagh and Murphy, vol. 1, p. 62.)

his estates his Protestant son would take them over and so they passed from grandfather to grandson but always remained a centre from which priests and Catholic teachers could serve the locality living in the Abbey though often having to disguise themselves as domestic servants in the blue and yellow livery of the Colcloughs.

"The immediate consequence of the withdrawal of support was geographical dispersal, firstly to America and the West Indies and later to Australia and New Zealand though there are few parts of the world where at some time or other Colcloughs have not lived for a time at least. Availability of grants of land meant that the first generation of Colclough colonists were generally agriculturists but with the second generation we find them entering the learned professions or the armed forces. The few who remained in the British Isles with support withdrawn descended very rapidly in the social scale."[722] Did we not see the same results in Wales in the dispersal of the Gaines family?

Much Research, Few Solutions

There is a goodly quantity of available information about the Colclough/Coakley/Cokeley family. In spite of that fact, I reluctantly report that, after months of effort aimed at identifying the individuals who occupied the period in our line from the time of Thomas of Currach to that of James Cokeley, American immigrant, I have been unable to fill in the blanks with assurance. You might recall that there was an unproven generation or so in the Gaines line, as well, but in that case all that was lacking was documentation which would prove some rather conclusive evidence of the correct line. Solid evidence and proof of it are both lacking for two, possibly three, generations of the Coakley family. A trip to the Virgin Islands or the Leewards would likely take care of some of the uncertainty, but that trip will not be made in the near future. Perhaps another trip to Ireland would help, but that trip will not happen before this book goes to press, either. Bear with me, and I will fill the void with general history, mostly through the observations of others who have written with authority on the subject. I am, at the very least, certain that this historic overview pertains directly to members of our family and many others who found themselves in similar circumstances. Through the observations of others I will be able to introduce some individuals who are excellent candidates for direct ancestry in this branch of the Coakley family.

Sixteen thirty-seven would have been an early date for Coakleys

[722] J. Colclough, Preface, pp. 2-3.

escaping the ravages of Cromwell's power, but we cannot be sure that one adventurous soul of that name did not answer the call of Gov. Anthony Brisket, who was originally from the Wexford area and who was trying to entice his countrymen to Montserrat at that time. "They answered his call and soon heavily outnumbered the English colonists."[723]

On 10/3/1716 a letter was written by one General Hamilton in which he reported the residents of Anguilla along with their households. Among these:
Edw Coakley..1 man..1 woman..0 children..4 Negroes..3 working Negroes
Tho Coakley..1 man..1 woman..9 children..22 Negroes..9 working Negroes
Edw Coakley..1 man..1 woman..5 children..12 Negroes..7 working Negroes[724]

"It was Edward Coakley who had to travel to Antigua to obtain probate of Governor Richardson's will from Sir William Mathews in 1742. Some of his relatives were among the brave and determined men who sixty-two years[725] before established the first plantations in the Virgin Islands."[726] That year would have been 1680, therefore it may have been the latter Edward, the one who had accumulated less property by 1716, who was a witness to the will of the Governor. On 2/1/1742 he appeared before "His Excellency, Captain General and Governor in Chief in and over all His Majesty's Leeward Charibbee Islands in America, Chancillor Vice Admiral & Ordinary of the same" Matthews to swear "upon the Holy Evangelists of Almighty God, that he was present and did see John Richardson, late Sign and Seal" (the will).[727]

Edward[728] is listed elsewhere as the father of John Coakley who died in St. Croix, leaving immense wealth including chests containing 200,000 pieces of eight[729] hidden under his bed. James is listed in almost the same

---

723 Richard S. Dunn, *Sugar and Slaves: The Rise of the Planter Class in the English West Indies, 1624-1713* (Chapel Hill, University of North Carolina Press, 1972), p. 122.

724 Vere Langford Oliver, ed., *Caribbeana: Being Miscellaneous Papers Relating to the History, Genealogy, Topography, and Antiquities of the British West Indies*, vol. 3 (London, Mitchell, Hughes and Clarke, 1909-1919), pp. 255-256.

725 The author is precise in this statement which affirms that Edward Coakley's family, at least, arrived in the islands c1680. This statement is confirmed by Dr. Helmut Blume, et al, *Baedeker's Caribbean Including Bermuda* (New York, Prentice Hall, n.d.), p. 58.

726 S. B. Jones, M.B.E., ETC., *Annals of Anguilla* 1650-1923 (Basseterre, St. Kitts, B. W. I., 1936), p. 7.

727 *Sugar, Rum and Tobacco*, pp. 45-50.

728 S. B. Jones reported that as late as 1937 a child named Edward Coakley Lake was a student in a school in Anguilla. (*op. cit.*, pp. 6-7)

729 Oliver, *Caribbeana*, vol. 5, p. 267. (On p. 72 of vol. 5 we find that a Dr. Coakley bought two square mahogany dining tables at 8 pounds, a Beaufetta for 6 pounds 2 shillings, a pair of brass mounted pistells at 6 pounds 2 shillings, and a feather bed, bedstead, mattress and pavilion [bed

breath as this John. Since they died within two years of one another it would seem they were likely brothers, or cousins, at least. So far there is no proof of this supposition.

Other early settlers on Anguilla, mostly Englishmen, arrived around 1650. Many of the inhabitants left Anguilla in 1680 to live on Virgin Gorda or Tortola.[730] By 1700, according to James Abraham, Tortola was inhabited by a number of settlers who had come from Anguilla, among which were the parents of John Coakley Lettsom. His mother, Mary Coakley, could well have been a daughter of one of the men mentioned above. Some time after 1672 Sir William Stapleton of Nevis, Governor of the Leeward Islands, moved a reported 80 inhabitants, mostly Welsh, Irish and English, from Tortola to St. Kitts.[731] It is further said that by 1689 the people of Anguilla were "so harassed by the French and Irish that Captain Thorn was compelled. . .to remove a number of them to Antigua."[732] As Abraham said, "It was a queer, violently discordant world. . .raucous (and) bizarre. . . ."[733] To the best of our knowledge the Colcloughs would have been classified as Irish Catholics. Would they have been among the group dreaded for their harassment of other settlers? I believe a distinction may be made here between the Irish and the Irish Catholics, but I am not without bias.

There were reasons other than French and Irish hostility for the departure of the English settlers from Anguilla. The island itself was hostile. ". . .(O)n the whole it is an ungrateful soil, yielding only to hard labour and giving enough during rainy seasons to supply man and beast, the chief products being pigeon peas, beans, sweet potatoes, (and) Indian corn. . . .Flat (and) treeless. . .the prevailing winds from northeast to southwest sweep over it continuously, modifying the climate to that of a sub-tropical country. There are no streams and the few wells afford only brackish water. In seasons of drought the sufferings of the inhabitants are intense, persons being compelled to get up at midnight and walk from three to four miles to secure a scanty supply of water trickling from the springs of the chief wells."[734]

---

canopy] at 7 pounds. Interesting proof that there were a number of Coakleys in the islands at this time.)

[730] There was a substantial colony of Quakers on Tortola in the early 18th century. It is known that some of the Coakleys were Quakers, at least for a while. It may have been that the names Benjamin, James, Daniel, Caleb and other "Biblical" names, uncommon in the Colclough family of Ireland, entered into the line because of the Quaker connection. It is also known that most of the Coakley Quakers in Ireland lived in the general vicinity of Cork. Thomas of Currach, probable ancestor, had settled near that area.

[731] Florence Lewisohn, p. 10.

[732] S. B. Jones, p. 6.

[733] Abraham, pp. 4-8.

[734] Lewisohn, p. 2.

S. B. Jones added that Anguilla was "filled with alligators and other noxious animals. . .and the island was frequently plundered by marauders." He allowed that it was good for raising tobacco, however, and that the cattle multiplied very fast.[735] For a parcel of land granted the colonist might pay, ". . . if required, a fat capon, a kid, and later one ear of Indian Corn on every Feast day of St. Michael the Angel."[736]

Other reports of the Irish emigration to and among the islands include the following:

"On Barbados, after the English Civil War (1642-1660) Oliver Cromwell's Commonwealth government accentuated the differences between the English factions (Roundheads - Parliamentary/Cavaliers - Royalist/Protestant). Members of both factions came to the islands, many of them able to purchase estates."[737] Were the English-speaking Irishmen, many of whom had been ardent Loyalists, considered among the English in this comment?

In 1678 then-Governor Stapleton compiled a census which showed the number of Irish among the populations of four islands: On Nevis there were 450 Irish men; on Antigua 360; on St. Christophers 187; and on Montserrat 769.[738]

"Many of the settlers were Irish - with Irish settlers forming 70 percent of the white population on Montserrat in 1678."[739] Surely some of these were Coakleys/Colcloughs. Our "cousin" and benefactor, John Colclough, knows that his ancestor was on Montserrat, at least for a time.

"In 1688 there were 90 surveyed plantations on St. Thomas with a total white plantations of 148 distributed as follows: 66 Dutch, 31 English, 17 Danes and Norwegians, 17 French, 4 Irish, 4 Flemish, 3 Germans, 3 Swedes, and one each of Scottish, Brazilian and Portuguese."[740] Were they among these on St. Thomas?

During the Nine Years' War (1688-1697) James II was deposed and

---

[735] Capt. Thomas Southey, Commander of the Royal Navy, *Chronological History of the West Indies*, vol. 2, p. 119., as quoted by S. B. Jones, pp. 2-3.
[736] S. B. Jones, pp. 3-4.
[737] Jan Rogozinski, *A Brief History of the Caribbean From the Arawak and the Carib to the Present, Revised Edition* (New York, Facts on File Inc., 1999), p. 74.
[738] Dunn, p. 127.
[739] Rogozinski, p. 76.
[740] William W. Boyer, *America's Virgin Islands: A History of Human Rights and Wrongs* (Durham, NC, Carolina Academic Press), pp. 10-11.

Irish Catholics on Nevis, Antigua, and Montserrat rebelled in support of their king. The Governor-general of the Leeward Islands, Christopher Codrington, managed to quell the rebellion.[741] (On pondering the given name James, which seems to have no precedent in the Coakley family, could G-g-g-g-g-grandfather James have been named in honor of the deposed monarch? Or was the Quaker influence such that he was awarded the customery "Biblical" name?)

"The objection to the Irish was principally because of their religion, as most of them were Catholics and, as events proved more than once, likely to join with their French[742] co-religionists against the Protestant English."[743]

"There is no mention in the official pedigrees of Colcloughs who emigrated to the West Indies, but (John Coakley) Lettsom, who was born in 1744, probably had (the following) information from his mother (the former Mary Coakley). Sir Dudley Colclough, Kt. of Duffrey Hall, born 1613, MP Enniscorthy, 1689, took the oath of the Confederate Catholics, and was robbed of his estates by Cromwell, but restored to them by Charles II."[744] "(The Colcloughs). . .were classed as 'old English' and no less than 14 Colcloughs suffered under the Williamite confiscation as 'Irish Papists.'"[745]

. . ."Different branches of (the Coakley/Colclough) families, during the Government of Ireland, went to Barbadoes, in favour of the Commonwealth; and settled afterwards in different islands among that large cluster known to us by the names of the Leeward and Windward Islands."[746]

. . ."the nineteenth century saw a worldwide scattering of the Colclough family. Adam of Duffry Hall died in 1793 and the great house of the Colcloughs gradually fell into disrepair and was subsequently demolished; another house was built on the site. . . Colcloughs moved to Carlow, Kilkenny and Laois. Their descendants may still be found in Australia, Canada, and the United States, from which many of them have returned on visits to Tintern Abbey to proudly research their illustrious forebears."[747]

---

[741] Rogozinski, p. 100.

[742] William, Lord Willoughby, Governor of Barbados and of the Leeward Islands, said in 1668 when the Irish had sworn loyalty to the English king, "I believe them till an enemy appear." (Sir Alan Burns, *History of the British West Indies,* London, George Allen & Unwin Ltd., 1965, p. 338.)

[743] Burns, p. 348.

[744] Letter to Miss Biddulph-Colclough of Tintern Abbey, December 10, 1931 as quoted by Abraham, p. 12.

[745] MacLysaght, *More Irish Families*, p. 60.

[746] Thomas Joseph Pettigrew, *Memoirs of the Life and Writings of the Late John Coakley Lettsom*, vol. 1 (London, Longman, Hurst, Rees, Orme and Brown, 1817), p. 5.

[747] Whelan, *Tintern*, p. 31.

At St. Croix, where the name Coakley was in evidence in 1769, there is a picturesque west-facing bay known as Coakley Bay.

"It is possible some of his family found it expedient to emigrate to Barbadoes during the Commonwealth. . ."[748]

"It would seem, from the above information that the Coakley family was disposing of their estates, either due to financial reasons or the fear of losing them to the state for political reasons."[749]

It is evident that there is general agreement about the dispersal of the Colclough family from Ireland, and that quite a number of authorities believe that one or more family lines lived in a variety of places in the West Indies. James, the Virginia immigrant, for one, was first located on Antigua as he was exchanging vows with Margaret Antonison sixty-five years after the earliest Irish emigrees were said to have appeared in the islands. From that time much of the story is known. We may never be able to account for the unknown.

---

[748] Abraham, p. 12.
[749] Charles Colclough, research notes, unp.

Appendix A

Another Possible Gaines (Games) Line

In Chapter 11 the most likely linkage between Sir Dafydd (Gam) ap Llewelyn and Thomas Gaines, American immigrant, is detailed. It is acknowledged, however, that it is possible that the Aberbran line is not the correct one. Since the study was made and the work done on the "Newton" family, I felt it appropriate to present that line, also, just in case. It is included below.

Jeuan or Edward Gam

son of **Morgan Gam** and **Margaret Lloyd**

brother of Alice m. Jenkin Stradling
Gwenllian m. Morgan Prees Gwilym
Gwallter of Porthgwyn
Meredith
Gwilym
Thomas
Llewelyn ap Morgan of Penfathrin m. Jennet Rhaglan
Jeuan hir, ancestor of the Gwyns of Bodwigad
David Gam
step-brother of Maud m. Owen Griffith ap Owen Gethin

m. **Anne Lloyd**

father of Agnes m. Jeuan Gwilym Fychan
Joice m. John Scudamore
Cissil m. Philip Vaughan of Tyleglas
Margaret Gam m. Thomas Evan Madoc of Slwch
Anne m. John Havard tew.
Joan m. Lewis Gunter
Gwilym m. Margaret Havard of Penkelly (Pencelly)
Morgan ap Jeuan m. Gwladis Bloet/Blewet

G-g-g-g-g-g-g-g-g-g-g-g-g-g-grandfather- 18th generation

Anne Lloyd

daughter of **Gwilyn Lloyd** (1473-)

m. **Jeuan** or **Edward ap Morgan**

mother of Agnes m. Jeuan Gwilym Fychan
Joice m. John Scudamore
Cissil m. Philip Vaughan of Tyleglas
Margaret m. Thomas Evan Madoc of Slwch
Anne m. John Havard
Joan m. Lewis Gunter
Gwilym m. Margaret Havard of Penkelly
Morgan ap Jeuan m. Gwladis Bloet

G-g-g-g-g-g-g-g-g-g-g-g-g-g-grandmother- 18th generation

Gwilym Lloyd

b. c1473 in Carregfawr, Brecon, Wales (This date is highly questionable!)

son of **Rhys Lloyd** and **Golewdydd Vychan** (LDS)

brother of **Margaret Lloyd** m. Morgan Gam
Lewis ap Gwilym Glwyd of Castell Hywel

father of **Anne Lloyd** m. Jeuan or Edward ap Morgan

G-g-g-g-g-g-g-g-g-g-g-g-g-g-g-grandfather- 19th generation

Morgan ap Jeuan

son of **Jeuan/Edward ap Morgan** and **Anne Lloyd**

brother of Agnes m. Jeuan Gwilym Fychan

Joice m. John Scudamore
Cissil m. Philip Vaughan of Tyleglas
Margaret m. Thomas Evan Madoc of Slwch
Anne m. John Havard tew
Joan m. Lewis Gunter
Gwilym m. Margaret Havard of Penkelly

m. **Gwladis Bloet** (Blewet) (c1446-)

Through his marriage to Gwladis, Morgan came into possession of *Llandevailog tre'r graig* in the hundred of Talgarth where he settled.[750]

father of Joan m. Morgan Thomas hir
John Games of Newton, Member of Parliament, County of Brecon, 1545; High Sheriff, Brecon, 1574; m. (1)Margaret Gwalter; 2)Margaret Morgan of Arxton

G-g-g-g-g-g-g-g-g-g-g-g-g-grandfather- 17th generation

Gwladis Bloet/Blewet

b. c1446 in Wales[751]

daughter of **Morgan Bloet** or Blewet and a daughter of William Bruchill

m. **Morgan ap Jeuan**

mother of Joan m. Morgan Thomas hir
John Games of Newton, MP of County Brecon, 1545; High Sheriff, Brecon, 1574; m. (1)Margaret Gwalter; (2)Margaret Morgan of Arxton

G-g-g-g-g-g-g-g-g-g-g-g-grandmother- 17th generation

[750] Jones, vol. 4, p. 171.
[751] LDS

Morgan Bloet or Blewet

m. a daughter of William Bruchill

father of **Gwladis Bloet** (c1446-) m. Morgan ap Jeuan

G-g-g-g-g-g-g-g-g-g-g-g-g-grandfather- 18th generation

___Bruchill

daughter of William Bruchill

m. **Morgan Bloet**/Blewet

mother of **Gwladis Bloet** (c1446-) m. Morgan ap Jeuan

G-g-g-g-g-g-g-g-g-g-g-g-g-grandmother- 18th generation

William Bruchill

father of ___Bruchill m. Morgan Bloet (Blewet)

G-g-g-g-g-g-g-g-g-g-g-g-g-g-grandfather- 19th generation

John Games of Newton[752]

son of **Morgan Games** and **Gwladis Bloet** (Blewet)

The fashion in names was changing about this time, and John was the first to use the last name of Games.

---

[752] An interesting anecdote pertaining to this family: . . . "(T)here are almshouses built here with a portion of garden ground attached to each. . .These were given by one of the family of Games of Newton, for the residence of twelve female decayed housekeepers of the town of Brecon. . .This excellent charity has conduced to support many old and infirm females, who have seen better days, at a time of life when they are unable to gain a livelihood; the houses are more than tolerable dwellings, having a walled court in front, in the middle of which, on a stone, is an inscription prohibiting blasphemy, adultery, fornication and profane oaths, under pain of exclusion, and enjoining a due attendance on the church and the sick of their own sisterhood; in addition to their habitation, rent-free, each of the females admitted receives ten shillings quarterly, and is provided with a flannel gown and petticoat at Christmas." (Jones, vol. 4, p. 169.)

brother of Joan Games m. Morgan Thomas hir

m. (1)Margaret Gwalter; (2)**Margaret Morgan** of Arxton

John inherited Newton and other lands in Saint David's and Llanspyddid through his first wife, Margaret Gwalter, daughter of Thomas Walter Jenkin Havard.

father, with Margaret Gwalter, of: Gwladis Games m. Christopher Vaughan of Tretower
Joan Games m. (1)Meredith Watkin; (2)Philip John of Marchogtir
father, with Margaret Morgan, of: **Edward Games of Newton** (-1564) m. Elizabeth Vaughan
Meredith Games of Buckland m. (1)Gwenllian Gwyn;[753] (2)Jane Ychan; (3)a daughter of Rhys Morgan John; (4)Elinor, daughter of Rhys ap Owen
Elizabeth Games m. William James
Joan Games m. James Parry of Poston

High Sheriff of County Brecon in 1574 and in 1587.
Member of Parliament 1545-1547

G-g-g-g-g-g-g-g-g-g-g-grandfather-16th generation

Margaret Morgan

daughter of **William Morgan of Arxton**

m. **John of Newton**, of Brecon County, MP 1545

mother of **Edward Games of Newton** (-1564) m. Elizabeth Vaughan
Meredith Games of Buckland m. (1)Gwenllian Gwyn; (2)Jane Ychan; (3)a daughter of Rhys Morgan John; (4)Elinor ap Rhys ap Owen, daughter of Rhys ap Owen
Elizabeth Games m. William James
Joan Games m. James Parry of Poston

G-g-g-g-g-g-g-g-g-g-g-grandmother- 16th generation

[753] Meredith Games's daughter, Elizabeth, became the second wife of Edward's son, Sir John Games of Newton (1559-1606).

William Morgan of Arxton

father of **Margaret Morgan** m. John of Newton

G-g-g-g-g-g-g-g-g-g-g-g-grandfather- 17th generation

Edward Games of Newton, Esq.

son of **John of Newton,** MP and **Margaret Morgan**, daughter of William
Morgan of Arxton

brother of **Meredith Games of Buckland**, MP Brecon 1554-1555, m.
(1)Gwenllian Gwyn of Trecastle; (2) Jane Ychan; (3)a daughter
of Rhys Morgan John; (4)Elinor ap Rhys ap Owen
Elizabeth Games m. William James
Joan Games m. James Parry of Poston
step-brother of Gwladis Games m. Christopher Vaughan of Tretower
Joan Games m. (1)Meredith Watkin; (2)Philip John of Marchogtir

m. **Elizabeth Vychan/Vaughan**, daughter of Sir William Vaughan of
Porthaml

"By the marriage of Edward Games of Newton with Elizabeth Anne, daughter of Sir William Vaughan of Porthaml. . .the estate of Peytyn Gwyn as well as Peytyn du, by some family arrangements and settlements, became the property of the Gameses of Newton, the lineal descendants of Sir David Gam . . ." and of his father, who had first purchased the properties.[754]

He was "called to the Bar."[755] This, I believe, suggests that he was a member of the legal profession.

father of Jane Games m. Richard Herbert of Penkelly
Margaret Games m. Thomas Powel Gwyn of Trecastle
Elizabeth Games m. James Thomas of Slwch
Gwladis Games m. William Solers of Porthamal
Sibil Games m. William Whitney of Green Pit

[754] Jones, 1898, p. 248.
[755] Jones, vol. 4, p. 277.

Sir John Games of Newton (-1606), High Sheriff of County Brecon, 1600; Member of Parliament 1587, m.(1)Elinor Gwyn; (2)Elizabeth Games, daughter of Meredith Games; (3)Catherine Bradshaw of Presteigne
Edward Games of Tregaer (-1564) m. Jennet Walbeoffe
Walter Games m. Alice Gunter
Christopher Games m. Margaret ap Thomas ap Hopkin Awbrey
Roger Games m. Alice Havard of Brecon
Thomas Games
Morgan Games

Edward Games of Newton, Esqr. is given the credit for having urged the Earl of Pembroke to seek a charter for the town of Brecknock from King Philip and Queen Mary in 1556. This charter, once granted, removed many of the restrictions imposed by the Marchers, including a 100 pound per year abatement of which the town was much in arrears. The town was also in arrears to Edward for "Parliament fees," and for that reason and as a "reward for good service" it gave to him the hospital and the lands belonging to it, which Edwin Poole still found to belong to the Games family at the time he published in 1886.[756]

Edward was Justice of the Peace at one time in the county of Brecon; he was also named the first Recorder of Brecknock (1557-1564) after the charter was granted. Poole reports that Edward was "several times Member of Parliament for the borough of Brecon (1542-1553), and High Sheriff for the county of Brecon in 1559."[757] Jones proclaims him to be "one of the most influential personages in Brecon of his day."

d. 1564

In the Brecknock Priory Church, in an area that was once within the communion rails, but is now in the Vicar's Chapel, Theophilus Jones locates the tomb of "Edward Games of Newton, 1564," in space otherwise described as that of the Prices of the Priory.[758] His body was placed there under the high altar in 1610.[759]

G-g-g-g-g-g-g-g-g-g-g-grandfather- 15th generation

---

[756] Poole, p. 34.
[757] Poole, p. 393.
[758] Poole, p. 45.
[759] Poole, p. 65.

Elizabeth Anne Vychan/Vaughan

b. c1513 in Porthamal, Brecon

daughter of **Sir William Vaughan of Porthamal** and **Katherine Havard**

m. (1)John Havard of Tredomen (2)**Edward Games of Newton** (-1564), High Sheriff Breconshire, 1558

mother of Jane Games m. Richard Herbert of Penkelly
Margaret Games m. Thomas Powel Gwyn of Trecastle
Elizabeth Games m. James Thomas of Slwch
Gwladis Games m. William Solers of Porthamal
Sibil Games m. William Whitney of Green Pit
Sir John Games of Newton (-1606), High Sheriff Breconshire, 1600; MP 1587, m.(1)Elinor Gwyn; (2) Elizabeth Games daughter of Meredith Games; (3)Catherine Bradshaw of Prestelgne
Edward Games of Tregaer (-1564) m. Jennet Walbeoffe
Walter Games m. Alice Gunter
Christopher Games m. Margaret ap Thomas ap Hopkin Awbrey
Roger Games m. Alice Havard of Brecon
Thomas Games
Morgan Games[760]

G-g-g-g-g-g-g-g-g-g-grandmother- 15th generation

Sir John Gaines of Newton

"John Gain" was knighted, according to a letter from Sir Albert Tillery, Secretary to the Registrar, in the middle of the 16th century. At that time the letters *es* were added by some family members to that name. The current spelling has been used, by some, since that time.

b. 1559

son of **Edward Games of Newton** (-1564) and **Elizabeth Vaughan** of Porthamal

[760] Latter Day Saints

Newton, near Brecon, was built by Sir John Games in 1582.

brother of Jane Games m. Richard Herbert of Penkelly
Margaret Games m. Thomas Power Gwyn of Trecastle
Elizabeth Games m. James Thomas of Slwch
Gwladis Games m. William Solers of Porthamal
Sibil Games m. William Whitney of Green Pit
Edward Games of Tregaer (-1564) m. Jennet Walbeoffe
Walter Games m. Alice Gunter
Christopher Games m. Margaret ap Thomas ap Hopkin Awbrey of Cantref
Roger Games m. Alice Havard of Brecon
Thomas Games[761]
Morgan Games

m. (1)Elinor Gwyn (2)**Elizabeth Games** (3)Catherine Bradshaw of Presteigne

father of Mary Gaines m. Charles Walcott
Edward Gaines of Newton, High Sheriff, Breconshire, 1623, m. Bridget Vaughan
John Gaines of Newton(-1656) m. Elizabeth Hoo of Skerming in Norfolk [762]

[761] This Thomas may be our immigrant forebear, Sir John our uncle. If so, some of the dates of these brothers may be in error. Since Sir John's story is quite well documented, I would suggest that either Edward and Elizabeth had their children over a long period of time, or that Thomas's dates may be incorrect. Either or both could be true.

"On the Usk River in Brecon, Wales, in the general area where early legends relate King Arthur had his residence and called meetings of his Knights of the Round Table, there stands an ancient farmhouse, the first part of which was built in the Twelfth Century. Sir David Gam's great-great-grandson, Sir John Games (1559-1606) came into possession of the ancient house, 'Newton' and enlarged it."[763]

"The reception room where one enters from the front door is nicely furnished with some antiques, but not with any that belong to the house. The Great Hall is huge, 50 by 20 feet with very high ceilings. There are two floor levels; the lord of the manor and his family dined at tables set in the raised portion and others at tables placed on the lower level of the floor. Near the ceiling and in the walls are openings from which music could be heard when played by the minstrels. The fireplace is about 10 feet wide and 6 feet high with a stone mantel over the top. On this stone is carved an inscription showing the ancestral line from Sir David Gam to Sir John Gaines and the Gaines coat of arms with the motto, "All Depends on God" (*Ar Dduw y gyd*). There is a big staircase of hand carved timbers, and a large chimney in the center of the house with four huge fireplaces connecting."[764]

Edward Poole, historian, said of the house: "This interesting specimen of the strong and not unsightly mansions of the Elizabethan age, (is) half fortress and half domestic residence. . . ."

Member of Parliament, 1587
High Sheriff of Brecon in 1600[765]

d. 1606

G-g-g-g-g-g-g-g-g-grandfather- 14th generation

Elizabeth Games

---

[762] This couple had a son named Hoo Games/Gaines who was said to have m. Blanch Kemeys. Family tradition suggests that Blanch m. Thomas, our immigrant forebear. It is clear that Blanch is our strongest connection with this line, but there is at least one major error in someone's records if she is actually our ancestor.

[763] L. P. Gaines, pp. 3-4.

[764] Sutherd, *Reprint*, 1972, pp. 18-21.

[765] The Games men are remembered as prominent, productive citizens. Between the lines one finds that some of them also used their immense influence to take advantage of situations and people. Pamela Redwood in her essay on "The Games Family versus the Borough of Brecon, 1589-1606," from *Brycheiniog*, pp. 10-15, cites some examples of less worthy behavior.

daughter of **Meredith Games of Buckland**, MP and **Gwenllian Gwyn** of Trecastle

m**.** **Sir John Gaines of Newton** (1559-1606)

mother of Mary Gaines m. Charles Walcott
Edward Gaines of Newton, high sheriff, Brecknockshire, 1623, m. Bridget Vaughan
John Gaines of Newton m. Elizabeth Hoo of Skerming in Norfolk.

G-g-g-g-g-g-g-g-g-grandmother- 14th generation

Meredith Games of Buckland

son of **John Games of Newton**, MP, Breconshire, 1545, and **Margaret Morgan**

brother of **Edward Games of Newton** (-1564) m. Elizabeth Anne Vaughan of Porthamal
Elizabeth Games m. William James
Joan Games m. James Parry of Poston
step-brother of Gwladis Games m. Christopher Vaughan of Tretower
Joan Games m. (1)Meredith Watkin; (2)Philip John of Marchogtir

m. (1)**Gwenllian Gwyn** of Trecastle (c1510-); (2)Jane Ychan; (3)daughter of Rhys Morgan John; (4)Elinor ap Owen, daughter of Rhys ap Owen.

father of John Games of Buckland, High Sheriff, Brecknockshire, 1604, m. Catherine Evans of Neath
Elizabeth Games, m. (1)Thomas Lewis of Brecon; (2)Sir John Games of Newton[766]
Catherine Games m. John Thomas Lewis of Ffrwdgrech
by 2nd marriage William Games (-1605) m. Elizabeth Goch
by 3rd William Games m. __ Capor
by 4th Gwenllian Games m. John Davis of Brecon (-9/24/1658)

Meredith Games was a Member of Parliament from Brecon in 1554

[766] Meredith's daughter, Elizabeth, m. Edward's son, Sir John Games of Newton (-1606). First cousins!

and 1555. He served as an alderman[767] in 1573, 1576, and in 1583.[768]

d. c1600

Identified as Meredith Games *of Buckland*, this man was the first to build a mansion where the present one now stands. It is supposed that Meredith either bought the land from the Watkin family, or that he received it as a grant from the Crown.[769]

A stone in the cemetery of Christ's College Church of Brecon states, "Here lieth the body of William, the son of Meredith Games, Esq., ap John ap Morgan ap Edward ap Morgan ap Sir David Gam, Knight; he married Elizabeth, viz., Llewelyn ap John ap Thomas ap Griffith ap Owen ap Griffith ap Owen Gethin; they had issue 10 children now living - 1605[770]

G-g-g-g-g-g-g-g-g-g-grandfather-15th generation

Gwenllian Gwyn

b. c1510 at Brecon

daughter of **Thomas Gwyn** of Trecastle (1490-)

m. **Meredith Games of Buckland**, MP Breconshire, 1554, 1555

mother of John Games of Buckland, high sheriff, County Brecon, 1604, m. Catherine Evans of Neath
Elizabeth Games m. (1)Thomas Lewis of Brecon; (2)Sir John Games of Newton
Catherine Games m. John Thomas Lewis of Ffrwdgrech

G-g-g-g-g-g-g-g-g-g-grandmother- 15th generation

[767] A Welsh/English alderman is a senior elected official who ranks next to the mayor in importance.
[768] Poole, *op. cit.*, p. 410.
[769] Poole, *op. cit.*, p. 103.
[770] Poole, *op. cit.*, p. 103.

Thomas Gwyn of Trecastle

b. 1490 (LDS)

m. **Elen Vaughan**, daughter of Roger Vaughan, Esq. of Porthaml

father of **Gwenllian Gwyn** (c1510-) m. Meredith Games of Buckland
Howel Gwyn, Esq., m. Jennet Llewelyn, daughter of Gwilym Llewelyn, Esq. of Garregfawr
John Gwyn, Esq., of Abercraf m. Anne Price, daughter of Thomas Price, Esq., of Abertreweren, Defynog (high sheriff for Brecon in 1670).

G-g-g-g-g-g-g-g-g-g-g-grandfather- 16th generation

Then and now, the Wilson children:
Jim, the twins, Martha and Emma, and Elisabeth (seated)

Appendix B

Unfinished Stories - The Living
Generations 1, A, B, C

The individuals in this chapter are struggling with complexities that other generations have not had to endure, and enjoying comforts and luxuries that other generations would not have been able to imagine. History is in the making here. I'll not waste your time by citing significant incidents or interesting tidbits; as William Wordsworth said, "The world is too much with us. . . ," and these individuals are part of all that is happening. The generations represented here, the first (Blanche Odessa Miller Wilson's and James Moore Wilson's children); and generations A (the offspring of my generation); B (the grandchildren of generation one); and C, and so forth, will not only be participants in the process of history, they will be expected to complete and continue this report, creating an expanded portrait of the make-up of a family.

Blanche and Moore had four children. I'm sure, though I never heard it voiced, that it was very important for Moore Wilson to have a male heir, someone to carry on the name. After all, none of his brothers had produced any heirs to the family name. Imagine the pleasure of the young couple at the arrival of their firstborn, a boy child, whom they proudly named for his father.

The James Moore Wilson, Jr. Family
Generation 1

James Moore Wilson, Jr.

b. 10/10/1930 in Lexington, Virginia.

Jim was one of a relatively few people who had the opportunity to be born in Stonewall Jackson's house in Lexington during the time it was used as a hospital. The home is now on the historic register and used as a museum.

Jim was the only child of Blanche and Moore to be born in a hospital. Mother decided that she did not like the impersonal care of an institution, and chose to have her other three children at home. A nurse was employed and the doctor, a friend, put on notice. It worked! Mother experienced childbirth well attended, in congenial surroundings.

son of **James Moore Wilson** (2/2/1898-3/18/1983) and **Blanche Odessa**

Miller (11/30/1896-3/27/1980) 6/2/1928

brother of Martha Miller Wilson (11/13/1932-) m. Walter Barrett Black (2/6/1932-) 8/27/1955
Emma Wade Wilson (11/13/1932-) m. Charles Willard Jordan (9/15/1933-) 9/13/1952
Elisabeth Anne Wilson (7/7/36-) m. (1) Martin Quinter Miller, Jr. (12/12/1930-) 1/13/1956; (2)William Long Hodges (7/22/1930-) 6/16/1972

Jim spent two years at Virginia Polytechnic Institute before he decided that his father knew more about agriculture than did the professors at Tech.

m. **Maude LaRue Fauber** (4/16/1929-) 4/11/1952

Jim and LaRue live on a farm we knew as "Mrs. Cupp's" because of the family who lived there when we were children growing up across the road. There was, however, a house there long before the Cupp family arrived, for a plat dated 1837 indicates it. Part of the house and a shop building situated behind the house may be that old. The one-story, plastered "shop" with heart pine floors and ceiling was once two stories and the front part of the house. Around 1900 this part was rolled away and a fine new building, built by Mr. J. A. B. Lotts, was added to the low, two-story log kitchen at the back, all of which provided the space necessary for Jim, LaRue, and eight very busy children, and here all of the young *Wilsons* in our family were raised.

father of **Glenn Franklin Wilson** (6/5/1953-) m. Jane Pendleton Campbell (2/17/1953-) 3/17/1973
Emily Faith Wilson (8/14/1954-) m. James Kilby Forkovitch (8/16/1949-) 4/29/1989
Kenneth Michael Wilson (6/25/1956-) m. Janet Marie Hendrix (7/9/1957-) 2/4/1978
Karen Denise Wilson (1/14/1958-) m. Thomas Calvin Ingram (9/15/1959-) 2/16/1977
Linda LaRue Wilson (1/29/1960-) m. David Pledger Murray (9/4/1959-) 6/26/1982
Jerry Lee Wilson (5/5/1962-) m. Paula McKemy (2/5/1964-) 12/10/1983

Laura Jean Wilson (4/9/1964-) m. (1)Daniel Naar Early (7/17/1958-) 9/27/1991 Divorced: (2)Toni Mancari

Lisa Marie Wilson (4/9/1964-) m. William Gaston Everhart (10/1/1957-) 6/18/1994 Divorced.

Jim worked as a second-shift machine operator at Westinghouse for 35 years and farmed during daylight hours. It is common knowledge that the farm no longer supports large families as it did in the days of Joseph Miller. For that matter, Joseph had a job (as a Brethren minister) on the side, also, although we do not know whether he was paid for his services. After Jim retired to full-time farming, he was heard to say that all he wanted of retirement was to farm and to make LaRue happy.

Jim is an elder at Mt. Carmel Presbyterian Church which he attends with his wife and children and grandchildren, as his father did before him.

Jim's and LaRue's daughter, Lisa Wilson Everhart, served for a time as the interim pastor of Timber Ridge Presbyterian Church. In this role, she and her father were both members of a commission to install the Rev. C. William Cox at Mt. Carmel Presbyterian Church 4/23/1995.

Maude LaRue Fauber

b. 4/16/1929 at "Skylark," the Fauber family home at Montebello, Virginia

daughter of **Hercy Franklin Fauber** (5/8/1882-2/17/1958) and **Lottie Virginia Campbell** (3/16/1889-11/30/1984) 6/30/1916 at Mt. Paran Church

m. **James Moore Wilson, Jr.** (10/10/1930-) 4/11/1952

mother of **Glenn Franklin Wilson** (6/5/1953-) m. Jane Pendleton Campbell (2/17/1953-) 3/17/1973

Emily Faith Wilson (8/14/1954-) m. James Kilby Forkovitch (8/16/1949-) 4/29/1989

Kenneth Michael Wilson (6/25/1956-) m. Janet Marie Hendrix (7/9/1957-) 2/4/1978

Karen Denise Wilson (1/14/1958-) m. Thomas Calvin Ingram (9/15/1959-) 2/16/1977

Linda LaRue Wilson (1/29/1960-) m. David Pledger Murray (9/4/1959-) 6/26/1982

Jerry Lee Wilson (5/5/1962-) m. Paula McKemy (2/5/1964-) 12/10/1983
Laura Jean Wilson (4/9/1964-) m. Daniel Naar Early (7/17/1958-) 9/27/1991. Divorced; (2)Tony Mancari
Lisa Marie Wilson (4/9/1964-) m. William Gaston Everhart (10/1/1957-) 6/18/1994

LaRue, while successfully raising this household of attractive children and restoring their interesting old home, had time for crafts and music. She is extremely skillful at both, rather, at everything she does!

She is an exceptional musician, playing guitar, mandolin, fiddle, and banjo, and, so far as I know, any other stringed instrument she picks up. She plays with several groups *for* many groups. LaRue learned to play at age eleven and says she has played "with the best (and worst) and has a great time!"

Generation A

Glenn Franklin Wilson

b. 6/5/1953 at Waynesboro Community Hospital, Waynesboro, Virginia

son of **James Moore Wilson, Jr.** (10/10/1930-) and **Maude LaRue Fauber** (4/16/1929-) 4/11/1952
For siblings, see p. 396-397.

m. **Jane Pendleton Campbell** (2/17/1953-) 3/17/1973 in Greenville, Virginia

father of **Stephanie Lynn Wilson** (11/4/1973-) m. Todd Eugene Wade (6/28/1973-) 10/3/1992
Ann Marie Wilson (5/2/1975-) m. Anthony Scott Nelson (1/29/1975)

Glenn rebuilds and restores old log buildings and builds Americana furniture. His accomplishments have been featured in several magazines. He has worked on such notable buildings as the mill and the shop at the Cyrus McCormick home in Raphine, Virginia, and he recently traveled to Dearborn, Michigan where he was employed by the Ford Museum to rebuild the log cabin home of William Holmes McGuffey, compiler of the famed McGuffey Readers. It seems that log cabin technology is something that hasn't been developed there.

The Glenn Wilson home is notable. He carefully tore down one that had been in the Wilson family four or five generations ago and rebuilt it as his own. This home had been that of Samuel Wilson and Drucilla Fauntleroy Larue, and possibly earlier generations of the family.

He and Jane are members of Mt. Carmel Presbyterian Church.

Jane Pendleton Campbell

b. 2/17/1953 at King's Daughters Hospital in Staunton, Virginia.

daughter of **John Thomas Campbell** and **Mabel Whitesell** of Greenville

m. **Glenn Franklin Wilson** 3/17/1973 at Greenville

mother of **Stephanie Lynn Wilson** (11/4/1973-) m. Todd Eugene Wade (6/28/1973-)10/3/1992
Ann Marie Wilson (5/2/1975-) m. Anthony Scott Nelson (1/29/1975-)

Emily Faith Wilson

b. 8/14/1954 at the Waynesboro Hospital

daughter of **James Moore Wilson, Jr.** (10/10/1930-) and **Maude LaRue Fauber** (4/16/1929-) 4/11/1952
For siblings, see p. 396-397.

m. **James Kilby Forkovitch** (8/16/1949-) 4/29/1989 at Mt. Carmel Presbyterian Church in Steele's Tavern, Virginia

Faith and Jim live near Harrisonburg, Virginia, with their cats.

Retired by the time she had reached the ripe old age of 45, Faith reports that she and Jim are involved in deep sea diving, piloting airplanes, golfing, whitewater rafting, skiing, sky diving, rock climbing, boating, and extensive travel. They own and rent two college fraternity houses, along with other properties, and operate a Christmas tree farm rated number one in Virginia in 1995. That year they provided the Christmas tree for Governor Wilder at the mansion in Richmond. Faith is a member of the board of the

Spotswood Country Club Golf LGA, and also serves on the Harrisonburg-Rockingham Free Clinic Fund Raising Board. In her spare time, she studies piano at Eastern Mennonite University.

James Kilby Forkovitch

b. 8/16/1949 in Harrisonburg, Virginia

son of **Nickolas John Forkovitch** and **Betty Ann McGrath**

m. **Emily Faith Wilson** (8/14/1954-) 4/29/1989

Jim is the Vice-President and General Manager of Howell Metal Company and co-owner of a 104-unit retirement community development project.

Faith and Jim share a great many interests and activities. Jim prefers the rock climbing, however, to the piano playing, which he rarely does anymore. He serves on the board of the Harrisonburg hospital in the Funds Division.

Kenneth Michael Wilson

b. 6/25/1956 in Waynesboro, Virginia.

son of **James Moore Wilson, Jr.** (10/10/30-) and **Maude LaRue Fauber** (4/16/1929-) 4/11/1952
for siblings see p. 396-397.

m. **Janet Hendrix** (7/9/1957-) 2/4/1978

father of **Eric Christopher Wilson** (6/26/1980-)
Heather Michelle Wilson (2/4/1983-)

Mike is a Maintenance Planner for McKee Foods in Stuarts Draft, Virginia. He also does some farming.

Mike, Janet, and their family live in the home which his great-grandfather, Samuel McCown Wilson, built around 1907 for his large family. They have restored and improved the home considerably, even putting in *bathrooms*, which Mike's great-grandmother had considered unsanitary and would not allow her husband to install in the new home, leaving instead a small empty room at the head of the main staircase.

In addition to his commitment to his home, family and job, Mike serves as Assistant Fire Chief for the Raphine Volunteer Fire Department. He is the Red Cross Disaster Co-ordinator and Shelter First Responder Medic with the Fire Department.

This family attends the Mt. Carmel Presbyterian Church.

Janet Marie Hendrix

b. 7/9/1957 in King's Daughters Hospital, Staunton,Virginia

daughter of **James Ray Hendrix** and **Ruth Boaz**

m. **Kenneth Michael Wilson** (6/25/1956-) 2/4/1978 at Central Methodist Church in Staunton

mother of **Eric Christopher Wilson** (6/26/1980-)
Heather Michelle Wilson (2/4/1983-)

Janet serves as the Billing and Collections Manager for the Rockbridge Area Community Services Board in Lexington, Virginia. Recent information included the fact that she was also attending college full time in order to complete her degree.

In her spare time she serves as a Volunteer Fireman with the Raphine Volunteer Fire Department. She is a Red Cross Disaster Coordinator and Shelter Coordinator.

Karen Denise Wilson

b. 1/14/1958 in Waynesboro, Virginia

daughter of **James Moore Wilson, Jr.** (10/10/1930-) and **Maude LaRue Fauber** (4/16/1929-) 4/11/1952
for siblings, see p. 396-397.

m. **Thomas Calvin Ingram** (9/15/1959-) 2/16/1977 in Staunton, Virginia

mother of **Samantha Jacqueline Ingram** (1/18/1978-) m. Brian Keith Morrison (2/17/1977-) 8/31/1996
Thomas Calvin (T. C.) **Ingram** (2/21/1982-)
Samuel Luke Ingram (7/26/1983-)
Tiffany Renee Ingram (12/21/1988-)

Calvin and Denise live with their family in Craigsville, where Denise works for Hershey Chocolate. She loves homemaking and taking care of her busy family. Her hobbies include sewing, gardening, and cooking. She modestly claimed that not everyone would enjoy her cooking as much as she does.

She belongs to the Craigsville Presbyterian Church.

Thomas Calvin Ingram

b. 9/15/1959 in Maryland

son of **Samuel Calvin Ingram** and **Lena Bell Alstock**

m. **Karen Denise Wilson** (1/14/1958-) 2/16/1977 in Staunton, Virginia

father of **Samantha Jacqueline Ingram** (1/18/1978-) m. Brian Keith Morrison (2/17/2977-) 8/31/1996
Thomas Calvin (T. C.) **Ingram** (2/21/1982-)
Samuel Luke Ingram (7/26/1983-)
Tiffany Renee Ingram (12/21/1988-)

Calvin works for the Town of Craigsville. He is a sportsman in his spare time, enjoying hunting and fishing.

Linda LaRue Wilson

b. 1/29/1960

daughter of **James Moore Wilson, Jr.** (10/10/1930-) and **Maude LaRue Fauber** (4/16/1929-) 4/11/1952
for siblings, see p. 396-397.

Linda earned a BA in Education from Berea College in Berea, Kentucky.

m. **David Pledger Murray** (9/4/1959-) 6/26/1982 at Mt. Carmel Presbyterian Church in Steeles Tavern, Virginia

mother of **Rebecca Wade Murray** (1/30/1986-)
Jacob David Murray (8/7/1990-)

Linda and David live in Harrisburg, North Carolina. She teaches sixth grade social studies in Cabarrus County Schools nearby. She and her family attend the Rocky River Presbyterian Church where she has served as an elder. She currently sings in the choir.

In her leisure time Linda enjoys sewing, remodeling, and gardening, not to mention construction. She and David have built their own home and have helped to build his parents' home. When their church takes on the building of a Habitat for Humanity house each year, she works on that, too.

David Pledger Murray

b. 9/4/1959 in Lexington, Missouri

son of **James Nelson Murray** and **Louise Ann Banguess**

m. **Linda LaRue Wilson** 6/26/1982 at Mt. Carmel Presbyterian Church in Steele's Tavern, Virginia

father of **Rebecca Wade Murray** (1/30/1986-)
Jacob David Murray (8/7/1990-)

David received his BA in Industrial Arts Education from Berea College in Berea, Kentucky. He teaches, as Linda does, in the Cabarrus County middle school where one of his jobs involves a class in Exploring Technologies, a computerized course including aerodynamics, robotics, video production, and other technical areas.

Linda reports with pride that David is also an accomplished woodworker, and that he has a beautiful voice and is often asked to solo in his choir. He is at this time an elder at Rocky River Presbyterian Church, and a very active member of the congregation.

As reported before, David is also a builder, having built his parents' and his own home, with Linda's help, and worked with Habitat for Humanity projects.

Jerry Lee Wilson

b. 5/5/1962 in Waynesboro, Virginia

son of **James Moore Wilson, Jr.** (10/10.1930-) and **Maude LaRue Fauber** (4/16/1929-) 4/11/1952
For siblings, see p. 396-397.

m. **Paula Jean McKemy** 12/10/1983 at Mt. Carmel Presbyterian Church in Steele's Tavern, Virginia.

father of **John Thomas Wilson** (7/21/1984-)
Danielle Leigh Wilson (10/16/1989-)

Jerry and Paula live in Rockbridge Baths, Virginia. He works as a Lineman for BARC, a power coop in Millboro.

Paula Jean McKemy

b. 2/5/1964 in Lexington, Virginia

daughter of **Paul R. McKemy, Sr.** and **Joan Fauber**

m. **Jerry Lee Wilson** 12/10/1983

mother of **John Thomas Wilson** (7/21/1984-)
Danielle Leigh Wilson (10/16/1989-)

Paula is a cafeteria worker in the Rockbridge County Schools.
This family attends the Bethesda Presbyterian Church.

Laura Jean Wilson

b. 4/9/1964, twin sister of Lisa Marie Wilson, in Waynesboro, Virginia

daughter of **James Moore Wilson, Jr.** (10/10/1930-) and **Maude LaRue Fauber** (4/16/1929-) 4/11/1952
For siblings, see p. 396-397.

m. (1)**Daniel Naar Early** (7/17/1958-) First Presbyterian Church, Harrisonburg, Virginia. Divorced; (2)Tony Mancari

mother of **Abbie Lisa Early** (2/5/1994-)

Laura has a BA in History and a BA in Appalachian Studies from Berea College in Berea, Kentucky.

She lives in Harrisonburg where she is the Director of Corporate Support for WVPT Public Television. She has won state and national awards for Public Broadcasting Corporate and Foundation Support. She has been the historical consultant for several regional documentaries.

Laura's hobbies include photography, hiking and sewing.

Daniel Naar Early

b. 7/17/1958 in Richmond, Virginia

son of **Dennis Norman Early** and **Yvonne Henton**

m. **Laura Jean Wilson** 9/27/1991 at the First Presbyterian Church in Harrisonburg, Virginia. Divorced.

father of **Abbie Lisa Early** (2/15/1994-)

Lisa Marie Wilson

b., the twin of Laura Jean Wilson, 4/9/1964 in Waynesboro, Virginia

daughter of **James Moore Wilson, Jr.** (10/10/1930-) and **Maude LaRue**

Fauber (4/16/1929-) 4/11/1952
For other siblings, see p. 396-397.

m. **William Gaston Everhart** (10/1/1957-) 6/18/1994 at Mt. Carmel Presbyterian Church in Steeles Tavern, Virginia. Divorced.

mother of **Anna Laura Everhart** (3/18/1996-)
Ashley Caperton Everhart (11/17/1997-)

We were all proud of Lisa when she became an ordained minister. She graduated from Berea College, Berea, Kentucky, in 1986 with a degree in Philosophy and Religion, after which she continued her education at the Lexington Theological Seminary in Lexington, Kentucky, earning a Master of Divinity degree in 1991. That fall she entered Union Theological Seminary in Richmond, Virginia to work on the Master of Theology degree, which was conferred in 1993. Lisa has since been trained in intentional interim ministry in the Presbyterian Church. She has served congregations in Kentucky, North Carolina, West Virginia and Virginia. At last notice she was the Interim Pastor of Sherando Presbyterian Church in Stephens City, Virginia.

William Gaston Everhart

b. 10/1/1957 in Wilmington, Delaware

son of **Leighton Phracner Everhart** and **Anna Caperton**

m. **Lisa Marie Wilson** 6/18/1994 at Mt. Carmel Presbyterian Church in Steeles Tavern, Virginia

father of **Anna Laura Everhart** (3/18/1996-)
Ashley Caperton Everhart (11/17/1997-)

Bill, a native of Wilmington, Delaware, graduated from Union Theological Seminary in Richmond, Virginia in 1994. In 2001 he earned the Doctor of Ministry degree in the field of contemporary worship from that institution. He currently serves the First Presbyterian Church of Waynesboro, Virginia.

Generation B

The members of this next generation, the g-grandchildren of Blanche and Moore, grandchildren of Jim and LaRue, have somewhat shorter histories. They have lived somewhat shorter lives!

Stephanie Lynn Wilson

b. 11/4/1973 in the Waynesboro Community Hospital

daughter of **Glenn Franklin Wilson** (6/5/1953-) and **Jane Pendleton Campbell** (2/17/1953-)

sister of Ann Marie Wilson

m. **Todd Eugene Wade** (6/28/1973-) 10/3/1992 at Mt. Carmel Presbyterian Church in Steeles Tavern, Virginia

mother of **Joshua Ty Wade** (7/21/1995-)
Dylan Jacob Wade (6/5/1997-)

Stephanie and Todd live with their sons in Staunton where Stephanie is a full-time mom and homemaker.

Todd Eugene Wade

b. 6/28/1973 in Waynesboro, Virginia

son of **Samuel Wallace Wade** and **Betty Lou Whitesell**

m. **Stephanie Lynn Wilson** (11/4/1973-) 10/3/1992 at Mt. Carmel Presbyterian Church in Steele's Tavern, Virginia

father of **Joshua Ty Wade** (7/21/1995-)
Dylan Jacob Wade (6/5/1997-)

Todd is a Line Operator for DuPont.

Ann Marie Wilson

b. 5/2/1975 in Waynesboro, Virginia

daughter of **Glenn Franklin Wilson** (6/5/1953-) and **Jane Pendleton Campbell** (2/17/1953-)

sister of Stephanie Lynn Wilson

m. **Anthony Scott Nelson** (1/29/1975-)

mother of **Stanley Hunter Nelson** (6/2/1995-)
Samuel Colt Nelson (10/7/1996-)

Ann Marie and Anthony live in Stuarts Draft, Virginia. She works for Neileson Company in Harrisonburg, Virginia.

Anthony Scott Nelson

b. 1/29/1975 in Waynesboro, Virginia

son of **Stanley Summers Nelson** and **Linda Turrell**

m. **Ann Marie Wilson** (5/2/1975-)

father of **Stanley Hunter Nelson** (6/3/1995-)
Samuel Colt Nelson (10/7/1996-)

He works for Alcoa and is a hunting and fishing enthusiast.

Eric Christopher Wilson

b. 6/26/1980 at Martha Jefferson Hospital in Charlottesville, Virginia

son of **Kenneth Michael Wilson** (6/25/1956-) and **Janet Marie Hendrix** (7/9/1957-)

brother of Heather Michelle Wilson

Eric graduated from Rockbridge County High School in 1999 and is studying forestry at Dabney Lancaster College. While at home he, like his parents, is a firefighter and a First Responder with the Raphine Volunteer Fire Department. He also has a job at White's Truck Stop in Raphine.

Heather Michelle Wilson

2/4/1983-2/8/2005 Heather's untimely death was the result of an automobile accident.

daughter of **Kenneth Michael Wilson** (6/25/1956-) and **Janet Marie Hendrix** (7/9/1957-)

sister of Eric Christopher Wilson

Heather graduated from high school in 2001. As a student she worked part-time at McDonalds and also did some baby-sitting. She was active in the Mt. Carmel youth program, and helped with Bible School there. She attended Blue Ridge Community College.

Samantha Jacqueline Ingram

b. 1/18/1978 at Kings Daughters Hospital in Staunton, Virginia

daughter of **Karen Denise Wilson** (1/14/1958-) and **Thomas Calvin Ingram** (9/15/1959-)
For siblings, see p. 402.

m. **Bryan Keith Morrison** (2/17/1977-) 8/31/1996 at Craigsville Presbyterian Church, Craigsville, Virginia

mother of **Justin Bryant Morrison** (5/8/1998-)
Jessica Cameron Morrison (6/23/2000-)

A 1996 graduate of Buffalo Gap High School, Samantha is working in children's clothing retail. This young couple lives in Staunton.

Bryan Keith Morrison

b. 2/17/1977 at Kings Daughters Hospital in Staunton, Virginia

son of **Mark Sterling Morrison** and **Martha Frazier**

m. **Samantha Jacqueline Ingram** (1/18/1978-) 8/31/1996 at Craigsville Presbyterian Church in Craigsville, Virginia

father of **Justin Bryant Morrison** (5/8/1898-)
Jessica Camron Morrison (6/23/2000-)

Bryan is an ASE certified mechanic at Montgomery Ward Auto Express.

Thomas Calvin (T. C.) Ingram, Jr.

b. 2/21/1982 in Staunton, Virginia

son of **Karen Denise Wilson** (1/14/1958-) and **Thomas Calvin Ingram** (9/15/1959-)
For siblings, see p. 402.

m. **April Nicole Campbell** 10/13/2001

father of **Cheyenne Marie Ingram** (1/19/2002-)

T. C. loves to tinker with motors and such, and enjoys hunting and fishing.

April Nicole Campbell

m. **Thomas Calvin (T. C.) Ingram, Jr.** 10/13/2001

mother of **Gage Nathaniel Simmions** (10/25/1998-)
Cheyenne Marie Ingram (1/19/2002-)

Samuel Luke Ingram

b. 7/26/1983 in Staunton, Virginia

son of **Karen Denise Wilson** (1/14/1958-) and **Thomas Calvin Ingram** (9/15/1959-)

For siblings, see p. 402.

This young man loves hunting and fishing and playing ball.

Tiffany Renee Ingram

b. 12/21/1988 in Staunton, Virginia

daughter of **Karen Denise Wilson** (1/14/1958-) and **Thomas Calvin Ingram** (9/15/1959-)
For siblings, see p. 402.

Tiffany's mother says that her daughter's favorite pastime is talking.

Rebecca Wade Murray

b. 1/30/1986 in Concord, North Carolina

daughter of **Linda LaRue Wilson** (1/29/1960-) and **David Pledger Murray** (9/4/1959-)

sister of Jacob David Murray (8/7/1990-)

Rebecca attends her family's church, where she sings in the choir with her parents. She also attends Central Cabarrus High School.

Jacob David Murray

b. 8/7/1990 in Concord, North Carolina

son of **Linda LaRue Wilson** (1/29/1960-) and **David Pledger Murray** (9/4/1959-)

brother of Rebecca Wade Murray (1/30/1986-)

Jacob, who is very interested in science, attends J. N. Fries Middle School.

John Thomas Wilson

b. 7/21/1984 in Lexington, Virginia

son of **Jerry Lee Wilson** (5/5/1962-) and **Paula McKemy** (2/5/1964-)

brother of Danielle Leigh Wilson (10/16/1989-)

Danielle Leigh Wilson

b. 10/16/1989 in Lexington, Virginia

daughter of **Jerry Lee Wilson** (5/5/1962-) and **Paula McKemy** (2/5/1964-)

sister of John Thomas Wilson (7/21/1984-)

Abbie Lisa Early

b. 2/15/1994 in Harrisonburg, Virginia

daughter of **Laura Jean Wilson** (4/9/1964-) and **Daniel Naar Early** (7/17/1958-)

Abbie, when in third grade, was reading on a fifth grade level. She loves science, math, reading, and antiques! She has an interest in acting, having played roles in several WVPT productions as well as a Civil War documentary which has won numerous national awards, including an Emmy.

Anna Laura Everhart

b. 3/18/1996 in Goldsboro, North Carolina

daughter of **Lisa Marie Wilson** (4/9/1964-) and **William Gaston Everhart** (10/1/1957-)

sister of Ashley Caperton Everhart (11/17/1997-)

Anna is a first grader who loves reading, writing, drawing and acting.

Ashley Caperton Everhart

b. 11/17/1997

daughter of **Lisa Marie Wilson** (4/9/1964-) and **William Gaston Everhart** (10/1/1957-)

sister of Anna Laura Everhart (3/28/1996-)

Ashley was, at last report, a vivacious pre-schooler at Good Shepherd Day School in Waynesboro, Virginia. She loves to play with big sister and enjoys computers and music.

Generation C

The children introduced below are the g-g-grandchildren of Blanche and Moore, the g-grandchildren of Jim and LaRue, and the grandchildren of Glenn and Janie. How time does fly!

Joshua Ty Wade

b. 7/21/1995 at Augusta Medical Center in Fishersville, Virginia

son of **Stephanie Lynn Wilson** (11/4/1973-) and **Todd Eugene Wade** (6/28/1973-)

brother of Dylan Jacob Wade (6/5/1997-)

Dylan Jacob Wade

b. 6/5/1997 in the Augusta Medical Center in Fishersville, Virginia

son of **Stephanie Lynn Wilson** (11/4/1973-) and **Todd Eugene Wade** (6/28/1973-)

brother of Joshua Ty Wade (7/21/1995-)

Stanley Hunter Nelson

b. 6/3/1995 at Augusta Medical Center in Fishersville, Virginia

son of **Ann Marie Wilson** (5/2/1975-) and **Anthony Scott Nelson** (1/29/1975-)

brother of Samuel Colt Nelson (10/7/1996-)

Samuel Colt Nelson

b. 10/7/1996 at Augusta Medical Center in Fishersville, Virginia

son of **Ann Marie Wilson** (5/2/1975-) and **Anthony Scott Nelson** (1/29/1975-)

brother of Stanley Hunter Nelson (6/3/1995-)

The family of James Moore Wilson, Jr. and Maude LaRue Fauber as seen on the steps of the Wilson family church, Mt. Carmel Presbyterian, in Steele's Tavern, Virginia.

The family of Martha Miller Wilson and Walter Barrett Black

Generation 1

The Twins

Martha was the second born in our family, though not by much. Emma was literally close on her heels! No one expected twins since ultrasound devices were not available in those days. But the one with dark curly hair arrived, closely followed by the not so curly-headed, not so dark-haired one. The twins were always a delight. The community found them an enjoyable novelty, and Mother spent endless hours with a hairbrush, a curling iron, a sewing machine, anything that would make these two little girls ever more delightful.

Martha and Emma were reported to have been quite close as toddlers, not only playing well together, but looking after one another. They even developed their own language, according to our parents. And they called each other the same name, which has followed them down to the present. That name was "Little Memmy," which may have been a blending of both their names.

Generation 1
The Martha Miller Wilson Family

Martha Miller Wilson

b. 11/13/1932 in Raphine, Rockbridge County, Virginia

daughter of **James Moore Wilson** (2/2/1898-3/18/1983) and **Blanche Odessa Miller** (11/30/1896-3/27/1980) 6/2/1928

sister of James Moore Wilson, Jr. (10/10/1930-) m. Maude LaRue Fauber (4/16/1929-) 4/11/1952
Emma Wade Wilson (11/13/1932-) twin; m. Charles Willard Jordan (9/15/1933-) 9/13/1952
Elisabeth Anne Wilson (7/7/1936-) m. (1)Martin Quinter Miller, Jr. (12/12/1930-) 1/13/1956; (2) William Long Hodges (7/22/1930-) 6/16/1972

Martha earned a B. S. in Home Economics at Longwood College in

1954. She taught briefly in the public schools of West Point, Virginia, and, after her marriage, worked as a dietary unit supervisor at Virginia Polytechnic Institute for three years. She left this job when her husband graduated from college.

m. **Walter Barrett Black** (2/6/1932-) 8/27/1955 at Mt. Carmel Presbyterian Church in Steele's Tavern, Virginia

mother of **Kathy Elisabeth Black** (6/23/1959-) m. (1)Samuel E. Stinnette (11/14/1958-) 4/9/1983. Divorced; (2)Michael Coffey (2/8/1959-) 12/16/2000
James David Black (7/2/1962-) m. Katherine Aline Trimble (5/17/1951-) 9/24/1988

After her children were grown Martha served as a librarian in the public schools of Hanover County, Virginia for fifteen years.

Martha and Pete built their home on eleven wooded acres in Hanover County, near Ashland, Virginia. Here Martha enjoys cooking, sewing, and gardening. In her retirement, she volunteers for a variety of organizations including Lewis Ginter Botanical Garden, Overbrook Presbyterian Church in Richmond, Hanover County Master Gardeners, and Virginia House. She also edits a woman's club newsletter. She commented that she had difficulty saying no to volunteer jobs.

Pete and Martha travel quite a bit, also. Whether visiting family, attending elderhostels, or traveling abroad, they are always on the go.

Walter Barrett Black

b. 2/6/1932 in Covington, Virginia but grew up, between 1934 and 1952, in Staunton, Virginia

son of **Ralph Wesley Black, Sr**. (3/24/1905-1/27/1994) and **Sue Barrett Smith** (10/29/05-5/15/1976)

m. **Martha Miller Wilson** (11/13/1932-) 8/27/1955 at Mt. Carmel Presbyterian Church in Steele's Tavern, Virginia

father of **Kathy Elisabeth Black** (6/23/1959-) m. (1)Samuel E. Stinnett

(1/14/1958-). Divorced; (2)Michael Coffey (2/8/1959-) 12/16/2000

James David Black (7/2/1962-) m. Katherine Aline Trimble (5/17/1951-) 9/24/1988

Pete served in Korea from 2/53-6/54 and was discharged with the rank of Sgt. First Class. In 1958 he received a BS degree in Architectural Engineering from Virginia Polytechnic Institute, and worked as a structural engineer for Reynolds Metals for 33 years

In his retirement he is a volunteer driver for the American Red Cross and a docent at the Virginia Aviation Museum. He has served as a member of the board of the Volunteers Association of the Science Museum of Virginia. He also spends some of his time practicing shots at the pool table in the downstairs room which he built for the purpose. He has "a passing interest in photography, music, art, crafts, languages, crosswords, automobiles, vintage aircraft, and in eliminating the stereotype of the engineer who knows nothing but numbers."

Generation A

Kathy Elisabeth Black

b. 6/23/1959 in Richmond, Virginia

daughter of **Walter Barrett Black** (2/6/1932-) and **Martha Miller Wilson** 11/13/1932-) 8/27/1955

sister of James David Black (7/2/1962-) m. Katherine Aline Trimble (5/17/1951-) 9/24/1988

m. (1)**Samuel Ernest Stinnette** (11/14/1958-) 4/9/1983. Divorced; (2)Michael Lynn Coffey, Sr.(2/8/1959-) 12/16/2000

mother of **Michael Scott Stinnette** (9/15/1987-)

Kathy graduated from James Madison University in 1981 with a degree in Art Education and a BFA. She teaches art in Oak Ridge, Tennessee.

Art is also one of her hobbies, along with hiking, reading and traveling.

Michael Lynn Coffey, Sr.

b. 2/8/1959

son of **Beverly** and **Mary Coffey**

m.(1)__; (2)**Kathy Elisabeth Black** (6/23/1959-) 12/16/2000

father of Michael Coffey, Jr. (2/28/1981-)
Stephen Charles Coffey (2/15/1988-)

Mike works for CDM as an environmental engineer. He was recently involved in cleaning up anthrax in Washington, D. C. Before he did this sort of thing he taught high school chemistry and biology. He has many interests, including flying (he holds his pilot's and instructor's licenses) and is also interested in photography, hiking, geology, dinosaurs, reading, travel, and almost anything labeled science.

Samuel Ernest Stinnette

b. 11/14/1958 in Amherst County, Virginia

son of **Sherwood Earl Stinnette** (4/10/1933-9/15/1992) and **Barbara Ann Wiley** (6/25/1935-)

m. **Kathy Elisabeth Black** (6/23/1959-) 4/9/1983. Divorced.

father of **Michael Scott Stinnette** (9/15/1987-)

James David Black

b. 7/2/1962 in Louisville, Kentucky

son of **Walter Barrett Black** (2/6/1932-) and **Martha Miller Wilson** (11/13/1932-)

brother of Kathy Elisabeth Black (6/23/1959-)

m. **Katherine Aline Trimble** (5/17/1951-) 9/24/1988 in Richmond, Virginia

father of **David Barrett Black** (10/21/1990-)

Jim graduated from Virginia Polytechnic Institute with a BS in economics in 1984. He pursued an interest in woodworking after college, starting his own business making furniture and reproductions. He changed his career to one involving computer technology in 1988-1989 and gained experience with several Richmond companies prior to becoming successful as an independent computer consultant in 1996. He is currently self-employed as a Computer Systems Analyst and Programmer.

In his spare time Jim enjoys woodworking and photography and *loves* sailing. He started karate instruction with David in 1997 and earned his Black Belt in 2003.

Jim and Katherine live in Mechanicsville, Virginia.

Katherine Aline Trimble

b. 5/17/1951 in Staunton, Virginia

daughter of **Robert Thomas Trimble** (7/5/1928-6/25/1993) and **Ruth Elizabeth LeCompte** (3/18/1934-10/25/2001) 10/20/1949

m. **James David Black** (7/2/1962-) in Richmond, Virginia 9/24/1988

mother of **David Barrett Black** (10/21/1990-)

Katherine grew up in the beautiful town of Staunton, Virginia. She graduated from Eastern Mennonite College with a degree in Nursing and began her career as a critical care nurse at the Medical College of Virginia Hospitals in 1973. She completed her Master's Degree in Nursing at MCV-VCU in 1981. She loved the fast-paced and challenging environment at MCV and remained there until May 1997 when she and Jim seized an opportunity for her to be a full-time homemaker. While at MCV she received awards for national critical care "Excellence in Administrative Practice" as well as Manager of the Year at the MCV hospital.

Katherine loves being a full-time "at home" wife to Jim and mother to David. She keeps busy with lots of new and expanded interests such as cooking, reading, gardening, photo scrapbooking, and yoga. Her opportunities to volunteer at David's school, New Hanover Presbyterian Church, the local hospital, and in their residential community have been an added blessing.

Generation B

Michael Scott Stinnette

b. 9/15/1987 in Oak Ridge, Tennessee

son of **Kathy Elisabeth Black** (6/23/1959-) and **Samuel Ernest Stinnette** (11/14/1958-) 4/9/1983

Michael has had many fascinating interests. He has concentrated on learning to speak Spanish and on learning to play the piano. And he has accomplished a great deal in these and other endeavors. At this time his mother says he is interested in teenage things, including sports, movies and music.

David Barrett Black

b. 10/21/1990 in Richmond, Virginia

son of **James David Black** (7/2/1962-) and **Katherine Aline Trimble** (5/17/1951-) 9/24/1988

David is in middle school. He enjoys school, riding his bike, swimming, playing tennis, helping his dad build a wooden kayak, painting mini-figures, reading, his dog Maggie, the cats Bud and Lou, and playing the piano, violin, and more recently, the guitar.

With freckles on his nose, beautiful blue eyes and a great smile, he has lots of friends. He is a really happy kid!

Generation 1
The Emma Wade Wilson Family

Emma Wade Wilson

b. 11/13/1932 in Raphine, Rockbridge County,Virginia

daughter of **James Moore Wilson** (2/2/1898-3/18/1983) and **Blanche Odessa Miller** (11/30/1896-3/27/1980) 6/2/1928

sister of James Moore Wilson, Jr. (10/10/1930-) m. Maude LaRue Fauber (4/16/1929-) 4/11/1952
Martha Miller Wilson (11/13/1932-) twin; m. Walter Barrett Black (2/6/1932-) 8/27/1955
Elisabeth Anne Wilson (7/7/1936-) m. (1)Martin Quinter Miller, Jr. (12/12/1930-); Divorced. (2)William Long Hodges (7/22/1930-) 6/16/1972

m. **Charles Willard Jordan** (9/15/1933-) 9/13/1952

mother of **Debra Jordan** (5/21/1953-) m. Allen Vernon Stout (2/5/1950-) 10/12/1984 - Divorced.
Martha Anne Jordan (3/7/1956-) m. John Herman Belz (11/3/1956-) 7/7/1979

Emma attained a BS in Elementary Education from Madison College. Her early married years were spent as a homemaker and busy mother, pursuing many sewing and craft interests. Teaching was added to the schedule after Debbie and Martha were in school.

Many of her "leisure" activities were those of her children. She served as a scout leader, Sunday school teacher, and children's choir mother, and was involved in PTA and school activities.

After 25 years in the classroom, retirement in 1991 provided time for very satisfying travel, reading, participation in church work, being a "volunteer," and helping with the research and writing of the family history, which she reports as "a wonderful experience."

Charles Willard Jordan

b. 9/15/1933 in Staunton, Virginia

son of **James Willard Jordan** (1/13/1915-1/15/1976) and **Georgia Alice Houser** (2/5/1918-7/29/2000)

m. **Emma Wade Wilson** (11/13/1932-) 9/13/1952

father of **Debra Jordan** (5/21/1953-) m. Allen Vernon Stout (2/5/1950-) 10/12/1984. Divorced.
Martha Anne Jordan (3/7/1956-) m. John Herman Belz (11/3/1956-) 7/7/1979

Charley's early working years, spent managing a camera department, were a happy blending of job and hobby since photography was a personal interest. Most of his years of work were spent as a purchasing manager for Smith's Transfer, a trucking company in Verona, Virginia. He retired after spending some time in office supply sales following the close of Smith's Transfer in 1987.

The decision of the Jordans, both Emma and Charley, to retire in 1991 was made so that they could enjoy an easier life and have some time for travel. Now they not only have time for the frequent visits to North Carolina and to California, where their daughters and grandchildren live, but for adventures in more remote places, from Alaska to Great Britain, and a number of places between.

Emma, in her spare time, has looked into Charley's ancestral background with him, and they report that his ancestors represent almost as many European nations as do our own. In the smaller world of Staunton, Virginia, Charley is busy with family and friends and the activities of the Staunton Civic Club and other organizations.

Generation A

Debra Jordan

b. 5/21/1953 in Staunton, Virginia

daughter of **Charles Willard Jordan** (9/15/1933-) and **Emma Wade Wilson** (11/13/1932-) 9/13/1952 sister of Martha Anne Jordan (3/7/1956-)

m. **Allen Vernon Stout, Jr.** (2/5/1950-) 10/12/1984 in Tampa, Florida

mother of **Jonathan Allen Stout** (1/29/1989-)
Katherine Elisabeth (Katie) Stout (5/3/1995-)

Debra, better known as Debbie, was the first-born in her generation on either side of her family. As a little girl she was a go-getter, mastering every challenge easily. She excelled in school and was very active in extracurricular activities, serving as a class officer and in other leadership roles. She was a member of the National Honor Society and was very involved in church and youth groups.

After several years in college, she decided the world of work was more to her liking. As a young adult she lived in both Florida and North Carolina, working with her husband until she became a full time mother and homemaker. She has always been a very supportive participant in activities that involve her children. She even home schooled Jonathan for two years while Katie was just a baby, proving that she was still a go-getter.

In addition to raising her family Debbie has provided a beautiful home for them, demonstrating her talent as a decorator.

She is living in Charlotte, North Carolina where she is very active in her church. Now a single mom, she remains very involved with her two children.

Martha Anne Jordan

b. 3/7/1956 in Staunton, Virginia

daughter of **Charles Willard Jordan** (9/15/1933-) and **Emma Wade Wilson** (11/13/1932-) 9/13/1952

sister of Debra Jordan (5/21/1953-)

m. **John Herman Belz** 7/7/1979 at Covenant Presbyterian Church in Staunton, Virginia

mother of **Christopher Scott Belz** (2/21/1985-)
Amanda Leigh Belz (6/4/1987-)

Martha graduated from Radford University in 1978, earning a BS in early childhood education. She and John moved one week after their marriage to San Jose, California, where they planned to live for just two years. They decided to stay after falling in love with the area, the climate, and the many people with whom they established strong relationships.

Martha was employed as a manager at Amdahl Corporation until the birth of their second child, Amanda. Since then she has been a homemaker who loves and appreciates John and their children and thoroughly enjoys the opportunity to be at home for them.

An active volunteer for the children's schools and activities, Martha is also a volunteer for Foothill Presbyterian Church in Personnel and Christian Education. She has a passion for travel and enjoys planning the trips as well. Other interests are music, gardening, entertaining, camping, skiing, football, and hockey.

John Herman Belz

b. 11/3/1956

son of **Paul Dewey Belz** (12/31/1920-) and **Gladys Arlene Bistine** (11/30/1921-5/3/2003)

m. **Martha Anne Jordan** (3/7/1956-) in Staunton, Virginia 7/7/1979

father of **Christopher Scott Belz** (2/21/1985-)
Amanda Leigh Belz (6/4/1987-)

John graduated from Virginia Polytechnic Institute in 1978 with a BS in electrical engineering and completed his master's degree there in 1979. A job opportunity took Martha and him to California, where he worked for Amdahl Corporation for over twenty years, advancing from CPU chip designer to Vice President of Engineering. In 2001 he left Amdahl and is now working at Veritas Software Corporation.

John, like Martha, volunteers in many different ways with his children's activities and at Foothill Presbyterian Church. His other interests include running marathons, traveling, camping, skiing, music, and home improvement.

Generation B

These are the children of Debbie and Allan and Martha and John, the grandchildren of Emma and Charley, and the g-grandchildren of Blanche and Moore.

Jonathan Allen Stout

b. 1/29/1989

son of **Debra Jordan** (5/21/1952-) and **Allen Vernon Stout, Jr.** (2/5/1950-)

brother of Katherine Elisabeth (Katie) Stout (5/3/1995-)

No one in the family doubted that Jonathan would be interested in and active in sports. His ability to dribble a regular-sized basketball as a three year old was a strong indication that he was athletically inclined. He has played basketball, soccer and hockey, and in the summer of 2002 he had a successful season as pitcher for his baseball team. He also loves skateboarding, swimming and video games.

Jonathan is in high school. He enjoys activities with his church group as well as with other friends.

Katherine Elisabeth Stout

b. 5/3/1995

daughter of **Debra Jordan** (5/21/1952-) and **Allen Vernon Stout, Jr.** (2/5/1950-)

sister of Jonathan Allen Stout (1/29/1989-)

Katie, the youngest of the Jordan family, has spent her eight years busily participating in school, gymnastics, dance, soccer, swimming, reading, and playing with her friends. She has learned to play the violin and has been playing the piano for about a year. Her family is delighted with her obvious musical ability. She loves animals and thinks she might want to be a veterinarian when she grows up.

Christopher Scott Belz

b. 2/21/1985 in San Jose, California

son of **Martha Anne Jordan** (3/7/1956-) and **John Herman Belz** (11/3/1956-) 7/7/1979

brother of Amanda Leigh Belz (6/4/1987-)

Christopher graduated from Valley Christian High School in San Jose in June 2003. He played flag football when he was younger, but preferred track in high school. Interested in music, he started with the piano and progressed to the saxaphone and clarinet. He has recently concentrated on playing the guitar. He is also a very active member of the Boy Scouts.

A recent high point, forgive the pun, was experienced in the summer of 2000 when Christopher and his dad traveled to Japan where the two of them climbed Mt. Fujiyama.

Christopher's lifelong interest has been cars. He is in college now and is considering a career in automotive design engineering, or in business, or perhaps law.

Amanda Leigh Belz

b. 6/4/1987 in San Jose, California

daughter of **Martha Anne Jordan** (3/7/1956-) and **John Herman Belz** (11/3/1956-) 7/7/1979

sister of Christopher Scott Belz (2/21/1985-)

Amanda has danced for seven years and has studied music, starting with piano and advancing to flute. She also sings in the girls' church choir and rings handbells with her parents and other adult bell ringers there.

She is active in scouting. In the summer of 2001 she climbed to the top of Yosemite's Half Dome with members of her troop. Now a junior at Valley Christian High School, she enjoys reading and writing stories. She thinks she may be interested in a career of teaching and writing.

The family of Emma Wade Wilson and Charles Willard Jordan

The family of Elisabeth Anne Wilson Hodges

The Elisabeth Anne Wilson Family

Generation 1

Elisabeth Anne Wilson

b. 7/7/1936 "at home" in Raphine, Rockbridge County, Virginia

daughter of **James Moore Wilson** (2/2/1898-3/18/1983) and **Blanche Odessa Miller** (11/30/1896-3/27/1980) 6/2/1928

sister of James Moore Wilson, Jr. (10/10/1930-) m. Maude LaRue Fauber (4/16/1929-) 4/11/952
Martha Miller Wilson (11/13/1932-) m. Walter Barrett Black (2/6/1932-) 8/27/1955
Emma Wade Wilson (11/13/1932-) m. Charles Willard Jordan (9/15/1933-) 9/13/1952

I received a BS in Elementary Education with a minor in English in the three wonderful years of budding responsibility that I spent at Longwood College. They were some of the best!

m. (1)**Martin Quinter Miller, Jr.** (12/12/1930-) 1/13/1956; (2)**William Long Hodges** (7/22/1930-) 6/16/1972 "at home" in Rockbridge County, Virginia

mother of **Sylvia Ellen Miller** (8/16/1958-) m. Lee Edward Lantz (4/2/1952) 5/22/1999

As the parent of a tiny daughter, I commuted from Staunton, Virginia, where we then lived, to Charlottesville to earn a MEd in Special Education. I taught the blind at the Virginia School for the Deaf and the Blind, and spent many years thereafter with the public schools of Lynchburg, working in several capacities. After going back to school once more, I served as a middle school librarian for the last twelve years of my career.

Happily retiring in 1991, I joined my husband in gardening, singing, and volunteering at St. Stephen's Episcopal Church and at the public schools which were attended by my grandchildren at the time. We also took on a heavy travel schedule, visiting every corner of Great Britain and much of

Europe, as far east as the Czech Republic and Slovakia. We also had a fantastic trip to China, as well as a jaunt to the islands of the Caribbean.

As I examine the missions of my life, I have had three: the first was to achieve success as a wife and mother; the second, to give my best toward the education of Virginia's children; the third, to write the history of our family and of the conditions which most affected the lives of those who preceded us. For some reason I feel that this is a job I was intended to complete. I am grateful to Emma Wilson Jordan for giving me the shove that started me on this venture, and to Bill, Emma, Martha, and others, for giving me immense help and encouragement along the way.

I have other interests, too, among which are my husband, who has been most supportive in many of my efforts, and my daughter, who has been the same. Being family with them is great! My grandchildren are wonderful, interesting people and I recognize them as my future. My recently-acquired son-in-law is a great comfort to me, a veritable saint on this earth! Life would not be the same without these well-loved people.

I also have wonderful friends with whom to share memories and experiences, and I continue to serve wherever the opportunity occurs. Life is rich.

William Long Hodges

b. 7/22/1930 in Lynchburg, Virginia

son of **James Barnett Hodges** (11/23/01-7/5/1993) and **Frances Hartwell Long** (9/6/1907-8/20/1979)

Bill grew up at Elk Hill on Perrowville Road in Forest, Virginia. His father had a large orchard there, and also raised sheep and cattle. Bill was raised to love farming and orcharding and not to mind the hard work they involved.

brother of Harriette Goodwillie Hodges Andrews (10/16/1932-)
James Barnette Hodges, Jr. (6/1/1935-)
Elizabeth Perry Hodges (7/18/1944-)
Thomas Goodwillie Hodges (7/23/1945-)

Bill graduated from Cornell University where he earned a MS in Pomology. His intention had been to come back to Virginia to raise fruit, but the United States Army interceded, and he served for two years during the

Korean War, in Germany.

m. (1)Ann Brown, mother of his four children:
Helen Warren Brown (3/1/1953-) m. Steve Richards (3/19/_)
Marianne Frances Hodges (8/3/1954-) m. John Cassedy (6/19/1948-)
William Long (Pete) Hodges, Jr. (12/8/1958-) m. (2)Frances Holiday Wilhelm (12/2/1957-); (3)Elizabeth Nash (8/8/1954-)
Ann Brown Hodges (12/26/1960-)
m. (2)**Elisabeth Anne Wilson (Miller)** (7/7/1936-) 6/16/1972 on the lawn at home in Raphine, Rockbridge County, Virginia

After returning to Virginia, Bill bought High Peak Orchard, a 600 acre place in Amherst County, where he grew apples and peaches for years, until he decided that he could not make a living in the orchard business. He then studied the insurance business and became an agent. This he continued for thirty years until his retirement in 1991.

Bill is a musician, a singer above all. He was born into a musical family that expected the tradition to be continued. He sang as a child with his family, at Episcopal High School, at Cornell, on the Kate Smith Show, at St. Stephen's, and everywhere else he paused for a moment. He has done considerable solo work as a tenor, singing "leads" in everything from the Gilbert and Sullivan light operas, Handel's *Messiah*, *Die Fledermaus*, and *Porgy and Bess*, to Sir Harry Lauder favorites and "Danny Boy" and the other beloved Irish songs. A recent achievement was that of singing *Carmina Burana* at Carnegie Hall in New York City. It should not be surprising that we met in a church choir.

He is a very busy person, spending much time and effort on his garden at St. Stephen's; on Kiwanis Club projects; on choral rehearsals and performances, as well as other musical challenges; on Master Gardener projects; on the James River Batteaux Festival; and a thousand other activities at home and elsewhere. In his spare time, he is tremendous help to me in my research. I appreciate his talents, his willingness to get involved, and his accomplishments. He's a great guy!

Martin Quinter Miller, Jr.

b. 12/12/1930

son of **Martin Quinter Miller, Sr.** (3/20/1906-) and **Leila Todd Maxwell** (11/18/1906-)

brother of Elizabeth Anne Miller (8/26/1934-) m. George Thomas Serrett (7/26/1935-)

father of **Sylvia Ellen Miller** (8/16/1858-) m. Laurence Erwin Judd (12/14/1952-) 8/6/1983; Lee Edward Lantz (4/2/1952-) 5/22/1999

Martin was educated at Bridgewater College and at the University of Virginia. His working years were spent teaching. He and Betty, his wife, live in Lynchburg, Virginia.

....

Leila Todd Maxwell and **Martin Quinter Miller, Sr.** were wonderful and supportive parents and grandparents who will always be remembered well by those who knew them.

Martin Quinter Miller, Sr., born at Beaver Creek in Rockingham County, Virginia, in 1906 was, as was Blanche Odessa Miller, a g-g-grandchild of Daniel Miller (3/23/1787-11/29/1851) and Anna Garber. His family shares with ours, therefore, all of those who came before. It might be said that my daughter and my grandchildren got a double dose of this proud lineage.

Generation A

Sylvia Ellen Miller

b. 8/16/1958 in King's Daughters Hospital in Staunton, Virginia

daughter of **Elisabeth Anne Wilson** (7/7/1936-) and **Martin Quinter Miller, Jr**. (12/12/1930-) 1/13/1956

m. Laurence Erwin Judd (12/14/1952-) 8/6/1983; Lee Edward Lantz (4/2/1952-) 5/22/1999

mother of **Ashley Alexander Judd** (4/6/1984-)
Stephen Laurence Judd (8/3/1987-)

As a little girl, this busy, green-eyed child enjoyed friends and horses. As she grew older she proved to be very talented at needlework and crafts, decorating, photography, and the arts.

Sylvia was educated at East Tennessee State University and Lynchburg College, where she received both a BA in Psychology and Sociology and an MEd in Agency Counseling. She has worked as a mental health therapist with the seriously mentally ill. She currently works for Centra Health's Lynchburg General Hospital Emergency Room in Lynchburg as a Mental Health Consultant and is studying for professional licensure.

She loves animals and has had a great variety of pets. In her spare time she enjoys gardening, cooking, decorating, and entertaining. Her husband says she also enjoys spending money.

Sylvia and Eddie and the children live in Lynchburg, Virginia.

Lee Edward Lantz

b. 4/2/1952 in Harrisonburg, Virginia

son of **Joseph Harry Lantz** (10/4/1922-) and **Lois Katherine Lineweaver** (6/6/1928-1/12/1998)

m. **Sylvia Ellen Miller Judd** (8/16/1958-) 5/22/1999

Eddie was educated at Virginia Polytechnic Institute, Madison College, and George Mason University, earning BS degrees in Psychology and in Biology and an MA in Counseling Psychology. He and Sylvia met at their jobs in the mental health field, where they still work together as Mental Health Consultants. Eddie is a Licensed Professional Counselor in the State of Virginia and also has a private counseling practice.

He enjoys traveling, reading and spending time with family and friends.

Eddie is, among other things, a wonderful parent to Alex and Stephen.

Laurence Erwin Judd

b. 12/14/1952 in Champaign Urbana, Illinois

son of **Donald Frank Judd** and **Carol Nellie Alexander**

m. **Sylvia Ellen Miller** (8/16/1958-) 8/6/1982; divorced in 1991

father of **Ashley Alexander Judd** (4/6/1981-)
Stephen Laurence Judd (8/3/1987-)

Generation B

These are the g-grandchildren of Blanche and Moore Wilson, and my grandchildren!

Ashley Alexander Judd

b. 4/6/1984 in Lynchburg, Virginia at Virginia Baptist Hospital

daughter of **Sylvia Ellen Miller** (8/16/1958-) and **Laurence Erwin Judd** (12/14/1952-)

sister of Stephen Laurence Judd (8/3/1987-)

m. **William Hunter Swann** (9/15/1978-) 5/15/2004 at St. Stephen's Episcopal Church, Forest, Virginia.

Alex, known by our friends for her "chocolate" eyes when she was a tiny little person, is now a college student. She enjoys clothes, jewelry, friends, reading and theatre. She wants to be an educator when she finishes school and plans to be a world traveler.

She became a heroine in the summer of 2001 when she and a friend were credited with saving the life of their guide who was hit in the head by a falling rock as the three of them descended Mt. Shasta in California.

A current description of Alex would be incomplete without the mention of her brand new husband, Hunter Swann, as they return from a honeymoon in Mexico to begin life together.

William Hunter Swann

b. 9/15/1978 in Lynchburg, Virginia

The newest family,
Ashley Alexander Judd and William Hunter Swann

son of **John Lloyd Swann** (12/3/1948-) and **Gloria Von Weiss** (5/4/1949-)

brother of Ann Williamson Swann (1/29/1974-) m. Robert Charles
Thompkins, Jr. (2/16/1970-)
Robert Lloyd Swann (3/14/1980-)

m. **Ashley Alexander Judd** (4/6/1984-) 5/15/2004

Hunter is anticipating a career in the Coast Guard. He is now Petty Officer Swann.

He enjoys outdoor activities, including biking, hiking and rock climbing. He chooses music and reading for his less strenuous activity. All in all, we think he is a great addition to the family!

Stephen Laurence Judd

b. 8/3/1987 in the Bedford, Virginia Hospital

son of **Sylvia Ellen Miller** (8/16/1958-) and Laurence Erwin Judd (12/14/1972-)

brother of Ashley Alexander Judd (4/6/1984-)

Stephen, currently a high school student, is really "into" sports. He has played soccer on a travel team, distinguished himself as a cross-country runner, participated in meets and races on bikes and mountain bikes, and broken his collar bone *twice* while skateboarding! Now he is shooting for the hoops! He attends New Vista School in Lynchburg, Virginia.

Handsome Stephen's eyes are as clear blue as his sister's are brown.

Grandchildren

It is these special people who carry the future of any family. A listing of those who will represent my brother, my sisters, and myself is complete herein, to date. We are very proud of these grandchildren and expect wonderful things of each and every one.

There are some other children, largely unknown to the other descendants of Blanche Odessa Miller and James Moore Wilson, who should be mentioned here. They are the grandchildren of William Long Hodges, my husband. I lay claim to some of them, as well, relative to how much opportunity I have had to come to know them. Some of them have lived their whole lives a long way from the place their parents were raised and the place in which we live! There is a kinship for all of us, however, in that Bill and all of his lineal descendants are also descended from Sir Davy Gam, who lived in medieval times. The good old Briton blood pulses in these veins also:

Mary Love Hodges
Robin Danielle Cassedy
Natalie Ann Cassedy
Sarah Elizabeth Richards
James Edward Richards
Amanda Marie Richards

Bill and I are proud of these children, too.

Bibliography

Abercrombie, Janice L. and Slatten, Richard, compilers, *Virginia Publick Claims: King George County*, Athens, GA, Iberian Publishing Co., 1991, p. 17.

Abraham, James Johnston, *John Coakley Lettsom, His Life, Times, Friends and Descendants*, London, William Heinemann Medical Books, Ltd, 1933, pp. 4-16, 49-64.

Ainsworth, John F. and MacLysaght, Edward, "Survey of Documents in Private Keeping," 2nd Series, *Analecta Hibernica*, No. 20, Dublin, Stationery Office, 1958, pp. 4-13, 25, 259.

Albemarle County Deed Book 1, p. 395.

Arndt, Betsy, Venice, FL, research reported to Emma Jordan 2/2001.

Auditor's Account Book, 1779, Virginia State Library, p. 177.

Augusta County Deed Book 4, pp. 277, 281.

Augusta County Deed Book 21, pp. 499, 501.

Augusta County Marriage Book, 1792, pp. 92-98a.

Augusta County Marriage Book 1, 1785-1786, p. 21.

Augusta County Will Book 4, p. 480.

Augusta County Will Book VI, pp. 429-431.

Augusta County Will Book 9, p. 417.

Augusta County Will Book 32, p. 219.

Bailey/Bond Genealogical Collection, Jones Memorial Library, notes.

Bailey, Brian, *Great Romantic Ruins of England and Wales*, New York, Crown Publishers, Inc., 1984.

Benchley, Peter, "The Bahamas," *National Geographic*, Vol. 162, No. 3, Sept. 1982, pp. 373-395.

Berleth, Richard, *The Twilight Lords*, New York, Alfred A. Knopf, 1978, p. 185.

Bixler, Irene, from her records.

Black, George F., *The Surnames of Scotland*, 4th ed., New York, New York Public Library, 1974, pp. 193-194, 796-797.

Blair, Charles William, *A History of Mossy Creek Presbyterian Church*, Bridgewater, VA, Bridgewater Beacon Printing, Inc., 2000, pp. 35, 255-274.

Blume, Helmut, et al, *Baedeker's Caribbean Including Bermuda*, New York, Prentice Hall, n.d., p. 58.

Bly, Daniel W., *From the Rhine to the Shenandoah: Eighteenth Century Swiss and German Pioneer Families. . .*, vol. 2, Baltimore, Gateway Press, Inc., 1996, pp. 3-4.

Boyd-Rush, Dorothy A., *Marriage Notices from Extant Issues of the "Rockingham Register," Harrisonburg, Virginia, 1822-1870*, Heritage Books, Inc., 1993, p. 246.

Boyer, William W., *America's Virgin Islands: A History of Human Rights and Wrongs*, Durham, North Carolina, Carolina Academic Press, Preface, pp. 10-12.
Brumbaugh, Martin Grove, A. M., Ph. D., *A History of the German Baptist Brethren in Europe and America*, Elgin, IL, Brethren Publishing House, 1906, pp. 1-109.
Buchanan, Paul C., *Long Families on the Rappahannock River Before 1800*, Springfield, VA, 1987, pp. 6-12.
Buchanan, Paul C., and Owens, Susie M., "Henry Long and Some Descendants of Colonial Virginia: Third Generation: Children of Bloomfield Long," *The Virginia Genealogist*, vol. 38, no. 3, pp. 47, 115-118, 120-121, 125, 192-193, 196-198.
Burke, Sir Bernard, C.B., LL.D., *Burke's Genealogical and Heraldic History of the Landed Gentry of Ireland*, London, Burke's Peerage Ltd., 1911, pp. 119-120; 4th edition, 1958, p. 44.
_____ *Burke's Irish Family Records*, London, Burke's Peerage Ltd., 1976, p. 254.
_____ *The General Armory of England, Scotland, Ireland and Wales; Comprising a Registry of Armorial Bearings from the Earliest to the Present Time*, London, Harrison, 59, Pall Mall, 1884, p. 213.
Burns, Alan, *History of the British West Indies*, London, George Allen & Unwin Ltd., 1954, pp. 338, 348.
Campbell, T. E., *Colonial Caroline: A History of Caroline County, Virginia*, Richmond, Dietz Press, Inc., 1954, p. 408.
Carlock, Walter, *The Studebaker Family in America, 1736-1976*, Tipp City, OH, The Studebaker National Family Association, 1976, pp. 3, 677.
Cerny, Johni and Zimmerman, Gary J., *Before Germanna*, American Genealogical Lending Library, 1990, pp. 1-27.
Chadwick, Nora, *The Celts*, London, Penguin, 1971, pp. 100-103.
Chalkley, Lyman, *Chronicles of the Scotch-Irish Settlement in Virginia: Extracted from the Original Court Records of Augusta County, 1745-1800*, vol. 2, Salem, MA, Higginson Book Co., 1912, pp. 92-98, 405, 431.
_____ *Chronicles of the Scotch-Irish Settlement in Virginia: Extracted from the Original Court Records of Augusta County, 1745-1800*, vol. 3, Baltimore, Genealogical Publishing Co., Inc., 1974, pp. 171, 405, 564.
Church of the Latter Day Saints, Salt Lake City, Utah, computerized records.
Clark, from the files of kd4tnq@netscape.net, p. 11.
Cloney, Sean, "The Colcloughs," *Tintern Abbey County Wexford: Cistercians and Colcloughs, Eight Centuries of Occupation*, Saltmills, County Wexford, Friends of Tintern, n.d., pp. 19-22, 36.
Coakley, Charles, Nova Scotia, research results.
Coakley, Marion L. of Dayton, VA, research and letters.
Coakley, Walter, notes.

Colclough, George Dewey, *Information Concerning The Colclough Family in the United States of America, England, and Ireland*, Burlington, NC, Burlington Letter Shop, 1969, unpaged.

Colclough, John, *A Chronological Index*, http://www.tourismresources.ie/colclough/pref.htm.

_____ Colclough Family Rally announcement.

Coldham, Peter Wilson, *English Adventurers and Emigrants, 1609-1660: Abstracts of Examinations in the High Court of Admiralty with Reference to Colonial America*, Baltimore, Genealogical Publishing Co., Inc., 1984.

Conrad, W. P., *From Terror to Freedom in the Cumberland Valley*, Greencastle, PA, Lilian S. Besore Memorial Library, 1976, p. 122.

Creque, Darwin D., *The U.S. Virgins and the Eastern Caribbean*, Philadelphia, Whitmore Publishing Co., 1968, pp. 25-49.

Crews, Irvin Burkett, "The Crews and the Irvin Families," Houston, TX, c1966, p. 6.

Crozier, William Armstrong, *Spotsylvania County Records, 1721-1800: Being Transactions from the Original Files at the County Courthouse. . .*, Baltimore, Southern Book Co., 1955, pp. 50, 61, 224-225, 255.

______ ed. *Virginia County Records of Spotsylvania County, 1721-1800*, vol. 1, Baltimore, Genealogical Publishing Co., 1978, pp. 15, 174, 206.

Culpeper County Deed Book K 1779-1781, pp. 89-91, 100-101.

Culpeper County Will Book A, 7/16/1756, pp. 133-134, 205.

Culpeper County Will Book K 1779-1781, pp. 181-183.

"Cultural Snapshots," *German Genealogical Digest*, vol. 15, no. 2, Summer 1999, pp. 60-61.

Driver, Carolyn Click and Gassett, Bertha Driver, *Descendants of Ludwig Treiber (Lewis Driver) and Barbara Sprenkle in The Shenandoah Valley of Virginia the United States of America*, 1990, pp. 3-3B, 367-368.

Driver, Robert J., ed., *52nd Virginia Infantry*, H. E. Howard, Lynchburg, VA, 1986, p. 127.

______*52nd Virginia Infantry*: Addendum for the Second Edition, n.d., p. 196.

Dunn, Richard S., *Sugar and Slaves: The Rise of the Planter Class in the English West Indies, 1624-1713*, Chapel Hill, University of North Carolina Press, 1972, pp. 122, 127.

Durant, Horatia, *Raglan Castle*, Risca, Great Britain, Starling Press Ltd., 1980, pp. 20-33.

Durnbaugh, Donald F., *The Brethren in Colonial America*, Elgin, Illinois, The Brethren Press, 1967, p. 255.

Eckenrode, H. J., *List of the Revolutionary Soldiers of Virginia: Special Report of the Department of the Archives and History for 1911*, Richmond, Davis Bottom, Superintendent of Public Printing, 1912,

p.104.
"Eire," *World Book Encyclopedia*, 1959 ed., vol. 5, p. 2239.
Fifth Virginia Convention Proceedings and notes 4-5.
First Marriage Record of Augusta County Virginia 1785-1813, Verona, Virginia, Augusta Heritage Press, Inc., 1985, p. 20.
Fothergill, Augusta B., and Naugle, John Mark, *Virginia Tax Payers 1782-87 Other Than Those Published by the United States Census Bureau*, Baltimore, Genealogical Publishing Co., 1966, p. 46.
Fox, Brian, *Wexford: A Touring Guide*, Wexford County, Ireland, South East Tourism, n.d., pp. 47-48, nos. 275, 627.
Freter, Bernard, Hagen, Germany, research and e-mail correspondence.
Gaines file, Rockingham Historical Society, Dayton, VA.
Gaines, Lewis Pendleton, *The Gaines Genealogy: Our Line from 1620 to 1918*, Calhoun, GA, T. H. Land, 1918, pp. 1-19.
Garber, Clark M., *The Garber Historical and Genealogical Record*, vol. 3, Butler, Ohio, 1964, pp. 8-9.
Garber, Steven R. and Masters, Jerry R., "Gerber, Garber and Garver Progenitors in Pennsylvania," *Pennsylvania Mennonite Heritage*, Vol. 22, No. 3, July 1999, pp. 25, 30-31.
Genealogies of Virginia Families: From Tyler's Quarterly Historical and Genealogical Magazine, Baltimore, Genealogical Publishing Co., Inc., 1981, pp. 176-185.
Glick, J. Paul, *A 3-Generation Genealogy of Rev. Joseph Miller of Beaver Creek Church, Rockingham County, Virginia*, Waynesboro, VA, 1966, pp. ix-xiii, xv-xvi, 30-33, 46-48.
Green, Raleigh Travers, comp., *Genealogical and Historical Notes on Culpeper County, Virginia*, Baltimore, Regional Publishing Co., 1983, pp. 14, 18, 36.
Groome, Francis H., ed., *Ordnance Gazateer of Scotland: A Survey of Scottish Topography, Statistical, Biographical and Historical*, Edinburgh, Thomas C. Jack, Grange Publishing Works, 1885, pp. 404-405.
Grun, Bernard, *The Timetables of History*, Third Revised Edition, New York, Simon & Schuster, 1991.
Gwathmey, John H., *Historical Register of Virginians in the Revolution: Soldiers, Sailors, Marines, 1775-1783*, Richmond, Dietz Press, Publishers, 1938, p.165.
Haley, Mary Tod, *Caroline County, A Pictorial History*, Norfolk, Donning Co., Publishers, 1985, pp. 10-12.
Hannau, Hans W., *Islands of the Bahamas*, New York, Hastings House Publishers, n.d., pp. 16-19, 105-106.
Hening, William Waller, *The Statutes at Large; Being a Collection of the Laws of Virginia from the First Session of the Legislature in the Year 1619*, vol. 7, Richmond, Franklin Press, 1820, pp. 323-330.
Herbert, Roberta Miller, from genealogical notes.

Hertzler, Patricia Heatwole, *The Story of Melvin Jasper Heatwole, Mollie Grace Coffman*, Powhatan, VA, 1983, p. 15.

Hollen, Mary, interview, fall of 1994.

Hore, Phillip Herbert, ed., *History of the Town and County of Wexford from the Earliest Times to the Rebellion of 1798*, London, E. Stock, 1901, pp. 181-183.

Houff, Robert E., *One Hundred and Twenty-Five Years for Christ, 1828-1953: A History of the Beaver Creek Congregation 1952*, pp. 5-6, 9-10.

Johnson, Robert E., *Scattered Leaves: Genealogy of the Johnson-Bond and Utermoehlen/Bredehoeft Families*, Sacramento, CA, n.d., pp. 8-10.

Jones, S. B., M.B.E., ETC., *Annals of Anguilla 1650-1923*, Basseterre, St. Kitts, B.W.I., 1936, pp. 2-4, 6-7.

Jones, Theophilus, *A History of Brecknockshire*, London, Edwin Davies, 1898 edition, pp. 79-129, 245-253, 510.

______*A History of Brecknockshire*, vol. 1, Wales, Blissett, Davies, et al, 1909, pp. 98, 160-161.

______*A History of the County of Brecknock*, vol. 2, The Brecknock Society, 1930, pp. 170, 172, 192.

______*A History of the County of Brecknock*, vol. 3, The Brecknock Society, 1930, p. 185, appendix.

______*A History of the County of Brecknock*, vol. 4, The Brecknock Society, 1930, pp. appendix x-xi, 69, 128, 148, 169, 171-172, 229, 233-234, 245, 248, 251, 271-278.

Kavanagh, Art and Murphy, Rory, *The Wexford Gentry*, vol.1, Bunclody, Ireland, Irish Family Names, 1994, pp. 62, 71, 78-82, 100-103.

______*The Wexford Gentry*, vol. 2, Bunclody, Ireland, Irish Family Names, 1996, pp.135-136.

Kaylor, Peter Cline, *Abstract of Land Grant Surveys, 1761-1791*, Dayton, VA, Shenandoah Press, Jan. 1938, p. 66.

Kent, Anthony, Kilmore Quay, Ireland, research.

Kenyon, John R., BA ALA, FSA, FRHistS, *Raglan Castle*, Cardiff, Cadw: Welsh Historical Monuments, 1994, p. 3.

Kernodle, P. J., *Lives of Christian Ministers*, Richmond, Central Publishing Co., 1909, pp. 380-381.

Kimmel, John M., *Chronicles of the Brethren: A Concise History of the Brethren or Dunker Church*, Brookville, Ohio, 1972.

King George County Deed Book 6, 1745-1784, p. 13.

King George County Deed Book 7, 1785-1793, p. 56.

King George County Order Book 4A, pp. 279, 365, 425, 434-436.

Kiracofe, James McCutcheon, letter to Caroline Virginia Coakley Kiracofe, 6/6/1875.

Kiracofe, Josiah Andrew, letter to Blanche Miller Wilson, Tuesday, October 31.

Kiracofe, Nelson Bittle, letter to his parents from a Civil War encampment.

Knittle, Walter Allen, Ph. D., *Early Eighteenth Century Palatine Emigration: A British Government Redemptioner Project to Manufacture Naval Stores*, Baltimore, Genealogical Publishing Co., 1965, pp. 47-50, 70, 103, 207-226.

Kuhns, Oscar, *The German and Swiss Settlements of Colonial Pennsylvania: A Study of the So-Called Pennsylvania Dutch*, Ann Arbor, Michigan, Gryphon Books, 1971, p. 40.

Lancaster, Esther, Halifax, Nova Scotia, research.

Latter Day Saints, computerized records.

Lewisohn, Florence, *Tales of Tortola and the British Virgin Islands*, Hollywood, FL, International Graphics, 1966, pp. 2, 10-11, 18.

Llyfrgellydd, *The National Library of Wales Journal*, vol. xxiv, Aberystwyth,1885-86, pp. 214, 221.

Long, Almyrta F., *The Long History*, vol. 2, n.d., pp. v-vii.

Long, Harvey Lawrence, AB, MA, JD, *The Big Long Family In America, 1736-1979: A Host of Descendants of John Long 1728-1791*, Ogle Co., IL, 1981, pp. iv-18, 207-226.

MacLysaght, Edward, D. Litt., M.R.I.A., *Irish Families: Their Names, Arms and Origins*, Dublin: Hodges Figgis & Co. Ltd., 1957, p. 281.

______*More Irish Families*, Galway, O'Gorman Ltd., 1960, pp. 60, 209.

______*The Surnames of Ireland*, 6th edition, Irish Academic Press, 1985, p. 294.

Mallott, Floyd E., *Studies in Brethren History*, Elgin, IL, Brethren Publishing House, 1954, pp. 40-353.

Mansfield Family in England and America, box 4, item 2, unpaged collection, DAR Library.

Mason, Floyd R. and Mason, Kathryn G., *John H. Garber and Barbara Miller of Pennsylvania, Maryland and Virginia*, Bridgewater, VA, 1995, p. 1088.

______ *The Michael Miller and Susanna Bechtol Family Record*, Bridgewater, VA, Bridgewater Beacon Printing, Inc., 1993, pp.1-54, 58-59, 64-66.

Mason, Floyd R., compiler, *Michael Miller of 1692 and His Descendants*, Bridgewater, VA, 1986, pp. 2, 7.

May, C. E., *Life Under Four Flags in North River Basin of Virginia*, Verona, VA, McClure Press, pp. 68-139, 178, 198-201, 213, 221, 231, 270-271, 445.

_____*My Augusta, A Spot of Earth, Not a Woman*, Bridgewater, VA, Good Printers, Inc., 1987, pp. 332-336.

Meade, William, Bishop, *Old Churches and Families of Virginia*, Philadelphia, J.B. Lippincott, 1857, p. 375.

_____*Old Churches, Ministers, and Families of Virginia*, vol. 2, compiled and reprinted by Jennings Cropper Wise, Philadelphia, Lippincott Co., 1931, pp. 75-76.

Mercatante, Anthony S., *The Facts on File Encyclopedia of World Mythology and Legend*, New York, Facts on File, 1988, p. 189.
Miller, Annie Elizabeth, *Carolina Pioneers and their Descendants*, Macon, GA, J. W. Burke Co., 1927, pp. 17-19.
Miller, Benjamin Kerlin, letters to Joseph Daniel Brower Miller, 1/13/1910, 9/11/1910.
Miller, Gene Edwin, *Some Brethren Families*, Irvine, CA, 10/1979, p. 1.
Miller, Lula Mae, *Johannes Friederick Kirshof: Early Settler and Patriarch of Northern Augusta County*, vol. 1, Verona, VA, McClure Printing Co., 1981, pp. 1-4, 5-20, 33-34, 265-328.
Morris, Jan, *The Matter of Wales*, Oxford, Oxford University Press, 1984, pp. 58-61, 65, 218, 321, 380-381.
Morton, Oren B., *A History of Rockbridge County Virginia*, Staunton, VA, The McClure Co., Inc., 1920.
Murphy, Derula, *Ireland*, Salem, New Hampshire, Salem House, 1985, pp. 33-34.
The New Encyclopedia Britannica, 1994 ed., vol. 2, p. 494; vol. 20, p. 607; vol. 29, pp. 122-123.
Nicklin, John Bailey Calvert, compiler, *St. Paul's Parish Register: Stafford and King George Counties, 1715-1798*, Baltimore, Genealogical Book Co., 1962, p. 10.
1990 Caribbean Islands Handbook, Prentice Hall, 1989, p. 55.
Nugent, Nell Marion, *Cavaliers and Pioneers, Abstracts of Land Patents and Grants, 1623-1800*, vol. 1, Richmond, Dietz Printing, 1934, p. 177; vol. 3, p. 312.
Oliver, Vere Langford, ed., *Caribbeana; Being Miscellaneous Papers Relating to the History, Genealogy, Topography, and Antiquities of the British West Indies*, vol. 3, London, Mitchell, Hughes and Clarke, 1909-1919, pp. 255-256.
______ ibid., vol. 5, pp. 49-50, 72, 267.
Orange County Deed Book 6, p. 182.
Orange County Deed Book 6/6/1749, p. 512.
Orange County Deed Book 16, p. 158.
Orange County Deed Book 21, 1795-1800, pp. 17, 108.
Orange County Order Book 4, pp. 341, 796.
Orange County Order Book 9, p. 85.
Orange County Will Book 1, p. 244.
"The Origin of Your Family Name," Blue Chip Products, 1995.
The Oxford Companion to British History, Oxford, Oxford University Press, 1997, p. 136.
Parks, D. L., research, letter, 5/19/1999.
Patterson, Dona Kirk, "Curry," in *Augusta County Heritage Book, 1732-1998*, Summersville, WV, Shirley Grose and Associates, 1999, p. 140.
Pettigrew, Thomas Joseph, *Memoirs of the Life and Writings of the Late John*

Coakley Lettsom, vol. 1, London, Longman, Hurst, Rees, Orme and Brown, 1817, p. 5.
Peyton, J. Lewis, *History of Augusta County, Virginia*, Bridgewater,VA, Charles R. Carrier, 1953, p. 239.
Phillips, Sir Thomas, Baronet, *Glamorganshire Pedigrees,* Worcester, England, Deighton and Co., 1845, p. 29.
Poole, Edwin, *The Illustrated History and Biography of Brecknockshire from the Earliest Times to the Present Day*, Brecknock, 1886, pp. 7, 9, 11, 14, 19, 34, 43-45, 65, 81, 91-94, 126, 149-150, 177, 196, 228, 246, 248, 259, 304, 324, 382, 393.
"Post Offices," *The Virginia Genealogist*, Vol. 23, January/March 1979, pp. 55-57.
Priode, Marguerite B., research.
Reid, Alan, *The Castles of Wales: Castellu Cymru*, London, George Philip, 1973, pp. 46-47, 121, 124-126, 135, 137-138.
Revolutionary Soldiers Auditor's Account Book (XV), 1783, p. 373.
Riley, Mary Reid, and Williams, MacFarland, research.
Rockingham County Burnt Deed Book 8, pp. 540-541.
Rockingham County Deed Book 4, p. 218.
Rockingham County Deed Book 5, p. 302.
Rockingham County Deed Book 8, pp. 112-113.
Rockingham County Deed Book 11, p. 523.
Rockingham County Deed Book 12, p. 491.
Rockingham County Deed Book 66, p. 512.
Rockingham County Deed Book 73, pp. 158-159.
Rockingham County Deed Book 94, pp. 253-254.
Rockingham County Deed Book 108, p. 373.
Rockingham County Deed Book 146, pp. 517-518.
Rockingham County Index of Marriage Registers, A-K, Bond 785.
Rockingham County Marriage Register, p. 182.
Rockingham County Marriage Register, Book 2, p. 89.
Rockingham County Marriage Register, Book 4, p. 176.
Rockingham County Register of Births 1862-1870, pp. 57, 73.
Rogozinski, Jan, *A Brief History of the Caribbean From the Arawak and the Carib to the Present*, Revised Edition, New York, Facts on File Inc., 1999, pp. 72-145.
Ruth, John L., '*Twas Seeding Time*, Scottdale, Herald Press, 1976, pp. 45-47, 100.
Sappington, Roger E., *The Brethren in Virginia: The History of the Church of the Brethren in Virginia*, Harrisonburg, VA, The Committee for Brethren History, 1973, pp. 1-9, 30-31, 37-40, 130-151.
Scheel, Eugene M., *Culpeper: A Virginia County's History Through 1920*, Culpeper, VA, Culpeper Historical Society, 1982, p. 21.
Scheldknecht, C. E., ed., *Monocacy and Cacoctin*, vol. 4, no. 1, Westminster,

MD, Family Line Publishing, 1989.
Schlien, Manfred, submission to LDS records and e-mail correspondence.
Schreiner-Yantis, Netti, and Love, Florene Speakman, compilers, *The 1787 Census of Virginia: An Accounting of the Name of Every White Male Tithable Over 21 Years*, Springfield, VA, Genealogical Books in Print, c1987, pp. 370-884.
"Second Germanna Colony of 1717," *The Germanna Record*, no. 6, June, 1965, p. 88.
Shenandoah County Court Records, Deed Book E, 1783-1786, p. 429.
Sheppard, I. A., letters to N. B. Kiracofe, 5/11/1870 and 9/9/1870.
Smith, George M., compiler, translator, *Hebron Church Register, 1750-1825, Madison, Virginia*, vol. 2, Edinburgh, VA, Shenandoah History Publishers, 1981, p. 41.
Southey, Thomas, *Chronological History of the West Indies*, vol. 2, London, Cass, 1968.
Sparacio, Ruth and Sparacio, Sam, *Spotsylvania County Order Book 1724-1729: Abstracts of Spotsylvania County, Virginia 1724-1730* (Part III) McLean, VA, Antient Press, 1990, p. 74.
______*Virginia County Court Records, Orange County, Virginia: Orders 1757-1759*, McLean, VA, The Antient Press, 1998, p. 43.
Spotsylvania County Deed Book A, p. 377.
Spotsylvania County Deed Book G, 1766-1771, p. 255.
Strassburger, Ralph Beaver, *Pennsylvania German Pioneers: A Publication of the Original Lists of Arrivals in the Port of Philadelphia from 1727 to 1808*, Baltimore, Genealogical Publishing Co., 1980, vol.1, pp. 3-6, 45.
Sutherd, Calvin E., *A Compilation of Gaines Family Data with Special Emphasis on the Lineage of William and Isabella (Pendleton) Gaines*, Fort Lauderdale, June 1969, p. 10.
______*A Compilation of Gaines Family Data with Special Emphasis on the Lineage of William and Isabella (Pendleton) Gaines*: Reprint of the Original Edition of 1969, Fort Lauderdale, August 1972, pp. viii, 9-12, 18-21, 34-36, 348-350.
______*Supplement to A Compilation of Gaines Family Data with Special Emphasis on the Lineage of William and Isabella (Pendleton) Gaines*, Fort Lauderdale, November, 1973, pp. 2-3, 5-7, 114-116.
Tyler, Lyon G., M.A., LL.D, ed., *Tyler's Quarterly Historical and Genealogical Magazine*, vol. 5, Richmond, Richmond Press, Inc., 1924, pp. 54-56.
The Vestry Book of Stratton Major Parish, King and Queen County, Virginia, 1729-1783, Richmond, The Library Board, 1931, pp. 11-63.
Virginia Land Office Patent Book 26, pp. 212, 315.
Virginia Land Office Patent Book 28, p. 454.
Virginia Land Office Patent Book 39, pp. 17, 81.

Virkus, Frederick Adams, ed., f.i.a.g., *The Compendium of American Genealogy*, vol. 6, Chicago, The Institute of American Genealogy, 1937, p. 776.

Vogt, John & Kethley, T. William, Jr., *Virginia Historic Marriage Register: Rockingham County Marriages, 1778-1850*, Athens, GA, Iberian Press, 1984, p. 199.

Wales in Pictures, Minneapolis, Lerner Publications Co., 1990, p. 21-23.

Wayland, John Walter, *Art Folio of the Shenandoah Valley*, Harrisonburg, John W. Wayland, 1924, n.p.

______*The German Element in the Shenandoah Valley of Virginia*, Bridgewater, C. J. Carrier Co., 1964, pp. 20-21, 125-130, 181-182, 186-187.

______*A History of Rockingham County Virginia*, Dayton, VA, Ruebush-Elkins Co., 1912, pp. 106-107, 112-113, 339-340.

______*A History of Shenandoah County, Virginia*, Strasburg, VA, Shenandoah Publishing House, Inc., 1976, p. 172.

______*Virginia Valley Records: Genealogical and Historical Materials of Rockingham County, Virginia and Related Regions*, Baltimore, Genealogical Publishing Co., Inc., 1985, pp. 106-107, 323.

Westergaard, Waldemar, *The Danish West Indies Under Company Rule, 1671-1754*, New York, Macmillan Co., 1917.

Whelan, Kevin, ed., *Tintern Abbey County Wexford: Cistercians and Colcloughs, Eight Centuries of Occupation*, Saltmills, County Wexford, Friends of Tintern, n.d., pp. 21-22, 27, 31, 36-37.

______*Wexford: History and Society*, Dublin, Geography Publications, 1987, pp. 131, 133-134, 137-138, 140-144, 168, 471.

Williams, Eric, *From Columbus to Castro: The History of the Caribbean 1492-1969*, New York, Harper & Row Publishers, 1970,

Wilson, Blanche Miller, to Elisabeth Wilson Hodges, letter "Mon. the 24th," bef1980; other letters and genealogical notes.

Wilson, James W., "The Mossy Creek Area of Augusta County Virginia During the Eighteenth Century: The Land and the People," a thesis submitted to the Graduate Faculty of James Madison University, August 1993, pp. 36-37, 40.

Wood, Sudie Rucker, compiler, *The Rucker Family Genealogy with Their Ancestors, Descendants and Connections*, Richmond, Old Dominion Press, 1932, pp. 120, 175, 436-437.

Wooddell, James, to Emma and Charley Jordan, 12/31/1998; to Elisabeth Hodges 3/11/1999.

World Book Encyclopedia, vol. 5, pp. 2211-2213.

York County, Pennsylvania Will Book A, 1749-1762, p. 47.

York County, Pennsylvania Will Book C, p. 74.

York County, Pennsylvania Will Book E, p. 187.

York County Orphan's Court Record Book E, p. 40.

Index

C

D

E

F

H

I

J

K

L

M

R

S

T

Y

Z